GW00545173

Robert Greenall was born in Hastings, England in 1966, and graduated in Russian from the University of Durham in 1989. He has lived in Moscow since 1990, working as an interpreter and translator for Novosti Publishers, ABC News, BBC TV News, and subsequently as Travel Editor of *Moscow Guardian*. He is currently Editor of the magazine *Russian Life*.

Following extensive travel in 1993, he wrote a guide to European Russia, *An Explorer's Guide to Russia* (1994), which has been saluted for its pioneering attempt to make many previously unknown areas of the country accessible to the independent traveller.

Critical praise for *An Explorer's Guide to Russia*:

"An absorbing account of a fascinating country"
Mail on Sunday

"Looks beyond the official Russia of the tour buses to try to discover something of the authentic spirit of this vast and complex land"
Chicago Tribune

"British writer and photographer Robert Greenall offers a wealth of historical information, maps and directories, plus tips on customs and habits..."
Time Magazine

"No tedious passages, nor unnecessary generalisations... A useful book with city maps, hotel lists and descriptions of museums, restaurants and unofficial sights which cannot even be found in the most complete domestic guidebooks. The book is written with a sincere liking for Russia and appeals to foreign travellers to be responsive, cordial and grateful guests. However, Greenall does not avoid unpleasant truths..."
Moscow News

Moscow
An Explorer's Guide

By Robert Greenall

Harbord Publishing

Art Research, Proofreading:
Ed Hogan, Lucy Lezhneva, Karen Mason.
Lay-out and Maps: Stanislav Mosolov.
Design: Atelier Works.

This edition first published in 1995 by
Harbord Publishing Limited, 58 Harbord Street,
London SW6 6PL, U.K.

Published in the United States and Canada by Zephyr Press,
13 Robinson Street, Somerville, MA 02145, U.S.A.

Text © 1995 by Robert Frank Turner Greenall

ISBN 1 899414 10 X (Harbord Publishing)
British Library Cataloguing in Publication data.
A CIP record for this book is available from the British Library.

ISBN 0-939010-51-8 (Zephyr Press)
Library of Congress Catalog Card No. 95-61100

Printed in England by Hartnolls Limited, Bodmin, Cornwall.

This book is sold subject to the condition that it shall not,
by way of trade or otherwise, be lent, re-sold, hired out
or otherwise circulated without the publisher's prior consent in
any form of binding or cover whatsoever other than that in
which it is published and without a similar condition including
this condition being imposed on the subsequent purchaser.

The author and editor have done their best to ensure the
accuracy of all information contained in this book. However,
they can accept no responsibility for any loss, injury, or
inconvenience sustained as a result of information or advice
contained herein.

Introduction   7

Practical Information   25

Central Moscow   55

Introduction

A City of Character

For such a vast, enigmatic and contradictory country as Russia, it is difficult to imagine a more suitable capital than Moscow. Set in the middle of European Russia's expanse of forest, field and rivers, it is a teeming circular zone where all her beauties, horrors, successes and failures seem compounded and magnified. Here East meets West with a dramatic friction — and many observers are captured by an inexplicable fascination.

Moscow is the Kremlin, the seat of immeasurable central power, both political and spiritual. But it is many other things, too: wide, dusty, polluted streets and monstrous tower blocks from the 1970's, teeming people-centres like the markets and railway stations, quiet monasteries and churches, and spacious parkland.

Today is certainly an exciting time to visit Moscow, perhaps unprecedentedly so. For a city with a population of over ten million people, spread over a landmass of nearly 900 square kilometres, and a rich cultural heritage which has been accumulated over the last nine centuries, Moscow was, until a few years ago, a surprisingly grey, pedestrian and oppressive place, lacking in many basic urban needs, to say nothing of cosmopolitanism.

The reforms of recent years, though, have transformed the city, with all the contradictions and peculiarities of the Russian character bubbling to the surface with striking results. On the one hand, streets which once trumpeted the achievements of socialism now flaunt flashy foreign boutiques; on the other, a resurgent Orthodox Church is returning to its churches, which for decades have lain abandoned and derelict.

People too have changed. Ten years ago you had to seek real human life well beneath the solemn surface, in the world of those relatively few people who were not afraid of, or had nothing to lose by, contacts with foreigners. Now, apart from an initial reserve towards strangers that is traditional for Russians, Muscovites are generally accepting and hospitable to foreigners.

A younger generation is meanwhile growing up free of past regimentation. Schoolchildren and teenagers have an energy and inquisitiveness which often amazes their parents, though to outsiders it may appear only natural. In appearance, too, they have been quick to absorb fashions from the rest of the world, while maintaining a style which is distinctly their own.

But society is also deeply split: after several years of political battle, people are vociferous and often angry. While some make money in Western firms, or, increasingly, in the Russian private sector, others are forced by poverty out onto the streets — either to beg, to steal, to sell their meagre possessions in spontaneous chaotic bazaars, or to spit venom at the government in communist and nationalist demonstrations.

While such activity seems now on the wane, and a repetition of unrest like that witnessed in 1991 and 1993 seems increasingly unlikely, there is more excitement in the economic sphere. At last Moscow resembles a world capital, with a range of expensive hotels, restaurants, cafés and nightclubs already well established — and the growth, albeit slow, of places accessible to lesser mortals.

Aesthetically too, the city has become brighter. Although some criticise the speed of change in its appearance as an example of window-dressing – the creation of a facade, or an attempt to cover up real problems – few would deny that Moscow is a more colourful city today than even three years ago.

Building work seems to be going on everywhere, the result of the efforts of the city's highly energetic mayor Yuri Luzhkov. The Tretyakov Gallery, the greatest collection of Russian art in the world, has reopened after restoration, while an enormous new World War II memorial complex has appeared at Poklonnaya Gora. In a few years the reconstruction of Russia's largest church, the Cathedral of Christ the Saviour, is scheduled for completion, as is a shopping complex-cum-underground mall on Manezh Square. The list goes on...

Although Moscow may be a modern city in the making, past experience of political upheaval and policy changes show that it may yet fail to be fully made. The capital is dragging a relatively backward country behind it – and though Moscow may be the heart of Russia, it is not all of Russia. Travel outside the city and you witness a completely different experience, where the old conservatism of the Party elites, combined with greater poverty, makes for a harder, greyer existence.

Nevertheless, Moscow may not at first seem a tourist city in the European sense. Lacking its quota of picturesque old buildings and quaint streets, its wide and increasingly traffic-choked main arteries hardly seem the place for leisurely strolls.

But such surface impressions belie the reality. As well as obvious central sights like the Kremlin and Red Square, Moscow's charm lies behind its facades, in its backstreets and courtyards. Exploring Moscow sometimes requires investigating inside buildings, whether visiting Russian friends or one of the many house- and apartment-museums where the memory of outstanding people is lovingly preserved in their former homes.

For such reasons, this guide-book takes a different approach from others and presents Moscow in a series of walks, which, though they don't avoid main thoroughfares altogether, give visitors a chance to see parts of Moscow which they might otherwise miss.

But even allowing for such detours, it would be impossible to tell everything about such a vast city – and there is no better source for further enlightenment than local people. There are a number of ways to establish contact with ordinary Russians, such as arranging accommodation through Moscow Bed & Breakfast (see pages 41–43); this has the double advantage of avoiding the impersonality and cost of hotel accommodation, which in Moscow is generally either very expensive or very bad, as well as giving a chance for real human communication.

As a way of simply meeting local people, Jim Haynes's *Russia: People to People* (Canongate Press and Zephyr Press, 1996) is a unique directory giving names and addresses and brief information about Russian citizens in both Moscow and St. Petersburg who are interested in meeting foreigners; some also offer bed and breakfast and guiding facilities.

Finally, for those who prefer guided tours to independent sightseeing, there is Patriarchi Dom, a popular tourist organisation with an excellent reputation in the local expatriate community. They have the advantage of small manageable groups, interesting and qualified guides and a wide range of tours both within and outside the city to cater for all tastes. Many of their tours are mentioned in the text: for further information call 255-4515.

Many visitors to Moscow, and indeed plenty of its native inhabitants, at times dislike this crowded, impersonal and occasionally ugly city. But Moscow nevertheless draws them back, seducing them with its scale, activity and vibrancy — one which can finally be more compelling than the peace and beauty of its northern rival, St. Petersburg.

Moscow has plenty of her own subtler charms, and the discerning, perceptive visitor will find much to his or her liking. This guide tries to reveal the city's hidden pleasures.

History

Kievan Rus' and the Founding of Moscow

The history of the race which later came to be known as the Russians begins somewhere between the 7th and 9th centuries. Slavic tribes in what is now Central Russia and Ukraine united around the city of Kiev and were subjected to the Varangian (Norse) rulers of Novgorod in 882. Kievan Rus', as it was called, converted to Christianity in 988, and developed into a major European power.

By the 12th century, however, Kiev had passed its golden age and was racked by internal divisions. Other princedoms, like that of Rostov-Suzdal in the northeast, became increasingly powerful, and its warrior-ruler Yuri Dolgoruky ("of the long arms", later himself Prince of Kiev) built numerous new fortress outposts, one of which was Moscow. The city's founding date is given as 1147, its first mention in the chronicles, where Dolgoruky refers to a banquet he held here for his southern ally Prince Svyatoslav.

The "Tatar Yoke" and Moscow's Rise

In 1237-38 disaster struck the Russian princedoms, as Mongol-Tatar hordes swept in from the East and subjugated almost all of them. Moscow, still just a little settlement in the forest on Borovitsky Hill (now the Kremlin), did not prove much of an obstacle. Perhaps because of this the enemy saw fit to make Muscovy head of its vassal Russian state and collector of its taxes. Tributes to the Khan gradually weakened other Russian cities, making them increasingly dependent on Moscow.

In 1328 Muscovite Prince Ivan Kalita (he was renowned for his greed — his name means "moneybags"), was made Grand Prince by the Khan, and the Metropolitan (then the head of the Russian Church), moved his seat from Vladimir to Moscow.

From then on Moscow started to take its fate into its own hands. In fact, it was Moscow's Prince Dmitry who first united Russia against the Khans. He defeated them soundly on the Don River at Kulikovo Field in 1380, thus earning himself the

title "Donskoy" (of the Don).
Though the Tatars were to
torment Russia with their looting
and pillaging for many centuries
to come, they no longer
controlled her.

The "Third Rome"

Moscow now went from strength
to strength, and with the fall of
Byzantium in 1453, Prince Ivan III
hastened to proclaim it the new
centre of the Orthodox world. It
became known as the "Third
Rome", received its first stone
buildings as well as the earliest
influence from Western architecture — a magnificent Kremlin built
in part by Italians.

A century later, the decline of
the Tatars put Moscow in control
of a united, centralised Russian
state. Prince Ivan IV ("the
Terrible") proclaimed himself the
first Russian Tsar in 1547 and
expanded his territory to the Tatar
Khanates of Kazan (1552) and
Astrakhan (1557). In 1582, the
Russian conquest of Siberia
began.

The Time of Troubles

Ivan's death in 1584 put an end
to Russian expansion, and his
weak son Fyodor, nominally Tsar,
became overshadowed by his
sister's husband, the boyar Boris
Godunov. In 1598 Fyodor died,
and Godunov was elected Tsar.
Rivals plotted against him, and
he was accused of responsibility
for the death of Ivan's second
son, Dmitry; on his death in 1605
Russia erupted into intrigue and
civil war. Two "False Dmitries"
appeared successively, both
backed by the Polish King, each
holding power briefly in turn.

Finally Moscow was occupied
by the Poles, then saved by a
militia force from the Volga under
the command of Suzdal Prince
Dmitry Pozharsky and merchant
Kozma Minin. Mikhail Romanov
was elected tsar by a meeting of
the boyars in council.

Tsar Mikhail, just 16 at his
election, proved capable of
uniting the squabbling nation,
and began a dynasty which
would last more than 300 years.

Moscow as Second City

The accession of Peter the Great
in 1689 was probably a step
forward for Russia, bringing
Western-style reforms as well as
new conquests and territories,
captured from the Turks in the
south and the Swedes in the
north.

It was bad news for Moscow,
however — Peter hated the city
and set about building his own
capital at St. Petersburg. A great
believer in Western values, Peter
found Moscow too backward and
isolated and needed a "window
on Europe".

After a brief return to favour
under Peter's grandson Peter II,
Moscow went into a protracted
decline. Hovering dangerously on
the brink of provincial obscurity, it
continued to develop in its own
special way. In 1762, German
Tsarina Catherine overthrew her
husband Peter III in a palace
coup, heralding a new era of
Russian prosperity.

Catherine the Great's reign
brought a measure of enlightenment, at least for the upper
classes, and in 1762 she freed
the nobility from most of their
obligations to her.

As a result, Moscow became a
"Nobles' Republic", a freer city
unrestrained by the oppressive
officialdom of St. Petersburg. The
city flourished, both intellectually
and culturally.

Destruction and Reconstruction

When, in 1812, Napoleon Bonaparte invaded Russia, he made Moscow the main target of his offensive. Using a scorched earth tactic to wear down the invaders, the Russian command led them right back to Moscow in the process. Though Napoleon entered the city, Tsar Alexander I refused to negotiate terms; Moscow's inhabitants burnt the city to prevent looting by the French, and Napoleon was forced to depart with his demoralised army.

A new city quickly rose from the ashes of the "Nobles' Republic", which in just over 10 years had gained a magnificent new appearance. Growth continued throughout the century, accelerating in the later decades of industrialisation. In 1871, Tsar Alexander II emancipated the serfs (semi-slaves, the subjects of Russia's near-feudal system), leaving hundreds of thousands of people free to move to the city and seek work at the new factories.

Revolution

By the early 20th century, industrialisation had given rise to a new militant urban working class and an emerging danger which the still backward and oppressive tsarist regime failed to see. Parties like the urban Social Democrats and rural Socialist Revolutionaries began to organise effectively for the overthrow of the regime.

When revolution broke out in 1905 following Russia's disastrous defeat in the war with Japan, its main theatre of activity was Moscow. The Presnya district in the west of the city was barricaded, and workers fought pitched battles with troops in the streets. The 1905 revolution was suppressed, but the cosmetic reforms by Tsar Nicholas II and his ministers which followed were insufficient, and the ravages of the disastrous 1914 war again drove Russia into economic collapse and revolution.

In February 1917 the Tsar abdicated and a provisional government was set up in Petrograd (St. Petersburg) by liberal members of the tsarist parliament, the Duma. The new government proved ineffective and lacked support, unlike the revolutionaries, whose authority grew every day in the workers' councils, the "Soviets". In October Vladimir Ilyich Lenin, leader of the most radical Social Democrat faction, the Bolsheviks, seized control of government in the main cities.

Moscow was a Bolshevik stronghold, where, after seven days of fighting, workers expelled provisional government troops from the Kremlin. With civil war breaking out in other parts of Russia, the young revolutionary state was threatened from many quarters, including several White armies which were approaching Petrograd directly. Lenin took the decision to move the capital back to the southern city in March 1918.

Bolshevism and the Stalin Years

Iron discipline and one-party rule under Lenin saw Bolshevik Russia successfully through the Civil War; the subsequent New Economic Policy (NEP) was an experiment with limited capitalism which brought a measure of prosperity during the early and middle 1920's. These policies were reversed following Lenin's death in 1924 by Josef Stalin, who emerged victorious from a complex power struggle among Communist Party factions.

By 1928-30 the country was moving toward totalitarian rule and a personality cult. Massive industrialisation, secret police terror and the creation of a huge army of political prisoners in the camps of the Gulag created a new kind of slavery. By now Moscow had become the capital of a highly centralised state, the Soviet Union.

World War II – "The Great Patriotic War"

Though the Molotov-Ribbentropp pact of 1939 initially kept Russia out of World War II, in June 1941 Hitler launched "Operation Barbarossa" and by winter German tanks were within a few kilometres of Moscow. (The point to which they advanced, now marked by a monument, is visible on the road into the city from Moscow's Sheremetyevo airport).

However, apart from the odd German bomb, the city itself was more or less spared the ravages of this war, as the Red Army resisted heroically and finally stopped the German advance. The city's heavy industry was moved back to Siberia, while central government evacuated to the city of Kuibyshev (now Samara) on the Volga.

Other cities, like Leningrad and Stalingrad, suffered greater hardship and destruction, and it was only after immense effort and loss of life (at least 20 million casualties through the duration of the war), including the Nazi slaughter of millions of civilians, that the Soviets finally drove the invader back to Berlin.

The Post-War Period, the "Thaw" and "Stagnation"

As Soviet influence tightened in Eastern Europe, and the Cold War began its first icy stage, Moscow too was oppressed by the paranoia of its aging dictator. Rarely leaving the Kremlin, Stalin delegated to the likes of Secret Police Chief Beria and Culture Minister Zhdanov. The latter became notorious for his role in the expulsion of Anna Akhmatova and Mikhail Zoshchenko from the Writer's Union in 1948, an act symptomatic of the authorities' continuing persecution of the intellectual elite in this period.

Stalin's rule continued until his death in 1953; over the next three years, a process of reform, named the "thaw", began, highlighted by the delivery of a special report on the Stalin era to the 20th Communist Party Congress by Nikita Khrushchev, the new General Secretary and effective ruler of the country.

In a significant break with Stalinism, millions of political prisoners were rehabilitated and released, and political and cultural life was allowed a measure of breathing space. However, Khrushchev's half-hearted reforms and often eccentric policies alienated his more conservative colleagues, and he was overthrown in 1964.

Emerging from a collective leadership to assume absolute power in the 1970's, the dull bureaucrat Leonid Brezhnev plunged the Soviet Union into a period of deathly stability, known nowadays as "stagnation". The costs of an aggressive policy abroad (notably the invasions of Czechoslovakia in 1968 and Afghanistan in 1980) and the squandering of natural resources left a legacy of economic hardship which the next generation of leaders has still not been able to deal with effectively.

It was a society that had much surface pomp and splendour, such as the 1980 Moscow Olympics (whose propaganda effect was lost because of a boycott by the U.S. and several other teams over the Afghan war), as well as formal parades which continued to mark major holidays.

Nevertheless, compared with current difficulties, many today remember these years as ones of relative prosperity, when the main elements of a decent life, including abundant and inexpensive food, were more or less assured. However, by the time Brezhnev and his briefly-lived successors, Andropov and Chernenko, had departed the scene in the mid-1980's, the Communist Party was suffering an irreversible diminution of power, felt at first psychologically, later politically.

Perestroika and Glasnost

These watchwords of the new General Secretary Mikhail Gorbachev brought immediate enthusiasm and relief to many after an uncertain *interregnum*, but this was followed by disillusionment; political reform, including tentative steps toward democracy, was not matched in the economic sphere. Striving towards reform, the country in fact teetered towards crisis.

The coup of August 1991, a botched attempt to return to old-style communism, saw Moscow once again witness to major political upheaval. As in 1905, the area of focus was not the Kremlin, but the Presnya area. The House of Soviets, better known as the "White House", became the rallying point of the democratic opposition, which stood firm under the leadership of Boris Yeltsin, the maverick former Sverdlovsk Party leader who had been elected Russian President earlier that year. The power of the Party was finally destroyed: the Soviet Union, founded in 1922, broke up into its constituent republics at the end of the year.

The New Russian Federation

At the beginning of 1992, Moscow suddenly found itself the capital of a different, smaller country, the Russian Federation. President Yeltsin and his reformers attempted to create a functioning market economy, simultaneously contesting this new direction with a parliament still dominated by former communists. Confrontational politics continued.

Economic hardship and steep inflation fuelled growing opposition to the new Russian government, although in many ways Russian citizens have proved, to date, incredibly patient when faced with changes which literally overturned the fabric of their lives. Communists and nationalists, now in opposition, found new champions in disillusioned reformers like parliamentary leader Ruslan Khasbulatov and Yeltsin's own vice president Alexander Rutskoi.

Deadlock deepened between the two sides, culminating in an absurd and tragic confrontation in September and October 1993; parliament defied Yeltsin's attempt to dissolve it, and stayed in its headquarters, the White House. Attempts to reach compromise failed, and on October 3rd Moscow was gripped by a wave of violence in which more than 150 people died.

Parliament supporters stormed the Mayor's Building, and tried to take over the TV centre at Ostankino. In response, Yeltsin ordered the military first to shell, and then storm the White House itself, arresting his rivals. New parliamentary elections were held in December to allay fears of dictatorship, and a new constitution was passed which at last set boundaries for the legislative and executive branches of power.

Today, Russian democracy is still shaky; the country remains in depression, while the popularity of its leaders, Yeltsin in particular, seems in terminal decline. New difficulties like the wasteful and unwinnable war in Chechnya have brought protest both at home and abroad. However, the consolidation of power of the new elite, one which nonetheless tolerates opposition parties and attacks in the press, seems to indicate that Russia is groping its way toward a new stability; considering its savage history, it is at least a relative step towards enlightenment.

Art and Architecture

The First Stone Churches

Like every other aspect of Russian life, the tendency to combine Eastern and Western influences is strikingly apparent in its architecture.

Early Russian building design is best represented today by churches, which for centuries were the only structures built in stone (early settlements were almost always entirely built of wood, and as a result nothing remains today of pre-15th century Moscow). Their design borrowed from the Byzantine "cross in square" plan (the shape of a cross filling a square base), they were topped by an onion dome or cupola, giving them an Eastern feel.

Art, other than heathen sculpture of the pre-Christian period, also came initially from Byzantium, in the form of frescoes and icons painted for these early churches. Before Moscow took centre stage in Russian history, various stone-building centres developed in Russia. In prosperous 11th century Kiev, huge, elaborate cathedrals were constructed, while in the more fractious 12th century, centres like Vladimir, Novgorod and Pskov began to produce more modest churches, with high domes and small bodies, in local styles. The impoverished years of the Tatar occupation put an end to stone-building, though the heritage of old Russia was passed down in wooden architecture.

The Unification of Russian Styles

The first post-Mongol stone churches, like the Cathedral in Moscow's Monastery of the Saviour and Andronicus, differed little from those which had been built 200 years previously. Its interior was painted by Andrey Rublyov, who developed the first genuinely Russian school of icon-painting, with a style that was highly poetic and contemplative, and is still regarded by many as the true highpoint of Russian art.

As Moscow grew in strength, it sought to unite the local architectural styles of old Russia, as well as incorporate outside influences. In such a way Ivan III hired architects from Italy, then in the full glory of the Renaissance, and sent them off to old Russian cities to study local features.

The most notable result was Aristotle Fioravanti's Kremlin Assumption Cathedral, based on a 12th century Vladimir church, coloured by Italianate touches.

In the wake of the Kremlin reconstructions, much of the 16th century saw intensive church building, leading to Moscow being christened "the city of forty times forty churches". Architects drew inspiration from wooden architecture, particularly the tent-roof style (the nearest Russian equivalent to spires in Western church architecture) and the covered stairways and blind arcades which often accompanied it. St. Basil's Cathedral and the Resurrection Church at Kolomenskoye are the most outstanding examples.

Taking Art to the People

In the next century Patriarch Nikon banned the tent-roof, considering it alien to Orthodox canons. By now, though, the architectural initiative was passing to the city's merchant guilds, who built small, festive churches like the Trinity Church in Nikitniki (see Walk 2) and St. Nicholas in Khamovniki (see Walk 6). This "democratisation" was also reflected in art, where masters like Simon Ushakov introduced landscapes and people into his icons and frescoes in a way that made them understandable to the ordinary man. In this period the first secular stone buildings appeared, distinguishable for their solid squat appearance with covered stairways and white-washed walls.

The Westernising influence of Peter the Great which saw the capital moved to St. Petersburg was strongly evident in Moscow, both in art and architecture. At the end of the 17th century, the Baroque made its appearance in Russia. In Moscow this was best reflected in the Naryshkin style, so called because of projects initiated by the Tsar's mother Natalya Naryshkina. Churches like the Intercession Church at Fili (see Greater Moscow, War Memorials) show an abundance of vertical highlights, carved portals and platbands, giving them an extravagant and festive appearance.

Russian Classicism

In painting, too, the emphasis shifted to secular portraiture, as Peter encouraged the first tentative steps of Russian artists in this direction. By the end of the 18th century, tastes had changed, and austere classical (sometimes called neo-classical) forms became prevalent. Architects like Vassily Bazhenov and Matvey Kazakov left their mark on Moscow with beautifully proportioned churches and town mansions, drawing on ancient Greek and Roman forms for inspiration.

The disaster of 1812 proved a watershed for Moscow Classicism. The reconstruction that followed saw the appearance of "Moscow Empire", embodied in numerous modest town houses, often built in stucco-faced wood and drawing inspiration from rural peasant styles.

By the middle of the 19th century, however, Classicism was already in decline, with the extravagances of Historicism, or Eclecticism, becoming pre-eminent.

In art these tendencies were reflected somewhat by the work of the "Itinerant" (Peredvizhniki) school, whose realist paintings often drew from history or folklore.

A Revival of Traditional Forms

The most significant trend to emerge was the attempt to revive elements of early Russian architecture, both monumental and folk. This took a number of forms, from the rather pompous and gargantuan official neo-Byzantine style of buildings like the Church of Christ the Saviour (destroyed in 1931, but now under reconstruction, *see* Walk 6), to the intimate and innovative folk style of the Abramtsevo circle (*see* Excursions, Abramtsevo).

In many cases, artists and architects worked in concert to discover and celebrate the Russian past, often with striking effects. As well as participating in the design of buildings, artists produced murals and mosaics for their exteriors, such as those for the Pertsov House, Tretyakov Gallery and many other buildings. Many included features of the Art Nouveau style, which brought the latest modern techniques and stylistic influence from Europe, such as flowing and naturalistic lines.

In Moscow the best work in this style was accomplished by Fyodor Shekhtel, famous in particular for the Yaroslavl Station (*see* Walk 10), Moscow Arts Theatre (*see* Walk 4) and a series of mansions built for Moscow's merchant families. In this period, small one- and two-storey houses began to be replaced by *dokhodniye doma*, stately private apartment blocks with five or more floors. Much of the building work of this period was carried out by prominent members of the new capitalist class, who also distinguished themselves as patrons of the arts.

While some encouraged local talent, like Savva Mamontov at his Abramtsevo workshops, others like Sergey Shchukin and Pavel Tretyakov amassed valuable collections of French Impressionists and Russian "Itinerants" respectively, which were later to make Moscow and St. Petersburg museums into major centres of world art.

Constructivism and Socialist Realism

War, revolution and civil war brought most building in Moscow to a halt for ten years. But the brave new styles of the revolutionary period were in due course reflected in architecture. Led by Konstantin Melnikov, the Constructivists fused the starkly modern visions of the Russian Futurist artists with the late-19th century Chicago school principle that form should follow function.

The poor economic conditions of the 1920's meant that far more constructivist buildings were designed than were ever erected, but the 1927 offices of *Izvestia* (*see* Walk 3) and the private house of Melnikov from the same year (*see* Walk 5) still seem fresh and inspired today. Futurism, while enjoying a prominent place in 1920's culture, was then almost forgotten in the changing ideological climate, to be truly revived only 60 years later during perestroika.

By 1935, Constructivism was long dead in the Soviet Union, killed by a culturally conservative leadership which favoured a grandiose monumental style with classical and traditional Russian overtones, commonly known as "Stalinist Gothic". The most dominant examples are Moscow's seven nearly identical "wedding cake" skyscrapers, which include the Foreign Ministry (see Walk 5) and Moscow State University. This was also the period when the "underground palaces" of the Moscow Metro, and the lavish multi-ethnic pavilions of the Exhibition of Economic Achievement (VDNKh) were begun. Such tendencies went hand in hand with Socialist Realism, the glorification of the communist "future" in painting and sculpture.

The Mutilation of Old Moscow

The decade of the 1930's is also remembered as a time of destruction in Moscow. Many old streets, particularly Tverskaya, were widened, their old buildings knocked down and replaced by grey granite blocks of the type mentioned above. Elsewhere individual buildings were destroyed, either because they were in the way, like the Sukharev Tower (see Walk 8), or because they were symbols of the old regime, like the Church of Christ the Saviour. Construction of the metro was made possible with bricks and materials from buildings thus destroyed.

The death of Stalin did nothing to reverse construction policy in Moscow. A second wave of modernisation began in 1954, bringing further, no less monstrous mutilation to large areas of the city. Prospekt Kalinina (now the New Arbat) was driven through part of the old Arbat quarter and lined with enormous shops, while building programmes in the suburbs went into overdrive, creating *khrushchoby*, five-storey apartment blocks whose nickname involved a word-play on the name of General Secretary Khrushchev and the word for slum, *trushchoba*.

Originally built with a maximum projected life of only 20 years, the majority of them remain standing, and occupied, to this day.

Modern Architecture

In the 1960's and 1970's, Russian architecture awoke from its 25-year sleep, with the appearance of buildings like the House of Soviets (the "White House") and the Comecon building, now the Mayor's Office (see Walk 5). Western architects were brought in for such projects as the International (Mezhdunarodnaya) and Cosmos Hotels.

But the results brought little comfort to ordinary Soviet citizens, as modern blocks of flats became progressively uglier, taller and less habitable. Although they may now epitomise the suburban hell of cities worldwide, with their skylines of 15-storey abominations, the stronger sense of local community has meant that they have not developed the sense of alienation associated with such buildings in the West. For many of their original inhabitants, moved from the crowding of shared apartments, these homes represented a real, unimaginable new life.

While perestroika virtually brought building in Moscow to a standstill, there was an explosion in previously underground and "dissident" art. Works lost, forgotten, or hidden away in the storerooms of museums over 50 years finally confronted the public both at home and abroad. When the initial enthusiasm died down and commercial interests began to dominate, Moscow took a natural place in the art world, with an emerging private gallery scene as adventurous as in any other European capital.

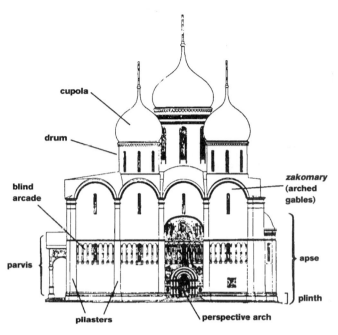

cupola

drum

blind arcade

parvis

pilasters

zakomary (arched gables)

apse

plinth

perspective arch

THE KREMLIN, CATHEDRAL OF THE DORMITION, 1475-79. Adapted from *A History of Russian Architecture* (Cambridge U.P., 1993) by William C. Brumfield, by permission of the author.

Architecture Glossary

Arcade: a series of arches supported by columns, piers, or pillars.

Belvedere: a raised turret or lantern on top of a house or other structure, situated so as to command a view.

Blind Arcading: decorative rows of arches carved into or applied to the outsides of walls, a particularly common feature of Vladimir-Suzdal architecture which was later adopted by the Moscow school.

Cupola: an onion dome of any size on a cylindrical base, or drum, crowning a church, bell tower, mosque or other structure.

Drum: the cylindrical base of a cupola.

Kokoshniki: semi-circular, gabled decorative panels that ring the bases of spires or of drums, in single or multiple courses, of uniform or varying sizes. The name is derived from the peaked *kokoshnik* headgear of medieval Russian women.

Naryshkin Baroque: an architectural style incorporating an abundance of vertical highlights, carved portals and

platbands. Named after Peter the Great's mother, Natalya Naryshkina, who favoured the style.

Platband: a decorative window surround of wood, tile, or carved stone.

Quincunx: an arrangement of five objects, with one placed at each corner of a rectangle and the fifth in the centre.

Risalits: in architecture, sections of the exterior walls of a building that project from the main line of the facade, usually symmetrical to the building's central axis.

Solium: the raised floor at the front of a church sanctuary.

Tent Roof: a steeply pitched church roof, generally constructed in the form of hexagonal or octagonal panels, diminishing in width from base to top.

Trapeza, or **Trapeznaya:** the western addition to a church, built to supplement the sanctuary, the worship space beneath the cupola(s).

Zakomary: arched gables that follow the contours of the vaulting of 11th and 12th century Russian churches.

In building, the 1990's have heralded an unprecedented boom, though architectural merit may not always be its distinguishing factor. From the official side, its main driving force is Mayor Yuri Luzhkov, a former construction engineer, who has embarked on gargantuan projects like the rebuilding of the Church of Christ the Saviour and an underground shopping mall adjacent to Red Square. The forces of private capital, in the form of banks and other flourishing commercial ventures, have been working in parallel, busy renovating and rebuilding countless old buildings in the centre for urgently-needed high-quality office and apartment space.

With the reopening of the city's Tretyakov Gallery after ten years of restoration, the full heritage of Russian art is once again on display. For more detailed notes on this, as well as descriptions of the work of major artists, see the chapter on the Tretyakov Gallery.

People and Everyday Life

Ethnic Mix

Unlike the diverse multiracial cities of Western Europe, Moscow may seem at first overwhelmingly monoethnic and Russian. However, it does have a good sprinkling of just about every nationality from the former Soviet Union, and a thriving foreign community which now numbers upwards of 100,000. Alongside Asian and African students, many of whom remain here (often reluctantly, and sometimes in considerable poverty)

from the days of Soviet-sponsored education programmes, there has been a progressive influx of Westerners, attracted initially by the adventure and latterly by expanding business opportunities. Most locals, it has to be said, find it difficult to understand why anyone should come voluntarily to live in a country which they themselves, to varying degrees, would be happy to leave.

Whereas in past centuries there used to be quarters in the city for major ethnic communities like the Ukrainians, Armenians or Tatars, they have all now been dispersed over the course of various housing programs. These non-Russians still have traditional places at which to gather, like mosques and synagogues, as well as restaurants preparing national cuisine and peasant markets (the domain of provincials from Ukraine, Moldova and the Caucasus). Some (but certainly not all) of the city's criminal gangs, are distinguished by their ethnic origin — there are Chechen, Dagestani, Azerbaijani and other "mafias".

The Russian Character

Russians are predominantly a slavic race, as classic Russian features tend to show — typically fair and stocky, with a tendency to grow outwards in later life, and warm and emotional in character. However, their turbulent history, including 150 years of Tatar domination, has complicated their genes. This major injection of oriental blood has given them many Asiatic traits, like hospitality towards strangers and a mysterious irrational cruelty.

In displaying feelings they may seem to Westerners remarkably honest. If, by avoiding inane or false smiling, they often appear glum or morose, when they show genuine mirth they are childishly innocent. If they like or don't like a person they will show it, and their relationships can veer between open hostility and undying love in a matter of minutes.

To Westerners, their behaviour can sometimes seem overpowering, both physically and mentally. Physical contact is common, no less between men than women, and a hand round the shoulders or on the knee is considered perfectly acceptable. Men will generally shake hands when greeting acquaintances, or kiss if they haven't seen each other for some time. People stand surprisingly close together, in a way that for outsiders would clearly be an invasion of personal space.

Russians share a great sense of community, a concept for which they have a special word, *sobornost*. This can make foreigners feel uncomfortable and not part of things; the position of honoured guest can be a hard one to relinquish. However, visitors to Moscow need not worry too much about such things — many people there are in constant contact with foreigners, speak proficient English and have a good understanding of what they are likely to be interested in, as you would expect in any major world city.

Daily Lives

Decades of communism, and traditional values, have both played a part in forming the Russian "work ethic", if it can be described in such terms. Many people still put their personal lives firmly before work, heritage of a past when job pressures were always miniscule compared with the difficulties of feeding

yourself, bringing up children and living in overcrowded accommodation.

Family and friends have always taken priority in Russia over the "common good", with the result that people relied on "connections" to get scarce goods or otherwise inaccessible services. A matriarchal system developed: the women had the tougher lot in life, but were also better prepared to cope than the men, whose inability to fulfil themselves often led to alcoholic oblivion.

Today Russian, and especially Moscow society, is split, between those who continue to endure personal hardship (and now real poverty), while receiving little money for little work, and a much smaller superclass which has made the transition to a capitalist life-style — where stressful jobs are relieved by a relatively comfortable domestic existence.

With increasing economic pressures, many of the former are forced to supplement their incomes or find cheaper ways to live. After the price reforms of 1992, people took advantage of the liberalisation of trade laws and went out on to the streets to sell whatever they could. Many began to rely increasingly on their *dachas* (country cottages) or *ogorod* (garden plots) for vegetables, spending their weekends, and summer holidays there, and even moving out of the city altogether to live more cheaply and less stressfully.

Those with cars took to earning extra money by carrying passengers. In the early days of reform, the discrepancies were most striking, when a skilled professional might earn more through one night's work as an unofficial taxi-driver than in his month's official salary.

Others, *chelnoki*, took advantage of price differences of goods on sale in neighbouring countries (particularly China and Turkey for clothing, and the Gulf for electrical goods) and travelled on "shop tours", bringing back large shipments of goods for sale in newly established street markets.

The reforms of the last few years have inevitably changed Russians as consumers. Shops are much better stocked than before 1992 (many were then often simply empty, with queues forming when anything remotely desirable went on sale), and many previously unknown products are now available in abundance. However, though there is clearly a demand for such things, many cannot afford them and, in the case of the older generation, simply don't understand what they are. Meanwhile, there can still be shortages in basic goods as before, and queues can occur for anything sold reasonably cheaply. Some, especially older women, still make a living by reselling simple goods bought in shops: the Pushkin Square underpass in the very centre of the city is still the nightly scene of this uninspiring spectacle.

One of the most immediate symbols of the new trading city which appeared at the turn of the decade was the street kiosk. Previously restricted to such things as cigarettes, ice-cream or newspapers, thousands sprang up all over the city selling everything from toy machine guns to condoms, making a huge difference to the physical appearance of the city. Recently, attempts have been made to curb their growth and even remove them, but the shortage of shop space ensures their continued survival. More private shops are appearing across Moscow, but the impermanence of the city's retail atmosphere still seems to favour kiosks.

Leisure Time

Russians are renowned for their love of celebrations, and will use any excuse to have a good time (*gulyat'*). When in solitude (not often for a nation which is very family-orientated, and tends to live in cramped conditions), Russians are avid readers, their current fare being detective stories, romantic fiction and tabloids, all of which have appeared in the last decade.

Evening pastimes such as theatre and cinema have suffered from the onslaught of television, while the unique and urgent role which some culture played under the former system vanished along with it. Cinemas in particular have suffered from falling audiences, this factor in itself a mirror of the Russian film industry's own crises.

The stuffy boredom of former state television is now long a thing of the past, with the last four years bringing successively the state-run but independent Russian State Television (RTR), the entertainment-based TV-6, and, most recently, top quality news provider NTV, which has also brought major Hollywood films to Russian screens for the first time.

Cable and satellite links are also in development, while radio airtime is now unrestricted for once-forbidden stations like Radio Liberty. Game shows, feature films and advertising (often of products that people cannot afford) attract a sizeable audience, although classic Soviet films are still as popular as anything else.

Attitudes Toward Westerners

Russia's relationship with the West has always been highly contradictory. While some people are deeply suspicious and even openly hostile – the euphoria of early perestroika has long passed – others may seem almost excessively receptive to Western ideas and materials. Throughout history these two groups have been struggling for power and influence, and at various points each has had its way.

Enforced ignorance about and negative reporting on the West under communism led to a reaction which saw extreme curiosity about the world which was opened up after Mikhail Gorbachev allowed private travel abroad in 1988. Though elements of xenophobia and nationalism are becoming stronger, in Moscow people are generally better educated and travelled, and now have a more balanced idea of the West. Developments in the media, and contact with the many foreigners in the city, have ensured that even those who have never been outside Russia have an understanding of the world which was unimaginable ten years ago.

Even in Moscow, however, you can expect to receive special treatment from many people. The more unscrupulous regard Westerners as a source of unlimited wealth, and may try to overcharge you for things they are selling or services they are offering, or, on the other hand, invite you to embark on business ventures with them.

This could be lucrative, but don't be too trusting: Russians have a great ability to talk, but may be less capable when it comes to follow-through. Whatever their financial aspira-

rent-a-car
CINEMA TRANS

15, Drouzhinnikovskaya Street
123242 Moscow, Russia
Phone: (7-095) 255-9873
Phone/fax: (7-095) 255-9348
Telex: 411070 CENTR SU

	Toyota Carina E	Volvo–940	Toyota Hiace (10 seats)
Per hour ($ rates)			
day time 8 am – 8 pm	20	25	25
night time 8 pm – 8 am	25	30	30
Airport transfers (3-hour use, incl. waiting at the airport)	50	60	70
Per day (10-hour use)	160	180	200

- Minimum use — 2 hours, maximum time is unlimited
- Considerable discounts for long term rentals
- Reservations: Monday–Friday, from 9 am to 6 pm

THE RIGHT CHOICE FOR THE MOSCOW VISITOR

CAR + DRIVER

tions, Russians' earthy generosity and hospitality, especially extravagant when directed towards visitors from afar, will likely make you feel at home and secure.

Try to respond in kind, and don't be afraid to show emotions – all too often Westerners are seen to be cold and unfriendly. If you do, chances are you will find loyal friends and lasting friendships.

Further Reading

Recent change has made many of the numerous studies, histories, travelogues and other titles on Moscow and Russia out of date. Listed here are key works of information, up-to-date guides and particularly revealing studies.

The Traveller's Yellow Pages and *Handbook for Moscow* (first edition, 1994). Business and services listings, plus short texts explaining practicalities. Available from: InfoServices, 1 St. Marks Place, Cold Spring Harbour, NY 11724 (tel: 516-549-0064).

Where in Moscow, edited by Paul E. Richardson (fifth edition, 1995). Concise yellow and white pages, useful for tourists. Also, *Russia Survival Guide: Business & Travel* (sixth edition, 1995). Available from Russian Information Services, 89 Main Street #2, Montpelier, VT 05602 (tel: 800-639-4301).

Glas: New Russian Writing. A unique and inspiring quarterly journal of contemporary Russian writing in English translation, *Glas* is available in the U.S. from Zephyr Press (tel: 617-628-9726); in the U.K. from Dept. of Russian Literature, Univ. of Birmingham (tel: 0121-414-6044); in Moscow, from editor Natalya Perova (tel: 441-9157).

An Explorer's Guide to Russia, by Robert Greenall. A comprehensive 1994 guide for the independent traveller to European Russia. Published in the U.S. by Zephyr Press, in the U.K. by Canongate Press.

Trekking in Russia and Central Asia, by Frith Maier (first edition, 1994). Definitive guide to the wildernesses of the former Soviet Union. Available in the U.S. from The Mountaineers, 1011 SW Klickitat Way, Seattle, Washington 98134; in Canada from Douglas & McIntyre Ltd., 1615 Venables Street, Vancouver, B.C. V5L 2H1; in the U.K. from Cordee, 3-A De Montfort Street, Leicester LE1 7HD.

Russia: People to People, edited by Jim Haynes. Contains personal details and contact information on 1,000 Russians of all ages, from Moscow and St. Petersburg, who are interested in meeting people from abroad. (1995, Zephyr Press, Canongate).

A History of Russian Architecture, by William C. Brumfield (Cambridge UP, 1993). The fullest subject-guide, comprehensive and well-illustrated.

Moscow: An Architectural History, by Kathleen Berton (I.B. Tauris). Expert study specific to Mosow, ideal advance research for future visitors.

Discovering Moscow: The Complete Companion Guide, by Helen Boldyreff Semler. The most thorough and satisfying cultural/historical guide to Moscow. Published by St. Martin's Press, New York, 1989.

Practical Information

Preparations

Visas

There are three main types of visa for travel to the Russian Federation. Each is generally valid for up to three months.

1. **Ordinary.** This requires an invitation from a Russian citizen from the first city you wish to visit, which must be processed at a local branch of OVIR (*Otdel Viz i Registratsiy*, Visa and Registration Department).

2. **Business.** Similar to the above, except that private individuals are replaced by the company you wish to visit. If you have a contact at an enterprise or other legitimate organisations you may be able to solicit from them a "business visit" invitation letter. Many business-class hotels also offer such visa support. Their letter can be very brief and vague as to your purposes, and will still likely be accepted by the Russian consulate or embassy to which you are applying.

3. **Tourist.** This is the kind of visa you will receive if you join a group tour, although individuals can also travel this way. It is now possible to obtain this kind of visa, without pre-booking hotel accommodation, via your local Intourist branch. For a fee of $75 (£50), this leaves you with the freedom to choose your own accommodation when you arrive.

Fortunately, various organisations will assist you in applying for an ordinary or business visa. They include travel agents who specialise in Russia and other C.I.S. destinations. Others who do this include the Travellers' Guest House in Moscow (*see* Listings, Accommodation at the back of this guide).

In the United States, contact the Center for International Education in Alexandria, VA (tel: 800-343-7114, fax: 703 931-4085) and Russian Travel Service in Fitzwilliam, NH (tel. & fax: 603-585-6534), who are also the agents for our recommended Bed & Breakfast services. In the UK, most of the London-based visa services as well as travel agents can arrange this: fees start from about £70.

Whether you submit the application to the Russian embassy or consulate on your own, or through a visa support agent, all applications require you to supply two passport-size photos and your passport (a photocopy of the main pages is also acceptable), plus the processing fee. Applications should be submitted as early as possible, since extra charges are payable for urgent visas.

Consular fees seem to differ drastically from country to country, though U.S. and U.K. fees are both reasonable. You are strongly advised to avoid applying for visas in former Soviet republics, where consulates tend to be highly inefficient or plain unscrupulous; expect either to be kept waiting in ugly queues, or charged unearthly amounts of money, or both.

NOTE: if you are planning to leave Russia in the course of your visit to travel to one of the former Soviet republics (particularly Latvia, Lithuania, Estonia or Ukraine), a standard single-entry visa is *not* sufficient to ensure that you will be allowed to cross the border back into Russia.

A double-entry visa, or multiple-entry visa, is necessary for this. Also, obviously, the requisite visa for the country you are visiting. Land borders are controlled, as are international airports.

Russian Embassies & Consulates

UK
Russian Embassy
18 Kensington Palace Gardens,
London W8 4QP.
Tel: (0171) 229-6412,
727-6888.

Russian Consulates
5 Kensington Palace Gardens,
London W8 4QP.
Tel: (0171) 229-3215,
229-3216.

58 Melville Street, Edinburgh
EH3 7HL.
Tel: (0131) 225-7098;
fax: (0131) 225-9587.

USA
Russian Embassy
1115-1125 16th St. NW,
Washington D.C., 20036.
Tel: (202) 628-7551, 7554.

Russian Consulate General
9 East 91st St., New York,
NY 10020.
Tel: (212) 348-0926;
fax: (212) 831-9162.

Russian Consulates
2790 Green St., San Francisco,
CA 94123.
Tel: (415) 202-9800;
fax: (415) 929-0306.

2323 Westin Building, 2001 6th
Avenue, Seattle, WA 98121.
Tel: (206) 728-1910;
fax: (206) 728-1871.

Canada
Russian Embassy
52 Range Road, Ottawa, Ontario
K1N 8G5.
Tel: (613) 236-7220;
fax: (613) 238-6158

Russian Consulate
3655 Avenue du Musée,
Montreal, P.Q. H36 2E1.
Tel: (514) 843-5901;
fax: (514) 842-2012.

Registration

When you arrive, you are required to register your visa within three days (although if you take longer to do this, the consequences may not be dire). This is most easily done by the hotel in which you are staying (an automatic procedure); if you were invited by an organisation, the procedure must be done by them (this may mean giving up your passport for a few days).

If you have an ordinary visa and are not staying in a hotel, you will have to go yourself to the Registration Department (UVIR) at Ulitsa Chernyshevskovo 42, Metro Kitai Gorod northern exit, then trolleybus #25 or #45, to the edge of the Garden Ring road. Opening hours are Mon, Tues, Thurs 10 am–1 pm and 3 pm–6 pm; Fri 10 am–1 pm, 3 pm–5 pm. Tel: 207-0113. Queues here are long – expect the procedure to be infuriating.

Loss of Documents

It is advisable to make a photocopy of your passport and visa before you leave, and keep them in a safe place separate from the documents themselves.

In event of loss, the first thing you should do is report it to the *militia* – not so much in the hope of recovering anything, but in order to obtain a certificate stating what you have lost. If you are travelling in a group tour, some of these procedures should be done on your behalf.

Passport. Report the loss immediately to your embassy. You will be required to provide passport photos and a photocopy if possible, pay a fee and fill in an application form. The process takes about two days.

Visa. Go to the central UVIR with your militia report as well as a letter from the person or company which invited you.

Customs Declaration. Go with your militia report to Moscow Central Customs, Ulitsa Marinoi Roshchy 12. Tel: 971-1178. The inspector at window #6 will provide you with a new declaration. In practice, if you will not be taking any currency with you when you leave the country, this last procedure may not be necessary.

Health and Insurance

Vaccinations

Recent outbreaks of contagious diseases in Moscow and other areas mean that some vaccinations are now necessary. Tetanus shots should be updated, while diptheria jabs are essential for Moscow, where dozens of people died of the disease in 1993. The hepatitis A vaccine is now recommended.

Should you fail to get vaccinated before departure, the medical centres listed in this guide (*see* Listings, Medical Centres) will provide this service, though fees are high, and some will charge you for an initial examination as well as the jab.

Health Care

With the opening of a number of Western-run and -backed medical centres, staffed by foreign-trained doctors, the choice in health care has improved greatly in Moscow over the last three years.

Their charges — which may include a mandatory joining fee for even the simplest treatment —

are high; in urgent cases they will facilitate evacuation, or hospitalisation in more prestigious and comfortable Moscow clinics such as the Kremlin Hospital. A proper insurance cover will do much to help with such eventualities.

If urgent hospitalisation is needed outside this system, foreigners can expect to be as well treated as possible given language problems and the delapidation of many Russian hospitals. Patients can request visits to/by embassy doctors, though these services are generally expensive, and may not always be available.

Insurance is therefore strongly recommended, and should be sufficient to cover the high level of charges you may incur, as well as giving provision for evacuation (air ambulance) if necessary.

What to Take with You

Food and Medications

Nowadays most Western food items and basic medications are obtainable in Moscow, though very often the prices are higher than at home and supplies of rarer items can be erratic. For convenience, however, it's a good idea to take things like vitamins and dietary food as you may have to spend time searching for them once in Russia.

Some form of insect repellant is vital in summer — the mosquitoes, especially in northern areas, are vicious, and shop supplies get snapped up quickly during the season.

If you're travelling outside Moscow for more than a day, be sure to take whatever items of personal comfort you hold dear with you – the chances are you won't find them where you're going.

Clothing

If you're travelling between April and October, some form of light waterproof clothing is essential. Although Moscow's summer weather can be very warm and dry, it is interspersed by heavy thunderstorms, while spells of colder weather are always likely.

In winter, take layers of warm clothing, and a hat; temperatures are generally below freezing. There will almost certainly be snow and ice, so wear shoes that have a good grip – pavements can be treacherous.

Presents

You should be prepared to give plenty of small gifts to Russian friends. Most major brands of alcohol, cigarettes, sweets and the like have been available in Moscow for several years, so people will be more appreciative of things which are special to where you come from.

Books or magazines in a foreign language spoken by the recipient always go down well, as do records, cassettes and CDs (though bear in mind that many Russians don't have CD players).

Travel to Moscow

By Air

Almost all major airlines have flights to Moscow. If you're travelling from Western Europe, cheaper options are generally on transit routes, such as those via Helsinki or Frankfurt. The new private Russian airline Transaero now has a remarkably cheap and comfortable flight from London Gatwick to Sheremetyevo 1 (slightly further from the centre than Sheremetyevo 2) with a 30-minute stop in Riga. Aeroflot Russian International Airlines still seems to lag behind its rivals in terms of service, and its prices are not even especially competitive when compared with European national carriers.

From the U.S., there are a multitude of options, with almost all major European carriers flying via their home capitals. Delta flies direct to Moscow from New York, while Aeroflot fly from New York, Chicago, San Francisco, Los Angeles, Miami, Seattle and Washington DC.

By Train

Arrival by train, via Europe or China, offers a distinct view of the country, although journeys are very lengthy.

1. If you're coming from the U.K. or anywhere in Northern Europe, you'll pass through the flat, rather dull countryside of Poland and Belorussia to arrive at the Belorussia Station in Moscow. The journey time from London (via Oostende or Hoek van Holland) is about 56 hours.

2. Forest and lake scenery is the attraction of the northern route, a daily train leaving Helsinki, Finland for Moscow and taking about 15 hours.

3. Three routes bring passengers from Southern Europe and the Balkans to Russia, via Ukraine (for which a transit visa is necessary). Those that cross from Hungary and Slovakia at Chop, and Romania at Vadul Siret offer spectacular views of the Carpathian mountains on the way.

If you're coming from Romania you should avoid the Ungeny route – this takes you through Moldova, for which you need an extra transit visa, and the break-away Transdniester Republic, scene of armed conflict a few years ago.

1. The Trans-Siberian Express runs between Moscow and Peking, with one route crossing the border directly, another travelling through Mongolia. Trains on the direct China-Russia route are more comfortable.

A spectacular route has opened up through Kyrgyzstan; this, again, requires extra transit visas.

Train tickets straight through to Moscow are not much cheaper than flying, after allowing for the various transit costs, although they allow the flexibility of open return date (tickets are normally valid two months). But based on your individual trip itinerary, there may be opportunities for a little added adventure. Avoid buying train tickets to Europe in Moscow: prices are considerably higher.

There are also a number of bus routes from Germany, France, Poland, Finland as well as Southern Europe and the Balkan countries. Check locally for details.

Customs Regulations

On entering the country, travellers are expected to fill in a customs declaration form stating the amount of currency held in cash, traveller's cheques etc., plus any valuable items that you want to take out with you. You should keep this form throughout your stay; on departure you will complete a similar form, both of which you will hand in as part of a procedure which seems to have lost its point some years ago.

There is no limit to the amount of money you can bring in, and the amount which you take out should not exceed that figure: proof of exchange certificates are no longer requested. (It's a good idea to make photocopies of credit cards, the main pages of your passport, and your visa, and to keep them in the same safe place as your customs declaration.)

It is forbidden to bring Russian currency and other purchasing documents into or out of the country, as well as narcotics and weapons, with the exception of those required for hunting, which need a special permit from the Interior Ministry.

There are also restrictions on what you can take out of Russia, which are changing constantly. Objects of artistic, historical or other cultural value, such as icons, can only be taken out with the authorisation of the Ministry of Culture and on payment of a special duty. Many art galleries will provide this service for you automatically if you purchase the works through them. If you attempt to export such works without permission, they will likely be confiscated at the border.

Crime and Security

Although foreign headlines are often gripped by news of Russia's rising crime rate, don't expect the streets of Moscow to be any worse than those of New York – in fact they are consider-ably safer.

Take the precautions neces-sary for any large city, and don't rule out the chance that you could become a target of crime. Foreigners may stand out less now than in the past – the flashiness of Russia's New Rich takes a great deal of beating – but some will still assume that visitors are loaded with money, as well as being more vulnerable due to their unfamiliarity with the local environment. Though clothes alone are unlikely to make you stand out, many Russians can generally tell foreigners by their expression and mannerisms, even if speech or skin colour don't give them away immediately.

Organised crime of the kind which dominates news headlines will not affect the short-term visitor – it already operates on a scale, compared to which the budget of most casual travellers is negligible. Petty crime is another matter, and it is here – from pick-pocketing, to street robbery – that you may experience trouble.

Bear in mind also that crime-fighting in Russia, especially directed towards small-scale or everyday offences, leaves much to be desired. Don't expect to rely on the *militia* (police) to be of much help if you become a victim: the service is as inefficent and badly financed as many other official bodies. While there are many honest and hard-working cops, others are thoroughly corrupt and would expect bribes for the most simple kinds of assistance. The most you are likely to receive from them for any petty crime are the documents necessary for an insurance claim.

Gypsies

Gypsies are a common phenomenon in Moscow: if they approach you and offer, for instance, to read your palm, it's best to remove yourself in another direction as quickly as possible. They can be very persistent, and it may be necessary to show more aggression than you are used to, or would like, to keep them away.

As in many European cities, gangs of gypsy children can be the most visible and aggressive thieves. Beware of unkempt, poor-looking children (often under age 14, because they cannot be arrested) and resist being sympathetic to their condition. You are in danger of being robbed as they surround you. Giving them money, rather than getting rid of them often has the opposite effect.

At Night

Be especially careful at night. Even if you are travelling, avoid hanging around metro stations, train stations, markets or airports if at all possible, and don't carry excessive amounts of money with you.

Don't get into private cars or taxis if there are two or more people already inside (this applies equally during daylight hours). Many Russians carry protective CS gas cannisters, *gazoviye ballonchiki*, but the best protection is to be aware of your surroundings.

Accommodation

If you're staying in a hotel which is anything but five-star, it is advisable to keep your door locked at all times and your valuables on your person. Don't have too much faith in hotel security, and beware of semi-official, unordered room service. Entrance guards, despite their often threatening appearance, can be slack and unobservant, and floor attendants are usually only elderly women.

If you're staying at a Russian home or in rented accommodation, never give your address to a stranger. If you're arranging to meet someone whom you don't know very well, try to do so on neutral ground.

Women Travellers

As in other countries of the world, unwelcome attention can be a problem, and you may be accosted on the street. Try not to be too friendly, especially if you're unsure of the context: don't respond to eye-contact, since that could be interpreted as a direct come-on.

Russian women are often much more restrained and surly with men, until they really know and trust them. Try not to walk alone at night, and if it's really necessary, walk fast and don't turn your head.

Money

Rubles or Dollars?

After years during which the dollar functioned as an alternative currency on Russian territory, a new law which took effect from the beginning of 1994 has made the ruble the country's only legal tender. All shops and other enterprises officially take rubles only, although some may be willing to let you exchange simultaneous to making purchases, or provide facilities on the spot.

Do not rely on this, however, and do not be fooled by prices written in dollars or deutschmarks (or in "y.e." – this is simply another way of saying dollars,

and has nothing to do with Japanese yen!): payment is by rubles at the current exchange rate, or by credit card (purchases will be billed in dollars).

For street or market purchases, taxi rides and other informal transactions it may still be possible to pay in dollars if you need to. In any case, be discrete when purchasing with dollars on the street, and keep bills tucked away in separate pockets.

Credit cards are accepted in an increasing number of locations, from hotels and restaurants to stores, although the fact that there are signs/stickers visible does not necessarily mean that one or other credit card is actually valid in the shop – check inside. Payment facilities by travellers' cheques are still rare.

Exchanging Money

In the last five years, the ruble's movement against the U.S. dollar has been uniformly downwards, despite times when the speed of fall stalls and an apparent period of short-lived stability sets in.

At print date, the exchange rate was approximately 4,500 rubles to one U.S. dollar, with the ruble having recovered some of its previous lost value. In the wake of a Central Bank edict promising to keep currency fluctuations within a limited range, the future may hold greater stability.

Changing money is not usually a problem in normal working hours, or at other times in main central areas – although on Sunday, even in the centre of the city there are few exchange offices open. Such locations are easy to identify, generally with signs in English or $ signs – in Cyrillic, the words are *obmen valyuty*, Обмен Валюты.

These offices are generally operated by banks and have ultra-tight security (i.e. armed toughs in khaki at the door, and special boxes for passing money through to a cashier behind protective glass screens), which makes them a pretty safe option. Such points accept dollars, sometimes deutschmarks, but rarely any other currency.

Make sure notes are not worn, ripped or written on – these are rarely accepted at full rate, although many exchange points will have a list of places that do accept them. If you cannot get to one of these, expect to sacrifice about ten percent of their face value for the convenience of rapid exchange. Some exchange points refuse to take dollars dated pre-1985. Most do not charge a commission for transactions, though you may find that the rate for changing less than $100 is less favourable.

Be very wary of changing with people on the street, especially if they appear from nowhere – the chances are they'll disappear again with your money. Sometimes people standing in a bank line with you will offer to sell you rubles – they may give you a better rate but make sure they produce their rubles before you show them your dollars – and remember that such transactions remain illegal.

Denominations

At present, notes are issued in denominations of 100; 200; 500; 1,000; 5,000; 10,000; 50,000 and 100,000 rubles. Old Soviet notes, dated 1961–1991, are no longer legal tender, nor are blue 5,000 and red 10,000 bills dated 1992. There are coins in denominations of 1, 5, 10, 20, 50 and 100 rubles.

Travellers' Cheques & Credit Cards

These can be changed in some hotels and banks, but don't rely on finding one of these places open at weekends and expect to pay a sizable commission. Make sure you always have some cash with you just in case, and for convenience bring some smaller denomination notes.

Withdrawing dollars by credit card is increasingly widespread, and avoids the need to keep large sums in cash. Although banks now deal with these transactions efficiently, their commission fees, which are charged on top of any commission made by the card-issuer, range from one percent (withdrawals on Visa from Inkombank) to as high as five percent. Check your notes, and do not hesitate to ask for smaller denominations if you need them.

Cost of Living

Moscow has a reputation as being one of the most expensive cities in the world. This assumption is usually confirmed by those who arrive as tourists or on business, and whose lives revolve around hotels, first class restaurants and tourist traps such as the Arbat.

There is also an iniquitous two-tier pricing system which applies to many hotels, internal rail and air tickets and even now some museums, whereby the very primitive distinction is made between Russian (sometimes C.I.S.) citizens and everyone else; the latter have to pay as much as 20 times the rate charged to the former. Whereas some of these prices for foreigners may be considered reasonable, others, particularly for hotels, are clearly too high.

It is still possible, however, to live cheaply in Moscow. You can stay in Bed & Breakfast accommodation (see advertisement on pages 41–43), use public transport at a fraction of the equivalent cost in the West, have lunch at one of the many bistros or fast-food venues and dinner, say, at one of the cheaper restaurants mentioned in this guide (local cuisines like Georgian are often the best value).

Even taxis are still considerably cheaper than in the West, despite the fact that, as a foreigner, you will probably pay more than a local.

It should be possible to keep on-the-ground expenses, including accommodation, to well below $100 a day, although going outside the above limits may see costs rising rapidly.

City Transport

Metro

Moscow's Metro is by far the fastest and most convenient form of public transport in the city. It consists of a circle line (*koltsevaya linia*) intersected by numerous radial (*radialniye linii*) lines. They operate from 5:30 am–1:30 am, though interchanges between stations close earlier, at about 1 am.

Fares
Payment is by green plastic jeton (currently costing R 600, or about 10 cents, available at windows inside the station), which is inserted into the turnstile as you enter. Thereafter you are free to travel as you please, for as long as you please until you

exit from another station. (Metro ticket offices also sell the smaller brown plastic telephone token which allows you to call from public telephones.)

If you are staying for a month or more, it may be more sensible to get a monthly pass, either for the metro alone (currently R 36,000, about $7) or for all means of transport (R 60,000, about $12). Just show your card to the attendant as you enter.

Orientation
Once on the platform, you will see a sign above your head listing the stations in each direction (if you are at a junction of several lines, signs will appear before the corresponding escalator at the top). If you intend to change, you can check which station to alight at from the diagram on the wall beyond the track. Interchange stations are given in red, and the stations on the intersecting line (colour coded) listed below those stations.

Once you are on the train, it is difficult to determine which station you are at by looking out of the window. Signs are rare, and trains can be very crowded. Listen for the taped announcement: the name of the station will be given first, followed by any connections from that station. Just before the doors close you will hear the warning *astarozhna, dveeri zakrivayootsa* ("attention, the doors are closing"), followed by the name of the next station. Recently, diagrams have appeared in trains with names of all stations on the given line marked in both Cyrillic and Roman script.

If the train is crowded and your station is next, ask the person in front of you *vy vykhodite?* ("are you getting out?"); if they are not, they will do their best to make way for you. If you wish to change to another line, look for the sign with a man walking down steps and the word *perekhod* (переход, transfer), and the name of the station you are changing to.

Some circle line stations have the same names as their radial counterparts, so in this case look for the name of the line. Tretyakovskaya and Kitai Gorod stations have mixed platforms, where you may not have to use the *perekhod* but simply need to cross to your train.

Exits from stations are marked simply by the word *vykhod* (выход or выход в город, exit). Many stations have two exits, and there are signs on the platform indicating which exit leads to which bus, trolleybus, and tram routes, and also directions to nearby streets and landmarks.

Overland Transport

Trolleybuses, trams and buses generally start later and finish earlier than the metro. Though you may be lucky late at night with stray buses, this cannot be relied on, and even at 10 pm waits can be long.

Most are more crowded and slower than the metro, and not recommended for longer journeys. Buses can be useful for travelling between places which are close geographically where there is no convenient metro connection, as well as for reaching distant suburbs from the last metro stop on a line and travelling to country areas.

Tickets (at the same price, or cheaper than the metro) can be purchased in strips of 10 from the driver or from special kiosks, as well as from metro ticket offices. For each journey you punch your ticket in one of the

franking gadgets along the walls of the bus.

There are periodic checks by inspectors: they will show identification and expect you to produce a monthly pass or punched ticket. If you don't have either, you will have to leave the bus with them at the next stop and pay the fine. Inspectors never appear during rush hour or late at night, and fines remain cheaper than monthly passes.

Orientation

Stops are marked by an "A" for buses and a "T" for trolleybuses and trams (some also have the alternative Russian "T", spelt like the letter "M", not to be confused with the sign for the Metro).

One side of the sign gives intervals during peak hours and the end destination of each route (some central stops have a complete list of stops). If you're not going to the end and have no transport map, you'll probably have to ask if the bus/trolleybus is going where you want, or rely on the bus itself, which generally lists the main stops on a board in the side window.

Often stops are not announced over the vehicle's loudspeaker, or the voice is incoherent, so unless you have instructions in advance you may need to ask where to get off. If you don't speak Russian, try writing down your destination on a scrap of paper.

Suburban Trains *(Electrichki)*

Most towns in *Moskovskaya Oblast'* (Moscow Region) are served by electric trains from the city's nine terminals. They are currently Russia's cheapest form of out-of-town transport – and it shows. In summer they are stifling, in winter freezing cold, and often dirty, smelly, slow and packed tight (especially at weekends when Muscovites travel backwards and forwards from their dachas).

Tickets are bought at the *prigorodnaya kassa* (пригородная касса), singles unless otherwise stated. To ask for a return, say "tooda i abratna". The same situation with inspectors and finding stops once on board applies as for overland municipal transport.

Taxis

Taxis are not always easy to find, but in Moscow you won't have much trouble getting a lift. Just hold out your arm at the roadside (with your palm spread, not with thumb extended as in the West).

You can flag down almost anyone, from trucks to Mercedes, and at night even buses. If you're going a short distance, ambulance drivers usually have the best rates and almost always stop. Don't worry about interfering with their work; they won't pick you up unless they're off duty!

When the car stops for you, you need to state your destination and agree on a price with the driver, even if the car appears to have a meter. Many will try to overcharge foreigners, so try to get an idea of approximate rates beforehand. Taxis hanging around airports, railway stations, hotels and other places where foreigners gather are expensive and not always safe.

It's not advisable to take a car in which there are already other passengers; woman should only travel alone at night by taxi if they are familiar with the local environment.

You can book radio taxis by phone, although an element of

Russian is necessary for this. These are reliable, and can work out cheaper despite the booking fee. Tel: 457-9005, 975-5101, 975-3101, 927-2108, 927-0000.

Driving in Moscow, Car Hire

Traffic rules in Russia are often quite bizarre, with elaborate one-way systems, U-turns and a distinct shortage of legal left turns (instead you'll have to do a U-turn followed by a right turn, or vice versa).

You are likely to be pulled over by the traffic militia (GAI, ГАИ) quite regularly; they usually stand by the roadside and usher you aside with hand signals. In such cases, you are justified in pretending that you don't understand (if this is the case). Failing that the proffering of a few dollars should satisfy them, although negotiating this may be tricky without language skills.

Russians drive aggressively, often failing to heed the rules and cutting in front at a moment's notice. Blame for a collision from behind always lies with the rear vehicle.

Filling up with petrol can sometimes be a problem, as stations are often invisible (on minor roads), closed or out of petrol. Don't leave yourself short, and be sure to get a map indicating their whereabouts in advance.

For these reasons, most car hire companies provide vehicles complete with drivers. For a full list of firms, see Listings, Car Hire at the end of this guide.

Travel to/from Airports

Arriving at one of Moscow's airports, especially at inconvenient night-time hours, can make for an expensive or unpleasant introduction to the city. At Sheremetyevo 2, in particular, try to get someone you know or an acquaintance to meet you.

Travel rates into the centre of the city offered by official companies at the airport are as much as $45-50: although private drivers will offer to take you for less, be wary about accepting their offers. Returning to the airport is much simpler and cheaper, with many drivers (especially those already on Leningradsky Prospekt) willing to make the detour and drop you off for the ruble equivalent of $10–15.

Although some who offer their services will try to convince arriving passengers that there is no other way of reaching the centre, all airports, including Sheremetyevo 2, are served by bus routes. This does not apply at night, and may involve longer than usual delays at non-peak hours, as well as being inconvenient if you have luggage.

To travel to Sheremetyevo 2 airport, there is an Express bus to/from Metro Rechnoi Voksal, as well as stopping buses #517 to/from Metro Planernaya, and #551 to/from Metro Rechnoi Voksal, all of which also serve Sheremetyevo 1. The stop is on the ground level of the airport, beyond the car park: tickets in strips must be bought from the driver, and two tickets endorsed for the journey, plus one for each large piece of baggage.

There is also an Express bus to the city air terminal, Aerovoksal, which leaves from the lower-level covered area, approximately every hour, first bus 5:30 am, last bus 10 pm (fares R 4,500 plus R 1,000 for each piece of luggage).

For Sheremetyevo 1 airport (for Aeroflot flights to St. Petersburg and the Russian

north, plus all Transaero flights, and other international destinations, including charter flights): as for Sheremetyevo 1.

For Vnukovo airport (flights to most southern and Siberian destinations), take bus #511 or #511-Э from Metro Yugo-Zapadnaya. For Domodedovo (flights to Central Asia and some Siberian destinations), take a suburban train from Paveletsky Vokzal.

Express buses to all internal flight airports leave the central air terminal, Aerovokzal (Metro Dinamo, Leningradsky Prospekt 37-A) between 5:30 am and 10 pm. Connecting buses also run between airports.

Communications

Postal Services

The Russian post office has improved considerably in recent years, but should still not be relied on for fast service. Registered (*zakazniye*) and express letters are only moderately faster and more reliable than ordinary airmail, although still cheaper than Western postal charges.

If you want to be really sure, though, and are in a hurry, the international mailing services (Federal Express, TNT Mailfast, DHL and others) are all represented in Moscow. Their offices can generally be found in major hotels, while the joint venture EMS Garantpost is based in several major Moscow post offices. Larger envelopes will be opened and inspected by customs (both incoming and outgoing), which holds them up for a further day: expect a delivery time of 3–4 days to the West for the courier companies (often longer for incoming mail), and 4–7 days with Garantpost.

If sending parcels by post, the usual practice is to take them to the post office unwrapped, where they will be inspected. If you don't have your own wrapping paper you will be given string and brown paper which is generally of inferior quality. Only a limited number of post offices take international parcels.

When addressing letters or postcards in Russia, you should put the country name at the beginning, preferably in both Cyrillic and Roman letters, and the number 500 in the bottom left corner (this simply shows the postman that the letter is going outside the former Soviet Union and replaces the six figure postal code for internal mail). If you're using a Russian envelope or postcard (as opposed to a blank Western envelope) there is a special place for the postcode, and a space at the bottom right for the sender's address. Stamps are generally, but not always, available in post offices.

Telephone: Local Calls

Local calls within Moscow from private phones are free, so asking your host if you can make a call is purely a matter of courtesy. Street payphones (taksofon, таксофон) are often broken, and it may require some persistence to find one that works.

Use the special brown plastic tokens (zheton, жетон), available from metro station ticket offices and post offices: in theory, each should give you three minutes, but in fact most seem to carry on indefinitely without your needing to insert another token. There is no way for people to call you back on these phones.

Long Distance Calls

Calls abroad can be made from most private phones, post offices, special inter-city payphone centres (peregovorny punkt, переговорный пункт), hotel rooms and card phones in some hotel lobbies, but not from ordinary payphones on the street.

From a private phone or hotel room, dial 8 for a line outside Moscow, wait for the tone, then 10 for an international line, then the country code etc. Make sure that you know the charges beforehand and agree about payment with your host. If you need to book a call through the operator, call 8 (wait for tone)-194.

In post offices you should go to the telefon (телефон) section, where you can book calls by writing the destination, phone number and duration of call on a piece of paper and paying the cashier. After some time, your name and booth number will be announced and you can take the call.

It is probably easier, though, to go to the peregovorny punkt (sometimes these are separate entities, sometimes inside post offices). Here you simply pay a deposit on entering, and are directed to a booth where you dial the number yourself. Procedure differs from place to place, so check whether you need to dial the first 8, and whether you need to press a button when connected. You can now make collect calls to the U.S. via AT&T, as well as charge card calls, by dialling 155-5042.

If you're calling to cities in Russia or the former Soviet Union, the same procedure applies as for dialling abroad. Dial "8", followed by the city/area code and number.

Charges

Telephone charges for inter-national calls differ depending on the time of day and type of phone used. As elsewhere in the world, calls are cheaper early in the morning and late at night.

Prices are now comparable, in some cases higher, than in the U.S. or Europe. Charges are lowest from private homes and state-financed organizations, while calls reserved through the operator or made from offices are charged at about twice the standard rate. In Moscow, you can find out rates for calls by dialling 07. Like anywhere else in the world rates from hotel room phones and payphones are higher still, usually increasing in proportion to the hotel's standard.

Useful Numbers

Fire	01
Militia (police)	02
Ambulance	03
Local information	09
Time	100

Telegrams

This is a most effective and cheap way to reach people, both inside and outside the former Soviet Union. Telegrams can be sent from any post office, or over the phone by dialling 927-2002, though for texts in English it's probably better to go to the former. Most post offices in the city have a telegram (*telegraf*, телеграф) service.

Major Post Offices
(with services provided)

Tsentralny Telegraf
Ulitsa Tverskaya 7, Metro Okhotny Ryad. Tel: 924-9004. For fax, telephone, telex.

Mezhdunarodny Pochtamt
Varshavskoye Shosse 37, Metro Nagatinskaya. Tel: 114-4584. For EMS Garantpost, inter-national parcels.

Tsentralny Pochtamt
Ulitsa Myasnitskaya 26, Metro Chistiye Prudy. Tel: 928-6311. For fax, telephone, EMS Garantpost.

Opening Times

Russian shops generally have long working hours, from 8 or 9 am to 7 pm (until 8 or 9 pm, for food shops). Former state shops have a lunch break (*pereryv*, перерыв) which runs either from 1–2 pm or 2–3 pm. You will find sometimes that shops (also museums, public buildings, restaurants, cafés) are closed for repairs, for "technical reasons" *(po tekhnicheskim prichinam)*, for inventory *(uchot)* or for cleaning *(sanitarny den')*.

Except for the last case, which is usually a fixed day towards the end of the month, these circumstances are almost impossible to predict – an infuriating fact of life in Moscow. Note that many such places will be closed on public holidays.

Banks are generally open 10 am–5 pm, while branches of the State Savings Bank (*Sberbank*), which also exchanges foreign currency, should list branches which remain open on holidays.

Almost all cultural events in Moscow – concerts, opera and ballet, theatres and film showings – start at 7 pm. In practice, curtain-up will normally be a few minutes later – punctuality has yet to make its mark here.

Public Holidays

In an overall system which seems a curious mix of old and new, the old Soviet-era holidays (such as New Year's Day, Women's Day and May Day) are still more important, and popularly celebrated festivities than their recent democratic counterparts (Sovereignty and Constitution Day).

Orthodox Church feast days are now also widely celebrated, particularly Easter. The Russian Orthodox Church still uses the old Gregorian calendar which runs twelve days behind the Western, or Julian, calendar: thus, Christmas is celebrated on January 7th, and the "Old" New Year on January 13th.

In some especially confusing cases, the previous working week will be adapted to suit a forthcoming holiday to combine it with the nearest weekend; normally, the previous Saturday becomes a working day.

Official holidays fall on the following days:

January 1st, 2nd - New Year's Holidays, a time of heavy drinking.
January 7th - Orthodox Christmas
March 8th - International Women's Day, a symbolic equivalent of Mother's Day in the West, when women are feted with flowers, chocolates and other gifts from their menfolk.
April - Orthodox Easter, the exact date of which varies from year to year.
May 1st, 2nd - Workers' Day, still celebrated in Russia though without the former pompous parades on Red Square.
May 9th - Victory Day, now being revived as a time for parades of veterans and present-day military. The German capitulation in 1945 was signed at midnight Moscow time, hence the holiday comes a day later than in the West.
June 12th - Sovereignty Day, anniversary of the 1991 elections for the Russian Parliament. A holiday that no one properly understands.
December 12th — Constitution Day, marking the 1993 yes-vote given to Russia's constitution.

Summer Shut-down

Most Muscovites spend their summer weekends and holidays out of Moscow if they possibly can. If they cannot afford holidays on the Mediterranean — Cyprus is the most popular destination for newly-wealthy Russians — or on their own, now almost as expensive, Black Sea coast, most will go to their dachas to relax, sunbathe, grow fruit and vegetables and generally cool off from the rigours of city life.

As a reflection of this, many official enterprises and even businesses drastically reduce the scale of their activity over the summer.

Culturally, too, the summer is a near dead-season for the city with very little theatrical or concert activity in evidence between the end of June and the beginning of September.

The phenomenon has its charms as well as its frustrations. On July and August weekends, in particular, Moscow can seem a different city with quiet pavements which at other times of the year would be packed with passers-by and major roads which are mercifully light of their usual heavy road traffic.

May We Recommend
MOSCOW BED & BREAKFAST

Get a taste of how Muscovites live, and let your host help acclimate you to the city! The publishers of *An Explorer's Guide to Moscow* invite you to contact their partners, Moscow Bed & Breakfast, who offer **accommodation, guide/interpreter, visa support,** and other contacts, bookable from the U.S. at a cost substantially below the rates of other such organizations.

Moscow B&B can meet you at the airport or train station, bring you to your bed & breakfast host, and pick you up at the end of your stay. They have also engaged guide/interpreters who are available to take you on excursions in and around the city, for either individual sight visits, or for engagements lasting several days or more. Another service is **ticket purchase,** for the Bolshoy and other performances as well as for train, bus or boat travel. You pay the cost of the ticket plus a small service charge. Visa support, including invitations, is available as well.

For **bed & breakfast,** daily rates range between $25 and $45, depending upon whether your host speaks English and on the location of the apartment (the center or suburbs). Dinner may be added for $8–10. Our agent, Russian Travel Service, charges a modest flat fee for each accommodation. **Guide/interpreters** are available at a rate of $10–$15 per hour, depending upon level of experience. (They can be engaged for half-days or full days as well.) Guides with less formal training are suitable for most tourists. A **car and driver** may be hired for traveling within the city or outside. You can book an interpreter (with or without a car) to accompany you on explorations of the Yaroslavl, Vladimir, and Tver Regions, as well as of more distant places. We also handle arrangements for **group travel.** For further information, advice, visa support, and complete booking assistance, please contact Russian Travel Service. If you speak Russian, you may contact Moscow Bed & Breakfast directly, by fax.

Note: Russian Travel Service also books bed & breakfast for St. Petersburg and Kiev.

Russian Travel Service	***Moscow Bed & Breakfast***
Attn: Helen Kates	Alla Kashtanova, Director
P.O. Box 311	Moscow, Russia
Fitzwilliam, NH 03447	tel. & fax:
tel. & fax:	(7)(095) 457-3508
(603) 585-6534	

◆ S A M P L E   L I S T I N G S ◆

These are some of the Moscow hosts and guide/
interpreters who are available for booking through
Moscow Bed & Breakfast.

BED & BREAKFAST

Metro KIEVSKAYA, just west of the center, across the
Moscow river. **Evgeny** and **Galina** are actors, and live in a
2-room apartment with their 9-year old daughter, Daria.
They speak English, and also have a car.

Metro KANTEMIROVSKAYA, south of the center near
Kolomenskoye Museum Preserve. **Dina** lives alone in a
2-bedroom apartment. She speaks English.

Metro CHISTY PRUDY, in the center near the Garden
Ring, a very beautiful part of old Moscow. **Galina** is 36,
and lives in a 4-bedroom apartment with her 16- and 12-
year-old sons, Ivan and Sergey. They can accommodate
four guests in 2 rooms.

Metro KRASNOPRESENSKAYA, on the Circle Line. **Boris**
is an actor, and has a one-bedroom apartment. He speaks
English, and offers his apartment for short lengths of time.

Near Metro DINAMO, north of the center. **Yelena** is a 35-
year-old economist, and lives alone in her 2-room apartment, in a green and peaceful part of Moscow. She speaks
English.

Near Metro OKTYABRSKOYE POLE, Khoroshovskoye
shossé district, NW of the center. **Tatyana** is 45 years old,
and lives in a 2-room apartment. She speaks English and
French.

Metro TUSHINSKAYA, NW from the center. **Malika** is a
vibrant middle-aged woman who has a two-room apartment. She teaches Russian language and literature, and
speaks Spanish.

Metro KIEVSKAYA, on the Circle Line. Both **Lucia** and
her husband **Sergey** are philologists. They have a small
black poodle; Lucia speaks English.

Near Metro RECHNOY VOKZAL (River Station), north of
the center. **Galina** is 50, and lives in a very comfortable 2-
room apartment. She is an engineer, and has a dog named
Collie.

Metro UNIVERSITET, near Moscow State University.
Alexender is 60, and has a 3-room apartment. He offers
two rooms for accommodation in this peaceful area.

Metro UNIVERSITET, near Moscow State University. **Olga** is an assistant director of the Moscow Art Theater. She lives with her mother and 8-year-old daughter in a 2-room apartment, and offers one room for accommodation of guests.

GUIDE / INTERPRETERS

Twenty-year-old **Vadim** lives in a Moscow suburb. He's studied in the U.S., where he practiced his English a lot, and can take part in some excursions outside of the city. He enjoys swimming, science fiction, theater, and music.

Olga is an actress who manages an art gallery. She's 35, and is fond of music, poetry, theater, and the piano. A very helpful and charming person.

Nadezhda is 40 years old, has worked as a dealer in an art gallery, and as an interpreter with Gosconcert, the state concert organization. She is an expert in Russian literature and art, and also enjoys traveling. She is willing and able to travel with visitors. She is an Orthodox Christian.

Natalya has been an interpreter with Aeroflot, and is now a supervisor with El Al Airlines in Moscow. She has worked as a tour guide, and also interpreted at meetings of all kinds. She is sometimes available to travel with tourists. She likes literature, theater, music, and art.

Lucia has graduated from the University of Sofia, Bulgaria. She teaches English and is also a professional interpreter, and likes to read history and French literature, and to attend theater, especially opera.

Raisa, 40, is a graduate in Technical Translation from the Institute of Foreign Languages, and worked abroad as an interpreter for several years. She is available to accompany visitors on trips outside of Moscow.

Forty-year-old **Marina** has three years experience as a guide/interpreter on Russian-American cruises. She can accompany visitors on tours of Moscow, and also of old Russian towns nearby.

Natalya likes literature, classical music, opera, and ballet. She is a teacher of English, and teaches Russian to foreigners. She is 39.

Lyuba has interpreted for American and Canadian tourists, and has served as an interpreter at international competitions. Her personal interests include music, theater, art, and politics; she also collects stamps. She can travel with tourists. Christian.

Customs and Habits

Russians have always been famous for their public sullenness and reserve. While developments of the last decade have made them more open and able to express themselves to strangers, they are still very modest in public and don't make unnecessarily overt displays of emotion. Foreigners (particularly some Americans) often stand out immediately for doing just this.

Attitudes toward foreigners vary in Moscow (and in Russia as a whole), and while open hostility is still relatively rare, some may resent loud behaviour. Try to be restrained, without going to the other extreme and becoming excessively timid.

The Rigours of Daily Life

Assertiveness is still very necessary in many areas of Russian daily life. On public transport, in shops, and in queues generally, some extra effort may be needed to get what you want, as staff are often infuriatingly passive and unhelpful. If you find shop assistants chatting to each other or to one of the customers, don't be afraid to interrupt or surprised if they seem annoyed at your doing so — it's how everyone behaves.

Queues in Russia have their own special rules, which are essential to know. The first thing you should do before joining one is establish who is last. Ask *kto paslyedny?* and expect the reply *ya* (I am). Failure to do this, particularly if the line is an ambiguous one with people standing or sitting around in no obvious order, will result in people not remembering when you arrived and refusing to let you go in front of them.

If you are having problems, for instance with finding your way, don't be afraid to ask — signposting and directions are universally recognised to be poor. People are almost always helpful and many Muscovites have some understanding of English.

Visiting Friends

The Moscow home is very different from the fast, savage world of Moscow street life. You will probably be given a lavish welcome and be considered an honoured guest, so try to rise to the occasion. Bring flowers for the hostess (make sure there's an odd number of them — even-numbered bouquets are only for funerals), and chocolates, alcohol, biscuits, books, cassettes from your own country, or anything you think is suitable. Children will like any Western sweets, chewing gum, coins, badges or other trinkets.

You may be fed to bursting point. Don't be afraid to help yourself or ask for more — it can only please your hostess. If you're drinking, try to master the Russians' down-in-one vodka technique (this will probably earn you great respect!), but know your own limits. Do as everyone else does and take a long drink of juice or eat a pickled cucumber to take the taste away. After everyone's had a few drinks it's easier to keep your glass full and avoid inviting further refills. Bottles, once finished, should not be left to stand on the table.

It's worth knowing a few basic codes of etiquette. Men almost always shake hands in greeting, with hugs and kisses reserved for more emotional occasions or closer friends. Women kiss one another, but not always — and rarely shake hands with men.

Never greet someone across the threshold: it is considered bad luck. Use the more formal greeting when first being introduced to someone, especially when they are of an older generation. See "Basic Expressions" in the Language section at the end of this chapter.

In Church

If you visit a Russian Orthodox church or monastery, note that men are required to remove their hats, and women to wear some form of headgear (in Old Believer churches, scarves are obligatory).

Shorts and mini-skirts are also frowned on, and photos can only be taken inside a church with special permission.

Eating and Drinking

Food

Although few may visit Russia for its cuisine — it has neither the rich variety of Southern European cooking nor the spicy intrigue of Asian dishes — there are enough tasty and filling choices to keep you satisfied and interested for some time at least, especially if you don't rely only on restaurants, but are fortunate enough to be invited to accept offers of Russian hospitality.

The basic Russian diet is simple. Traditional peasant cooking usually involved one or more of the following staple vegetables: potatoes (*kartoshka*), turnips (*repa*), onions (*luk*), cucumbers (*ogurtsy*), beetroot (*svyokla*) and cabbage (*kapoosta*), of which the perishable ones are pickled for the winter. Salted cabbage or cucumbers are still commonly used as garnishes.

Other fruits and vegetables appear in season, so in July look for strawberries (*kloobnika*) and raspberries (*malina*), in August and September for melons (*dynya*) and water-melons (*arbooz*). Sour cranberries (*klyookva*) help to liven up the monotonous winter diet, while apples (*yabloka*), and to some extent tangerines (*mandariny*) and persimmons (*khurma*), are the only source of winter vitamins for most Russians. Vegetables are generally served in salads as *zakuski*, starters, while fruit is served as a dessert.

Mushrooms (*griby*) are widely enjoyed, and one of the most popular Russian pastimes in autumn is an outing to the forest for mushroom-picking. They can be fried (*zharenniye*), pickled (*marinovanniye*), or baked in a delicious sour cream sauce to produce *zhulyen*, julienne. They can be served as a main dish, or instead of soup, as a first course.

Soup (*sup*) is a vital part of lunch (*obyed*) in Russia — in fact, it is commonly held that eating lunch without it will upset your stomach. The most famous variety is *borshch*, its beautiful red colour originating from its main ingredient, beetroot. Others include the hearty *solyanka*, with tomato, fish and meat as the main ingredients, which in more sophisticated company may be topped with olives and lemon. *Shchi* is cabbage soup, and *okroshka* a cold soup made with *kvas* (see Drink).

Milk products, like *smetana* (sour cream) and yoghurts of various flavours and thicknesses, originated in the south. The commonest is *kefir*, a kind of plain yoghurt. Others are *prostakvasha*, similar to petits suisses, and *ryazhenka*, a delicious creamy yoghurt. *Tvorog* is similar to cottage cheese, and normally eaten with *smetana*. It's also a nutritious source of vitamins and protein if you're having diet problems. Milk itself can be scarce, especially in summer, and the flavour not very pleasant to the Western palate — Russian pasteurising techniques leave something to be desired. UHT milk is probably the safest, and is widely available in Moscow, whole and semi-skimmed, but not skimmed: the Russian taste for fatty foods still prevails.

Bread is normally eaten with every meal, traditionally black rye bread (*rzhanoy khleb*), heavy and slightly sour tasting. White wheat bread (*baton*) has appeared more recently and is still considered to be superior, and at last Muscovites seem to be developing a taste for wholemeal bread (*baton s otrubyami*).

Russians love to bake all kinds of pastry (*pirogi*), with fillings ranging from savoury fish and cabbage to sweeter cranberries. Pancakes (*bliny*) are virtually a national dish, dating from pagan times, and can be eaten as a delicacy with caviar (*bliny s ikroy*).

Cereals too are a staple. They are usually prepared as a *kasha*, that is, boiled in water with salt and butter. Most common are *grechka* (buckwheat), *mannaya* (semolina) and *ovsyanka* (oats).

Meat (*myasa*) was rarely eaten in old Russia, since people gave it up during Lent and other fasts, which totalled 240 days a year. Peasants ate fish in abundance, however, with plentiful river species proving a favourite for feast days. Herring (*selyodka*) became a fitting accompaniment to vodka, while the traditional dried fish called *vobla* was eaten with beer. Fish were the source of old Russia's only delicacies:

red salmon caviar (*krasnaya ikra*), or black sturgeon caviar (*chornaya ikra*) and sturgeon (*osetrina*). Today, raw or smoked fish is often served as an appetiser.

Although meat became wide-spread in Russia only during this century, it is now firmly established as the main source of protein, at least in urban areas. *Kolbasa* (German sausage) is also very popular, particularly as an appetiser or as a snack with bread (*buterbrod*). Much of today's Russian cuisine is centred around meat, though vegetarianism is now gaining popularity, both among devout Orthodox christians for whom meat is a decadent luxury and among Western-leaning progressive youth.

Typical meat dishes include *pelmeni,* a kind of ravioli or dumplings, and *zharkoye*, a hot-pot which, if prepared properly, ends up covered in dough, sealing the top so that the flavour is cooked in. *Kotlety,* cutlets, are the Russian equivalent of hamburgers, while *shashlyki* are shish kebabs, an import from the Caucasus, especially popular on picnics.

At the end of a meal tea (*chay*) is normally drunk, though coffee (*kofye*) is also now popular. Russians take both without milk but with lots of sugar. Indian tea is the most popular, and is sometimes supplemented with herbs.

Tea is often served with *varenye*, a very sweet liquid jam, almost always home-made and delicious. Alternatives, often taken as well as jam, are cake (*tort*) and sweets (*konfyety*), or in poorer families *pryaniki*, heavy, hard little cakes originating from the special patterned cakes made for festivals.

Drink

The Russian national drink remains vodka – consumed, if statistics are to be believed, copiously by the working male (and also female) population. The most common brands are Russkaya, Pshenichnaya and Stolichnaya, acceptable in quality as long as you buy the production of the Kristall factory in Moscow (other labels may look the same but the quality differs drastically from factory to factory – the Azerbaijani version, for instance, is closer to paint-stripper).

Nowadays imports like Absolut and Rasputin and private producers like the Smirnov family (now making vodka again in Russia after winning an international court case with the American Smirnoff company over the right to the name) provide a healthy choice for the consumer. Other than brands familiar in the West, vodkas like Posolskaya, Zolotoye Koltso and Sibirskaya are a must for the connoisseur. If you like flavoured vodkas, the fruity Kubanskaya, herbal Zubrovka (bison vodka!) and the butterscotchy Starka should not be missed.

The other popular hard liquor in Russia is *konyak* (cognac), mainly a Caucasian drink, but also highly popular in Russia. Quality ranges from Azerbaijani (again, often paint-stripper), through Dagestani and Georgian, to Armenian Ararat brands and the excellent Moldavian "Bely Aist" (White Stork).

Fortified wine (*vino*) is less popular in Moscow, with the exception of some cheap Azerbaijani and Dagestani sweet wines, known deceptively as *portvein* and loved by drunks who can't afford vodka.

Dry wines are enjoyed in more enlightened circles, although the very decent local Georgian and Moldavian types have recently been virtually eclipsed by the appearance of French, Spanish and New World wines. If you can find them, try semi-dries like Tsinandali (white) or Kindzmarauli, Khvanchkara and Odzhaleshi (red). Drier wines like Ereti and Mukuzani are slightly sour, but this does not detract from their appeal.

The best Moldavian wines are those which mix a range of grapes, though the Cabernets, Sauvignons, Aligotes and Rkatsitelis are good on their own too. The best sweet wines – a glorious range of sherries, ports and madeiras – come from the Crimea's Massandra factory.

Local sparkling wine (*shampanskoye*) is still inexpensive, popular and abundant, always on the table at any celebration and staple for women at such gatherings. Usually it is quite drinkable, but again quality does vary (you can distinguish the Azerbaijani brands today by the fact that their labels are written in Turkish!). The best is from the Crimea, from the Novy Svyet factory.

For Russians beer (*pivo*) is scarcely considered an alcoholic drink, though their own is generally stronger than Western varieties. More commonly it is treated as a soft drink by men, sometimes to chase down vodka or as "hair of the dog". Contrary to expectations, and to the convictions of many Russians, much of their beer is often just as good as many of the weak European imports now so common in Russia.

While Russian beer is considerably cheaper, it is not always pasteurised, so be sure to check production dates on the labels. If it's cloudy, or has plankton swimming in it, don't touch it. The commonest brands – like Zhigulyovskoye, Yachmenny Kolos and Moskovskoye – are nothing to write home about.

The best brands are Tverskoye from Tver, Baltika from St. Petersburg, Samco from the southern city of Penza, all producing a range of dark and light beers, and Khamovniki in Moscow, producing mainly light beers.

Russia's western neighbours, Belarus and Ukraine, are considered to produce better beer, and the former at least is widely available in Moscow – look out for Lidskaye, Starozhitnaye and Burshteyn in particular. The best Czech, Slovak and German brands are still available in abundance. Once popular brands from Latvia and Lithuania have all but disappeared from the shops.

For a non-alcoholic alternative, try *kvas*, treated as a soft drink but in fact slightly alcoholic. Made from fermented black bread, it is sold widely on tap in summer and was recently found to be still more popular than rival foreign soft drinks.

A note about drinking water: always boil tap water. In Moscow it is generally regarded as being safe, although you can never be sure, as a few cases of cholera in 1993 and 1995 demonstrated.

Western mineral water is generally available. The Russian variety is usually fizzy and often tastes strongly of minerals. The best are Narzan (almost tasteless) and Yessentuki (with a thick salty taste), both from the northern Caucasus spas. Water from holy springs bottled by the Orthodox Church has also made an appearance recently.

Buying Alcohol

Be careful when buying hard liquor on the street or in kiosks – there have been countless incidences of doctoring, and there are many underground stills producing poor quality spirit in bottles with seemingly respectable but bogus labels. Stick to the shops, and if buying imported liquor, make sure it has the little paper strip with the duty stamp (*actsiznaya marka*) over the top. Buying beer and wine is a safer bet, since faking them is less profitable.

Eating Out

After years in the culinary wasteland, Moscow now has an impressive array of foreign, private and cooperative restaurants. Although recently there has been a spate of medium-priced establishments opening, average prices are generally high, with an evening meal at most coming in at about $50. Such prices are enough to make them inaccessible to the great majority of the city's residents.

There are broadly three different types of restaurant in Moscow. At the top of the range are a number of first class establishments, sometimes but not always in the Western-run hotels; often importing all their ingredients from abroad, they have prices which match. The best of them may be gourmet delights, but are suitable only for expense accounts and special celebrations.

The former state restaurants – in Intourist and other hotels, and at a series of other locations such as the Praga or Uzbekistan – have a distinct style of dining which in the evenings normally involves an elaborate, noisy, and sometimes scandalous floor show. They are still favourite venues for wedding parties, but are rarely to be recommended for their food.

The third sector, the handful of private restaurants to have appeared in recent years, offer the most hope for the future. Although some obviously fall into the above first-class category, others are increasingly aware of the need to be competitive in price: the initiative has been led in particular by the Rosinter Joint Venture chain, which has opened Mexican, Italian, Spanish and Swiss restaurants across the city, as well as fast-food outlets. Prices here are no more than at comparable establishments in, say, London.

Chinese, Indian, French and Italian restaurants also abound, varying from completely authentic national fare to decidedly poor Russian imitations of the same. Of the former Soviet cuisines, Georgian is considered the best, with its greater emphasis on spices and beans, and a resemblance to Turkish dishes. Prices are generally lower than for Russian food, while quality and atmosphere are often higher.

For value, try the number of set lunch menus being offered for an average of $15-20, both at major hotels and at a number of restaurants. Another Moscow expatriate tradition is the Sunday brunch, a buffet with unlimited helpings hosted by most of the major hotels throughout the day on Sundays.

Cafés & Cheaper Eating

Sadly, the cheap seedy cafés which once filled Moscow have mostly been refurbished – they remain as bland and plasticky as before, but have now become overpriced. But though super-bargains are a thing of the past, it is still possible to eat cheaply in Moscow; in this guide we indicate as many such places as possible.

Stoloviye, cheap cafeterias, often serve inedible food and are probably best avoided. Expect to find the local menfolk swigging vodka by the beakerful and the fiercest local babushkas working behind the counter. The same applies to snack bars (*zaku-sochniye*), dumpling bars (*pelmenniye*), frankfurter bars (*sosisochniye*), sandwich bars (*buterbrodniye*) etc. Bear in mind, though, that there are always exceptions to the rule.

Street vendors sell meat pies which quickly become cold, stodgy, and greasy – try to catch them while they're hot and fresh. Many kiosks sell microwaved pizza or frankfurters. Ice-cream, however, is generally creamy and tasty, and frequently sold on street corners or kiosks.

Cakes and buns (*pirozhniye*) are also in abundance, but are often too stale and/or sweet for western tastebuds.

Tipping and Service

There is no standard system in Russian restaurants for service charges and the addition of tax. Some restaurants will add on 10 or even 15 percent for service, others not. Most include tax (currently 21.5 percent) in menu prices, although others will add it on later. If you're treated to a musical or other entertainment, expect to pay for that as well.

If in doubt, check before you eat, otherwise you might find yourself with a larger bill than expected. Tips for cloakroom attendants are optional, rarely more than a few thousand rubles.

Russian Language

Russian is a language in the Eastern Slavonic group, using the Cyrillic alphabet, devised in the 9th century on the basis of some Greek influence. The language is closest to Ukrainian and Belorussian, but a knowledge of Polish, Bulgarian, Czech or Serbo-Croat also makes learning easier.

The Alphabet

Аа   *a*, as in "car".

Бб   *b*, hardening to *p* at word-end or before consonant.

Вв   *v*, hardening to *f* at word-end or before consonant.

Гг   *g*, hardening to *k* at word-end or before consonant. его or ого at the end of a word, or in сегодня is always pronounced *yevo* or *ovo*.

Дд   *d*, hardening to *t* at word-end or before consonant.

Ее   *ye*, as in "yesterday".

Её   *yo*, as in "yob", always stressed.

Жж   *zh, j, g* as in the second g in "garage".

Зз   *z*

Ии   *ee*

Йй   *y*, at beginning or end of word. If at end, to lengthen vowel: it does not have own sound.

Кк   *k*

Лл   *l*

Мм   *m*

Нн   *n*

Оо   *o* as in "short", when unstressed becomes like the "a" in "ran".

Пп   *p*

Рр   *r*, always rolled.

Сс   *s*

Тт   *t*

Уу   *oo*

Фф   *f*

Хх   *kh*, like the German or Celtic *ch*.

Цц   *ts*, as in "floats".

Чч   *ch* as in "check".

Шш   hard *sh* as in "shop".

Щщ   soft *sh* as in "shin".

ъ   the hard sign: a pre-revolutionary letter, now used in only a handful of words to denote a break between letters, e.g. въезд (driveway), *vuy-yezd*.

Ыы   a soft *i* with a hint of the *ir* sound in "bird", or like the French *oeil*.

ь   the soft sign, used only to soften consonants.

Ээ   *e* as in "egg".

Юю   *yu* as in "yule".

Яя   *ya* as in "yarn".

Stress

Every Russian word of two or more syllables is stressed, but the place of stress is rarely predictable. To help with pronunciation in this brief introduction, we have marked each stressed syllable with an acute accent.

Pronouns and Proper Forms of Address

In Russian, as in some other European languages, different pronouns are used depending upon the speaker's relationship to the listener.

When addressing a stranger, an acquaintance or an elder, the plural pronoun вы (*vy*) is used. For good friends, relatives and children, on the other hand, the singular form ты (*ty*) is acceptable. In the examples which follow, the singular form is always given first.

In the following transliterations, the English letters used do not necessarily correspond to those given above, but are intended to aid in the most accurate pronunciation. They differ in turn from transliterations of place-names elsewhere in this guide, which are the generally accepted

English spellings and not always a reliable guide to exactly how they should be pronounced.

Note that single-letter words like "s" and "v" are pronounced by combining it with the next word.

Basic Expressions

yes *da* (да)
no *nyet* (нет)
good day, afternoon *dóbry den* (добрый день)
good morning *dóbroyah oótra* (доброе утро)
good evening *dóbry vyécher* (добрый вечер)
goodnight *spakóiny nóchi* (спокойной ночи)
hello (formal) *zdrástvooy-zdrástvooytye* (здравствуй, здравствуйте)
hi! *privyét* (привет)
goodbye *da svidánya* (до свидания)
'bye *paká* (пока)
all the best *vsivó kharósheva, dóbrava* (всего хорошего, доброго)
how are you? *kuk dilá?/kuk zhéezn?* (как дела/как жизнь?)
nice to meet you *ótchin pryát-no* (очень приятно)
it's good to see you *rud tibyá/vas vídit'* (рад тебя/вас видеть)
do you speak English? *ty guvaréesh/vy guvaréetye pa-angleesky?* (ты говоришь/вы говорите по английски)
thank you very much *spahsée-ba balshóye* (спасибо большое)
I don't understand Russian *ya nye punimáyu pa-róoski* (я не понимаю по русски)
please, you're welcome *pahzhálusta* (пожалуйста)
sorry, excuse me *eezveenée, eezveenéetye* (извини, извините)
that's okay, it's nothing *neechevó* (ничего)

good, fine *khurashó* (хорошо)
I'm okay, it's okay *narmálna* (нормально)
bad *plókha* (плохо)
my name is *minyá zuvóot* (меня зовут)
what is your name? *kuk tibyá/vas zuvóot?* (как тебя/вас зовут?)
I'm American, English (male/female) *ya amerikányets/amerikánka, angleechánin/angleechánka* (я американец/американка, англичанин/англичанка)
I (don't) want *ya (nye) khuchóo* (я хочу, я не хочу)
how old are you? *skólka tibyá/vam lyet?* (сколько тебе/вам лет?)
congratulations *puzdravlyáyu* (поздравляю)
help me *pumagéetye mnye* (помогите мне)
I'm hungry *ya khuchóo yest'* (я хочу есть)
I'm thirsty *ya khuchóo peet'* (я хочу пить)
I'm tired *ya oostáhl* (я устал)
I'm lost *ya zabloodéelsa* (я заблудился)
it's very important *éta ótchin váhzhna* (это очень важно)
it's urgent *éta sróchna* (это срочно)

Questions

where? *gdye?* (где?)
when? *kagdá?* (когда?)
what? *shto?* (что?)
how? *kak?* (как?)
how much? *skólka?* (сколько?)
who? *kto?* (кто?)
why? *pachemóo?* (почему?)

Orientation

how can I get to? *kak mnye praití/prayékhat da?* (как мне пройти/проехать до?)
where is...? *gdye zdyes...?* (где здесь?)

Practical Information | Russian Language

how long does it take to get to...? *skólka eetée/yékhat da?* (сколько идти/ехать до?)
to the left *nalyévo* (налево)
to the right *napráva* (направо)
straight ahead *pryáma* (прямо)
far away *dalikó* (далеко)
nearby *bléezka* (близко)

Transport

the metro *mitró* (метро)
where's the nearest metro station? *gdye bleezháishaya stántseeya mitró* (где ближайшая станция метро?)
token, jeton *zhitón* (жетон)
monthly pass *prayezdnóy* (проездной)
exit *víykhud v górud* (выход в город)
walkway (to another station) *pirikhód* (переход)
train station *vakzáhl* (вокзал)
train *póyezd* (поезд)
railway *zhelyéznaya duróga* (железная дорога)
airport *aerapórt* (аэропорт)
airplane *sumalyót* (самолет)
enquiries *spráhvachnuye byooró* (справочное бюро)
are there any tickets for..? *yest beelyéty na?* (есть билеты на?)
can I have a ticket for... *dáitye mnye beelyét na...* (дайте мне билет на...)
sleeper *es veh* (св)
couchette *koopéh* (купе)
check-in *rigistrátseeya* (регистрация)
boarding *pusádka* (посадка)
flight number *nómer réisa* (номер рейса)
taxi *tuksée* (такси)
bus *avtóboos* (автобус)
trolleybus *trullyéyboos* (троллейбус)
tram *trumvái* (трамвай)

Hotels

hotel *gustéenitsa* (гостиница)
receptionist *udmeeneestrátur* (администратор)

passport *pásspart* (паспорт)
visa *véeza* (виза)
luggage *bagásh* (багаж)
floor lady *dizhóornaya* (дежурная)
room *nómer* (номер)
key *klyooch* (ключ)
does the room have a bathroom? *nómer s oodóbstvumee?* (номер с удобствами?)
does the room have a phone? *nómer s tiliphónum?* (номер с телефоном?)
how can I phone long distance? *kuk zvanéet' pa myezhgórudoo?* (как звонить по межгороду?)
how can I make an international call? *kuk zvanéet' zuh grunéetsoo?* (как звонить за границу?)

Eating Out

restaurant *ristarán* (ресторан)
café *kuféh* (кафе)
cafeteria *stulóvaya* (столовая)
I'd like to book a table for two, three, four people *ya khuchóo zukazát stólik na dvaíkh, traíkh, chétveríyk chelovyek* (я хочу заказать столик на двоих, троих, четверых человек)
hors d'oeuvres *zukóoskee* (закуски)
first course *pyérvuye blyóoda* (первые блюда)
main course *fturíye blyóoda* (вторые блюда)
meat *myasníye blyóoda* (мясные блюда)
fish *réebnuye blyóoda* (рыбные блюда)
poultry *ptéetsa* (птица)
salad *sulát* (салат)
vegetables *óvashee* (овощи)
cheese *seer* (сыр)
fruit *fróokty* (фрукты)
dessert *dessért* (десерт)
ice-cream *murózhennuye* (мороженное)

wines, spirits *speertníye napéetki* (спиртные напитки)
boiled *vuryóny* (вареный)
fried *zháhreny* (жареный)
baked *zupichónny* (запеченный)
can I have the bill please? *pushitáitye pazháhlusta* (посчитайте пожалуйста)

Numbers

one (masc., fem., neuter) *adyéen, udná, udnó* (один, одна, одно)
two (masc, fem) *dva, dvye* (два, две)
three *tree* (три)
four *chitéerye* (четыре)
five *pyat'* (пять)
six *shest'* (шесть)
seven *syem'* (семь)
eight *vósyem'* (восемь)
nine *dyévit'* (девять)
ten *dyésit'* (десять)
eleven *adyéennatsat'* (одиннадцать)
twelve *dvyenátsat'* (двенадцать)
twenty *dvátsat'* (двадцать)
thirty *trítsat'* (тридцать)
forty *sórak* (сорок)
fifty *pidisyat* (пятьдесят)
sixty *shisdisyát* (шестьдесят)
seventy *syémdisit* (семьдесят)
eighty *vósyemdisit* (восемьдесят)
ninety *divyanósta* (девяносто)
one hundred *sto* (сто)
two hundred *dvyésti* (двести)
five hundred *pitsót* (пятьсот)
one thousand *tíssha* (тысяча)
a thousand rubles (slang) *shtóoka* (штука)
one million *milleeyón* (миллион)

Shopping

how much does it cost? *skólka stóyit?* (сколько стоит?)
could I have a look at? *pukazhéetye pahzháhulsta* (покажите пожалуйста)

shop assistant *prudavyéts/prudavshéetsa* (продавец/продавщица)
who's last in line? *kto paslyédny?* (кто последний?)
cashier's desk *kássa* (касса)
do you have any...? *oo vas yest'...?* (у вас есть?)

Russian Words to Recognise

переход crossing, walkway, e.g. between stations (*pirikhód*)
вход entrance (*fkhod*)
выход exit (*v'ykhad*)
посторонним вход воспрещен no admission (*pustarónnim fkhod vusprishyón*)
администратор hotel receptionist (*udmeeneestrátur*)
касса cash desk, ticket office (*kássa*)
театр theatre (*teyátr*)
кинотеатр cinema (*keenateyátr*)
сувениры souvenirs (*soovenéery*)
хлеб bread, baker's (*khlyeb*)
овощи vegetables, vegetable shop (*óvashee*)
рынок market (*rínak*)
продукты grocer's (*pradóokty*)
гастроном food shop (*gastranóm*)
туалет toilet (*twalyét*)
аптека drugstore (*uptyéka*)
книги bookstore (*knyéegee*)
почта post office (*póchta*)
банк bank (*bunk*)
обмен валюты exchange office (*ubmyén valyóoty*)
молоко milk store (*mulakó*)
мясо-рыба meat and fish store (*myása-ríba*)
камера хранения left luggage office (*kámera khranyéniya*)
закрыт на ремонт closed for repairs (*zakrít na rimónt*)
закрыт на учет closed for inventory (*zakrít na oochót*)
перерыв lunchbreak (*pirirív*)
здесь не курят no smoking (*zdyes nye kóoryat*)

Guide Symbols

☖   Historic Building or Monument
🏛   Museum, Art Gallery
⛪   Church
🍴   Restaurant
☕   Café
🍸   Bar
🍟   Fast Food
🎁   Shopping
💿   Music Club, Night Club
☺   Theatre
🎥   Cinema, Film
🎼   Concert Hall

Sources of Information

With no clearly functioning Tourist Office in the city, the Information Bureaux/Booking Offices of major hotels are useful sources of information, although reserving services through them may be expensive.

The popular guiding service Patriarchi Dom offers a wide range of tours and excursions, both within Moscow and to major sights beyond, many of which are mentioned in the text. For full information and details of their future tours, contact them on tel.: 255-4515. The former official state tourist organisation, Intourist, also offers daily City Tours, as well as periodic excursions through the Kremlin and Armoury Museum, and Diamond Fund, also to the Tretyakov Gallery and Pushkin Museum. For details and prices, tel.: 292-2365, 292-1278.

Moscow has a wide choice of English-language press, including two daily newspapers, *Moscow Times* and *Moscow Tribune*, both of which have programme details for the upcoming week in their Friday editions. *Moscow Revue* is a monthly colour Arts and Entertainment magazine.

Index of Advertisers

Central Moscow

Central Moscow | General Map

1. The Kremlin

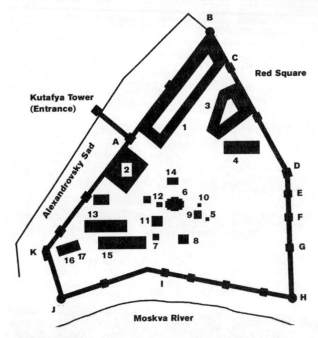

KREMLIN TOWERS
A: Trinity Tower
B: Corner Arsenal Tower
C: St. Nicholas Tower
D: Saviour's Tower
E: Tsar's Tower
F: Alarm Tower
G: SS. Constantine and Helen Tower
H: Beklemishev (Moskva River) Tower
I: Secrets Tower
J: Water-Drawing Tower
K: Borovitskaya Tower

MAIN MONUMENTS:
1: The Arsenal
2: Palace of Congresses

3: The Senate
4: The President's Residence
5: Tsar Cannon and Tsar Bell
6: Assumption Cathedral
7: Annunciation Cathedral
8: Cathedral of the Archangel Michael
9: Ivan the Great Bell-tower
10: Filaret's Extension
11: The Palace of Facets
12: Church of the Deposition of the Robe
13: Terem Palace
14: The Patriarch's Palace
15: The Great Kremlin Palace
16: The Armoury
17: The Diamond Fund

A walk through Moscow's central fortress, the seat of government from 1276 to 1712, and again from March 1918 to the present day. The word "Kremlin" (*kreml'* in Russian) describes the fortified strongholds built to protect early Russian towns from hostile raiders. These towns later developed outside their kremlins, making the latter obsolete for their original purposes. Their monuments, if still standing, are today most frequently used as museums or for administrative purposes.

Moscow's Kremlin encompasses the offices and chambers of the Russian president, as well as several museums and churches, now once again used for church services on major holidays. For most people, though, the symbolic significance is greater – the Kremlin stands for Russian statehood, or as the nerve centre of a world superpower.

The oldest structures here, the walls and churches, date from the 15th and 16th centuries, when Prince Ivan III was raising up his "Third Rome". As a whole, though, it is a great mixture of styles, and the beauty of the main square belies the disfigurement of the 1930's, when other fine buildings were destroyed. One small piece only of these vanished structures, the Red Porch, has been rebuilt.

STARTS & ENDS FROM: Metro Biblioteka imeni Lenina, Alexandrovsky Sad.

Alexander Garden
(Alexandrovsky Sad)
Exit the metro and walk to the Alexander Garden, running parallel to the Kremlin wall. Beneath it flows the Neglinka River, a rather smelly tributary of the Moskva. Near its confluence with the Moskva, by what is now the Kremlin's Borovitsky Tower, Yuri Dolgoruky founded the city. The Neglinka was diverted into underground pipes after the fire of 1812, and Osip Bove, the principal architect of the city's reconstruction, replaced it with the present garden.

The main monuments in the garden are an obelisk, dating from 1913, commemorating 300 years of the Romanov dynasty, and the Tomb of the Unknown Soldier, a World War II memorial, long a popular place for newlyweds to come and be photographed. The grotto in the Kremlin wall was also built by Bove.

The Kremlin Entrance
The Kremlin is entered through the peculiar hollow white tower near the back facade of the Manezh. This is the Kutafya Tower, which takes its name from an old Russian word meaning "clumsy old woman". (The other entrances – on Red Square and

near the Bolshoy Kamenny Bridge on the opposite side – are for officials only). Deposit any bags you have in the left luggage here, buy your tickets in the kiosk: you will need to decide beforehand which of the museums you want to visit.

Ticket prices are as follows (prices for Russian citizens in brackets): Kremlin territory admission R 500 (R 500), Assumption Cathedral R 25,000 (R 2,000), Archangel, Annunciation Cathedrals R 20,000 (R 2,000), Patriarch's Palace, Deposition Church R 15,000 (R 1,000), Armoury ruble equivalent of $12 (R 5,000).

Admission to the Diamond Fund is separate – pay R 79,000 (R 12,500) for an excursion on entry. Student categories are approximately half the respective adult prices.

Excursions cost R 36,000 (R 24,000 in Russian, if you have an interpreter of your own or don't need one).

☛ Kremlin territory and museums open Fri–Weds 10 am–6 pm. Tel: 202-9223. Armoury, tel: 921-4720. Diamond Fund, tel: 229-2036.

The Walls and Towers

From the Kutafya Tower, cross the bridge over the Alexander Garden to the Trinity Tower in the main wall. Before entering the Kremlin, look along the wall which is at its highest elevation here. It dates from the 15th century, though there were three previous walls, the most famous of them built in the 14th century. Made of white stone, it earned Moscow the nickname *Belokamennaya* (white stone), which stuck, even after the wall fell into ruin.

The present walls, however, are mainly red brick, and were built by the "Friazin brothers": Friazin was not a family name, but a Russian word for the Genoese, specialists in fortress building, many of whom worked on Moscow's Kremlin. This pair, working in renaissance style, gave the fortress what was then considered a very un-Russian appearance.

They also built the towers, of which there are twenty, though the upper parts visible today were added only in the 17th century. For this purpose Tsars Mikhail and Alexey rounded up the best masons in the country, threatening their families with prison until they turned up to work.

Each one is different from the next, and some deserve special attention. Looking towards the left from where you are now standing, the main towers are:

Trinity Tower
(Troitskaya Bashnya)
Ahead of you is the tallest tower (80 metres). This is the entrance for the humblest of the humble, hence its current role as the tourists' access. It was named by Alexey after the mission of the Trinity-St. Sergius Lavra (*see* Sergiyev Posad) which once stood nearby.

Corner Arsenal Tower
(Uglovaya Arsenalnaya Bashnya)
This tower was built over a secret underground spring, thus making it a source of water in time of siege.

St. Nicholas Tower
(Nikolskaya Bashnya)
This tower is unusual for its Gothic style, and is a good example of the variation to be found in the towers' architecture.

Saviour's Tower
(Spasskaya Bashnya)
If the Kremlin is a symbol of
Moscow and Russia, this tower is
a symbol of the Kremlin. It
became the main entrance and
was treated with due respect by
those who entered by it — there
was a rule that everyone had to
take off their hats as they passed
through, and failure to do so
incurred the punishment of bowing fifty times before the tower.

The lower part was built by
another Italian, Petro Solari, who
created an effect that was, aptly,
both extravagant and threatening.
The upper part, including the
clock, was added in 1625,
mounted by the Englishman
Christopher Galloway. Its post-
revolutionary replacement still
chimes out every day to millions
of radio listeners.

Tsar's Tower
(Tsarskaya Bashnya)
Built in 1680, this is the
youngest of the Kremlin's towers.
It seems more like a throne than
a tower, and that's just what it is
— the original wooden structure
was used by Ivan the Terrible to
observe ceremonies in Red
Square.

Alarm Tower
(Nabatnaya Bashnya)
This tower once contained a bell
that sounded the alarm when the
city was being attacked. In 1771,
during a time of plague, a group
of malefactors rang the bell and
the whole crazed city ran for the
shelter of the Kremlin. The cul-
prits were never found, and
Catherine the Great vented her
anger on the bell itself, pulling
out its tongue. It now stands in
the Armoury museum.

SS. Constantine and Helen
Tower *(Konstantino-Yeleninskaya
Bashnya)*
Prince Dmitry Donskoy passed
through this tower's predecessor
on his way to and from victory
against the Tatars at Kulikovo
Field. The thick walls of the current structure were believed to
hide a torture chamber.

Beklemishev or Moskva River
Tower *(Beklemishevskaya-
Moskvoretskaya Bashnya)*
A slender yet sturdy tower, it
guards the most vulnerable
approaches to the Kremlin. It is
named after a 16th-century
nobleman, whose residence
adjoined it and who is still
believed to haunt the tower.

Secrets Tower
(Tainitskaya Bashnya)
The oldest tower (built in 1485),
its name is explained by the
underground passages leading
from it. In addition to being a
place for drawing water from the
Moskva River, it is believed to be
linked to the mysterious library of
Ivan the Terrible, full of rare and
fabulous manuscripts, which has
yet to be rediscovered.

Water-Drawing Tower
(Vodovzvodnaya Bashnya)
Water used to be pumped from

Central Moscow | The Kremlin

the river via this tower and carried into the Kremlin on an aqueduct to irrigate the gardens and supply the palaces. The current structure is post-1812.

Borovitskaya Tower
(Borovitskaya Bashnya)
The original "tradesman's entrance", this tower was used as a back door for furtive appearances and disappearances by Russian leaders. Its name comes from the word *bor*, which recalls the forest that covered this area when Moscow was founded.

The Arsenal
Returning to the start of the walk, enter the Trinity Gate. Immediately on the left inside is the Arsenal, now the headquarters of the Kremlin Guard. Built by Peter the Great for weapon manufacturing and storage, it became in 1812 a museum commemorating the victory against Napoleon. Some of the cannons displayed outside were captured from the retreating French army.

Palace of Congresses
To your right is the only modern building in the Kremlin, the Palace of Congresses. It was built in 1961, in the Khrushchev days of bravado and communist rhetoric, by a collective of five architects led by Mikhail Posokhin to host the upcoming Communist Party Congress (also to match the grandeur of Peking's equivalent central Party buildings). The builders sank the structure 15 metres into the ground, so that it wouldn't overshadow other Kremlin buildings.

For many years it served as a venue both for gatherings of top Party officials as well as for cultural performances, principally ballet. The latter has now become its only occupation, with the huge stage and auditorium (with seating for 5,800) accommodating the resident Kremlin Palace Ballet Company as well as visiting companies.

The Senate
As you continue past the Palace of Congresses, you'll see on the left, across the drive, a bright yellow building in classical style behind a small garden. This is the Senate, one of the many Moscow masterpieces of 18th-century architect **Matvey Kazakov**, favoured by Catherine the Great for his restrained, functional style.

Its most notable feature is the rotunda, a symbol of happiness, which Catherine hoped to establish through the rule of law. Inside the building the offices used by Lenin after the Revolution were preserved, until their recent removal to his country museum-estate at Leninskiye Gorky. It was from these offices that Lenin ran the early Bolshevik state after the government moved back to Moscow in March 1918.

The President's Residence
To the right of the Senate is a much later building painted in a similar colour, perhaps to camouflage its architectural deficiencies. Built in 1935, it formerly housed the Presidium of the Supreme Soviet, a kind of inner standing parliament – in pre-perestroika days the full parliament only needed to meet for a few days a year, since there was no genuine debate. Now it is the official residence of the Russian president.

Tsar Cannon and Tsar Bell
As you approach Cathedral Square, you will see the Kremlin's twin oddities, the largest cannon in the world, which has never been fired, and

the largest bell in the world, which has never been rung.

The Tsar Cannon, weighing 40 tonnes and boasting a barrel five metres long, never had occasion to be used: Moscow's enemies would take one look at it, the idea went, and turn tail. It was commissioned by Ivan the Terrible's son Fyodor, and has a relief of him just behind the muzzle. On the carriage, meanwhile, the depiction of a lion savaging a snake symbolises Russian power, always victorious over its enemies.

The Tsar Bell, weighing 200 tonnes, was an impossible proposition right from the start. Things kept going wrong during its construction, until it finally cracked in a fire. Begun in the 1730's during Anna Ivanovna's reign, it was only lifted out of its pit, into which it had fallen during a casting mishap, 100 years later. The 11-tonne fragment which broke off it at that time has lain beside it ever since.

Assumption Cathedral
(Uspensky Sobor)
On entering the square, your attention will be taken immediately by the largest of the churches, the magnificent Assumption (or Dormition) Cathedral on your right.

During the process of unification of Russia under Moscow in the 15th century, Prince Ivan III decided to create a cathedral that would become the focal point of Russian Orthodoxy. He needed a highly skilled architect, of a kind Russia was at that time unable to provide: obliged to look abroad, he finally chose the Bolognese, Aristotle Fioravanti, to build Russia's greatest church. Fioravanti was dispatched to Vladimir, Pskov and Novgorod to acquaint himself with the varieties

of Russian style. He did this thoroughly, and the Assumption Cathedral (1475–79) is the result.

Most of all, the Cathedral resembles the Assumption Cathedral in Vladimir, its massive bulk topped by *zakomary*, arched gables which follow the contours of the vaults inside, and five domes. The belt of arcades intended to relieve the austerity of the walls (located just below mid-height), and the large window slits below the semicircular arches that crown the walls, are also features of the older cathedral.

The Assumption Cathedral served as a burial place for Orthodox patriarchs and for the coronation of tsars. Inside, the walls were painted mainly in the mid-17th century, their themes copied from original 15th-century works by the great Russian master Dionysius.

A few of his simple and delicate earlier paintings are preserved below the main iconostasis. Their main theme is the Assumption of the Virgin Mary into heaven, the backbone of the new dogma of Russian Orthodoxy. This replaced the Byzantine tradition of devoting the main cathedral to St. Sophia, or the Wisdom of God; the Assumption, in Orthodoxy, was the means by which that wisdom was brought to humankind.

The iconostasis also has a purpose – to demonstrate the unity of Russia. The lowest tier contains icons captured from Moscow's defeated rival cities, most notably Novgorod and Vladimir. On the rear wall to the right of the entrance is another of these, a 15th-century copy of the Virgin of Vladimir, a Byzantine icon used by successive Russian capitals to proclaim their superiority. The original arrived in Moscow in 1395, but after the Revolution was transferred by Lenin to the Tretyakov Gallery.

Note also the solid silver chandelier. Napoleon, who used the cathedral as a stable during his occupation of Moscow, on departure looted all the gold and silver inside. This was later recaptured, and the silver remoulded into the chandelier.

Annunciation Cathedral
(Blagoveshchensky Sobor)
The Annunciation Cathedral, on the back of the square to the left, was the second of today's Kremlin churches to be built. As this was intended for the tsars' private worship, it was built without foreign help by Pskov masters. The original, also in the Vladimir style, was quite modest, but was enlarged in Ivan the Terrible's time.

The result is a festive nine-domed church with gilded copper roofing. One necessary innovation was a porch, built when Ivan was forbidden to enter the church for services after he contravened Orthodox doctrine by marrying a fourth time.

The most interesting features inside are the early-15th century icons, preserved from the previous cathedral on the site and miraculously rediscovered, under layers of later painting, in the 20th century. They demonstrate a rare collaboration between the two greatest artists of the day, **Theophanes the Greek** and **Andrey Rublyov**. Compare Theophanes' harsh, dramatic figures in the deisus tier (second from the bottom), with Rublyov's rounder, softer images (St. Peter and the Archangel Michael).

The earliest wall paintings in this cathedral date from 1508, and were also rediscovered this century after being thought to be lost. They are the work of Dionysius' son **Theodosius**, and include pairs of Russian and Byzantine saints, such as St. George together with St. Demetrius of Thessalonica, on the right hand pillar as you face the altar. Their purpose was to demonstrate the Russian church as heir to that of Byzantium.

Cathedral of the Archangel Michael
(Arkhangelsky Sobor)
The Cathedral of the Archangel Michael, the third on the square, shows a much more obvious foreign influence — in fact, it is commonly referred to as a "Russian church in an Italian robe". Its builder was a Venetian called **Alevisio**, who was commissioned by the dying Ivan III in 1505. Alevisio's most noticeable contribution was the scallop-shell decoration inside the semi-circular *zakomary*, later copied by other Russian architects.

The interior of the cathedral became the burial place of grand princes and tsars, from Ivan Kalita in the 14th century to Ivan V in 1696. Ivan's younger brother Peter the Great then decreed that tsars should be buried in the SS. Peter and Paul Cathedral in St. Petersburg. Nonetheless his Moscow-loving grandson Peter preferred to stay here, and after dying of smallpox in 1730 was buried here.

The frescoes were painted by talented 17th-century masters, including **Simon Ushakov** (*see* Walk 2), mostly on historical and military themes. The cathedral's patron was Michael, captain of the heavenly host, and consequently a number of the paintings celebrate Russia's campaigns. Many tsars are depicted, and there are also likenesses of all of the Russian princes whose principalities had joined Moscow.

Ivan the Great Bell-tower
(Ivan Veliky)
To the right as you enter the square from the Tsar Bell is the bell-tower, known as Ivan the Great (not to be confused with Ivan III, who shared this title) after the patron saint of the builder of the original, Grand Prince Ivan Kalita.

The lower octagonal portion was rebuilt in 1505–08, and filled with trophies by Ivan the Terrible, including bells from newly annexed Novgorod, and Baltic cities captured in the Livonian war. The part above it, which brought the tower to a height of 270 metres, was added by Tsar Boris Godunov.

Filaret's Extension
(Filaretovskaya Pristroika)
This adjoining belfry was named after Patriarch Filaret, who moved the patriarch's sacristy into this building. Built in 1635, it was blown up by Napoleon, then reconstructed exactly as before. It now serves as a temporary exhibition hall.

The Palace of Facets
(Granovitaya Palata)
The last structure in the square, opposite Ivan the Great, is the Palace of Facets, designed for the great feasts of the tsars, such as that held after the capture of Kazan. Built by two of Ivan III's Italians, **Petro Solari** and **Marco Ruffo**, it is in renaissance style and has no hint of Russian influence. It is not generally open to the public, which makes its lavish interiors, painted first by Simon Ushakov and then elaborated by Palekh artists, on golden backgrounds, all the more tantalising.

The Red Porch (*Krasnoye*

Kryltso), on its left side, was used by the Tsar to ascend to his coronation. The original was destroyed in 1933 to make way for a dining room for delegates to the 17th Party Congress. In 1993, Boris Yeltsin donated money from his personal fund to rebuild it, thus making it the first example of reconstruction of ancient monuments destroyed by Stalin. The new structure, however, has been sharply criticised by some architects, who believe it was built too hastily and is too obviously a copy.

Church of the Deposition of the Robe
(Tserkov' Rizpolozheniya)
This charming little church stands just behind the Assumption Cathedral, and is also open as a museum. It was built in 1486 by Pskov architects, in celebration of what was thought to be a case of divine intervention. A Tatar army en route to another sacking of Moscow suddenly got cold feet and withdrew. This miracle happened on the eve of the feast of the Deposition. The church now houses a wooden sculpture exhibition.

Terem Palace
(Teremnoy Dvorets)
There are several other palaces and churches hidden behind the main square buildings, most of them inaccessible. The most striking and visible is the Terem Palace, built in the 17th century and thereafter used as royal chambers. A *terem* is an upper chamber housing wives and children of the noble owner, often decorated in suitably colourful, fairytale and traditionally Russian style. In this case, it has an unmistakable gleaming red and white chessboard roof, as well as beautifully carved window frames.

Adjoining the Palace you can see one of several small churches, the Upper Saviour's Cathedral (*Verkhospassky Sobor*), built for private worship. Its eleven cupolas are unique, their drums encased in "shirts" of decorative tiling. The circular gaps in the tiling, which now reveal the red brick beneath, were once filled by bronze mountings depicting saints.

The Patriarch's Palace
(*Patriarshy Dvorets*)
On the other side of the Assumption Cathedral, with its entrance outside the square, the Patriarch's Palace was built in the mid-16th century by Patriarch Nikon. It incorporates the Church of the Twelve Apostles (*Tserkov' Dvenadsati Apostolov*), which replaced the above church as a private place of worship for the patriarchs.

Architecturally, it combines notable features of its neighbours – the drums of the Annunciation Cathedral, the *zakomary* of the Assumption, and the mass of the Archangel Michael. It is now a museum of 17th-century applied art, and its treasures provide a worthy alternative to the less accessible Armoury.

The Hall of the Cross, the first pillarless hall of this size built in Russia, is the most striking room in the museum. It contains gold and silver ware from Russia and Western Europe, notably an ornamental stove for making chrism (anointing oil used in church services) and a collection of German clocks, like the amusing Augsburg Bacchus. The church interior contains icons from other defunct Kremlin churches; some paintings by Simon Ushakov remain in the drum.

The Great Kremlin Palace
(*Bolshoy Kremlyovsky Dvorets*)
Walking to the end of the square overlooking the Moskva River, you will see to your right the Great Kremlin Palace, built by **Konstantin Thon** after the triumph of 1812 and used as a Moscow residence of the Tsars. There is no public access to the spectacular interior, but it is frequently seen on television in its role as the official presidential reception area for foreign delegations.

The Armoury
(*Oruzheinaya Palata*)
Look farther down the hill along the avenue which leads to the Borovitskaya Tower, and you will see the Armoury to your right, past the facade of the palace. Also built by Thon, the Armoury is Russia's oldest and most treasured museum. Although established as an armoury by Vassily III in 1511, its collection originated much earlier, from the weapons and battle regalia that each Muscovite prince received from his ancestors.

However, as the Tsar's court grew rich under Ivan III, it became a workshop for craftsmen of many trades. When Peter the Great packed them off to St. Petersburg, the original Moscow building became a museum. The collection was poorly looked after, and many items were lost, especially during the 1812 war, when it was evacuated to Nizhny Novgorod. Only in 1851 was it installed in its current location.

Its earliest exhibits, which include the chalice that belonged to Yuri Dolgoruky (in Hall II), date from the 12th century. Exhibits are not organised chronologically – rather, each room is devoted to a particular kind of artefact: weapons (Hall I), gold and silver

(Halls II and V), jewellery (Hall III), vestments (Hall IV), royal regalia (Hall VI), harnesses (Hall VII) and carriages (Hall VIII).

Although the golden age of the armoury was in the 17th century under Tsar Alexey Mikhailovich, some of the finest treasures are gifts from abroad, such as two thrones, one made of diamonds and the other of gold leaf studded with precious stones, both sent by Persia (in Hall VI), or the carriage given to Boris Godunov by Queen Elizabeth I of England (in Hall VIII).

Fabergé, Russia's most famous jewellers, are well represented in Hall III, with their characteristic Easter eggs containing exquisite miniatures – notably a Trans-Siberian express train and the sumptuous Catherine Palace outside St. Petersburg.

The Diamond Fund
(Almazny Fond)
The other part of the museum contains a collection of diamonds, opened to public view only in 1967. Its treasures include a diamond and pearl tiara made for Catherine the Great by the 18th-century craftsman Posier.

Among its grand set stones are the 300-carat Orlov Diamond, once the eye of a god in an Indian temple, presented to Catherine by her favourite, Count Grigory Orlov. The Shah Diamond was given to Nicholas I by the Persian ruler after the murder in Tehran of Alexander Griboyedov, who was serving as the Tsar's envoy.

The museum also has exhibits from this century, when the opening of new mines made the Soviet Union one of the world's largest diamond producers.

NB: These last two museums are open by excursion only, and each requires a separate admission.

WE CAN HANDLE ALL YOUR C.I.S. TRAVEL NEEDS – WHEN PLANNING YOUR VISIT, AND ON THE GROUND.

- Discounted Economy, Business & First Class Airfares
- Visa support for Russia: single- & multi-entry
- Internal CIS plane & rail tickets
- Hotel accommodation
- Corporate accounts

Alpha-Omega has offices in Leeds, Moscow and Almaty, and representatives in St. Petersburg, Kiev and Tashkent. Contact us – for the fullest service.

In the U.K.:
Borodin House,
6, Beaconsfield Court,
Garforth, Leeds
Tel.: (0113) 286-2121
Fax: (0113) 286-4964

In Moscow: Tel./fax: 956-2997

In Almaty: Tel.: (3272) 509-944
Fax: (3272) 509-573

ALPHA-OMEGA TRAVEL LIMITED

2. Kitai Gorod and the Central Squares

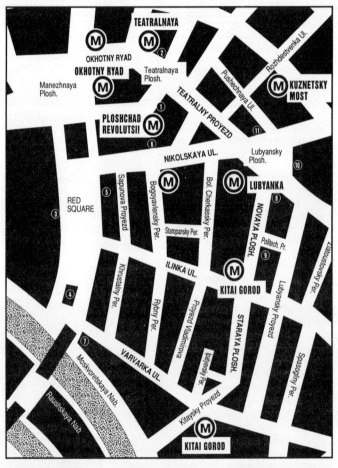

1. Hotel Metropol
2. Bolshoi Theatre
3. Lenin Mausoleum
4. St. Basil's
5. GUM
6. Epiphany Monastery
7. Rossiya Hotel
8. Mayakovsky Museum
9. Polytechnic Museum
10. Lubyanka
11. Detsky Mir

This tour of the centre and the old trading quarter takes you to Moscow's three main central squares – Theatre, Manezh and Red Square – through the old streets of the Kitai Gorod district and concludes at the KGB headquarters at Lubyanka Square.

A relatively small area, it encompasses trading quarters – past (Kitai Gorod), present (GUM) and future (the underground Manezh complex); military parade grounds, Red Square for the Soviet Union, for its predecessors Theatre Square; Moscow's first educational establishment; a gathering place of theatricals and ticket speculators near the Bolshoi, and of nationalists, who demonstrate and sell literature across the square.

STARTS FROM: Metro Ploshchad Revolutsii, Teatralnaya
ENDS AT: Metro Lubyanka

Theatre Square
(Teatralnaya Ploshchad)
Emerge from the western exit of Ploshchad Revolutsii (back carriage, if travelling from Arbatskaya), or the southern exit of Teatralnaya (front carriage, if travelling from Tverskaya) onto Teatralnaya Ploshchad (Theatre Square). So-called because of the three theatres dominating the northern side, its current appearance makes it difficult to imagine that this area was once a stinking bog, the flood plain of the nearby Neglinka River (now channelled underground), and used as a rubbish dump by the well-to-do inhabitants of the city centre.

Only after the 1812 fire was it filled in and a parade ground built, surrounded by a classical ensemble built on wooden piles (which still support the Bolshoi Theatre

today). The square's present layout dates from 1911.

Walk to the right round the square, keeping the high walls on your right. These walls were built originally by Prince Vassily III in the 16th century to protect the main trading area of the city, Kitai Gorod, to be visited later on this tour: one explanation of the area's name comes from *kita*, the word for the baskets filled with earth that were used to build the wall. Historians agree that it does not mean, literally, "Chinatown", as the Russian would suggest. Look up to the building dominating the corner of the square behind the wall, and you'll see part of the old printing house mentioned later in the walk.

In the centre of a minisquare on the right, you will pass a curious pile of stone blocks. This was the site of the statue of Yakov Sverdlov, a comrade of Lenin and the first titular head of the new communist state. The statue (along with the square, which was named after him during the Soviet years) fell victim to the popular euphoria following the failed August 1991 coup. Now the site has fallen prey to anti-semitic graffiti – Sverdlov was a Jew (*see* Walk 6).

HOTEL METROPOL

🏨 Metropol Hotel

On the side of the square facing you is one of Moscow's finest examples of art nouveau architecture, which at the time of its building filled conservative citizens with horror. It was built at the turn of the century by **William Walcott**, an architect of English descent born near Odessa and best known in the West for his whimsical sketches of ancient classical buildings.

At the beginning of the 1990's Finnish builders restored it from Intourist drabness to its former five-star glory. Look up to see the two large mosaics created by **Mikhail Vrubel** in rounded pediments at gable height directly above the main entrances. They were inspired by Edmond Rostand's play *La Princesse Lointaine*. Meanwhile, above the second floor is a quotation from Friedrich Nietzsche: "It's the same old story, when you build a house, you notice that you've learnt something."

Metropol Restaurants

As well as being one of Moscow's most exclusive hotels, whose recent guests have included the likes of Michael Jackson and Sophia Loren, the Metropol has a high concentration of top-class restaurants and cafés. The most palatial in appearance is undoubtedly the **Metropol Zal**, the main dining room, where buffet lunch beneath the splendid concave painted glazed roof will run to about $55.

For a glimpse of the lives of the court princes in 16th century Russia, try the **Boyarsky Zal**, where period Russian cuisine is accompanied by folk music. The prices are equally princely, and even the appetisers can top $50. For an equally pocket-draining experience, but in a lavish European atmosphere more in tune with the hotel's own image, visit the **Evropeisky Zal** on the ground floor whose windows look out onto the square.

Continuing along the main facade of the hotel brings you to the entrance of two of the Metropol's more modest eateries: for the determinedly sweet tooth, the **Café Confectionery** has a selection of exotic cakes, tea and coffee ideal for an afternoon of leisure, while opposite the secluded **Artists' Bar** offers drinks and a quiet place to sit through until midnight.

☛ *Boyarsky Zal, open 7 pm–11 pm; tel: 927-6089. Evropeisky Zal open 11:30 am–10:30 pm; tel: 927-6039. Metropol Zal open 7–11 am, noon–4 pm, 7–11 pm; tel: 927-6061.*

Café Confectionery open 10 am–8 pm Mon-Sat; tel: 927-6066. Artists' Bar open noon–midnight; tel: 927-6065. CC.

Teatro Restaurant

Around the corner, although within the same building as the Metropol, the more artistic and less extravagant also have a choice: the Teatro restaurant provides exquisite seafood, specialising in lobster, with a background of works by contemporary Russian artists.

☛ *Open 11 am–2 am. Tel: 927-6739. CC.*

Karl Marx Statue, Fountain

Turn your attention now to the middle of the square, cut by the main road *Okhotny Ryad* (Hunter's Row). On the southern side is a statue of Karl Marx, who survived the 1991 onslaught against his revolutionary followers. It was erected by Lev Kerbel in 1961 to mark the 22nd Congress of the Communist Party of the Soviet Union (CPSU): for 30 years Okhotny Ryad and its extensions Mokhovaya Ulitsa and Teatralny Proezd bore the name Prospekt Marksa.

Further back towards the Kitai Gorod wall, note a much earlier feature of the square, a fountain sculpted by **Ivan Vitali** in 1835, portraying young boys in classical style holding up a large goblet. Currently it is dwarfed by an auxiliary section of the Manezh Square construction work.

Maly Theatre

Across Okhotny Ryad from the Metropol, the Maly Theatre was reconstructed in 1824 by **Osip Bove**, the main architect of Moscow's rebuilding after 1812, from a private house. It was famous in the early part of the last century as a catalyst for intellectual opposition, performing plays by such irreverent figures as Griboyedov, Gogol and Ostrovsky, the last of whom was always particularly linked with the theatre – his statue now stands outside its main entrance.

The exquisite and ornate auditorium seems smaller than its capacity of 1,000 suggests. The Maly's repertoire today concentrates on the Russian classics, frequently history plays, with productions whose dramatic style is rarely ground-breaking.

Bolshoi Theatre

Dominating Theatre Square, this giant theatre, the centrepiece of Bove's ensemble dates from the same period as the Maly. Its ponderous eight-columned ionic portico is topped by a bronze figure of Phoebus restraining four bolting horses, described jokingly by turn-of-the-century social historian Vladimir Gilyarovsky as the only sober coachman in Moscow. With severe subsidence undermining its whole structure, the Bolshoi is long overdue for major repairs which threaten to close the theatre for some years.

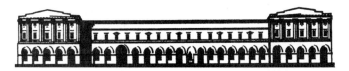

The Bolshoi's auditorium is famous for its size — six balconies high, with seats for 2,500 spectators — and acoustics, to say nothing of the opera and ballet performed in it, still a major draw for tourists.

Recent financial and staff problems have brought the Bolshoi to national attention, culminating in February 1995 with the resignation of Yuri Grigorovich, Artistic Director here for 30 years. His replacement by former ballet soloist Vladimir Vasilyev has given many hope that the Bolshoi will receive a breath of fresh artistic life.

The curtain goes up here nightly at 7 pm (except Mondays, the Bolshoi's day off); on Sundays, there is a matinee at noon and the usual evening performance at 7 pm. However, the theatre is closed in summer from the end of June until the beginning of September.

Touts outside the theatre offer tickets which range in price from a few dollars upwards, depending on the performance, how far up the seats are in the theatre, and what they think your spending power is. For a more reliable advance purchase, and choice of the best seats in the house, visit the EPS Box office on the ground floor of the Metropol. Here, tickets start from $15-$20. Tel: 927-6982/83.

🎭 Central Children's Theatre

The third main component of the theatrical ensemble was almost entirely reconstructed from Bove's original building in 1882 by B. Friedenberg in neo-classical style. It took on its present function in 1936, after serving as a branch of the Bolshoi, Maly and Moscow Arts Theatres.

It also houses the Bolshoi Theatre box office, frequented by those who cannot afford the prices of the entrepreneurs on the square and have little hope of more than the most distant seat.

From here, leave the square and follow Okhotny Ryad towards Manezh Square, first glancing right up Pushkinskaya Ulitsa.

☕ Avantazh Café

Next door to the metro entrance, this is a reliable source of sandwiches and mushroom julienne during the day. In the evenings it maintains its reputation as a gay café: a few years ago, the gardens in front of the Bolshoi Theatre were renowned as a gay pick-up area, though the appearance of gay bars and clubs in the city recently has seen the area become increasingly unsavoury.

⛲ House of Trade Unions
(Dom Soyuzov)
This stately 18th-century mansion, dwarfed on all sides by Stalin-era hulks, is just across Pushkinskaya Ulitsa on the corner. It was built by architect Matvey Kazakov for Prince Dolgorukov, a hero of the campaign to annex the Crimea, but was soon taken over by the local nobility and became the Nobles' Assembly.

In Soviet times it was converted to the House of Trade Unions, and became the scene of many of the most notorious of the "show trials" engineered by Stalin in the 1930s. It's best seen from the inside: try to get to a concert in the magnificent Hall of Columns. Lenin lay in state here after his death, and the premises are still frequently used for important ceremonies and celebrations.

But there is a typical element of irony in the building's new role; while the Hall of Columns resonates with classical music and political speeches from organisations like the Communist Party, another part of the building is occupied by Alexander's Night Club.

State Duma
(Gosudarstvennaya Duma)
Continuing along Okhotny Ryad as far as the junction with Tverskaya Ulitsa (to your right), you pass the building of the State Duma, the lower house of the Russian parliament, which has been located here since 1994. In Soviet times the building housed the State Planning Committee, a massive bureaucratic body responsible for coordinating Five-Year Plans designed to increase industrial and agricultural production.

Moskva Hotel
The huge Stalin-era structure on your left is the main hotel for deputies and other officials from the provinces. If you look at the facade of the hotel from Manezh Square, you will see that it is asymmetrical, probably the result of Stalin's intellectual shortcomings.

During its planning, Stalin was presented with a drawing in which the architect portrayed two different versions of the wings. Instead of choosing between the options, he appeared not to understand and told the architect to build the hotel as he had drawn it. The architect, not wishing to risk a dispute with the Great Leader, kept silent and did as he was told.

🍴 El Rincon Espanol
Just inside the entrance from the Manezh is one of the old-

est and liveliest of Moscow's foreign bars, El Rincon Espanol. Few places in Moscow can boast such consistent popularity, with food, music and waiters who are traditionally Spanish.
☛ Open noon–11:45 pm. Tel: 292-2893. CC.

Paradise

At the back end of the hotel, opposite the House of Trade Unions, is the Paradise Bar and Restaurant, whose rather bland interior belies the competent European cuisine.
☛ Open 9 am–midnight (breakfast 9 am–noon). Tel: 292-2030. CC.

National Hotel

To your right, on the far corner of Tverskaya, this grandiose hotel, mixing Art Nouveau and neo-classical styles, once also played host to Lenin — hence the huge revolutionary mosaic on the wall (see Walk 3).

Manezh Square

(Manezhnaya Ploshchad)
Cross Okhotny Ryad via the pedestrian subway to emerge into a mass of concrete and bulldozers. The extensive construction work visible ahead and to your right is a combination of restoratory and new projects, whose aim is to improve central Moscow. In the process of building a new underground development, including a shopping mall, one of the ambitious plans of Mayor Yuri Luzhkov, a number of unique architectural finds have been made.

This square is named after the large columned building at its far end, built after 1812 to celebrate the rout of the French invasion and used originally as a stable and arena for military exercises; it is now a concert hall and exhibition space. The building is now threatened by its own poor state of repair, and by the nearby building work.

The entrance to Red Square ahead of you is blocked for the reconstruction of the "Resurrection Gates" and "Chapel of Our Lady of Iberia", destroyed by Stalin.

The red-brick History Museum to your right and former Lenin Museum to your left are both being restored too. The latter was the Moscow City Duma (Council) before the Revolution, and is currently being reconstructed to house the Moscow History Museum. But unlike most building projects here, strung out over many years, these are all going ahead at a furious pace.

History Museum

The red brick State History Museum was built in 1883 in the ostentatious pseudo-Russian style of the day. Its size is astounding: 47 rooms and four million exhibits, not just Russian, spanning the period from the Stone Age to the present day. It is closed for restoration for the foreseeable future.

To reach Red Square turn left back towards the metro past street-sellers peddling a curious combination of Moscow maps and guides, and nationalist literature (the latter clearly doesn't pay on its own!), then right up steps through milling crowds of clothes sellers, and right along Nikolskaya Ulitsa at the top to emerge opposite the Kremlin.

Alternatively, for easier and quioter aooooo walk right along Manezh Square, then left when you reach the Kremlin, keeping the Kremlin Wall on your right.

Zhukov Statue

In front of the History Museum, this monument dates from May 9th 1995, the 50th anniversary of victory against Nazi Germany. Sculpted by Vyacheslav Klykov, it depicts Marshal Georgi Zhukov, now recognised as the Soviet Union's chief war hero.

In his lifetime, he remained in the shadow of Stalin, and his official disfavour continued under Khrushchev. Recent reassessments of the war have restored his reputation as strategic genius.

However, the monument has been severely criticised, both for its cold rigidity and for its position, currently overlooking a building site. Many say his rightful position is on Red Square, along with other defenders of Russia in times of need, Minin and Pozharsky.

Red Square
(Krasnaya Ploshchad)

Despite the obvious communist overtones of this name, its origin is much earlier, and is not on the Mayor's list of city names to be changed: the word *krasnaya* means "beautiful" in old Russian.

Over the centuries the square has served various functions – as a market, place of execution and venue for state ceremonies, from that marking the capture of Kazan to the shows of military strength which comprised the Soviet May Day and Revolution Day parades.

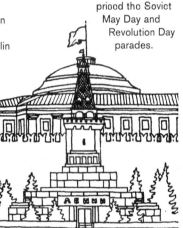

Lenin Mausoleum

Beside the Kremlin Wall stands what was once the most sacred shrine of communism, where for decades crowds queued to see the embalmed body of the leader of the world proletariat, or at least get a glimpse of the famous Post No. 1 – the goose-stepping Kremlin guards on sentry duty at its entrance, who were finally removed from their ceremonial vigil in October 1993.

Although the mausoleum currently remains open to the

public, Lenin's fate still seems uncertain. Guarded now by a solitary militiaman, the red (for communism) and black (for mourning) marble of Alexey Shchusev's great tomb promises an equally rich interior, and eerie echoes of a pagan temple.

Passing through the mausoleum, the steady stream of visitors moves on to the graves of other notables buried beneath the Kremlin Wall – dictator Josef Stalin (whose grave is frequently buried in floral tributes), apparatchik-in-chief Leonid Brezhnev and Western communist John Reed, author of *Ten Days That Shook the World*, among them.
☛ *Tues–Thurs, Sat & Sun 10 am–1 pm, no cameras or bags allowed, admission free.*

† St. Basil's Cathedral
(Pokrovsky Sobor)
Straight ahead you will see the Cathedral of the Intercession, better known as St. Basil's. Built in 1552 in honour of Ivan the Terrible's capture of Kazan, the stronghold of Russia's traditional

Tatar enemy, its more common name, paradoxically, is taken from that of the ragged holy man who predicted the evil deeds of the Tsar and condemned him to eternal damnation.

Despite its throng of brightly patterned domes and cupolas, the core church is quite simple, built in the tent-roof style that would later be banned in the 17th century by Patriarch Nikon. Most of its features are borrowed from Russian wooden church architecture.

Inside St. Basil's is a branch of the History Museum which contains exhibits portraying Russian history and the history of the cathedral in the 16th and 17th centuries, including a weapons and armour collection, icons and frescoes of the church.
☛ *Open Weds–Mon 9:30 am–5 pm. Tel: 298-3304.*

GUM
The side of the square opposite the Kremlin Wall is occupied by GUM (its name stands for "State Department Store", although it has now become a highly profitable joint-stock company).

Formerly known as the Upper Trading Arcades, this splendid glass-roofed three-storied shopping centre was built at the end of the last century to replace old merchant stalls, and housed more than 200 private shops.

Once rather drab and frequented by provincials, it has now turned sharply upmarket, its valuable real estate leased by multinational retailers like Christian Dior, Benetton and Karstadt.

Snacks in GUM

In the old days of chaotic trading in Kitai Gorod, each type of product had its own row of stalls. Among these was the "Glutton's Row", where Muscovites could expect to fill themselves for just a couple of kopecks.

Those days of cheap food are long gone, but for higher prices and some discomfort visitors to GUM and its environs have a wider than ever choice to satisfy their hunger and thirst.

The fastest option is probably **Rostik's**, the fried chicken parlour on the first floor of GUM at the Nikolskaya end, though your meal is unlikely to be especially nourishing. If you want a genuine Russian meal, try **Russkaya Kukhnya** on the first floor, first line. Expect a long wait, though, as serving girls seem unable to cope with the volume of customers. The grey Soviet-era café complex on the second floor is quieter, and here you can experience genuine pre-reform catering.

Other options are distinctly international. **Italian Dream**, on the ground floor between the first and second lines is very crowded and you'll have to stand. Brazil is represented by **Copacabana** on the first floor second line, though the food seems to fall slightly short of Brazilian. The most expensive, but probably best option, is the Chinese **Golden Dragon** on the first floor, third line.

Lobnoye Myesto (Execution Block)

Two monuments stand at the St. Basil's end of Red Square. One is the Lobnoye Myesto, or Place of Execution, where heads rolled in public – notably those of the instigators of the "Streltsy" rebellion against Peter the Great. However, this podium's more common use was for the reading of edicts and decrees.

The second monument is an 1818 statue by **Ivan Martos** of **Kosma Minin** and Prince **Dmitry Pozharsky**, who liberated Moscow from the Poles in 1612. Now dwarfed by the cathedral behind it, this statue once stood in a much more prominent position at the other end of the square, in front of the church on the corner of Nikolskaya Ulitsa.

Kazan Cathedral
(Kazansky Sobor)

Situated at the corner of Red Square closest to the Manezh, the Kazan Cathedral is a reconstruction, built at lightning speed in 1993 on the site of the church that was pulled down in the 1930's. Fortunately, during its demolition, leading Soviet restorer **Pyotr Baranovsky** took photos and measurements in the hope that it might one day rise again.

It, too, commemorates the events of 1612, and in particular the icon of the Kazan Virgin, which accompanied Prince Pozharsky on his campaigns. Church processions, attended by the Tsar himself, would come here from the Kremlin's Assumption Cathedral. A plaque just inside the church entrance pays tribute to President Boris Yeltsin and Mayor Yuri Luzhkov, who helped finance rebuilding.

Nikolskaya Ulitsa

Proceed along Nikolskaya, one of the three main streets of Kitai Gorod and one of Moscow's liveliest, which begins to the left of GUM's long Red Square frontage. Though originally a quarter inhabited by merchants, most were evicted by Ivan III and replaced by the nobles and clergy who had previously resided in the Kremlin. But the trading stalls remained till the Revolution, and the bazaar-like atmosphere still survives today. Nikolskaya in particular is now flush with expensive shops and banks.

Monastery of the Saviour Behind-the-Icon-Stalls

(Zaikonospassky Monastyr')
Nikolskaya had another name and another function before the Revolution: as Ulitsa Prosveshcheniya (Enlightenment Street), it was the first centre of academic life in the city. Enter the first courtyard on the left, which is graced by a fascinating Moscow Baroque church with balconies.

This is all that remains of the Monastery of the Saviour Behind-the-Icon-Stalls. Once part of Moscow's first higher education establishment, the Slavic-Greek-Latin Academy, where scientist and linguist **Mikhail Lomonosov** studied, it is now in a semi-derelict condition, though the lower church is once again functioning.

Lomonosov was later to become famous in a number of fields. Notably, he helped to regularise the first Russian literary language, unifying what had previously been a mess of colloquial regional dialects, and rules for poetry. He also devised the curriculum for Moscow University, founded by Catherine the Great in 1755 in a building later replaced by the History Museum, also on Nikolskaya which in those days extended right into the Kremlin.

The Printing House

(Pechatny Dvor)
Slightly further down the street, on the left is the Printing Press. The rather garish gothic building you see today replaced Ivan the Terrible's original press in the last century, but behind it the old proof-readers' building still stands.

It was here that Russia's first book, an edition of the Acts of the Apostles, was printed in 1564. Unfortunately access to the building is difficult and you may have to content yourself with the view of it from Theatre Square (see start of walk).

Slavyansky Bazar

At No. 13 is Moscow's oldest restaurant, frequented by government ministers, Siberian gold prospectors and rich landowners in the second half of the 19th century, while the ordinary Moscow public was still used to traditional eating places, known as *traktirs*.

Here, in 1897, an 18-hour lunch between Konstantin Stanislavsky and Vladimir Nemirovich-Danchenko led to the creation of the Moscow

Arts Theatre (*see* Walk 4). It is currently closed after a fire which gutted the building two years ago.

 Epiphany Monastery
(Bogoyavlensky Monastyr')
Turn right down Bogoyavlensky Pereulok past the derelict monastery of the same name. The Epiphany Monastery is the second oldest in Moscow, having been founded in the forest in 1296 by Prince Daniel, son of Alexander Nevsky and the first Prince of Muscovy.

The Cathedral (now shrouded in scaffolding) is one of the finest examples of Moscow Baroque; its lace-like stone carved platbands are still visible in places.

Stock Exchange Square
(Birzhevaya Ploshchad)
At the crossroads with Ulitsa Ilyinka is Stock Exchange Square, once the hub of financial activity in the city. Today's post-communist high finance, however, seems to have found it inadequate for its needs and is now more dispersed, though the Moscow Stock Exchange (the MTsFB, one of many) is now based here again.

The old Stock Exchange itself, standing opposite in the late classical building with ionic columns, is now the Russian Chamber of Commerce and Industry. To the left is the former Trinity-St. Sergius hostel, mission of the famous monastery (*see* Excursions, Sergiyev Posad) and now a part of Russia's Supreme Court.

 Old Square Piano Bar, U Arsentyicha
Take a detour from the square down Staropansky Pereulok to these two very welcome watering holes, on opposite sides of Bolshoy Cherkassky Pereulok.

The Piano Bar is a safe, reasonably-priced basement haven from the rigours of Moscow, with Scandinavian interior decorating its basement premises and attentive staff. Expect to pay well under $50 a head for a full meal, or you can settle for a drink and snack.
☛*Open 5 pm–5 am.*
Tel: 298-4688. Cash only.

 U Arsentyicha, meanwhile is a revived *traktir* (the Russian equivalent of an inn) renowned in the last century for its high class fish dishes. These have returned, at relatively low prices, and are accompanied by highly acclaimed beer, made on site to a Bavarian recipe and with Bavarian ingredients. Prices here are slightly cheaper than the above.
☛*Open noon–11 pm.*
Tel: 927-0755. CC.

Fyodor Restaurant & Bar
The turn-of-the-century town house at 19 Lubyansky Proyezd has been converted into an attractive Russian restaurant. Specialities include many traditional dishes, served with a complementary "one for the road", a final shot of vodka, complete with pickled cucumber. Its basement is now an atmospheric bar.
☛*Open daily noon until last guest leaves. Tel: 923-2578.*

Rybny Pereulok

Cross the square and walk down the little back street opposite. The right hand side is dominated by the Old Merchant Arcade, a classical pre-Napoleonic masterpiece by **Giacomo Quarenghi**. Now used as warehouses, it's worth exploration all the same.

Ulitsa Varvarka

Coming out onto Ulitsa Varvarka, the third of Kitai Gorod's roughly parallel thoroughfares, you will find one of the most extraordinary sights of contemporary Moscow: a cluster of attractive merchant churches and 16th century secular stone buildings, all dwarfed by the hideous eyesore of the 1960's-era Hotel Rossiya. The post-communist era has added another twist, with some of these ancient buildings now occupied by souvenir shops catering to tourists staying at the hotel.

Hotel Rossiya
Inhabited at various times by tourists and officials and regarded now as a middle-of-the-range hotel, the Rossiya also has a reputation as one of the hotbeds of mafia life in the city.

There are three attractions which might persuade you to come here: for the view – the only good excuse for dining in the top floor restaurant; for a night out in the expensive Manhattan Express nightclub, unremarkable but for the occasional concert or reception; or to taste the delicacies of the Japanese cuisine at the Tokyo restaurant, where the food is cooked in front of you.

With its entrance facing the Moskva River, the Rossiya Concert Hall has played host to all the major names of Russian entertainment as well as a wide range of visitors.

Armadillo Bar

Situated in Khrustalny Pereulok, this is a classic Tex-Mex bar, no longer exotic for the discerning Muscovite. Lively and American dominated, it features local versions of country and rockabilly music, a curiosity in themselves, as well as pool/billiards tables and darts.
☛ *Open 5 pm–5 am, weekends from noon. Tel: 298-5091. Cash only.*

Old English Embassy

(Staroye Angliiskoye Podvorye)
This pleasing 16th century stone house dates from the period of Ivan the Terrible's infatuation with Elizabethan England. The Tsar was charmed by Sir Richard Chancellor, a sea-captain shipwrecked off the coast of what is now Arkhangelsk. As a result of this meeting, and of his subsequent fascination with all things English, Ivan went so far as to propose marriage to Elizabeth.

Though this was not to be, England received "most favoured nation" status, and this well-located little house was made available for trade missions. Elizabeth never visited Russia, but in October

1994 her incumbent name-sake became the first reigning British monarch to do so; a plaque on the wall here marks the historic occasion.

The building is now a museum, showing exhibitions on relations between the two countries.

☛ *Open Tues, Sat, Sun 10 am–6 pm; Weds–Fri 11 am–7 pm, closed Mon. Tel: 298-3961.*

♜ Romanov Palace Chambers

(Palaty Romanovykh)
Nearby is a small museum devoted to the lives of the Boyar Romanovs, who once occupied this now recon-structed and colourfully painted house. The head of the household was **Nikita Romanov**, grandfather of Tsar Mikhail. As Ivan the Terrible's brother-in-law, Nikita had a softening influ-ence, and probably curbed some of the worst excesses of the regime while he remained in favour.

With its unusual ceramic stoves, gilded Flanders leather wall-coverings and carved wooden ceilings, it presents a unique picture of 17th century luxury. The low, narrow passageways, though endearing, are a nightmare for any tall visitor.

☛ *Open daily except Tues and last Mon of each month 10 am–6 pm (Weds, 11 am–7 pm). Tel: 298-3235/3706.*

Three Houses Art Gallery

A small cozy upstairs gallery selling a fine selection of non-official art from the

1960's and the present day, also jewellery, lacquer boxes.
☛ *Open daily 10 am–8 pm. Tel: 298-3948.*

✝ St. Maxim's/St. George's Churches

(Tserkov' Maksima Blazhennovo, Georgievskaya Tserkov')
Two souvenir shops, both in former churches, offer a reasonable selection of local crafts, as well as the chance to admire 19th century paint-ed ceilings. St. Maxim the Blessed, at No. 6, has a mainly religious flavour, while St. George's, at No. 12, is large, musty and chaotic.

✝ Trinity Church at Nikitniki

(Tserkov' Troitsy v Nikitnikakh)
Walk down Varvarka to the end, leaving the Kremlin to your back, then turn left onto Staraya Ploshchad, one side of the huge Ilyinsky Square which stretches up the hill-side. Just on the left down a sidestreet, Nikitnikov Pereulok, you will see the fairytale Church of the Trinity at Nikitniki, considered the finest of Moscow's merchant churches.

Its most striking feature is the painting inside, done by Moscow master Simon Ushakov. In a colour-livened tableau, he was able to con-vert the stories of the New Testament into a visible lan-guage for ordinary people, sometimes adding a humor-ous detail from contemporary life to spice it up. It is cur-rently a museum.
☛ *Open daily except Tues, 10 am–6 pm. Tel: 298-3451.*

Old Square

(Staraya Ploshchad)
At the upper end of the square is the building that once made this name notorious – the headquarters of the Soviet Communist Party Central Committee. Now it is occupied by the Administration of the Russian President (the apparatus of the executive branch of power) and the Administration and Duma of the Moscow Region.

If you want to see more of Kitai Gorod, turn left from here, down either Ulitsa Ilyinka or Nikolskaya, which will take you back to Red Square. Otherwise, continue straight to Lubyanka Square (*Lubyanskaya Ploshchad*), a feature of Russia's more immediate past.

Pleven Monument

This unusual monument on your right by the Kitai Gorod metro entrances is in fact a tiny chapel, built by Vladimir Sherwood to commemorate the taking of Pleven in 1877, Russia's contribution to the liberation of the Bulgarian nation, fellow Slavs, from the Ottoman Empire. The anniversary of Bulgarian independence is still celebrated here.

Moscow City Museum

Just past the approach from Ulitsa Ilyinka, the colourful classical church of St. John the Divine Under-the-Willow now houses the City of Moscow museum. If the exhibition seems small and disappointing, it is only because of a lack of space.

In fact the museum has over a million exhibits, with paintings, drawings, maps and various city treasures, most now in storage. There are plans to move to the former Lenin Museum.
☞ *Open Tues–Sun 10 am–6 pm; Weds, Fri 11 am–7 pm. Tel: 924-8490.*

Polytechnic Museum

The enormous late-19th century building across the road on your right is the Polytechnic Museum, a scientific mecca for Russian schoolchildren. Its vast halls are filled with everything from early clocks and cameras to intricate models of catalytic crackers and the like.

It falls far short of the London Science Museum in terms of size, colour and push-button visual aids, and there is an emphasis on guided tours and live lectures. Even so, it is instructive for its national (and Soviet) slant on world science. Guided tours can be arranged in English.

The museum is also famous as a venue for poetry evenings, a phenomenon of the sixties; officially banned 30 years ago, they are now enjoying a revival. Once graced by the appearance of the likes of Boris Pasternak, it is now favoured by the 1960's generation, figures like Yevgeny Yevtushenko and Andrey Voznesensky.
☞ *Open Tues–Sun 10 am–5:30 pm (Tues, Thurs 1 pm–8:30 pm). Tel: 223-0756.*

Children's World

(Dyetsky Mir)
The building ahead of you as you enter the square is *Dyetsky Mir*, the largest children's shop in the country. With its labyrinthine halls and

Moscow's Past and Present Come Together at Fyodor Restaurant and Bar, Offering the Best of Russian Cuisine to Moscow Residents and Visitors Alike.

For an experience of Moscow traditions, visit our historic restaurant, named after Fyodor Savelyev, one of the original builders of the Bely Gorod area of the city, which grew up in the late 16th century as Moscow expanded beyond the territory of the Kremlin and Kitay Gorod. The restaurant's premises, built for the Blandov family of "milk kings", retain many of their art nouveau splendours.

Our menu includes many specialities of Russian cuisine, such as Tsarski soup, *okroshka*, Knyazheskaya sirloin, jellied crabs *a la Potyomkin*, sturgeon "Fyodora", Petrovski *kvas* with horseradish, the famed "Tsar" wine and the special "Blandov" milkshake. Following the ancient Russian custom, before you leave we offer you free of charge the traditional "one for the road" — a shot of vodka, served with pickled cucumber!

Fyodor Restaurant and Bar is open daily, from noon till the very last guest leaves, at 19 Lubyanski Proezd, near to Metro "Kitai Gorod". For reservations, tel.: 923-2578.

corridors, it gives a much better idea of Soviet-era shopping than the modernised GUM. However, the thriving black market in Pampers nappies at the entrance and the presence of such names as Lego and Winkler's World inside show that times have changed.

In fact, in this mercantile age, children's goods are not always viable on their own, and adult products seem equally abundant. A classic example is the car showroom downstairs, where toy Lamborghinis share display windows with full-size Cadillacs.

The Lubyanka

In a bizarre juxtaposition, Dyetsky Mir has three notorious neighbours, farther round to your right. The "Lubyanka" was the headquarters of the Soviet secret police, best known to the West as the KGB, but now undergoing regular name changes. In the cellars of the middle building, Stalin's police chief Lavrenty Beria used to interrogate prisoners before they were shipped off to the Gulag — that is, if they survived the process.

Appropriately, given the above, the memorial stone on the side of the square near the Polytechnic Museum is from the Solovyetsky Islands, one of the worst of the 1930's labour camps. It was erected there in 1990 by "Memorial", an organisation devoted to discovering the truth about the Stalinist repressions.

In the centre once stood a statue of **Felix Dzerzhinsky** (1877-1926), founder of the first communist secret police,

the Cheka. The removal of his statue in August 1991 became a powerful visual image for the fall of the old regime.

The KGB Museum

This relatively impartial account of the history of Russian and Soviet intelligence is situated on the first floor of the building housing the "Sedmoy Kontinent" supermarket. Opened in 1984 by **Yuri Andropov**, KGB head turned General Secretary, the museum was originally meant to instruct KGB staff and was closed to the general public. Access is still restricted and to get there you'll have to take a group tour: tours are organised regularly by Patriarchi Dom.

Although it tells the story of counter-intelligence since the 14th century, the main focus of the museum is on the Soviet era. There are profiles of the organisation's leaders, most of whom were executed, an account of the 1930s terror, wartime intelligence, and inevitably the Cold War, with its elaborate bugging devices, transmitters and codes.

The most recent exhibits are from the work of the Federal Security Service (FSB) in intercepting icon- and drug-smugglers. The latest addition to the collection is sobering — an anti-aircraft gun stolen from a military base in Omsk bound for the rebels in Chechnya.

Mayakovsky Museum

If the culmination of this walk seems too gloomy, you can strike a more light-hearted note by walking a few yards up Myasnitskaya Ulitsa to a bust of a bald-looking man and what looks at first sight like a pile of junk. This is the entrance to the innovative Vladimir Mayakovsky Museum, opened in its present form in 1989.

It is a shrine to Russia's greatest futurist poet, a man who devoted his life to the Revolution and then lost his way just as Stalin was beginning to flex his muscles. From top to bottom, it feels something like the backstage area of a modern theatre, with mangled iron railings and furniture suspended at unlikely angles. Mayakovsky's manuscripts hang frozen in glass while writing implements lie chaotically on sloping sawn-off desks.

The museum traces the poet's life, starting from childhood in Georgia and moving to his earliest involvement with the underground revolutionary movement. His attitude to power is summed up in one exhibit, a giant green armchair with a cracked portrait of Tsarist Interior Minister Stolypin on the seat: this reformist politician was a hated figure for revolutionaries.

You now climb right to the top of the building, to the room where Mayakovsky shot himself in 1930, and work your way down. Other rooms demonstrate his talent for making revolutionary posters, and his impressions from trips abroad. But once Soviet power was firmly established, clouds appeared on the horizon – the deaths of Lenin (1924) and of fellow poet Sergey Yesenin (1925), both feature prominently.

In the penultimate room, a sinister negative picture of Stalin appears on a heap of pipes, screws and machinery. In the final room, Mayakovsky's death mask lies on top of a huge white coffin, too large even for a man who seemed larger than life.

 Open Fri–Tues 10 am–6 pm, Thurs 1 9 pm, closed Weds and last Fri of month. Tel: 921-9560/9387.

🎁 Biblio-Globus Bookshop

Situated on the right side of Ulitsa Myasnitskaya, this busy bookshop has the city's best collection of art books, with new books downstairs and second hand books upstairs. Check prices before making a purchase – you may find they vary (on the same book) from place to place.

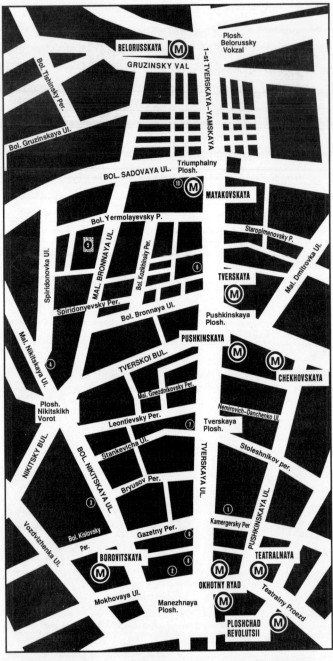

1. Moscow Arts Theatre
2. Moscow University
3. Conservatory
4. Gorky House Museum
5. Patriarch's Ponds
6. Revolution Museum
7. Moscow City Government
8. Intourist Hotel
9. Central Telegraph
10. Tchaikovsky Hall

3. Tverskaya

An ancient road from the Kremlin to Russia's major cities – first Tver, later St. Petersburg – Tverskaya has always been one of Russia's main thoroughfares. It originated as a trade route, and from the 18th century came to be used for the conduct of royal processions from the new northern capital.

All but a handful of its original buildings were removed during the 1930's, and the road was widened and reconstructed according to a new city plan: the few pre-revolutionary structures that remained were moved back several feet from their original positions. In 1932, the street was renamed Gorky Street, in honour of Maxim Gorky, one of the most revered Soviet writers.

Today Tverskaya is increasingly the display window of Moscow, its formerly dour Soviet facades filling over the last two years with a glittering range of foreign brand-name boutiques. Although its giant buildings and heavy traffic are not ideal for strolling, Tverskaya deserves to be explored once on foot – with enough time to savour its hidden details.

STARTS AT: Metro Okhotny Ryad
ENDS AT: Metro Belorusskaya

DIRECTIONS: Odd-numbered addresses are on the left side as you walk up Tverskaya from Manezh Square, even-numbered on the right. After Triumfalnaya Ploshchad, the street is called 1-ya Tverskaya Yamskaya, and the numbers begin again from 1. Length beginning to end: 2.5 km.

TRANSPORT: intermediary metro stations are Pushkinskaya/Tverskaya and Mayakovskaya; trolleybuses #1, #12 and #20 run the length of the street.

 National Hotel (No. 1)
This turn-of-the-century hotel with its fine views over the Kremlin, which begins the street, is most famous for the fact that Lenin stayed here. For many years lumped together under single management with its neighbour,

the Intourist, the National reopened in 1995 after a lengthy reconstruction as Moscow's latest five-star hotel, its glorious art nouveau interiors lovingly restored.

With a more intimate feel than its traditional rival, the Metropol, and a range of cafés and restaurants like the **"Moskva"** (serving Russian cuisine) and **"St. Petersburg"** (European cuisine), it promises to add a welcome new choice to central Moscow. Its innovations include smaller halls for banquets and private parties, and the stylish "Winter Garden" atrium café on the ground floor.

A branch of **Maxim's** is situated on the ground floor of the National Hotel. Prices are considerably higher than in other restaurants in Pierre Cardin's chain, easily topping the $100 mark for an evening meal.
☛ *Open: 11 am–midnight (closed Sundays). Tel: 258-7148/7060.*

Intourist Hotel (No. 3)

Before the appearance of western-managed Joint Venture hotels, the Intourist counted as one of Moscow's best: its central location may have been convenient, but its visual charm has never been evident. The Intourist has always had something of a seedy reputation, connected mainly with the nightly abundance of prostitutes, both inside and out. This is no longer a unique phenomenon, but it was here that it all started.

Unless you're staying here, the hotel's own restaurants – the **Skazka** (noon–3 pm, 7 pm–11 pm), with its abundance of folk motifs, and the massive, noisy **Golden Hall** (noon–5 pm, 7 pm–midnight), both serving Russian cuisine – probably deserve a miss, especially because they have recently been joined by many other foreign eateries.

A very decent Italian restaurant on the 3rd floor, **Santa Lucia**, serves mainly pasta and seafood from noon till the last guest leaves. *(Tel: 956-8413. CC).*

Lily Wong's is an American-style Chinese restaurant offering a popular $19.50 set lunch (noon–3 pm) and $29.50 "early bird menu" (3 pm–6:30 pm). Its entrance is from Tverskaya, next to the National. *(Tel: 956-8301. CC).*

A small **Azteca**, one of two restaurants of the same name in Moscow serving Mexican food, is perched on the Intourist's 20th and 21st floors, with a speciality in early morning breakfasts for around $5. Otherwise, you should find average Moscow prices here, i.e. an evening meal priced at around $40-$50 per person. (*Open 24 hours. Tel: 956-8490. CC for purchases of over $50*).

Newest addition of all is another branch of the well-established pizza outlet, **Patio Pizza**. (*Open 24 hours. Tel: 292-0891. CC*).

 La Cantina (No. 5)
The ground floor of the Yermolova theatre (*see* Walk 4) is occupied by La Cantina, a Mexican restaurant. Prices here are high, as you would expect from such a central location, and the food rates fair to good. Service is efficient, and the staff anglophone, a rarity outside the city's Irish bars. Live evening music with emphasis on blues and country.
☛*Open 8 am–midnight. Tel: 926-3684. CC.*

 Kombi's (No. 4)
This first floor restaurant is part of Moscow's best fast food chain, providing cheap, fresh and filling sandwiches delivered with almost unbelievably polite service. The entrance is opposite the Intourist. A second restaurant is sited further up Tverskaya on Triumfalnaya Ploshchad, and others are dotted around the city.

 Central Post Office (No. 7)
(*Tsentralny Telegraf*)
Built by **Ivan Rerberg** in 1927, this enormous grey building with the globe combines constructivist features of the 1920's with the

nascent Stalinist style. Here, during the repressive 1930's and later, foreign correspondents had to come to file their dispatches: with a single location, it was much easier to censor them.

With some sections open 24 hours a day, this is an easy location for sending registered letters, faxes and telegrams, or making international phone calls.

 Club Moskovskii (No. 6)
New Moscow night-club entertainment on a grand scale – with restaurant, bar, casino and discoteque. You'll spot the building straight away from its outside murals.
☛*Open noon–8 pm, 10 pm–6 am. Tel: 292-1282. CC.*

 Savvinsky Monastery Mission (No. 6)
(*Savvinskoye Podvorye*)
The offices of a large monastery outside Moscow (*see* Excursions, Zvenigorod), this building dates from 1907 and has a beautiful facade decorated with ceramic tiles and other features of 17th-century architecture. In the 1930's, it was obscured by a new building, and access is only through the archway of No. 6.

Bryusovsky Pereulok - Ulitsa Nezhdanovoy
This road to the left is named after James Bruce, Peter the

Great's Field Marshal of Scots origin who lived at its other end (*see* Walk 4). In the Soviet era it was renamed after Bolshoi Theatre singer Antonina Nezhdanova, who lived at No. 7; it now appears to use both names. The House of Composers, headquarters of the Composer's Union, is at No. 8/10.

Church of the Resurrection
(Tserkov' Voskresenya)
This little church is much loved by the inhabitants of central Moscow. Like most churches which survived the Soviet era intact, this one contains several icons saved from less fortunate places – an example is the Virgin of the Passions on the southern wall, from the Monastery which was once situated on Pushkin Square.

Tverskaya Ploshchad
This square's pre-1991 name, Sovetskaya Ploshchad, would seem to be more appropriate – almost nothing from before the Revolution remains here. The statue of Yuri Dolgoruky, Moscow's founder, in its centre, was erected in 1954 to commemorate the 800th anniversary of the city.

Aragvi Restaurant
The grandfather of Georgian restaurants in Moscow and, appropriately, favoured by Stalin. One of the better examples of Soviet state catering, it now seems moderately priced.
☛Open noon–11 pm. Tel: 229-3762. Cash only.

Uncle Guilly's (U Dyadi Gilyaya)
Now run by an American firm, this restaurant in Stoleshnikov Pereulok (leading off the square) is named after Vladimir Gilyarovsky, a turn-of-the-century writer famous for his book *Moscow and Muscovites*. Providing colourful descriptions and anecdotes, Gilyarovsky was not afraid to show the seamier side of life in the city. The speciality here is steak, with atmospheric cellar dining and friendly service.
☛Open noon–midnight. Tel: 229-2050, 229-4750. CC.

Moscow Government Building (No. 11)
The original building, designed by Matvey Kazakov for Moscow's military governor generals, was just three storeys high – the remaining two were added in 1939, when it was moved back 14 metres from its original place on the street.

One of its residents was Prince Dolgorukov, an extraordinarily naive descendant of the founder of Moscow. He held fabulous balls and unsuspectingly hobnobbed with the city's top criminals, who hid behind respectable charity organisations. One of these, a gang leader called Shpeyer, managed to "sell" the residence to an English lord, who, after the deed had been witnessed in a fake notary office, moved his luggage right into the governor's office before the scam was exposed.

Tsentralnaya Hotel (No. 10)

Once the place where the legions of foreign communists, effective exiles in Moscow, were accommodated in the Stalin years, the hotel had an unhappy reputation. Many of its inhabitants fell victim to the changing winds of political allegiances, and disappeared during night-time visits from the secret police.

Today it is far short of Intourist standards and probably best avoided. A grandly decorated ground floor dining room may be worth visiting for lunch.

 ### Moscow Bombay

The name of this restaurant, situated at No. 3 on the side-street Ulitsa Nemirovicha-Danchenko, expresses the nature of its cuisine, Russo-Indian – and Moscow-Bombay is a worthy attempt to combine the two influences. Such innovations as the cauliflower and potato curry (part of a substantial vegetarian choice) make it well worth a visit. Expect to pay around $50 for two.
☛ *Open noon–11 pm. Tel: 292-9731. Accepts Mastercard and Eurocard.*

 ### Pizza Hut (No. 12)

The smaller of two such restaurants in Moscow, this Pizza Hut was opened in 1990 as a joint venture with Moscow City Catering Committee. For a year or two it was one of the few rallying-points for deprived Moscow expatriates: business remains brisk despite new competition.
☛ *Open 11 am–10 pm. Tel: 229-2013. CC.*

 ### Filippov Bakery (No. 10)

The bread shop situated at No. 10 was the site of Moscow's most famous 19th century bakery, Filippov's, known particularly for its *kalatches* (traditional Russian figure-of-eight pastries with fillings) and meat pies. Its enterprising owner even managed, through a special freezing process, to deliver to Siberia, as well as to the Tsar's court in St. Petersburg, explaining that the River Neva's water was unsuitable for baking.

The origin of Filippov's currant rolls provides an entertaining story. One day the city governor found a cockroach in his roll. Summoning Filippov, he demanded an explanation. The resourceful Filippov promptly gulped down the roll himself, claimed that it was a currant and immediately ordered his bakers to start a new production line!

This building was damaged by the first shots of the 1905 revolution, when gunfire shattered its windows.

 ### Yeliseyevsky Food Shop (No. 14)

Approaching Pushkin Square, "Gastronom No. 1" is on the corner of Kozitsky Pereulok. It's Moscow's premiere food store – certainly in terms of its sumptuous decor, if not its selection – and is housed in what was the mansion of the noble Volkonsky family, which at the end of the 19th century fell into the hands of the new entrepreneurial class.

It was opened as a shop in 1901 by a St. Petersburg merchant who enraptured Muscovites by introducing them for the first time to exotic fruits such as bananas and pineapples. His wine shop caused controversy – he had to move it right to the back of the shop, so that it stood more than 45 feet from the nearest church, and thus became legal. Now wine is sold near the entrance – the law, and the church in question, have long since ceased to exist.

Night Flight (No. 17)
Moscow's first night club of its kind (opened 1991), the Swedish-owned Night Flight was notorious for its over-30 age requirement for men, and its aggressive prostitutes, who were said to seize on men as soon as they entered.

Now it's just another night club-cum-restaurant, with high regular menu prices but good and innovative food. The special lunch menu may be worth checking out. ☛ Open noon–5 am. Tel: 229-4165. CC.

Pushkin Square
(Pushkinskaya Ploshchad)
This large Moscow square occupies a prominent place in the city's everyday life, and is a frequent meeting place for Muscovites.

It was originally the site of the **Convent of the Passion**, founded by Tsar Mikhail in the 17th century in honour of a miracle-working icon brought here from Nizhny Novgorod. The convent was destroyed after the Revolution and the square reconstructed totally. Even the Pushkin statue, originally on the west side, was moved across to its present position.

A more recent landmark, Russia's first McDonald's, stands on the west side of the square. In the early days of its existence, McDonald's became a tourist attraction on a par with the Lenin Mausoleum, with a queue which often stretched right round the square. A combination of the opening of two more restaurants of the chain, inflation, and the novelty wearing off, makes entrance easy and rapid these days.

Pushkin Statue
This monument to the brooding poet was erected in 1880 by Alexander

Opekushin in a ceremony accompanied by lively festivities, which marked Russia's first real celebration of its national literature. Fellow writers Fyodor Dostoyevsky and Ivan Turgenev made eloquent speeches to mark the occasion.

ИЗВЕСТИЯ

Izvestia Building

The severe building on the far side of the square, including the metro entrance, is perhaps Moscow's most famous work in constructivist style. Built by Grigory Barkhin in 1927, it houses the editorial offices of the newspaper *Izvestia*, once the organ of the Soviet government and now Russia's leading democratically-orientated newspaper. The equivalent of the *Independent* or the *New York Times*, it is not afraid to take a harshly critical view of the government.

Trinity Motors Building (No. 18)

This fine art nouveau facade was built as the publishing house of Ivan Sytin, who rose from bookshop attendant to media mogul in just 15 years. He established *Russkoye Slovo* (Russian Word), a prominent pre-revolutionary newspaper.

Since the Revolution, the building has been used by the undistinguished newspaper *Trud*, at one time the organ of the official Soviet Trade Union movement. The ground floor is now occupied by an American car showroom.

Credit Bank

Turn to the right on to Nastasinsky Pereulok for a glance at another architectural feast. The bank, built in 1916 by Vladimir Pokrovsky, mixes old Russian, Moorish and Gothic styles.

Revolution Museum (No. 21)

Built in 1780 for Count Razumovsky, this classical mansion was for a time used for secret masonic gatherings. It's best known, however, for its role in the last century as the English Club, regarded as the most snobbish and conservative in Moscow, and not in fact English at all. For while the only club to allow gambling, it saw many a hereditary estate frittered away in its gaming halls.

In 1924 the building became the Revolution Museum, and now contains a detailed display of just about everything you can imagine that is connected to Russia's various revolutions – one which has sometimes involved rapid ideological U-turns in an attempt to remain objective. In recent years, an exhibition on the failed coup of August 1991 was added.

Unless you have an interest in the historical detail of these events, you may be content with the outdoor exhibits, such as a damaged trolleybus from August 1991. ☛ *Open Tues–Sun 10 am–6 pm (Weds 11 am–7pm), closed Mon and last day of each month. Tel: 299-9863/6274.*

Stanislavsky Drama Theatre (No. 23)

This theatre was created from an operatic-dramatic

Central Moscow | Tverskaya

studio begun in 1935, where the renowned director **Konstantin Stanislavsky** worked during his last years. With the help of some promising young directors and designers, it has staged some of the most interesting productions of recent years – including plays featuring **Pyotr Mamonov**, a rock singer turned actor, famous for his extraordinary facial and bodily contortions.

The Theatre's ground-floor buffet has been converted into a stylish restaurant-club, with a wide choice of beverages and quality live jazz or pop in the evenings. It is now part of a members' club, which also includes a restaurant with mainly French cuisine and carvery lunches. ☛*Open 1 pm–4 pm, 6 pm-6 am. Tel: 564-8004. Major credit cards, except AmEx.*

Young Viewers' Theatre (MTYuZ)

Down the next left turn, Pereulok Sadovskikh, are these former residential buildings, converted into a theatre for a Soviet-era troupe which has occupied the space since 1943.

Today the theatre is famous for the husband-wife artistic partnership of Kama Ginkas and Henrietta Yanovskaya. Yanovskaya's long-running production of Mikhail Bulgakov's *Heart of a Dog*, a satire on early Soviet communism, was one of the early hits of perestroika.

Yakor Restaurant

Just beyond the theatre, this restaurant should in no way be confused with the nearby Anchor (*Yakor* in Russian) in the Palace Hotel. This one also specialises in fish, in a traditionally Russian and less fussy fashion. Prices come in at about $50 for two. ☛*Open noon–10 pm. Tel: 299-2951, 209-5444. Cash only.*

Galerie les Oreades - Union of Artists Exhibition Hall (No. 25)

A combination of Parisian art gallery and Russian craft centre. For shoppers, the choice here is not large, but you can be sure of quality, and may find some lesser known village crafts here – such as a display of clay dolls from the north Russian town of Kargopol. ☛*Open 11 am–7 pm. Tel: 299-2289. Cash only.*

Baku-Livan (No. 24)

This Lebanese/Azerbaijani kebab house serves traditional middle-eastern fare like falafels and doners, and is one of the very cheapest and quickest eating options in central Moscow.

The Baku restaurant next door provides a similar but more varied menu, together with a somewhat sleazy evening variety show, for considerably higher prices, up to $50 a head.

 Kebab House open 10 am–10 pm, restaurant 11 am–5 pm, 6–11 pm. Tel: 299-8506. Major CC in restaurant.

Tandoor Restaurant (No. 30)

This temple of colonial decay is everything you would expect from an Indian restaurant in Delhi, transplanted perfectly into a flaking Soviet era interior. With its democratic prices (around $50 for a meal for two), Tandoor is an oasis for the less wealthy in search of a meal on Tverskaya.

 Open noon–11 pm. Tel: 209-5565. Major CC.

Mayakovsky Statue

A giant statue of the great revolutionary poet, Vladimir Mayakovsky (*see* Walk 2 for his museum) provides the main landmark of **Triumphal Square (Triumfalnaya Ploshchad)**. The work of Alexander Kibalnikov, erected in 1958, it shows the poet as a speaker at a rally – the way that communism preferred to depict him.

It's a spot which inspires fond memories among Moscow's 1960's generation, who used to gather here for informal concerts and poetry readings.

Peking Hotel

A Stalinist-style building on the far side of the square, akin to but not identical with the "wedding cake" series, this mediocre state hotel is best known for Moscow's first ever Chinese restaurant, opened in 1957, three years before the souring of

relations between the two communist giants.

Reopened after a major overhaul, again by the Chinese, a few years ago, it seems to arouse every emotion from rapture to despair among patrons. If you try it, good luck! Prices are about average for Moscow – up to $50 a head for a full evening meal.

 Open noon–4 pm, 6 pm–11 pm. Tel: 209-1387. CC.

American Bar & Grill

Next door to Kombi's (at No. 32/1, 1-ya Tverskaya-Yamskaya) this is the number one venue in Moscow for American food and atmosphere. Open 24 hours a day, its breakfasts are popular, while later in the day it fills up quickly, meaning you may have to wait a while for a table.

 Open 24 hours. Tel: 251-7999. CC.

Patio Pasta (No. 3)

Unlike its pizza brethren in the Rosinter chain, this restaurant seems to fall slightly short of Italian style culinary quality. Come for the generous salad bar and garlic bread and avoid the rather stodgy pasta.

 Open noon–midnight. Tel: 251-5861. CC.

Karousel (No. 7)

What could be just another sleazy overpriced Russian restaurant has been trans-

formed by a talented Italian chef into a genuinely high class eatery – stick to the chef's specials and be prepared to pay around $60-$70 per person for food. Avoid the nightclub and casino (at No. 9) at all costs.
☛ Open noon–6 am. Tel: 251-6444. CC.

 Slastyona Confectionery Shop (No. 12)
The fabulous displays of Russian-made boxes of chocolate and sweets is evidence that this is the main retail outlet of the Red October chocolate factory (see Walk 7).

 Booklover's Corner (No. 22)
(Lavka Knigolyuba)
A musty little shop selling antiques, second-hand books and bric-à-brac – it looks good for minor souvenirs, such as cutlery and trinkets.

 Laguna Restaurant (No. 15)
Average prices ($50 per head) for standard Russo-European fare. Staff friendly.
☛ Open noon–midnight. Tel: 251-9381. Major CC.

 Alexandrovsky Restaurant (No. 17)
Though nothing to do with the Palace Hotel next door, this restaurant has a magnificent 19th century interior and a portrait of reforming Tsar Alexander II, after whom it was named, on the wall. The cuisine is traditionally Russian, and suitably regal, although hardly worth the $75-plus you're likely to pay.
☛ Open noon–midnight. Tel: 251-7987. Major CC.

THE PALACE

Palace Hotel (No. 19)
A sparkling clean, modern, efficient, definitely five-star hotel run by the Austrian Marco Polo chain. All three of its restaurants are top class: the **Anchor** (open noon–5 pm, 7 pm–1:30 am) serving delicious fish dishes in an interior like a frigate's deck; the **Lomonosov** (open noon–3 pm, 7 pm–11 pm), with European and Russian cuisine, and the **Vienna** (open 5 pm–11 pm), whose food and decor (sketches of the city) match its name.
☛ Tel: 956-3152. CC.

 Ploshchad Tverskoy Zastavy
This square, the boundary between Tverskaya Ulitsa and Leningradsky Prospekt, was the site of the Triumphal Arch (see Greater Moscow, War Memorials), and served in its time as the main entrance to the city on the route from St. Petersburg.

Belorussia Station
(Byelorussky Vokzal)
This huge palatial terminus on the left dates from 1909, and is the main starting point for journeys to Northern Europe. It has been the scene of many momentous returns, like that of the Soviet troops in 1945, and the last Russian soldiers returning from Germany in 1994.

The statue of Maxim Gorky commemorates the writer's return from Italy in 1928. Running along the street to its left, Gruzinsky Val, is Moscow's largest street flower market.

4. Artistic Moscow

(See map for Walk 3).

Starting from Tverskaya and passing along Bolshaya Nikitskaya (formerly Gertsena) Ulitsa, this is a walk with an artistic flavour, which takes you through the Moscow of the great theatre directors, Konstantin Stanislavsky and Vsevolod Meyerhold, as well as writer and dramatist Mikhail Bulgakov, who immortalised the streets of the city in his novel *Master and Margarita*.

It also affords the opportunity to see some of the finest examples of Moscow's Art Nouveau, the works of architect Fyodor Shekhtel.

STARTS FROM: Metro Okhotny Ryad
ENDS AT: Metro Mayakovskaya

 Chekhov Arts Theatre *(MKhAT imeni Chekhova)* Leave the southwestern exit of Metro Okhotny Ryad (last carriage if coming from Biblioteka im. Lenina) and walk up Tverskaya on its right hand side to the second turning right, Kamergersky Pereulok. One of the city's theatrical landmarks, the Arts Theatre, or MKhAT as it is simply known by its Russian acronymn, was originally a chamber theatre which was rebuilt by **Fyodor Shekhtel** in 1902. The theatre's seagull motif, designed by Shekhtel, echoes Chekhov's famous play.

It was here that the creative pair of **Konstantin Stanislavsky** (1863–1938) and **Vladimir Nemirovich-Danchenko** (1858–1943) revolutionised European drama, through their famous "method" acting technique. Their interpretations of the work of Anton Chekhov were crucial in establishing his reputation after earlier setbacks – their first success a production of *The Seagull* in December 1898.

The theatre's current name dates from the mid-1980's, when the original company split up following an acerbic quarrel, with half remaining in the old building under artistic director Oleg Yefremov, while the other half moved, with company actress Tatiana Doronina, to a new building, named after Gorky, on Tverskoy Bulvar (see later in walk).

Its intimate period interior is one of the most charming spaces in Moscow. The theatre's long central gallery has a tangible sense of history to it, lined with ranks of black and white photographs of all the great names – actors, directors, writers – who have worked there, as well as commemorative statues of Chekhov, Stanislavsky and Nemirovich-Danchenko. There is a museum on site (of which the Stanislavsky Museum, see later in walk, is a branch), tracing the history of the theatre and containing props, sketches and personal possessions of actors, but it's currently closed for repairs. (Tel: 229-0080).

 MKhAT Club Restaurant
Next door to the theatre – in fact, using part of its buffet space – this restaurant serves European cuisine in a pleasant turn-of-the century atmosphere. Prices are moderate for Moscow.
Open noon–4 pm and 6 pm–3 am. Tel: 229-9106. Cash only.

 Ristorante Artistico
Extravagant art nouveau-style decor here befits Ristorante Artistico's location opposite a great theatre. A stylish and intimate Italian restaurant, its

small menu includes excellent pasta dishes, and an emphasis on veal, plus sumptuous desserts. Around $50 a head.
Open noon–midnight. Tel: 292-0673. Major CC.

Yermolova Theatre
Returning to Tverskaya, look opposite to No. 5, an older building sandwiched between two monsters (one Stalinist, one modern).

Named after the actress Maria Yermolova (whose house-museum will be visited later in this walk), this theatre is best known as the stage of **Vsevolod Meyerhold** (1874–1940), the talented experimental director of the 1920's and 1930's, who worked closely with futurists like Mayakovsky and reworked 19th century classics to produce Russia's finest avant-garde drama. He worked here 1931–38, before falling victim to Stalin's terror and dying in prison in 1940.

Moscow University
Turn right at the bottom of Tverskaya onto Manezh Square (*see* Walk 2). The ensemble of classical buildings which follow on your right houses several faculties of Moscow University, which were built on land purchased

by Catherine the Great in 1785 and designed by architect Matvey Kazakov.

This was the centre of the complex for a century and a half, before its removal to the Lenin Hills after World War II. The building on the other side of Bolshaya Nikitskaya, also part of the University, is post-1812, and in its forecourt is a statue of Mikhail Lomonosov (1711-1765), a great all-rounder of Russian science, linguistics and history who founded the University in 1755 (see Walk 2).

Ulitsa Bolshaya Nikitskaya

Once the beginning of the Moscow-Novgorod road, this street took its name from the Convent of St. Nikita, founded by the noble Nikita Romanov (see Walk 2) in the 16th century.

Later, it became the haunt of Moscow's enlightened aristocracy, and was frequently visited by **Alexander Herzen**; the street was named after him in the Soviet era, and that name, Ulitsa Gertsena, is still used by many Muscovites. It retains its cultured atmosphere, enhanced by the dual presence of the University and Moscow Conservatory.

Bruce Mansion

The house at No. 14 once belonged to James William Bruce, a direct descendant of the Scottish King Robert and a commander of Peter the Great's artillery at the battle of Poltava.

In addition to his military skills, Bruce was known to practise the black arts, and on one occasion succeeded in hypnotising the Tsar and his courtiers into believing

they were about to be washed into the River Neva in St. Petersburg by a flood. The house was partly rebuilt by his namesake and grand-nephew, who served as military governor-general of Moscow at the end of the 18th century.

Zoological Museum

Opened in 1805 under the auspices of Moscow University, this museum is one of the top ten of its kind in the world. It contains such delights as a stuffed panda and sea cow skeleton, as well as unique Mochulsky beetle and earthworm collections.

☛ *Open 10 am–5 pm daily except Mon and the last Tues of the month. Tel: 203-8923 (taped message), 203-3569.*

Moscow Conservatory

Housed in several buildings on the opposite side of the street, the Conservatory is one of Moscow's cultural centrepieces. It is both an internationally acclaimed music school and a concert venue whose Grand and Small Halls have witnessed performances by all the great Russian musicians, as well as premieres from composers such as Dmitry Shostakovich, Sergey Prokofiev and Alfred Schnittke.

The Conservatory occupies two buildings. The main one, an 18th century palace, was designed by Kazakov for Yekaterina Vorontsova-Dashkova, art patroness and friend of Catherine the Great. It was purchased in 1859 by Conservatory founder Nikolay Rubinstein, son of a pencil manufacturer, whose love of music was matched by his fund-raising abilities. He was helped by the fact that architect Vassily Zagorsky, whose alterations included filling in the main courtyard to create the auditorium, refused a fee for his services. It opened in 1866.

The second, No. 11, is even older, a converted boyar mansion whose acoustics make a perfect setting for the vocal department. The great Pyotr Tchaikovsky taught here from the beginning, but didn't live to the first concert in 1898 (he died in 1893). He is remembered every four years at an international competition which awards prizes in the fields of piano, violin, cello and voice – the next Tchaikovsky Competition is due to be held in 1998.

The statue to him in the forecourt, erected in 1954, is by Vera Mukhina, better known for her enormous "Worker and Peasant Girl" outside the Exhibition of Economic Achievements. If you're visiting the Grand Hall for a concert, you can't but notice the portraits of eminent composers which run along the upper walls of the grandiose auditorium.

Olady Café
The cheap tasty Russian pancakes served here with chocolate and jam fillings have made this little café a mecca for penniless University students for years. Now it is run jointly with the Dzhairo Express bar next door, which serves Middle Eastern fast food. This building once housed a book shop where the poet Sergey Yesenin sometimes worked behind the counter.

Little Ascension Church
(Tserkov' Malovo Voznesenya)
The tiny Baroque church opposite was built by Zakhary Chernyshev, Moscow's first governor-general, in the mid-18th century. A classic example of how such buildings were neglected and left to rot under communism, it has now been returned to the church, and was fully restored to mark Victory Day celebrations in 1995.

St. Andrew's Anglican Church
Peeping through from Ulitsa Stankevicha is the tower of a typical English gothic church. After years as a recording studio attached to the state record company Melodiya, it was given back to its original owners, the Anglican community, in 1994 at the time of Queen Elizabeth II's visit to Moscow. The Queen attended a service here and met expatriate children.

Mayakovsky Theatre
Built in 1866 as the Paradise Theatre, the building acquired its current name in the 1930's: the irony to it is that Vsevolod Meyerhold, who staged Mayakovsky's plays here during his brief directorship in 1922, was later arrested for "crimes" which included these productions.

In its earlier life, the theatre was once hired so that the Moscow Arts Theatre could stage a special performance of *The Seagull* for its author. Chekhov had missed the season proper – he was recovering from a cold caught following his distress at the play's first, failed run in St. Petersburg!

Today the theatre stages lavish productions of comedy and the classics, with a troupe which includes some of Russia's finest actors.

Leontyevsky Pereulok

For an optional extension to this walk, turn right before the TASS building back in the direction of Tverskaya Ulitsa and Pushkin Square.

Until recently known as Ulitsa Stanislavskovo, Leontyevsky Pereulok is a pretty street which combines various architectural styles: neo-baroque, classical and neo-Byzantine are all represented, and many buildings are occupied by embassies.

🏛 Stanislavsky House Museum

Of all Moscow's little house-museums, this is one of the finest and most unusual, and probably has the friendliest and most helpful staff. The celebrated director lived here 1921–38, though the museum retains even earlier decor from the 19th century.

It is in two parts, with visitors entering via the Onegin Hall, the opera studio Stanislavsky created for the Bolshoi Theatre. Here in 1922 Stanislavsky premiered his version of Tchaikovsky's opera *Eugene Onegin*. From the adjoining Blue Room, used for breaks in work, you enter the apartment proper through a medieval-style door. This and other features betray Stanislavsky's fascination with the chivalry of the Middle Ages.

One priceless exhibit is the Edison phonograph, one of only three in Russia – the

others belonged to Fyodor Shaliapin and Lev Tolstoy. Downstairs is an exhibition of costumes and props from various productions, collected by Stanislavsky from rural Russia and abroad.

☛ *Open Thurs, Sat, Sun 11 am–6 pm; Weds, Fri 2 pm–8 pm, closed last Thurs of month. Tel: 229-2855.*

😃 GITIS Theatre – The Bat Cabaret

(Letuchaya Mysh')
Turn left off Leontyevsky Pereulok onto Bolshoy Gnezdnikovsky Pereulok. On the right, close to its junction with Pushkinskaya, is the theatre of the State Theatrical Institute (GITIS), now most famous for the performances of the Bat Cabaret.

Started in a cellar of the Pertsov House (*see* Walk 6) in 1908 by wealthy Armenian playboy Nikolay Tarasov, it was attached to the Moscow Arts Theatre, whom it ridiculed in friendly fashion. Having achieved immense popularity in Russia, most of its members emigrated after the Revolution and continued their work successfully abroad throughout the 1920's. The cabaret was revived in Moscow in 1990, and its hilarious contemporary satire packs the small auditorium to bursting point.

The apartment building above the theatre was originally a bachelor residence: its rooms are spacious, but have only tiny kitchens. A sense of its original style survives if you glimpse into the ground floor hall.

Konyonkov Museum

Turning left onto Tverskaya Ulitsa and then immediately left again onto Tverskoy Bulvar, here a pleasant, tree-lined avenue, the last entrance of the corner house brings you to this unique museum, dedicated to Sergei Konyonkov (1874–1971), a man who devoted over 80 years of his life to wood sculpture.

Konyonkov began his extraordinary life in the forests near Smolensk, commanded the barricades in 1905, spent over 20 years in the U.S. (without learning English) and returned in 1945 to spend the rest of his days in this little apartment-studio.

He made the furniture here himself, simple stools and benches with hidden animals and pagan gods. Note the stool with the cat underneath, and the chair concealing a house spirit. Most of the exhibits are in his studio, and each deserves special attention: a severe figure of Paganini brandishing a violin; a flat-faced marble Bach with a snake-like wig, busy straining his deaf ears to listen to music; or his linden wood figure of Christ — only the head and feet carved, the rest of the body left in the form of a solid tree trunk.
☛ *Open Weds–Sun 11 am–7 pm, closed last Fri of month. Tel: 229-4472.*

Gorky Arts Theatre
(MKhAT imeni Gorkovo)
On the left hand side of the boulevard, this building is glaringly out of place, its red tufa windowless facade set back from the road among smaller 19th century houses. This is the home of the breakaway half of the Moscow Arts Theatre, led by Tatiana Doronina.

Yakovlev Mansion
Cross the boulevard at this point. The house at No. 25 is most famous as the birthplace of Alexander Herzen (*see* Walk 5), a statue of whom stands in the courtyard. Since the 1920's, it has been the Gorky Literary Institute, the most prestigious graduate institution for the country's writers.

The outbuilding on the left has plaques in memory of writers who lived here. One was **Osip Mandelstam** (1891-1938), the great poet who died in a labour camp after composing a poem which decried Stalin as a tyrant. He is remembered with a flat human silhouette, into which his signature has been etched.

The second, lesser known in the West, is **Andrei Platonov** (1899-1951), a novelist of working-class origins whose sympathy for society's mis-fits and Dostoyevskian moral preoccupations made him one of Russia's most influential 20th century writers.

Pushkin Theatre
This former noble's mansion was opened as a theatre in 1914 by Alexander Tairov, a talented experimental director of the Meyerhold genera-

tion. He was one of the few directors to stage European drama in the 1920's and 1930's, as well as being allowed to tour abroad.

Today, its own productions are fairly standard repertory material, but the stage also hosts interesting touring companies, as well as groups which lack their own permanent performance space. Watch the notices!

 Yermolova Flat-Museum
This cozy upper flat preserves the memory of Maria Yermolova (1853–1928), darling of the Maly Theatre and Russia's greatest tragic actress who lived here from 1889 until her death. The height of her career coincided with the works of **Alexander Ostrovsky**, but her greatest performance was as Joan of Arc in Schiller's *Maid of Orleans*, a part she played for 18 years.

The exhibition includes playbills and programmes, and the rooms, preserved unchanged, where Yermolova lived in her later years: after the Revolution the rest of the house was allotted to poor families.
☛*Open Weds–Mon noon–7 pm, closed last Mon of month. Tel: 290-0215/5920.*

 Panda Restaurant
This top-notch Chinese restaurant is run by a New Yorker manager who oper-

ates a high-class chain in the States. Expect to pay for the excellence of the food – $50 a head is the bare minimum.
☛*Open noon–11 pm. Tel: 298-6565, 202-8313. Major CC.*

Nikitskiye Vorota
You now emerge onto this square, once known as Moscow's "Latin Quarter" because of its lively student inhabitants. It seems distinguished and erudite even today, with its collection of second-hand and antiquarian bookstalls. Mark Rozovsky's Theatre Studio **"U Nikitskikh Vorot"** creates high quality chamber work on a tiny stage in a building on the square.

Across Bolshaya Nikitskaya is the tiny white Church of St. Theodore Studitus, built in 1623 by Tsar Mikhail's father, Patriarch Filaret. Mutilated and obscured from view by the Bolsheviks, it is now visible again and in the process of restoration.

The square is dominated by the ITAR TASS (formerly just TASS) building with its monumental globe entrance; the TASS news agency was once notorious as the mouthpiece of Soviet ideology.

Now its canteen, located in one of the older buildings back along the Boulevard has become **Fantasia**, an Italian restaurant – best to sample their delicious desserts rather than the average, overpriced main courses.

☞ *Open 10 am–2 am. Tel: 292-0216. Cash only.*

† Great Ascension Church
(Tserkov' Bolshovo Voznesenya)
Turning right down Malaya Nikitskaya, the severe classical church ahead was built over several decades, its construction delayed by the Napoleonic Wars. Although it was only finished in 1840, Pushkin was married here in 1831. This was not an auspicious occasion, however, with a dropped crucifix and candles blown out by a draught taken as a bad omen. Six years later the poet was killed in a duel.

Ryabushinsky Mansion, Gorky House Museum
Opposite the church is the Gorky House Museum, otherwise known as the Ryabushinsky Mansion after the art-patron banker for whom it was built in 1902–6 by **Fyodor Shekhtel** (1859-1926).

One of Moscow's best examples of art nouveau architecture, it's interesting particularly for its use of marine themes in the interior designs – blue and green stained glass windows with liquid curves, an amazing wavy staircase, and mosaics surrounding the house's exterior just below the eaves. Make sure you visit the curious secret chapel in the dome – Ryabushinsky was an Old Believer.

In 1931 the house became the residence of Maxim Gorky, the writer considered to be the father of Socialist Realism, upon his return to the U.S.S.R. from several years abroad. He died here in 1936: according to unsubstantiated rumour, his death was instigated by Stalin and effected by mixing poison with the paint of his bedroom walls. The museum focuses on his life here.

☞ *Open Thurs, Sat, Sun 10 am–5 pm; Weds, Fri noon–7 pm, closed last Thurs of month. Tel: 290-5130.*

Foreign Language Bookshop
(Inostranniye Knigi)
Take a detour up Malaya Nikitskaya to visit this little bookshop, doubling as an antiques shop, with a collection of second hand books in English and other major European languages. There's an extensive section of art and travel books, as well as dictionaries and technical manuals.

Ulitsa Spiridonovka, Blok Statue
The Gorky House Museum stands at the corner of Ulitsa Malaya Nikitskaya and Spiridonovka, a quiet but proud street which preserves much of the self-assured outlook of the turn of the century, when it was colonised by progressive elements of the prosperous young merchant class.

Another writer to live on this street was symbolist **Alexander Blok** (1880–1921), considered the greatest poet of Russia's Silver

Age – he briefly occupied the house immediately to the right of the statue. Blok was another tragic figure of Russian literature: despite considerable acclaim before the Revolution, his poem *The Twelve* was interpreted by his liberal colleagues as an expression of support for the Bolsheviks, and he died disillusioned and dispirited.

Savva Morozov Mansion

This baronial castle at No. 17 is also the work of Shekhtel, though its style is a complete contrast to his smaller Ryabushinsky Mansion. It was built for Savva Morozov, member of another progressive family of Old Believers which arrived in Moscow at the beginning of the 19th century, entered textile manufacturing, and later came to the forefront of the cultural, social, and financial life of the city, right up to the Revolution. The building is now used by the Foreign Ministry for receiving guests from abroad.

Ekipazh Club

Entered through a courtyard to the left before the hotel, this club is a combination of restaurant and jazz venue, and considered one of Moscow's most stylish, aimed at a clientele with more imagination than spending power. Its fare is innovative, with exotic salads and a cocktail selection larger than the combined food and drink menu.
☛ *Open Mon–Fri 5 pm–5 am, Sat, Sun 1 pm–5 am. CC.*

Marco Polo Presnja Hotel

Turn right onto Spiridonievsky Pereulok. A short way along on the left is the quietest of Moscow's Western-owned hotels, run by the Austrian Marco Polo chain. It has a small, highly acclaimed French restaurant with near-perfect cuisine and Bolshoi-trained musicians. Expect to pay around $100 a head for a meal.
☛ *Open 12–3 pm, 7–11 pm. Tel: 203-6689, 956-3010. CC.*

Ulitsa Malaya Bronnaya

This attractive street, running perpendicular to Spiridonievsky Pereulok, has had a very varied history. Its name comes from the first inhabitants, a guild making weapons and armour (*bron'* in Russian) in the 16th and 17th centuries. The small theatre, in its time the stage of eminent director Anatoly Ephros, is earning a new reputation for the work of his young successor, Sergei Zhenovach.

In the 19th century it was taken over by students, and is now a fashionable area – once home to members of the Soviet creative intelligentsia, it is now popular with wealthy expatriates and New Russians.

Café Begemot

Just across Ulitsa Malaya Bronnaya at No. 10, this is a cheap and pleasant but uninspiring café. Its name comes from Behemoth, the demon cat in Mikhail Bulgakov's novel *Master and Margarita*, most of the action of which takes place nearby.
☛ *Open 10 am–midnight (1–11 pm Sundays).*

Patriarch's Ponds

(Patriarshiye Prudy)

Walk away from the centre along Malaya Bronnaya through to a tree-shaded park surrounding a still sheet of water. This is Patriarch's Ponds, once part of a system of reservoirs created to provide fish for the Patriarch's table. Over the centuries the ponds fell into disuse, but after 1812 one was restored, which remains here today.

Along the far, northern edge of the pond are a series of animals carved in relief on stands, characters from the stories of 19th century writer **Ivan Krylov**, most famous for translating La Fontaine's fables into Russian. His statue stands here.

This place is better known, however, for its part in the satirical novel of Mikhail Bulgakov, *Master and Margarita*. The novel opens here, on the now-defunct tram tracks beside the pond, when Berlioz, editor at a Soviet literary organisation, slips on some spilt sunflower oil and is decapitated by a passing tram – the first of many outrageous acts of sorcery that engulf the city.

 ## Café Margarita

This little café on Malaya Bronnaya can be spotted by its metal door, complete with bright illustrations from the novel. Once a cheap student gathering place, it went upmarket a few years ago – but not all the way. Still accessible by Moscow price standards, it retains some of its previous charm.

☛ *Open 2 pm–midnight. Tel: 299-6534. Cash only.*

 ## Nikita Mikhalkov's House

Turn right past the café up Maly Kozikhin Pereulok. On the left at No. 11 is the house-cum-workplace of film director Nikita Mikhalkov. After a series of highly acclaimed films, his latest, *Burnt by the Sun*, received the 1995 Oscar for Best Foreign Film.

On its far wall is the emblem of his production company, "Tri-T" ("Three T-s"); its name is an acronym of the words for "comradeship, creativity and labour".

 ## Tryokhprudny Pereulok

Turn left at the top of the lane. On your left you will pass two more art nouveau style houses by Fyodor Shekhtel. First is the attractive printing house at No. 9, distinguished by its thematic reliefs and high Scandinavian-type roof. Marina Tsvetayeva, born in a house nearby that no longer stands, published her first book of poems here.

As you follow the road round to the left you pass the Uruguayan Embassy at Ulitsa Zholtovskovo, 28. As the initials "F.S." written over the porch indicate, this was the architect's own house.

 ## Bulgakov's Apartment

Cut back away from the centre through the square to emerge onto the Garden Ring (*see* Walk 6), and turn right. A few blocks up at No. 10, a plaque on the wall marks the house where Bulgakov lived. Through the courtyard and up the second stairway on the left is his flat, No. 50, portrayed in *Master*

and Margarita as the home base of the demons, as they wreak havoc on the city's complacent officialdom.

In pre-perestroika days, when Bulgakov was still an object of official disapproval, this stairwell became a gathering place for Moscow's rebellious youth, with whom the novel struck a chord. Artists painted characters from the book, Christ figures and abstractions on the walls, interspersed with quotes and slogans, while punks, hippies and other "outcasts" gathered on the landings and sang songs.

Some of the paintings remain today, though the standard of the contributions appears to have fallen. The apartment was briefly opened as a museum, but is currently used as an art gallery portraying work close in spirit to Bulgakov's writing.

 011

Across the Ring, entered through the courtyard of No. 10 is a restaurant and nightclub complex, whose odd name is explained by the Serbian origins of its proprietors – 011 is the telephone code for Belgrade. The food here is good but expensive, and the decor luxuriously dark and nostalgic. Its nightclub, open 11 pm–6 am, is popular with US expatriates.
☞ *Restaurant open 1 pm–midnight. Tel: 299-3964. CC.*

 Tchaikovsky Concert Hall

Three cultural venues are located next door to one another on **Triumfalnaya**

 Ploshchad – the **Mossoviet** and **Satira Theatres** and **Tchaikovsky Concert Hall**. Both theatres manage to maintain steady audiences, and Mossovet's small "beneath the roof" stage is also a leader in experimentation.

The Tchaikovsky Hall is the most interesting, both for its history and for the content of its performances. Construction was originally begun on this site for a theatre for Vsevolod Meyerhold. But after Meyerhold's arrest in 1938, the building was adapted into a concert hall. Since then it has regularly staged over 300 symphony and chamber concerts a year, including several festivals, with performances of national Russian dance, organ and choral music among its specialities.
☞ *Tel. 299 3487.*

 Moskva Cinema

Across the square is this small cinema, known also as the "House of Khanzhonkov" after Russia's first film industry magnate, Alexander Khanzhonkov (*see* Walk 5), whose company was based here. With the grander Kinocentre, it is one of the few cinemas in Moscow to show quality Soviet and Russian films in repertory
☞ *Tel: 252-7222/5860.*

5. Arbat, Old and New

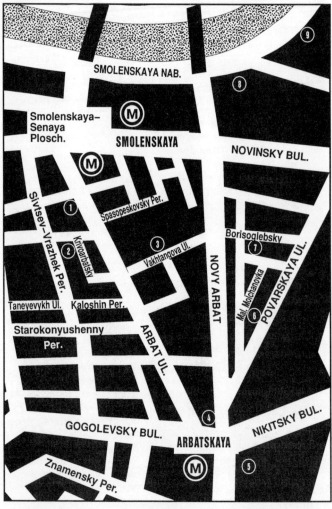

1. Puskin, Bely Museums
2. Melnikov House
3. Scriabin Museum
4. Praga Restaurant
5. Arseny Morozov Mansion
6. Lermontov Museum
7. Tsvetayeva Museum
8. Mayor's Building
9. White House

The Old Arbat (Stary Arbat)

The creation of Moscow's first pedestrian precinct, the Old Arbat, coincided with the beginning of glasnost, when the new atmosphere of freedom brought buskers, street artists and Krishna supporters out into the open. Over the years of reform it has developed further – smart clothes and souvenir shops, cafés (many less than smart), entertainers of every description and the inevitable crowds.

The earliest historical records of the street appear during an account of a major city fire in 1493; its name most likely originates from the Arabic word for "suburb" (which the Arbat then was) In the last century its relative quiet, and absence of industry and commerce made it a favourite neighbourhood for the aristocracy and creative intelligentsia – at one stage the population here was believed to number one noble for every seven ordinary residents.

Its special attraction endured into Soviet times, although its once grand apartments were turned into *kommunalkas* (communal flats), and by the 1970's the traditional Arbat people were being eased out by a new class, the functionaries of the Party bureaucracy. This phenomenon led poet Andrey Voznesensky to compare the Arbat to Chekhov's Cherry Orchard, another Russian institution being "chopped up" to make way for the new era.

STARTS AT: Metro Smolenskaya
ENDS AT: Metro Arbatskaya

DIRECTIONS: Walking from Smolenskaya, odd-numbered buildings are on the right, even-numbered on the left.

Smolenskaya Ploshchad

The western end of the Old Arbat leads out onto the Garden Ring road (*see* Walk 6) at this large chaotic square, once Moscow's haymarket. Look upwards, and you'll see the exotic tracery of the "wedding cake" **Foreign Ministry,** while opposite rise the twin tower blocks of the rather seedy Intourist Belgrade Hotel.

Pushkin & Bely Apartment Museums (Nos. 53–55)

A short walk away from the main road brings you, on the right hand side, to the Pushkin Flat Museum, the poet's Moscow residence after 1826. He lived here while courting his future wife, Natalya Goncharova, in the two years in which his "head spun" before he won her hand in marriage in 1830.

From that time on, though, Moscow began to go sour on Pushkin, as he was worn down by the local gossip. "I'm not alone, nor are there two of us," he wrote, referring to that most pernicious element of the Russian family, the meddlesome mother-in-law. The couple left for St. Petersburg soon after, never to return.

The ground floor of the museum has nothing to do with Pushkin's life in the flat – indeed, he lived on the first floor. Instead it shows a fascinating exhibition of sketches and prints of Moscow at the time of Pushkin's childhood (that is, before the 1812 fire).

Upstairs the arrangement is a little peculiar. Almost devoid of Pushkin's belongings, the museum is made up of a series of what seem like little shrines – tables or desks adorned with portraits of Alexander and Natalya. Of all Russia's literary heroes, so many of whom are lovingly remembered with house-museums, Pushkin is the most worshipped.

Another part of the building is occupied by a tiny museum to Andrey Bely, the prominent symbolist writer from the beginning of the century, best known for his novel *Petersburg*. Born here in 1880, Bely spent the first 26 years of his life in the flat and it became one of the spiritual and intellectual centres of the city, remaining so even after his departure. The most interesting exhibit is the "Line of Life", a complex diagram showing how moods, relationships and cultural influences affected his works.

 Both museums are open Weds–Sun 11 am–6 pm, closed last Fri of the month. The Pushkin Museum is by guided tour only (every 30 minutes in Russian, or in English by special arrangement). Tel: 241-3010/4212.

Arbat Hotel

Just off the Arbat on Plotnikov Pereulok stands this exclusive luxury hotel in quiet surroundings. It includes a restaurant of the same name with a wide selection of French wines for connoisseurs, ranging in price from $12 to $750. The French cuisine on offer here is equally pricey – expect your bill, apart from drinks, to top $50 per person.

 Open noon–midnight. Tel: 244-7641. Major CC.

Bar Italia (No. 49)

The groundbreaker of a recent Italian invasion of the Arbat, this once rather pricey restaurant and bar now suffers from fierce competition. The Pizzeria at No. 45 is under the same ownership.

 Open noon–midnight. Tel: 241-4342. CC.

Georgian Cultural Centre (No. 42)

This was once the residence of Yekaterina Ushakova, a blonde beauty with whom Pushkin fell in love prior to meeting his future bride Natalya Goncharova. Now its interiors provide a backdrop for a reasonably priced Georgian restaurant, **Mziuri** (downstairs), and an exhibition space and souvenir shop selling traditional Georgian paintings, ceramics and other artworks (upstairs).

The ground floor, however, has in recent years turned completely commercial, one room selling alcohol, cigarettes and some expensive jewellery, the other serving as a nightclub.

☛ *Mziuri is open noon–11:30 pm. Tel: 241-0313.*

Spasopeskovsky Pereulok

The next left turn after the Georgian Centre takes you to the pretty **Church of the Saviour on the Sands** (*Tserkov' Spasa na Peskakh*), built in 1711 and immortalised by the artist Vassily Polyenov in his famous painting "Moscow Courtyard" (*Moskovsky Dvorik*).

Just ahead is a small garden, planned by the architect Nikolay Lvov in memory of Pushkin. Lvov's own house, at No. 8, is now the Somali Embassy. Next door to it, in a somewhat unfortunate accident of geography, stands **Spaso House**, built in neo-Empire style on the eve of World War I by the self-made financier Nikolay Vtorov. Since 1933 it has been the residence of the U.S. ambassador.

Krivoarbatsky Pereulok

Returning to the Arbat, the next right turn is this odd L-shaped street leading back to the previous right turn, Plotnikov Pereulok. Its walls at this end are covered in graffiti, and may be accompanied by crowds of young people singing and strumming away in the doorways beneath.

The wall is dedicated to Viktor Tsoy, a Kazakhstan-born ethnic Korean singer-songwriter who died in a car crash in 1990. He fronted Kino, a gloomy black-clad foursome and one of the leaders of the St. Petersburg underground rock explosion of the early eighties. Their hit, "We Are Waiting for Change", became one of the anthems of perestroika.

▲ Melnikov House

At No. 10 on Krivoarbatsky Pereulok is one of Moscow's most unusual buildings, the house of constructivist architect Konstantin Melnikov (1890-1974).

It consists of two concrete cylinders cut into each other, with frequent hexagonal windows, demonstrating extraordinary skill in using the minimum of building materials to create maximum effect.

It was built in 1927, and the cultural climate of the time ensured that this was virtually the last chance Melnikov had to express himself freely in his work – his later plans were drowned in the Stalin era's sea of Neo-Classicism.

Samotsvety Shop (No. 35)

Returning to the Old Arbat, this building is one of the finest examples on the street of pre-revolutionary apartment houses. It was built for the elite, hence the decorative facade with knights and towers, equating it with a castle.

The name of the shop on the ground floor means "semi-precious stone" – this is one of Moscow's largest jewellers.

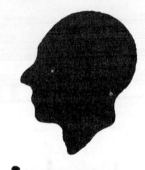

🎭 Vakhtangov Theatre (No. 20)

The current theatre was built in 1947 on the site of the original, a 19th century mansion, after the latter was destroyed by a German bomb during World War II. Considered one of the most prestigious of Moscow's classical theatres, it was established by Yevgeny Vakhtangov, a pupil of Konstantin Stanislavsky, in 1921; his profile and signature (above) remain its emblem to this day.

Nearing the end of his life, Vakhtangov staged the theatre's first and most famous production, the humorous and lyrical fairy story *Princess Turandot*, which is still performed today. Under current director Mikhail Ulyanov, it has been resting on its laurels for much of the last decade, although recent smaller scale productions like Ostrovsky's *Guilty Without Guilt* have been hailed as highlights.

🏛 Scriabin Apartment Museum

Take the left turn just before the theatre onto Ulitsa Vakhtangova, and follow it half way up to No. 11, the former apartment of the turn-of-the-century composer Alexander Scriabin (1872-1915). Bold and almost naively fresh, his compositions were described by Boris Pasternak as a "feast of Russian culture".

Scriabin spent his later, most productive years here and created such works as *Prometheus* and *A Poem of Ecstasy*. He entertained many visitors, including symbolist poet Konstantin Balmont and fellow composer Sergey Rakhmaninov.

This tiny museum retains the lofty rooms, sober but tasteful colours, and pleasing art nouveau furniture of his time. One room contains the bed where he died in 1915, by a strange coincidence on the day the three-year lease on his flat ran out. Its downstairs rooms are the venue for frequent piano and chamber music concerts.

Near to the Scriabin Museum, the house at No. 7 contains a pedigree cat market, where on Saturdays and Sundays you can come to choose between a selection of mainly British prize felines at very reasonable prices. *Museum open Weds–Sun 10 am–6 pm, closed last day of month. Tel: 241-0302.*

🏛 Alexander Herzen Museum

Return to and cross over the Arbat, taking the next right turn, Kaloshin Pereulok, down to Sivtsev Vrazhek

Ulitsa, a quieter street parallel to the Arbat – and much more representative of how this area used to be.

Its most notable landmark is the museum at No. 27 devoted to Alexander Herzen (1812–1870), the 19th century writer and proselytiser seen by revolutionaries as the link between the liberal Decembrist rebellion and the rise of socialism at the end of the century. He lived here 1843–46, and gathered a circle of progressive intellectuals, who thrashed out the world's problems here in typically heated Russian fashion.

The exhibition traces his life from the Decembrist uprising in 1825, when at age 13 he first took an interest in social policy, to the newspaper *Kolokol* (Bell), through which he raged from London exile at the tyranny of tsarism.

☛ *Open Tues, Thurs, Sat, Sun 11 am–7 pm; Weds, Fri 2 pm–9 pm, closed Mon and last day of month. Tel: 241-5859.*

Ulitsa Taneyevykh

At No. 5 on this street, beyond Sivtsev Vrazhek, is one of the city's most beautiful examples of Moscow Empire style – a wooden house with characteristic mezzanine, and plaster friezes of lions and griffons.

Japanese Noodles (No. 31)

Returning to the Arbat, this little café, while not culinarily exceptional, is both pleasant and exotic enough to provide a steady stream of visitors to sample its noodle soups and saké.

It shares a building with more characteristic Arbat enterprises, an antique shop and another selling lace patterned artefacts, one of Russia's traditional crafts.

☛ *Open 10 am–11 pm. Tel: 241-0886. Cash only.*

Baskin Robbins.

▼• Baskin Robbins Ice Cream Parlour (No. 20)

In a country which is very fond of its ice cream, this, the first of the American chain's parlours in Moscow, has had mixed success. It was opened in 1990 by Dennis Thatcher during his wife's high profile political "honeymoon" with Mikhail Gorbachev, when the British leader's distinctive walk-about style impressed locals.

Baskin Robbins had an instant popularity comparable only to McDonald's (*see* Walk 3). Several dozen price hikes later, it is clearly inaccessible to average Russians and has suffered from competition with the domestic "Pingvin" chain.

Kupina (No. 18)

A classic example of the smart antique shops now appearing on the Arbat. A second shop further up at No. 4 specialises in icons.

☛ *Open 10 am–8 pm. Tel: 291-1147.*

Porokhovshchikov House

Taking the next right turn, Starokonyushenny Pereulok, you will immediately see a beautifully constructed wooden house with decorations and carved platbands in traditional Russian style.

Built in 1870, it takes its name from its sponsor, a wealthy businessman best known for building the Slavyansky Bazar restaurant (see Walk 2). Its model received an award at the World Exhibition in Paris as the embodiment of true Russian style.

A-3 Gallery
Also on Starokonyushenny, this gallery, run by the Culture and Arts Department of the Central Administrative District, displays fine collections of modern art from Russia and abroad. It is currently gathering together the best of such works to create a museum of modern art.
☞ *Open Weds–Sun 11 am–7 pm. Tel: 291-8484.*

San Marco Pizzeria (No. 25)
This was the house where Porokhovshchikov lived. Under his auspices the Association of Russian Doctors set up its first clinic and chemist's shop here.

Now it is the best of the Arbat's pizzerias. It can be crowded, but people don't linger – it's a place for eating deliciously, rather than spending time or money.
☞ *Open noon–11 pm. Tel: 291-7089. CC, except AmEx.*

Tsvety
This tiny detached one-storey flower shop on the left seems at first glance unspectacular. What is surprising is that it has been trading flowers for nearly 200 years, from the days of the Church of St. Nicholas which once stood nearby.

Wall of Peace
(Stena Mira)
Just opposite the pizzeria is a section of wall covered in tiles. It dates from the early, romantic days of perestroika, when an American journalist with the appropriate name of Helen Marx went around Children's Homes collecting paintings on the theme of world peace. Local artists also participated to produce what we see today.

Praga Restaurant (No. 2)
This extraordinary building on the corner of the two Arbat streets is known as "the iron" (*utyug*) for its strange wedge shape. It has had a chequered history, beginning its public existence as a rather seedy *traktir* in the 1880's.

In 1896 it was won by the merchant Pyotr Tararykin in a game of left-handed billiards, and under its new owner gained a stylish new profile, based on exquisite French cuisine, iron-disciplined waiters drawn from the depths of Yaroslavl province, and an intricate system of halls and closets for every type of occasion. It became the social centre of the Arbat, frequented by the progressive intelligentsia but in no way exclusive.

In Stalin's time, the Praga became a special canteen for Party functionaries, reopening as a restaurant only in 1954 after his death. It then recovered something of its reputation, but like most of the best state restaurants of the Soviet era it has now been thoroughly upstaged by new rivals. This is probably a place to visit out of curiosity rather than a desire to eat good food.

Expect edible, if bland, Russian and Czech fare and the finest Czech beer.

☛ *Open 11 am−midnight. Tel: 290-6171. Cash only.*

Tomsky's Gogol Monument

In the distance, on the right as you face out of the street onto Arbatskiye Vorota Ploshchad, at the beginning of Gogolevsky Bulvar, part of the Boulevard Ring (see Walk 6), is a statue of Nikolay Gogol, Russia's greatest satirist. Known as "the soldier", this haughty and grandiose monument is one of the more unlikely attempts by Stalin to "reconstruct" Moscow.

Riding down the boulevard one day in the early 1950's, the dictator decided that the original 19th century statue looked too forlorn and pathetic, and so promptly had it replaced by something more to his taste. Unfortunately, "the soldier" has nothing whatsoever in common with the sad and complex character that was Nikolay Gogol.

The Arts Cinema

(Khudozhestvenny Kinotcatr) Crossing the flyover bridge over the Boulevard and then through the underpass − it frequently doubles up as a concert venue for young rock groups, as well as doing a brisk trade in kittens and puppies − the low white building ahead of the square is Moscow's oldest surviving cinema, and the first to be built in the city for the express purpose of showing films. In 1909 it opened with the Parisian drama *Georgette*, and showings

were interspersed with concerts by a symphony orchestra.

It was soon acquired by Alexander Khanzhonkov, pioneer of the Russian film industry, who commissioned Fyodor Shekhtel to reconstruct it. It remained Moscow's main cinema until the appearance of the Rossiya (see Walk 3) in 1961.

Ministry of Defence

The huge modern white building which now dominates the cinema is the visible portion of a sizeable townlet behind, reflecting the large and unwieldy nature of the ministry itself. This area has been the headquarters of the Red Army since the Civil War.

Note also the entrance to Arbatskaya metro station, to the right of the cinema. It was built in the 1930's in a star shape, as a tribute to the army.

Arseny Morozov Mansion

On the left across Ulitsa Vozdvizhenka, this "Moorish castle", its towers studded

Central Moscow | Arbat, Old and New

with shell motifs, is based on a house in Portugal spotted by the playboy industrialist Arseny Morozov during his travels.

Its design so outraged Lev Tolstoy that he called it "a stupid place built for some stupid useless person". Now called the "House of Friendship", it doubles as a venue for concerts and lectures, which afford opportunities to see its equally eclectic interior – including a hunting hall with carved animal heads, a Greek atrium and a room decorated in Renaissance style.

Andreyev's Gogol Monument

Cross back through the underpass and again across beneath the New Arbat, and walk up 200 metres or so along the outer side of the Boulevard Ring (Suvorovsky Bulvar).

In the small courtyard to the left stands the original statue of Gogol, a slumped, suffering, contemplative figure, above a frieze depicting tragi-comic animated characters from various of his works.

Its new site is actually more appropriate – the building to the right, now a library, was where he instructed a servant to burn the manuscript of *Dead Souls*, the masterpiece that had become too much for him to finish and which seems to have killed him. The writer died there two days later.

Moscow's only restaurant with authentic Taiwanese cuisine, **TAIPEI** offers a delicious menu prepared by our native Taiwanese chefs from the finest imported ingredients.The splendour of our oriental interior as well as the attention of our expert waiting staff guarantee you a truly enjoyable evening out. We look forward to your visit.

TAIPEI REJTAURANT IJ OPEN 11 AM – 11 PM at 13 VOLKOV PEREULOK (METRO "BARRIKADNAYA"). TEL.: 255-9934, 255-0176, 255-0441

The New Arbat (Novy Arbat)

Until 1962, this area of Moscow was just like all the other little neighbourhoods of the Arbat district, and included the charming Dog's Square (*Sobachya Ploshchadka*), associated with poets Alexander Pushkin, Marina Tsvetayeva and others.

In that year, it was all bulldozed to make way for a grand new highway, known by locals as the "artificial jaw", and designed to bring the mass May Day processions straight to Red Square. On either side, high rise blocks were built – on the right conventionally shaped, on the left designed to resemble open books.

Now it is a major shoppers' thoroughfare, and plans exist to make it a pedestrian-only precinct, or even create new underground complexes like that planned for Manezh Square (*see* Walk 2). It extends as far as the Moskva River, to the place known as Free Russia Square, scene of Russia's most recent political upheavals.

STARTS AT: Metro Arbatskaya
ENDS AT: Metro Krasnopresnenskaya

DIRECTIONS: Either continue from the finishing point of the above "Old Arbat" walk, or start from Metro Arbatskaya (light and dark blue lines, last carriage if coming from Kievskaya).
TRANSPORT: trolleybus #2 runs the length of the New Arbat street. Length from beginning to end: 1 km.

✝ Church of St. Simeon the Stylite (right side)
(Tserkov' Simeona Stolpnika)
The survival of this, the only old structure on the street seems truly miraculous. Built in the 17th century, this pretty church was where

Count Sheremetyev wed his bride, the serf actress Praskovia Zhemchugova-Kovalyova. The class status of the bride may have been what led the communist authorities to spare it.

🏛 Lermontov House Museum
This charming wooden house just off Novy Arbat on Ulitsa Malaya Molchanovka (turn right past the church, then take the little road off to the left) is typical of Russian house-museums, combining collections of manuscripts with recreations of the writer's living arrangements.

Mikhail Lermontov, the 19th century poet who briefly assumed the mantle of Pushkin after his death only to be killed himself in a duel at the tender age of 26, lived here with his grandmother for two years while he studied at Moscow University.

☛ *Open Thurs, Sat, Sun 11 am–5 pm; Weds, Fri 2 pm–5 pm; closed Mon, Tues, last day of month. Tel: 291-1860.*

The House of Books (right side, No. 26)
(Dom Knigi)
Moscow's largest book shop provides wide scope for browsing, although the first thing you'll notice here is that what is in fact on sale does not accord with the section headings, which have survived from an earlier decade.

There is an antiquarian section (ground floor on the left), a foreign languages section selling novels and magazines in English (ground floor on the right), records (first floor in the middle) and art books and guidebooks (first floor on the left).

Valdai Centre, Arbat Irish House (left side)
This recently built mini shopping mall mainly contains pricey foreign boutiques, plus two eateries: the Palms Coffee Shop, an Indian-run café, ideal for people-watching, and the Shakherazade restaurant, providing European cuisine with Middle Eastern spices and sauces.

☛ *Open noon–midnight. Tel: 291-9004, 203-4962. CC.*

Linked to it by a pedestrian arcade, the **Irish House**, the first foreign supermarket in central Moscow, opened in early 1991 to a fanfare of applause from the expatriate community. With food and

household goods sections, and the popular **Shamrock Bar**, it became an oasis for the homesick.

Today, the Irish are no longer in charge and the clientele is now mainly prosperous Russians, while the contrast with the smartly-refurbished Soviet **Novoarbatsky Gastronom** (foodstore) downstairs is hardly an acute one: note, though, that the Irish House has check-outs, while the Novoarbatsky still uses the old *kassa* system.

Moscow's small but prominent Irish community stages an annual St. Patrick's Day procession, popular with Russians and foreigners alike, along Novy Arbat.

Sports Bar (right side)
The ultimate in Moscow theme bars, American-style. Here you can play billiards or darts, watch 43 television screens or admire the vehicles on display, including bikes, buggies and even a Cadillac. There's live evening music and special lunch menus, but the bar has never managed to establish an identity beyond its physical appearance.

☛ *Open noon–5 am. Tel: 290-4311/4498.*

Bar Elephant (right side)
A little known, and also rather expensive watering-hole, Elephant has the advantages of being civilised

and quiet, as well as offering Tuborg beer on tap.

☞ *Open 1 pm–midnight. Tel: 200-5492.*

Institute of Beauty (left side)

Although this may sound like something out of George Orwell's *1984*, it is in fact one of the country's top medical institutions – Moscow's mecca for those with skin complaints or needing cosmetic surgery.

Tsvetayeva Museum

The next turn to the right off the New Arbat, Boriso-glebsky Pereulok (formerly Ulitsa Pisemskovo), brings you to the house where 20th century poet Marina Tsvetayeva spent the first years of her marriage, and endured the hardships of the Revolution and Civil War. Later derelict for decades and miraculously saved from destruction by Tsvetayeva's friends, it has finally opened as a museum.

It recaptures beautifully Tsvetayeva's early years here, though most exhibits are not authentic and have been donated by well-wishers. Each room has a unique, almost eccentric character, facilitated by art nouveau decor and individual objects, like the numerous animal skins and the picture of her idol Napoleon, placed in an icon stand.

Special use is made of light, as in the first room, the "Sea Bottom", where blue light comes in through the glass ceiling at dusk, and in husband Sergey Efron's bedroom, the "Attic Palace", where light from the morning sun is projected in a cross

shape from the dormer window onto the opposite wall.

The museum guides speak also of the hardship years, when 40 other people were crammed into the house. Tsvetayeva lived in dire poverty, losing her second daughter and for a time her husband, who went missing in the Civil War.

☞ *The museum is only open two days a week, Weds and Thurs, noon–5 pm. Tel: 202-3543.*

Jupiter Photo Shop (left side)

Moscow's largest photo shop and, ironically, one of the few places you still can have (poor quality) Russian and ORWO (East German) film processed. You will always find a second-hand market in Soviet cameras outside the shop.

Metelitsa Night Club (left side)

 More entertainment complex than just disco, Metelitsa's greatest boast is Russia's largest gaming hall, the Cherry Casino. It is a very exclusive night club, with high admission fees, tight security, smart dress and performances by top names in Russian show business. Favoured by Moscow's criminal elite.

☞ *Open 1 pm–6 am. Tel: 291-1130. Major CC.*

Oktyabr Cinema (right side)

This rather bland building is Moscow's second largest cinema, smaller than the Rossiya by only 20 seats. Its smaller second screen is one of very few in Russia to show films in Dolby stereo.

Roditi Centre, Tropicana (left side)

This British joint venture, situated beneath the distinctive globe (once an advertisement for Aeroflot) is one of several Western-style department stores that have recently appeared in the city. Prices tend towards the low end.

In the same building, Moscow's only Polynesian restaurant, **Tropicana**, offers exotic oriental cuisine, drawing on Chinese and Filipino roots, and a beguiling range of cocktails. There's an evening Variety show, too.
☛ *Tropicana, open 4 pm–6 am. Tel: 291-1134/2045. Major CC.*

The Mayor's Office

Another "open-book" design building on the right near the river bridge, this is part of a complex once considered one of the successes of modern Soviet architecture. It was built in 1967 to house Comecon, the Eastern bloc's equivalent of the EEC. When the organisation was disbanded, it became the headquarters of the administration of Moscow's Mayor.

In October 1993 it was stormed by supporters of the Russian parliament, before they themselves were bombarded into submission.

White House

(Byely Dom, Dom Pravitelstva)

The building across the square will be familiar to anyone who has followed events in Russia over the past five years. Built in 1980 in white marble, with a red granite base and grand front steps, it became the House of Soviets for the Russian Soviet Federated Socialist Republic (RSFSR) – in plainer language, parliament building for the Russian Federation.

It was the power base of Boris Yeltsin, elected Speaker in 1990 and then President of Russia in 1991, and thus the centre of resistance when top members of Mikhail Gorbachev's Soviet government declared a state of emergency in August 1991.

In a pronounced irony of fate, two years later Yeltsin would dissolve this very same parliament. This time the parliamentarians were equally defiant; led by Speaker Ruslan Khasbulatov and Vice-President Alexander Rutskoy, the White House again became a symbol of rebellion in October 1993.

Yeltsin ordered the army to shell those left barricaded in the White House; casualties were heavy, while the bombed-out building was badly blackened. Repaired in record time (by a Turkish construction company),it reopened as Government House early in 1994.

Note also the little Humpback Bridge behind the complex, a symbol of a much earlier conflict, the Revolution of 1905. It was part of the barricades put up by workers in Presnya, then the centre of resistance.

From here, walk back to Metro Krasnopresnenskaya, past the low brick wall of the U.S. Embassy. The new building visible in the compound centre is so riddled with bugging devices placed there during construction that it remains unoccupied.

TROPICANA —

Find the Luxurious Paradise of Polynesia in the Heart of Moscow

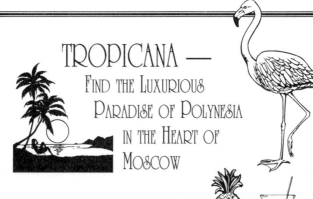

At Tropicana, a tropical oasis on the New Arbat, which for two years has been delighting guests with its unique interior decoration, truly exotic cuisine with a choice of authentic Polynesian specialities, as well as Chinese and European dishes. Our enticing range of cocktails is prepared by our experienced barmen from Germany, Singapore and Polynesia – and during our 6-8 pm Happy Hour, two cocktails come for the price of one.

If you're looking for brilliant entertainment, don't miss our evening Variety Show, which sparkles like a firework with its original numbers, bright costumes and beautiful performers. Our service is always attentive, and our prices are reasonable. For gamblers and those who enjoy the thrill of risk, our casino is open all night, with tables for American Roulette, Black Jack, as well as "Golden Oasis" and Stud Poker.

Tropicana is at New Arbat Street 21 (under the Globe). Tel: 291-1134, tel./fax: 291-2045.

Restaurant and Casino open: 4 pm - 6 am. Variety Show starts at 11 pm, with entry, including show, to the restaurant after 8 pm: Monday-Thursday $6, Friday-Sunday $10. Free guarded parking available.

TROPICANA — Moscow's Exotic Favourite. Don't Miss it on your visit...

6. Nobles' Moscow

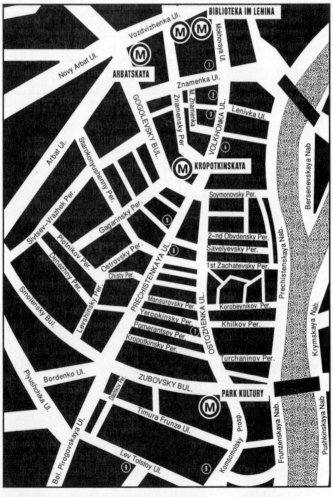

1. Pashkov House
2. Pushkin Fine Arts Museum
3. Museum of Private Collections
4. Cathedral of Christ the Saviour
5. Pushkin Museum
6. Tolstoy Museum
7. Languages University
8. St. Nicholas in Khamovniki
9. Tolstoy Museum Estate

This walk offers a parade of the finest classical mansions in the city, with a particular emphasis on "Empire" style, which was prevalent in the reconstruction period after the great fire of 1812.

Moscow's Empire style differed considerably from its European counterparts and coincided with a revival of Russian folk traditions and motifs, and a return to simplicity made necessary by the financial difficulties of the post-war period. Russia's favourite building material, wood, was used, often covered with stucco to give the appearance of stone.

This was the Moscow of the progressive nobility, who settled here, mostly on Ulitsa Prechistenka, during the reign of Catherine the Great. Their impoverished, more down-to-earth post-1812 successors created the area as it remains today. Two other major Moscow landmarks are also featured here: the site of the Church of Christ the Saviour, today scene of frantic construction work, and the estate of novelist Lev Tolstoy.

An optional extension of the walk includes a visit to the New Tretyakov Gallery, housing post-1917 Russian art.

STARTS AT: Metro Biblioteka imeni Lenina
ENDS AT: Metro Park Kultury

The Lenin Library
(Biblioteka imeni Lenina)
This imposing grey building with severe square columns dominating the metro exit was built over three decades of the Soviet era and shows features of both Constructivism and the Stalinist version of Neo-Classicism. Its enormous mass contains one of the world's largest libraries, with 30 million titles in 247 languages.

Shchusev Museum of Architecture
Turn left out of the metro onto Ulitsa Vozdvizhenka.

The classical nobles' estate at No. 5 is the building of the Architecture Museum, currently under restoration. The only part functioning is a temporary exhibition hall in the 17th-century Apothecary Shop (*Aptekarsky Dvor*) next door on Starov Pereulok. It was here that herbal medicinal potions were prepared for the Tsar's court during epidemics. These potions were made available to other layers of society, beginning with underprivileged groups like widows and orphans, once the courtiers had taken their fill.

The same complex also includes the manor house next door which once belonged to Prince Dmitry Shuisky, brother of Tsar

Vassily, the general who lost Moscow to the Poles in 1612.

☞ *Open Tues–Fri 10 am– 6 pm; Sat, Sun 10 am– 4 pm. Tel: 290-4855.*

Pashkov House

Continue along Starov Pereulok, which is still sign- posted by its old name, Ulitsa Marksa i Engelsa. Soon on your left, after the enormous grey building of the library, you come to the grand front entrance to one of Moscow's most legend- rich and romantic houses, the residence of one-time Siberian Governor Pyotr Pashkov. It is normally seen from the river side where it looms stately, impenetrable and mysterious.

In fact, it was just what it seems – an attempt to impress the Kremlin which stands opposite. The Pashkov House was almost certainly the work of Vassily Bazhenov, an architect of the late-18th century whose innovative fantasies were slightly too wayward for mainstream tastes. Bazhenov was regularly snubbed by Empress Catherine; she frequently suspended his work and refused to use the buildings he built, such as Tsaritsyno. The Pashkov House was one project that succeeded, and could be viewed as a form of revenge for the way that the Kremlin had treated him.

The building demonstrates Bazhenov's extensive know- ledge of ancient classical rules and would set the standard for Moscow archi- tecture for several decades. Most outstanding are the elegant proportions – a sub- stantial main house flanked by porticoed side wings and topped by a belvedere.

The house is now part of the Lenin Library, and houses early manuscripts from the former Rumyantsev collection. Though it's not open to the public, current visitors to Moscow can count themselves lucky – for years the facade was decked in scaffolding.

Near this entrance is the manor Church of St. Nicholas *(Tserkov Nikoly na Staroy Vagankovke)*, frequented in the last century by the writer Nikolay Gogol as a place of prayer.

Rosie O'Grady's

On the other side of Ulitsa Znamenka, Rosie O'Grady's is Moscow's best known Irish bar, which first appeared around the time of the August 1991 coup, when Western bars were still rare in Moscow. Always popular, it is now favoured by the city's "money men" and a sizeable Russian crowd.

☞ *Open noon–1 am. Tel: 203-9087. Major CC.*

† Church of St. Antipy by ■ the Carriage House

(Tserkov' Antipiya na Kolymazhnom Dvore) Continue past the entrance of Rosie O'Grady's down Malaya Znamenka (also known as Znamensky Pereulok) to this church building. A peculiar combina- tion of asymmetrical 16th- century church and 18th- century additions, it marks a site whose sinister nature is equalled only by the Lubyanka.

This was the headquarters of the *oprichnina*, Ivan the Terrible's secret police, and it is thought that the church was built by its leader, Ivan's deranged henchman "Baby" Skuratov, who was recently found to be buried here.

Vyazemsky/Dolgoruky Palace

Previous owners of this rather dull classical mansion, situated on the right before the bend in the road, and the buildings which pre-ceeded it, were not marked for their good fortune. In the 16th century, Prince Afanasy Vyazemsky was tortured to death by "Baby" Skuratov out of jealousy, while a century later Ivan Dolgoruky would be exiled to Siberia for falsifying Tsar Peter II's will.

In Soviet times the build-ing became, for no obvious reason, the Marx and Engels Museum, and it now houses, in part, the new Nobles' Assembly, a focal point for emigré aristocrats, as well as citizens trying to rediscover their possible noble ancestry.

Lopukhin House

Another noble's mansion on the same corner belonged to the family of the first wife of Peter the Great, Yevdokia Lopukhina, who later fell into disgrace and was banished to the Novodevichy Convent. The Lopukhin House now contains the International Roerich Centre, dedicated to two Russian artists, **Nikolay Roerich** (1874-1946) and his son **Svyatoslav**.

Both spent much of their lives in India and studied the cultures and peoples of the Himalayas, a theme that continues to be developed by the Centre. A small shop on the site sells Indian crafts, incense and literature on Oriental spiritualism.

Next door is a small museum dedicated to Nikolay , who was in his earlier years an artist of the "World of Art" (*Mir Iskusstvo*) movement.
☛*Open Tues, Thurs & Sat 11 am–7 pm.*

🍴 Patio Pizza

Emerge on Ulitsa Volkhonka beside the Pushkin Fine Arts Museum (*see* separate chapter). This sparklingly clean restaurant opposite, with views of the Moskva river, replaced an old Moscow "pizzeria", dating from the 1970's, when a group of Italians came to Moscow to start a chain of inexpensive restaurants specialising in one of their national dishes.

Soon becoming disillus-ioned, they departed, leaving in their place a new Soviet-style "pizza", a piece of dough doused in fake tomato sauce and sprinkled with negligible amounts of grated cheese, which can still be found in many street kiosks.

Now, thankfully, real pizza is back, and this restaurant differs little in standard from anywhere in the West. A second branch has been opened at the Intourist Hotel.
☛*Open noon–midnight. Tel: 201-5000. Major CC.*

🏛 Church of Christ the Saviour

(Khram Khrista Spasitelya)
As you turn right up Ulitsa Volkhonka past the Pushkin Museum, the building site on the left is immediately visible. Visitors to Moscow a few years ago will remember this as the site of the huge circular open-air heated Moskva swimming pool. Surrounded by parkland and seats for spectators, it was a truly Russian phenomenon: supremely glorious, awe-inspiring and wasteful. Passing by here in winter, clouds of steam blanketed the entire area, steadily eroding the foundations of the older buildings nearby.

Many Muscovites do not regret its passing — it represented one of the greatest grievances that the city had against Stalin, namely the destruction of the Cathedral of Christ the Saviour in 1931. Footage of the demolition of this enormous church has now been widely seen throughout the world.

The church itself was intended as a monument to the 1812 victory. Begun only in 1837, it was finished 46 years later, emerging as a symbol of both Orthodoxy and Tsarism. It was built by **Konstantin Thon**, an architect famous for his churches in the neo-Byzantine style beloved of the old regime. Hence, Stalin's wish to destroy it, and replace it with something even grander — a gigantic Palace of Soviets topped by a statue of Lenin which would often have been shrouded in clouds. The soft riverside soil proved unable to cope with such a weight, however, and eventually the swimming pool was built instead.

In 1994, a decision was taken by Moscow's Mayor to rebuild the church, planning completion of its main body in time for the 850th anniversary of the city's founding in 1997. This drew immediate questions, ranging from the financing and timetable of the project, to whether the cathedral could faithfully be reconstructed from nothing. Some even compared it to the "shock projects" of the communist era, when quality was generally sacrificed in favour of speed.

As is immediately apparent, construction work is proceeding at a rapid pace. The prefabricated building on the edge of the site houses a small museum with exhibits relating to the original building as well as to the reconstruction project.

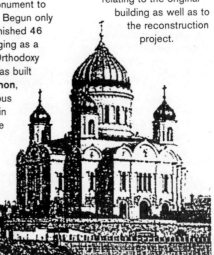

Boulevard Ring

(Bulvarnoye Koltso)
Passing the cathedral site, you now emerge on a square through which passes the Boulevard Ring, a semi-circle running between Moscow river embankments. This used to be the outer limit of the "White City" (*Bely Gorod*), an overspill from the Kremlin which was inhabited by minor courtiers and merchants. The area earned its name because its residents were "whitened", or exempted from city taxes.

In the 16th century, Ivan the Terrible moved his *oprichnina* here and built a wall around the city. When the wall was dismantled in the late-18th century, some of its stone was used to build the Moscow Governor's residence on Tverskaya, now headquarters of the Moscow City Duma. The current boulevard, favoured by Muscovites for inner-city strolling, was created on its site.

Pertsov House

On the left down at the very start of the boulevard, where it meets the embankment, is an extraordinary building with triangular shapes and fairytale illustrations, known as the Pertsov House. Designed by the "Itinerant" (*peredvizhnik*) artist **Sergey Malyutin**, it is really just an ordinary block of flats from the turn of the century, and is an excellent example of how the Itinerant movement applied its artistic creed to the architecture of Art Nouveau.

It was in an abandoned cellar of this building that Nikolay Tarasov launched the **Bat Cabaret** in 1908 (see

Walk 4). On entering the cellar, the founders of the troupe were met by a bat flying up from below – hence the company's name.

TrenMos Bar and Bistro

Return to the square past this corner restaurant. TrenMos stands for Trenton-Moscow, the former being the home town of the entrepreneur who started this, the first such American joint venture in Russia. TrenMos has a solid, steady reputation as a restaurant serving European and American cuisine. One recent innovation was the introduction of a bagel stall.

☛ *Usual hours noon–5 pm, 7 pm–11 pm. Currently closed for renovation.*

Prechistenskiye Vorota

This square is one of the former gates of the White City. *Prechistenka* comes from the Russian word *chisty* meaning "pure", and refers to the Convent of the New Virgin (Novodevichy), to which the street and its extension lead.

The statue between the two roads to the left is of Karl Marx's friend and co-writer Friedrich Engels, erected in 1975 to replace old houses knocked down for Richard Nixon's visit to Moscow three years earlier.

The peculiar pair of buildings connected by an arch-

Central Moscow | Nobles' Moscow

way in the centre of the boulevard ahead are the entrance and exit to Moscow's first metro station, Kropotkinskaya. It is named after Pyotr Kropotkin, the anarchist prince — during the Soviet era, Prechistenka square and street were also known by his name.

Ulitsa Prechistenka

The strange thing about this street is its near uniformity, a rare thing indeed in Moscow. It is lined with Empire style houses designed by two of the period's greatest architects, **Osip Bove** and **Afanasy Grigoriev** for the enlightened nobility of the era. The sheer quantity of columned porticos fronting directly onto the street seems to hem it in; it also suffers from the effects of exhaust fumes and foundation shaking juggernauts.

One stylistic exception is the 17th-century chambers on the left behind the Engels statue, at one time the dwelling of Prince Mikhail Golitsyn, admiral of the Russian fleet during Peter the Great's reign. Until recently, it served as a cinema: the red building here is now part of the National Archives.

Imperial Restaurant
The first right turn, Chertolsky Pereulok, takes you to this excellent Russian-style restaurant with a great French wine selection and an old world decor enhanced by the owners' extensive antique collection. In June 1994, Imperial became the first Moscow restaurant to win the International Certificate of Quality. Expect to pay about $50 per person for an evening meal.
 Open noon–11 pm. Tel: 291-6063. Major CC.

Pushkin Literary Museum
On the right of Prechistenka at No. 12 is the house of the Selesnyov and Khrushchev families, one of the best examples of Moscow Empire, made of wood reinforced with stucco. It boasts two columned facades, the main triumphal one looking onto Prechistenka and a more modest and intimate one on Khrushchovsky Pereulok, also sculpted reliefs over the windows by Ivan Vitali and a stone base in Russian peasant architecture tradition.

A museum to Alexander Pushkin, the early-19th century Russian poet, whose near-perfect combination of restraint and emotion has made him revered by generations of Russians, opened here in 1961. Pushkin never lived in the house, but was frequently in the area, visiting his many friends among the resident intelligentsia.

Creating the museum was a rather too hasty measure, as it didn't contain a single exhibit until some time after its opening. Now it appears to have gone to the opposite extreme and is fairly bursting with Pushkiniana. Among exhibits you can see 600 books from Pushkin's personal library (which ran to 5,000 works), and copies of his works in every conceivable language.

☞ *Open Fri–Sun 10 am–6 pm; Weds, Thurs 11 am–7 pm; Tues excursions only. Tel: 202-2321.*

Lev Tolstoy Literary Museum

The Lopukhin House at No. 11 is smaller and more conventional than its neighbour, No. 12, though both were built by Afanasy Grigoriev. As a museum, it's interesting for its *War and Peace* section and has some fine interiors. Unless you're a real Tolstoy devotee you'll do better to save your energy for his estate which is the culmination of this walk.

☞ *Open Tues–Sun 11 am–5 pm, closed last Fri of month. Tel: 202-2190.*

Krizis Zhanra Café

In a courtyard off Ostrovsky Pereulok, this hot and smoky little cellar bar is an oasis for Moscow's bohemians. It's well known for its live music, mainly jazz and rock ballads, and tasty snacks, including a decent selection for vegetarians. Prices are reasonable, at $3-4 a main dish, with a small cover charge ($3) in the evenings for music.

The only problem may be finding it. Ostrovsky Pereulok is the third street right off Prechistenka when walking from Kropotkinskaya: follow it for 5 minutes until you see a church on your left, then turn immediately right, and right

again into the courtyard. The basement entrance is 50 metres further, on the right.

☞ *Open daily noon–00:30 am. Tel: 243-8605.*

Yermolov Mansion

The most extravagant of Prechistenka mansions, that at No. 20, was built for the grim and melancholic General Alexey Yermolov, famous for his campaigns against the Chechens and other north Caucasian tribes in the early part of the 19th century. Its facade is crammed with motifs – scallop shells, eagles and heraldry, which compensate for an otherwise rather dull exterior.

Among subsequent residents were poet **Sergey Yesenin** and his wife, the American dancer **Isadora Duncan**. It was here that Yesenin wrote "I love you" in lipstick on the bedroom mirror.

Mama Zoya's

This basement Georgian restaurant on Sechenovsky Pereulok may not be quite in tune with the local classical environment, but it's rich in atmosphere nonetheless – informal, delicious and chaotic, everything a Georgian restaurant should be.

Mama Zoya's is one of the city's cheapest and best eating options; in the evenings there's likely to be music on offer as well. The effort to find it will be well rewarded: Sechenovsky Pereulok is fourth left off Prechistenka from Kropotkinskaya, and the entrance to the restaurant is from the courtyard behind building No. 8.

☞ *Open 11 am–10 pm. Tel: 201-7743. Cash only.*

Dolgorukov and Tuchkov Mansions

Like several of the houses in the area, these two adjoining mansions (Nos. 19 & 21) were originally built in the late-18th century and reconstructed after the 1812 fire. The first is more interesting architecturally, built by Matvey Kazakov, with a central columned portico and loggias on each side.

The second, by contrast, was more noteworthy for its residents, who seemed to be almost exclusively gamblers and/or art collectors. The last inhabitant, Ivan Morozov, was an eminent collector of the works of French Impressionists and contemporary Russian artists. Though the collection was later to be nationalised and dispersed to other museums, the house's tradition continued and it is now used by the Academy of Arts as an exhibition centre, with an emphasis on traditional, more established artists.

Okhotnikov Mansion

For a view behind the facade of a Prechistenka mansion, visit No. 32, once the house of the guards officer Okhotnikov. In the late 19th century it became one of the most prestigious schools in the country, the Polivanov gymnasium.

Now it is a music school and occasionally serves as a venue for plays and chamber concerts. The outbuildings to the rear are also worth investigation, forming a pleasant semicircular courtyard, while the interior staircase and hall retain much of their original charm.

Kropotkinskaya 36

This 1920's-style restaurant appeared in 1987, heralded as the first private restaurant in the city. Though it maintains its standards, it now differs little from numerous rivals in the area in both price and Russian fare: you'll pay about $50 a head.
Open noon–5 pm, 6 pm–11 pm. Tel: 201-7500. Major CC.

Australian Embassy

Turn left onto Kropotkinsky Pereulok. On the right you pass the Australian Embassy, an unusually austere and geometrical art nouveau masterpiece by Fyodor Shekhtel.

Turgenev House

Emerging onto Ulitsa Ostozhenka, the little wooden house visible on your left across the road at No. 37 was home of writer Ivan Turgenev's mother Varvara, with whom he stayed while visiting Moscow. She was known as a tyrannical woman who beat servants and children with equal and frightening regularity. After quarrelling with her sons and rejecting Ivan's attempts at reconciliation, she died a lonely death in 1850.

Moscow Linguistic University

The sumptuous palace on the near side of Ostozhenka, just to your left, is yet another example of 18th-century Classicism, built for Pyotr Yeropkin, a hero of the 1771 Great Plague. An army general, Yeropkin took control where Moscow's civil authorities had failed, isolated the epidemic and prevented panic.

The building was later a school, attended by philosopher Vladimir Solovyov and satirical writer Ivan Goncharov. It is now the country's most prestigious language institute, and one of the likely destinations of foreign students who come to Moscow to study Russian (including the author of this guide).

Proviant Warehouses
(Proviantskiye Sklady)
Turning right, away from the university, you pass a heavily guarded gateway on your right, from which black cars occasionally emerge. The buildings behind are former food storage depots, built during the 1812 reconstruction, and currently a focus of controversy: they are now used as garages for the Ministry of Defence, but their future is threatened by petrol fumes eating away at them from within.

Despite calls to move the cars out, however, the generals who travel in them are in no hurry to do so. There is a better view of the warehouses from across the Garden Ring Road.

Garden Ring Road
(Sadovoye Koltso)
Since its widening by Stalin in the 1930's reconstruction of the city, this large, fume-choked and accident-plagued road has kept little which recalls its name.

Its origins, however, lie back in the 16th century, when the Crimean Khan, Kaza Girei, was terrorising Moscow residents who lived outside the White City. An earthern rampart and wooden walls were built in a full

circle that covered the vulnerable southern approaches to the city. The area inside was known as the Earth Town (*Zemlyanoy Gorod*).

By 1812 these fortifications had fallen into complete disrepair, and in the post-war reconstruction local residents were encouraged to plant gardens on either side of where they had once stood – hence the street's current name.

✝ Church of St. Nicholas in Khamovniki
(Tserkov' Nikoly v Khamovnikakh)
Approaching Metro Park Kultury, the end of the walk, a further two sites which lie just a short distance ahead are definitely worth a visit.

Proceed up Komsomolsky Prospekt for 200 metres, and the distinctive exterior of the Church of St. Nicholas in Khamovniki comes into view on the right. One of the most colourful churches in Moscow, its exterior decoration is based on the embroidery for which members of its patron community were known. Inside are several purportedly miracle-working icons.

Guria Restaurant
Cross Komsomolsky Prospekt from the church, and duck into the courtyard which opens up behind the buildings on the street to find Guria, a Georgian café in the same mould as Mama Zoya's, and like it a marvel of cheap and quick eating. In fact, they are sister ventures, this, the original, being run by Zoya's husband.

There's rarely a queue here, although be prepared

to share a table: Guria has long been popular with foreigners (they can usually rustle up an English menu), particularly the students living across the road in the Linguistics Univiersity hostel.
 Open noon–10 pm. Cash only. Tel: 246-0378.

🏛 Lev Tolstoy Museum Estate

Cross back to the St. Nicholas church, turn up onto Ulitsa Lva Tolstovo and walk to the Lev Tolstoy Museum Estate, a wooden cottage once surrounded by countryside – at the turn of the century this area was still outside the city limits.

Tolstoy lived here with his family from 1895–1901, by then an increasingly isolated figure leading an unnecessarily austere existence. His way of life is treated very positively in the museum, with the great man's bicycle, dumbbells and shoemaking tools all occupying prominent positions among his belongings. The museum also makes an effort to portray his family – his musical sons, his daughters Tatyana, the artist of the family, and Marie, whose austere lifestyle most closely reflected the writer's own.
Open Tues–Sun 10 am–5 pm. Tel: 246-9444.

Crimea Bridge

(Krymsky Most)
Returning to Park Kultury, you can extend the walk by crossing over the bridge to Gorky Park, the Central House of Artists and the New Tretyakov Gallery. In this case, the finishing point is Metro Oktyabrskaya, a five-minute walk beyond the bridge.

The square which you have now reached, and the adjoining bridge, mark the point where the Crimean Tatars forded the Moskva River on their raids. The current bridge, built by Soviet architect Alexander Vlasov, dates from the 1930's, and is Moscow's only suspension bridge.

Gorky Park, Central House of Artists

Crossing over the bridge, you come to Gorky Park, with its collection of boating lakes, an amusement park and grounds which extend into the open country which runs along the banks of the river. Popular with Muscovites as a place for family outings on summer weekends, it also has one of the river-boat stops for the pleasure boats which run along the Moskva River.

On the other side of the bridge, the huge modern building is the **Central House of Artists**, whose huge spaces accommodate a wide variety of rotating exhibitions, which usually occupy one or two of its halls for a week or more. They range from major international exhibitions to shows of more domestic character.

In terms of its gift shops, art book stalls and café, it has more to offer the visitor than the original Tretyakov Gallery building.

🏛 Open-Air Sculptures

In the gardens behind the complex is a small display which appeared after the August 1991 coup. Several of the statues which were removed by demonstrators have found their resting

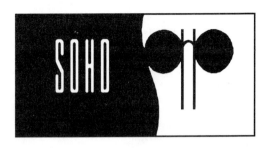

MOSCOW SOHO - WHERE THE ENTERTAINMENT NEVER STOPS

There's always something going on at MOSCOW SOHO, with its combination of Night Club, the PILOT Youth Club, Restaurant and Bar...

At PILOT, it's a live music stage and huge dance floor with groups appearing several days a week. Open 24 hours, SOHO is a more intimate night club, a favourite HAUNT of Moscow's arts and style crowd. Its extravagant decor includes 22 TV screens showing satellite channels, electronic games, bowling-alley, American snooker, darts. A special $15 BUSINESS LUNCH served noon-4 pm has become a favourite with locals, while the a la carte menu gives a choice of more exotic DELIGHTS.

MOSCOW SOHO is at Trekhgorny Val, 6, close to the International Trade Centre and Metro 1905 Goda. Tel.: 205-6209, 255-1552.

place here, including "Iron Felix" Dzerzhinsky, first head of the Soviet secret police, who formerly stood outside the KGB Headquarters at Lubyanka Square.

Beside him, lying appropriately on his side after being broken off his pedestal, is a marble Stalin. Nearby the grim, sinewy figure of Yakov Sverdlov, the first Head of State of Soviet Russia, looks down on visitors condescendingly, while the seated figure of his successor Mikhail Kalinin faces away. Opposite him, three plaster busts, of Brezhnev, Lenin and Stalin, stare vacantly out of the grass, and behind them a metal banner proclaims "The USSR, the Bastion of Peace."

🏛 The New Tretyakov

The Krymsky Val complex accommodates the New Tretyakov Gallery, a continuation of the Russian Art collection which begins from 1917. Many of the names represented here also appear in the main gallery, especially the early rooms which show Futurism. Subsequent rooms display the work of proletarian movements, culminating in the monolithic style of Socialist Realism, Stalin's approved art of the 1930's.

In recent years, many works of formerly "unofficial" artists have appeared too. Although unnumbered, the order of the halls, beginning on the building's 2nd floor, is easy to follow. The 1st floor often accommodates major temporary retrospective exhibitions, frequently of the Russian masters.

Hall 1. The exhibition opens with Kazimir Malevich's famous "Black Square", the ultimate in Suprematism, a renunciation of the reproduction of nature in favour of a specially created independent world of new forms.

For a brief period after the Revolution, modernists established a virtual artistic dictatorship in Russia, one which was briefly in tune with the official ideology. Malevich set up a suprematist art school in Vitebsk called UNOVIS (Asserters of New Art), together with such artists as Ilya Chashnik, also represented here.

Meanwhile, a rival group called OBMOKhU (Society of Young Artists), close to the constructivist style in architecture, was formed by Alexander Rodchenko, the Stenberg brothers and others.

Hall 2. Not only Futurists supported the Revolution, and artists like Kuzma Petrov-Vodkin sought to exalt the proletarian classes. In his "1918 in Petrograd" he portrays a simple peasant girl caught in the throes of revolution. Close in style to icon images of the Virgin and Child, it became known as the "Petrograd Madonna".

Hall 3. A room of portraits, by artists who were already known before the Revolution, like Aristarkh Lentulov and Pyotr Konchalovsky, members of the "Jack of Diamonds" group.

Halls 4–6. These rooms contain revolutionary art, which chart the beginnings of Socialist Realism — paintings glorifying achievements in industry and agriculture.

Here you can see such works as Boris Kustodiev's "Bolshevik", a giant carrying the red flag as the masses teem below him, and Isaac Brodsky's "Lenin at Smolny" – showing the leader of the Revolution planning his next move with great concentration.

Two more artists, Alexander Deineka and Yuri Pimenov, portray the new Soviet man and the optimism of the era, with works like "Building New Factories" and "Heavy Industry".

Halls 7–8. These small rooms, on the other side of the foyer, reached via several temporary exhibition halls, include a portrait of Lev Tolstoy by sculptor Anna Golubkina and works on new technological achievements like "The Metro Escalator" and "The First Russian Airship" by Alexander Labas.

Hall 9. Here you can see many of those artists whose work wasn't close enough to the new canons. Some paintings in this large room are on display courtesy of the artists' families – a few years ago, they would never have appeared here. Note Rublyov's work, including the "Portrait of Stalin Reading *Pravda*", showing the dictator as a cunning swarthy Caucasian.

Halls 10–11. A return to the wholesome world of happy, strong, well-fed collective farm workers – the staple of Socialist Realism.

Hall 12. Frescoes by Vladimir Favorsky from a maternity home in praise of motherhood – an example of communism imitating church art for its own pseudo-religious purposes.

Hall 13. I. Frikh-Khar's "Life is Getting Better", a highly entertaining majolica bas-relief showing festivities in an Azerbaijani collective farm.

Hall 14. The exhibition now moves completely into the monumental work of the Stalin era. Boris Ioganson's "Interrogation of the Communists" shows heroism in the face of Tsarist oppression, while Mitrofan Grekov's series on Budyonny's First Horse Army glories in victories of the Civil War.

Hall 15. Another subject for socialist realist art was sport, best represented here by Deineka's "Goalkeeper" at full stretch.

Halls 16–17. Two rooms which deal directly with Stalin's "Personality Cult", showing idealised portraits of the dictator. Sergey Gerasimov shows Stalin and his henchman Voroshilov before the Kremlin Wall, while Vassily Yefanov's "Unforgettable Meeting" sees him at a dinner being introduced to an enraptured young woman.

Hall 18. The exhibition ends with something of a return to normality, with works that draw directly from traditional Russian art. Among them are portraits of Dostoyevsky by sculptor Sergey Konyonkov (for his museum, *see* Walk 4), Konchalovsky's portrait of the theatre director Vsevolod Meyerhold reclining with a pipe, and works by Mikhail Nesterov, making an unexpected appearance after his religious paintings in the Old Gallery.

7. Beyond the Moscow River

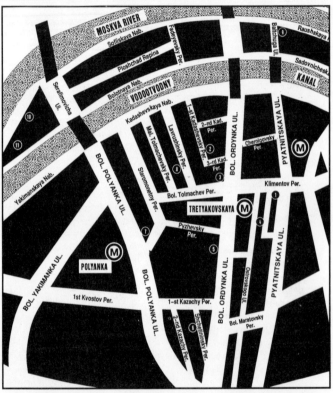

1. St. Clement's Church
2. Resurrection Church v Kadahakh
3. Church of Our Lady
4. Ostrovsky Museum
5. Sisterhood SS. Martha and Mary
6. Tropinin Museum
7. St. Grigory Neokesariisky
8. Tretyakov Gallery
9. Hotel Baltschug
10. Kirillov Chambers
11. Red October

This excursion takes you through the area known as *Zamoskvorechye*, literally "beyond the Moskva River". Once a marshy lowland area exposed to attack from the south during the Tatar raids, it seemed an unlikely place for people to settle. Nevertheless, it was very fertile, and situated on the southern trade route: as a result, it became farm land for Kremlin princes and home to many families.

By the 17th century, it was a centre for traders, crafts-men serving the Tsar's court, the military – including the crack regiment of musketeers, known as the "Streltsy" – and even a community of Cossacks. Following the Streltsy rebellion against Peter the Great, the area lost much of its importance in the city.

Only in the 19th century, with the replacement of rural estates by the town houses and shops of the new educ-ated bourgeoisie, did its status change. Today, Zamoskvorechye is distinguished as one of the areas of Moscow least affected by the rigours of modern life.

STARTS FROM: Metro Novokuznetskaya
ENDS AT: Udarnik Cinema, a short walk across the river to Metro Biblioteka im. Lenina or Borovitskaya

Pyatnitskaya Ulitsa

Exit from the metro turning right onto Pyatnitskaya Ulitsa, a busy shopping street and one of the three main arteries of the Zamoskvorechye area.

The local scenery is dominated by **St. Clements** on the left behind you as you emerge from the metro; the palatial baroque church was built by Count Bestuzhev (*see* Walk 10) to celebrate the successful coup d'état staged by his lover Empress Elizabeth in 1741. This was also the site of a battle in the 1612 war against the Poles, when **Prince Pozharsky** was

fighting his way towards the occupied Kremlin.

 Moscow Culture Fund
(*Moskovsky Fond Kultury*)
An overloaded little shop at No. 16 with very reasonable prices, the Moscow Culture Fund is a place where you're sure to find some unusual souvenirs to fit your taste. Note particularly the fine Georgian vases, custom jewellery, leather work and accessories.

 Tolstoy Museum
Turning right in the direction of the Moskva River, you pass almost immediately on your left a branch of the Lev Tolstoy museum at No. 12.

This building has a very tenuous link with the great writer – it was the quarters of servants of the merchant Vargin, who owned several

apartment blocks in the area. The young Tolstoy rented one of these flats on his return from the Caucasus. Exhibitions here are temporary, taken from the collection of the main museum on Prechistenka (see Walk 6). Behind is the modern building of Ingosstrakh, once the Soviet state insurance company.
☛ Open Tues–Sun 10 am–6 pm; Weds & Fri noon–7 pm. Tel: 231-6440.

Chernigovsky Pereulok
Take this lane, the first left off Pyatnitskaya distinguished by the large bell-tower on the corner. The small Baroque church on the left is that of
✝ **St. John the Baptist Beneath the Forest**
(Tserkov' Ioanna Predtechi pod Borom), built on the site of the oldest church in the Zamoskvorechye. Its rather unlikely name is explained by the features across the river – in the days of the first church, the Kremlin was still a forested area.

Just opposite is the
✝ **Church of SS. Michael and Theodore of Chernigov**, which was built on the site of the grisly demise of these two martyrs in the year 1330. They were trampled to death underneath wooden planks by the soldiers of Tatar leader Batiy Khan for refusing to worship his gods.

☕ Ordynka 13
There seems rather a shortage of good cafés and restaurants in this part of Moscow. As you emerge onto Ulitsa Bolshaya Ordynka (see below), you may be persuaded to try this cosy but rather nondescript cellar bar. With features like German beer on tap, plastic flowers and commercial radio in the background, it is typical of the mid-1990's Moscow café, its sterile cleanliness a reaction to the bland filth of its Soviet predecessors.

The Barrel-makers Guild
(Kadashevskaya Sloboda)
Cross the street into Vtoroy (2nd) Kadashevsky Pereulok, once the centre of the Zamoskvorechye and the home of barrel-makers for the tsar's household. Their
✝ **Resurrection Church** in Moscow Baroque style is the most notable landmark of the area, its main body and nearby bell-tower so slender that they seem stretched from above. The Resurrection Church also includes a number of motifs from both wooden Russian and classical architecture.

Bolshaya Ordynka
Return by Trety (3rd) Kadashevsky Pereulok to Bolshaya Ordynka. This street is a rarity in Moscow, graced by wooden houses and beautiful churches for much of its length. It was once the main route taken by Moscow's attackers from the south, and its name implies just this – the Russian word orda means horde.

Just opposite, at No. 17, is the house where St. Petersburg poetess Anna Akhmatova often stayed when in Moscow.

✝ Church of Our Lady, Joy of All the Afflicted
(Tserkov' Vsyekh Skorbyashchikh Radosti)
Turn right and walk down to

For the delights of authentic Chinese cuisine, visit the Zolotoi Drakon (Golden Dragon) restaurants, now at a variety of locations in Moscow. Open daily from 12 noon to 5 am.

ZOLOTOI DRAKON NA KALANCHEVKE
With Karaoke Bar & Casino
Ulitsa Kalanchevskaya 15–A
(Metro Komsomolskaya, Krasniye Vorota)
Tel.: 975–5566

ZOLOTOI DRAKON NA ORDYNKE
Ulitsa Bolshaya Ordynka 59
(Metro Dobrininskaya, Polyanka,
Tretyakovskaya)
Tel.: 231–9251

ZOLOTOI DRAKON–BOHAI NA PLYUSHCHIKE
With Restaurant & Shop
Ulitsa Plyushchika 64
(Metro Sportivnaya, Smolenskaya)
Tel.: 248–3602

"PYATERKA" BAR
Smolenskaya Ploshchad 6/13
(Metro Smolenskaya)
Tel.: 241–6344

"EVROPA–ASIA" NIGHT CLUB
Izmailovsky Val, 2
(Metro Semyonovskaya)
Tel.: 369–1226

ZOLOTOI DRAKON IN GUM
(Aisle 3, 2nd Floor)
Tel.: 929–3311

the little round Empire-style Church of Our Lady, Joy of All the Afflicted. While the main part was built by **Osip Bove** after the 1812 fire, the bell-tower and trapezium are among the few surviving Moscow works of **Vassily Bazhenov**.

One of Moscow's better preserved churches, it's definitely worth a look inside – the columned rotunda, which serves as a summer church, is truly magnificent. It seems hardly Orthodox, what with the marble angels of the choirs in the trapezium, which is used as the winter church, and the Flemish painting of Christ to the right of the entrance into the rotunda. On the left aisle is the icon of Our Lady, Joy of All the Afflicted, who performed a miracle cure on the sister of Patriarch Joachim in the 17th century.

The Dolgov family, who financed the building, had their mansion just opposite at No. 21.

🏛 Alexander Ostrovsky Museum

One of the roads leading off the little square over Metro Tretyakovskaya is Ulitsa Ostrovskovo: it runs to the left, in parallel with Ordynka. It is named after **Alexander Ostrovsky**, the 19th-century playwright known for such progressive social dramas as *The Thunderstorm* and *Wolves and Sheep*.

Ostrovsky was very fond of the Zamoskvorechye area of Moscow, and many of his plays deal with local middle class life. He was born in the pretty half-stone, half-wood house on the left at No. 9. Although he was only three

when his family moved, and lived for most of his life elsewhere in Moscow, this is his only house that has survived.

It is little known but well preserved: the ground floor devoted to his lawyer father while the upper rooms tell the stories of his plays. Ostrovsky was extremely prolific, staging 46 plays at the Maly Theatre (*see* Walk 2). *Open Weds–Mon 1 pm– 8 pm, closed last Mon of month. Tel: 233-8684.*

✝ Church of St. Nicholas in Pyzhi

(Tserkov' Nikoly v Pyzhakh) On the right of the street is the back entrance of this church, another fine example of the Moscow ornamental style so effectively embodied in the Trinity Church at Nikitniki (*see* Walk 2). Its builders, the Streltsy from Colonel Pyzhov's regiment, participated in the rebellion against Peter the Great and were executed in 1698. The back entrance is usually closed so you may have to return to Bolshaya Ordynka to continue further.

✝ Sisterhood of SS. Martha and Mary

(Marfo-Mariinskaya Obitel) Just opposite on Bolshaya Ordynka, barely visible through the trees, is the Sisterhood of SS. Martha and Mary. The remarkable little Art Nouveau church was commissioned in 1908 by Princess Elizabeth, the last Tsar's sister-in-law, after a terrorist bomb had killed her husband. Her intention was to devote the rest of her life to charity, and the surrounding buildings became a hospice for the sick.

The contrast between the fate of this woman, later beaten to death by the Bolsheviks, and that of the church's architect Alexey Shchusev, whose career reached a peak with his design of the Lenin Mausoleum, is extraordinarily poignant. With its simple, squat white stone body, the church is most reminiscent of early Pskov architecture, although it is in fact conceptually closer to Moscow's **Church of the Saviour in the Forest**, a charming, simple structure built in the Kremlin in the 14th century and destroyed by Stalin in the 1930's.

The stone carvings on the outside walls are a reminder of another feature of early Russian art: the white stone churches of the pre-Mongolian school of Vladimir-Suzdal. Its interior has paintings and icons by Vasnetsov's contemporary **Mikhail Nesterov**, but with the church undergoing delicate restoration work you'll need a special pass to enter.

The hospice buildings, however, are accessible but dilapidated. The original nuns somehow kept the charitable spirit alive through the decades of communism, and in 1990 the sisterhood was revived here. They now occupy some rooms of the polyclinic which uses the buildings.

Unfortunately, they have since been plagued with problems, as they find themselves sharing the buildings with offices of the rabid nationalist movement *Pamyat*, as well as an Orthodox gymnasium of very dubious reputation.

 U Babushki Restaurant
The name of this restaurant, situated at Ordynka 42, meaning "At Grannie's", is something of a misnomer – it's actually run by two actresses. This, however, does not deflect from the quality of the food, which can be even better than home cooking, and specialises in Russian cuisine. Babochka, a French restaurant on the same site, is considerably pricier.
☛ *Both restaurants open noon–11 pm. U Babushki, tel: 230-2797. Babochka, tel: 233-2110.*

 Golden Dragon Restaurant
At Ordynka 59, this fairly-priced eatery, one of a chain of Chinese restaurants, is outstanding for its bright modern decor, tea-drinking ceremonies and opportunity to view ancient cooking methods.
☛ *Open noon–5 am. Tel: 231-9251. Major CC.*

 Tropinin Museum
Turn right onto Pervy (1st) Kazachy Pereulok, one of the streets of the Cossack community in Moscow, and left down Shchetininsky Pereulok. On the right in a two-storey classical mansion is this small museum of 18th- and 19th-century Russian portraiture, mainly the work of serf painter Vassily Tropinin, famous for being one of the first to make ordinary working people his subjects.

Several of his contemporaries are also represented, like Dmitry Levitsky and Orest Kiprensky, with portraits of the General

Alexander Suvorov and the actress Yekaterina Semyonova respectively. Works by all of these artists appear in the Tretyakov Gallery. The temporary exhibitions here are often worth visiting.

☞ *Open 10 am–5:30 pm; Tues, Thurs 1 pm–8:30 pm, closed Mon. Tel: 231-1799.*

Ulitsa Bolshaya Polyanka

Return to Pervy (1st) Kazachy Pereulok, and follow it to the end to join Bolshaya Polyanka, Zamoskvorechye's third main street. On the corner is the Cossack community's focal point, the Petrine Baroque **Church of the Assumption**, built 1697.

Turn right and head for the rather faded but ornate church dominating the skyline, **St. Gregory Neokesariisky**. Built by Tsar Alexey Mikhailovich in 1679, it was the first Moscow church worked on by Russia's leading ceramicist **Stepan Polubes** (*see* Walk 11). His "peacock's eye" tiling, in a band below the eaves, was first used on the New Jerusalem Monastery outside the city (*see* Excursions).

Bolshoi Tolmachevsky Pereulok

Take the right turn just before the church, Staromonetny Pereulok, and walk behind it to the second right turn, Bolshoi Tolmachevsky. This was once the centre of the guild of interpreters, *tolmachy*, who served foreign dignitaries in their negotiations with the authorities during the 16th–17th centuries.

Earlier the street had been closely associated with the Tatar community: while Tatar armies came via Ordynka to attack Moscow, their more peaceful fellows came to trade, and settled in the Zamoskvorechye. Little remains of their presence here although an Islamic Cultural Centre has been set up on Maly Tatarsky Pereulok, beyond Novokuznetskaya Ulitsa, and plays an increasingly important role in the city's cultural life.

The mansion on the right hand side at No. 3 is the most striking of the area's town estates. It was built for the Demidovs, a family of Urals industrialists, and the railings at the front, prepared at one of their metallurgy plants, are a masterpiece of wrought iron casting.

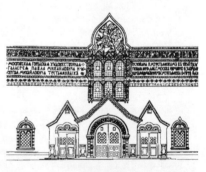

Lavrushinsky Pereulok

Turn left and walk past the **Tretyakov Gallery** (for a full guide, see Tretyakov Gallery chapter) down this newly-restored pedestrian precinct. It is unique in Moscow for its leisurely pace and relative calm (a contrast to the noisy Arbat), and is certainly one of the more successful of Mayor Yuri Luzhkov's Moscow reconstruction projects. On the left you pass several typical 17th-century town houses, newly restored.

Drainage Canal
(Vodootvodny Kanal)
You emerge by the hump-back iron ornamental foot-bridge over the Vodootvodny Kanal, dug in 1785 to allay flooding in the Zamosk-vorechye. Despite the unpleasant sounding name (it's known in local parlance simply as the "Ditch"), its embankments are not entirely displeasing to the eye, and the view to the right has echoes of St. Petersburg.

Everest Gallery
Turn right and follow the embankment as far as the end of Pyatnitskaya, then turn left and cross the canal. On the left on the third floor of No. 2 Ulitsa Baltchuga is a gallery displaying quality Russian art from 16th-century icons to post-modernism, much of which is bound for auction. It is worth just coming to look, although some art is for sale.

Hotel Baltschug Kempinski
Another five-star Moscow hotel, run by the German Kempinski chain, the Baltschug stands on the Moskva River embankment. Despite its name (*baltchug* is the Tatar word for mud) it is a stylish place, completely rebuilt, except for the 1898 facade, at the beginning of the 1990's.

The hotel overlooks the Kremlin and St. Basil's and boasts a top-floor bar with a library of classic novels. Its restaurants are **"Le Romanoff"**, whose royal atmosphere is enhanced by custom-made German furniture and an excellent selection of wines, and the **Baltschug**, with a more European emphasis and all-day smorgasbord for around $45. Prices match the high quality of service and degree of comfort.

On the ground floor the **Café Kranzler** offers a welcome atmosphere for morning coffee or afternoon tea, complete with a rich assortment of pastries.
☛ *Le Romanoff is open 6 pm–11 pm; Baltschug 7 am–10:30 am, noon–3 pm and 6 pm–11 pm; Café Kranzler 10 am–11 pm. Hotel tel: 230-6500.*

⛲ Sophiyiskaya Naberezhnaya
Turn left under the bridge and follow the Moskva River embankment for an unmatched view of the Kremlin and its churches.

The red and yellow build-ing which you pass, now part of the Ministry of Defence, was once owned by the noble Gagarin family and was in its time one of the largest buildings in Moscow. In the last century it passed into the hands of the wealthy wine merchant Vassily Kokorev, who, in a famous and inflammatory speech in 1857 at the Merchant's Assembly called for glasnost, by which he meant civil rights and emancipation of the serfs. As a result, the mayor banned him from speaking at table again.

Also part of the ensemble is the enormous adjoining bell-tower. Through its entrance is a courtyard, and beyond it the 17th-century **St. Sophia's Church**.

Slightly further along the embankment is the building of the British Embassy, one of the most luxurious and well-placed foreign representations in Moscow. Leaders of the Soviet Union long resented its prime view onto the Kremlin, and vainly exerted pressure to move diplomats to another location.

The "House on the Embankment"

(Dom na Naberezhnoy)
Continue beneath the river bridge into the next part of the embankment, Bersenevskaya Naberezhnaya. The building complex on your left is a series of apartment blocks built for government officials during the Stalin era. Its sinister-sounding nickname, "The House on the Embankment", was popularised in a novel by **Yuri Trifonov**, later adapted as a play by **Yuri Lyubimov** at the Taganka Theatre.

Built in 1931 by architect Boris Yofan, its prestigiously-sized and -decorated apartments were allocated to the political leaders and military men of the first generation of communism, as well as to favoured artists, writers and others. During Stalin's purges night-time visits from the secret police, heralding arrest and likely imprisonment, were a regular feature.

Its inhabitants included Georgi Dimitrov, the Bulgarian communist tried in Nazi Germany in 1933 for burning down the Reichstag and later resident in Moscow, as well as Lazar Kaganovich, Stalin's henchman and one of the planners of Moscow's reconstruction.

Facing the embankment is the Estrada Theatre, established in 1961. Roughly translated as "variety", the word *estrada* has not gone out of fashion in Russian as it did in English, and refers as much to modern pop as to music hall type entertainment. This theatre is a popular venue for all kinds of major artistes from home and abroad.

The Chambers of Averky Kirillov

Next on the left through an entrance gate you can see the **Church of St. Nicholas**, a pretty white church with abundant *kokoshniki*. It dates from 1656, when it was built together with the adjacent manor house. They combine to make the best preserved 17th-century monument of their kind in Moscow: recent restoration work in the church revealed a beautifully-preserved but empty Italian marble iconostasis.

The manor house is visible directly from the embankment, presenting a fine example of early Russian Baroque, believed to be built by Menshikov Tower architect **Ivan Zarudny** (*see* Walk 9). The estate, however, is thought to be cursed, as all the owners of this and previous palaces died violent deaths. The last was Averky Kirillov, Secretary-Scribe to the Duma in the days of Tsar Alexey Mikhailovich, who was killed during the Streltsy rebellion in 1682.

Red October Chocolate Factory

The huge red-brick complex at the end of this little peninsula was built in 1889 for Friedrich von Einem, a failed German confectioner who had come to Russia, like many a latter-day entrepreneur, to make a new start. He achieved an excellent reputation, one which survived nationalisation after the Revolution and will probably survive present business hardships. Red October, as the factory is still called, produces Russia's finest chocolates.

Access to the factory is restricted to group visits, so it makes sense to join the excellent Patriarchi Dom tour. You will be shown the small museum on site and the factory floor, where you can be mesmerised by the oozing of liquid chocolate and caramel, and take advantage of the ample opportunities for tasting the product! Finally, save your appetite for tea afterwards, when other untried varieties will be placed before you.

Udarnik Cinema

Retrace your steps to the river bridge and turn right beside the "House on the Embankment". Also part of this complex is one of Moscow's largest and most prestigious cinemas. The word *Udarnik* means "shockworker", referring to the "heroes of labour" of the early socialist years.

Eldorado Restaurant

On the opposite corner beyond the Drainage Canal bridge is a Finnish supermarket and restaurant complex that manages to be both chic and brisk. The restaurant is an oasis for international and innovative seafood dishes. Expect to pay $30–50 per person.
☛ *Open 24 hours. Tel: 230-3683, 238-8611 (restaurant) or 230-3662 (supermarket). CC.*

Sally O'Brien's

The new Irish bar next door, **Sally O'Brien's**, is rather lacklustre compared with its more long-established rivals Rosie O'Grady's and the Shamrock Bar. Main meals, pub style, are available, priced around $10–$15 a dish.
☛ *Open noon–1 am. Tel: 230-0059. CC.*

Dorian Gray Restaurant

This Italian restaurant is further along the embankment. The reason for calling it "Dorian Gray" remains a secret – perhaps the owners wish to attract Wildean dandies with money to burn: expect to pay about $80 per head for a full meal.
☛ *Open noon–midnight. Tel: 237-6342. CC.*

Moosehead Bar

Walk down Ulitsa Bolshaya Polyanka in the direction of Metro Dobryninskaya to the Moosehead Bar at No. 54.

A lively Canadian-run cellar bar with a trendy, mainly expat crowd, Moosehead has live jazz and blues in the evenings and tasty bar food. One of its attractive specials is the weekend breakfast, a full meal served from 10 am–5 pm (around $10).
☛ *Open weekdays noon–5 am; Sat & Sun 10 am–5 am. Tel: 230-7333. CC for purchases over $20.*

Central Moscow | Beyond the Moscow River

8. Petrovka and Neglinka

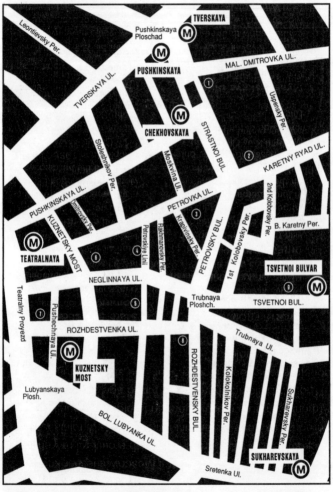

1. Church of the Nativity of the Virgin
2. Hermitage Theatre
3. Higher Monastery of St. Peter
4. Budapest Hotel
5. Sandunovsky Baths
6. Petrovsky Passage
7. Savoy Hotel
8. Nativity Convent
9. Old Circus

A tour around the area due north of the Kremlin. Near the shops of Kuznetsky Most, a brisk trading street, are two of Moscow's smaller, northern semi-circle of monasteries which offer a chance to escape from the bustle of the city.

The route follows in part the underground Neglinka River, along Petrovka and Rozhdestvenka streets, before moving further to the hills above to the site of what was once one of the city's most lively pre-revolutionary markets.

STARTS FROM: Metro Chekhovskaya
ENDS: Metro Sukharevskaya

Ulitsa Malaya Dmitrovka

Leaving Metro Chekhovskaya, follow the path of the mammoth building of the Rossiya Cinema, Moscow's largest movie house, and cross over the Boulevard. Ahead, Malaya Dmitrovka leads north away from the centre in the direction of the town of Dmitrov (after which the street is named).

Anton Chekhov spent his last years in Moscow in this area, and in Soviet times the street was named after him – this name, Ulitsa Chekhova, remains popular with many Muscovites today. It was on Malaya Dmitrovka that Moscow's first tram was built at the end of last century to bring workers into the centre from the new suburbs.

On the right hand side is the beautiful white 17th-century **Church of the Nativity of the Virgin in Putinki** (*Tserkov' Rozhdestva Bogoroditsy v Putinkakh*), unique for its multiple tent-roof spires, which were banned shortly after its construction by the reforming Patriarch Nikon. It was the last Moscow church to have this feature, though instead of serving as a roof as in earlier examples the spires are purely decorative.

🎭 Lenkom Theatre

A little further along Malaya Dmitrovka is the Lenkom Theatre. The building, whose official title is the more ideologically weighty Theatre of the Leninist Communist Youth League, originally housed the Merchants' Club from 1909.

The theatre, dating from 1927, was set up by exponents of proletarian art, and is now run by the talented director Mark Zakharov. His trademark style – opulent, often musical productions which exploit the potential of theatre to the full – has made its stage one of the most popular in Moscow; the company includes some of the greatest names of the Russian theatre, such as Inna Churikova and Oleg Yankovsky.

Harking back to the building's pre-revolutionary origins, Lenkom's small stage area returned to its original purpose in 1993, in the form

of the 2 x 2 Club, an intimate, exclusive nightspot.
☛ Open Weds–Sun 11 pm–5 am. Tel: 209-5346.

Strastnoy Bulvar

Walk back to the Boulevard Ring, here named Strastnoy Bulvar, and turn left, away from Pushkin Square. At the end of the last century, this was considered the most beautiful section of the Boulevard: in 1872 a member of the Naryshkin family planted a garden here.

Walking along it, the former palace of the Princes Gagarin stands on your left, with generous side wings and a twelve-columned portico. Built by **Matvey Kazakov**, it has served as a hospital since 1833.

Strastnoy 7 Restaurant

On the left is this little restaurant, offering mainly European cuisine in unusual gothic/avant-garde surroundings. Prices are moderate for Moscow.
☛ Open noon–11 pm. Tel: 299-0498. CC accepted.

Theatrical Books

(Teatralniye Knigi)
Across the Boulevard, a small bookshop specialises in books by the ART theatrical publishing house. There are some works in English and French for sale.
☛ Open Mon–Fri 11 am–6 pm. Tel: 229-9484.

Karetny Ryad

This part of the Boulevard ends at Petrovskiye Vorota, where it intersects with Ulitsa Petrovka. The extension of Ulitsa Petrovka to the left, away from the centre, is Karetny Ryad.

However, the big Stalinist building on its right-hand side is well-known to Muscovites as Petrovka 38, the headquarters of Moscow's Chief Directorate of the Interior Ministry, the equivalent of London's Scotland Yard.

Opposite is the **Hermitage Garden**, site of several theatres and a nightclub. It first appeared as a public garden on the site of a noble's estate at the end of the last century. The designer of the garden, M. Lentovsky, acquired the nickname "Wizard and Magician", as a result of the electric lighting display he created here; it was one of the first places in the city to be thus lit.

The attractive main theatre at the front has the same name as the garden, though it has had its own troupe only since 1959. Previously it housed other companies, including the Moscow Arts Theatre, which occupied the space before moving to its permanent stage on Kamergersky Pereulok: today, under director Mikhail Levitin, it has established a reputation for adapting the works of the 1930's absurdist writers of the OBERIU period.

To its rear is the Sfera Theatre-Studio, a red brick building which was the site of Moscow's first film showing.

The Hermitage Nightclub in the rear of the theatre building, meanwhile, maintains its reputation as one of the trendiest as well as most informal Moscow nightspots, with a young and cosmopolitan crowd.

📢 *Open Fri–Sun 10 pm–6 am. Tel: 299-1160, 299-7519 (recorded message).*

Ulitsa Petrovka

Turn back towards the centre and cross over the Boulevard to the main part of Ulitsa Petrovka. The street is named after the monastery whose belltower you see ahead and served as its direct route to the Kremlin. In later centuries it developed as a bustling shopping street with an abundance of stalls and later arcades.

🏛️ ✝️ ⬛ High Monastery of St. Peter

(Vysokopetrovsky Monastyr')
This impressive baroque ensemble had its origins in the 14th century, a time when two types of monastery were under construction in Moscow. To the south, a semicircle of fortress monasteries was built to keep out Tatars and other invaders. Meanwhile, in the quieter north of the city, closer to the centre, several more appeared, also in a defensive ring, but in fact serving a more familiar purpose as centres of contemplative monastic life.

Here, most current buildings date from the end of the 17th century and were financed by Natalya Naryshkina, mother of Peter the Great, whose imagination and enthusiasm for the architecture of the day resulted in a style, Naryshkin Baroque, being named after her family. However, the style is not much in evidence here and is best seen by visiting the

Intercession Church at Fili (*see* Greater Moscow, War Memorials).

It's hard to get inside the complex, but a walk around the walls reveals most of the buildings. The oldest is the small, white, single-cupola Church of Peter the Metropolitan, built by the Genoese Alevisio in the 15th century. Like the monastery itself, it is named after the famous church leader who brought the seat of Russian Orthodoxy from Vladimir to Moscow.

Note also the festive ✝️ ⬛ **Church of St. Sergius of Radonezh**, on a high arched base, the best example here of the baroque style. The church commemorates Peter's victory against his sister, the former regent Sophia; Peter had been saved from capture by taking shelter in the **Trinity St. Sergius Monastery**, of which St. Sergius was the founder.

🏛️ Literary Museum, Rosizo

The walls and residential buildings of the monastery were also built by the Naryshkins to commemorate the birth of Peter, the heir to the throne. The block facing Ulitsa Petrovka houses two "museums" although both are in fact simply exhibition halls.

The first, ROSIZO (*open daily except Mon and Fri, noon–7 pm*) contains mainly arts and crafts. The second, misleadingly called the State Literature Museum (*open Thurs, Sat, Sun 11 am–6 pm; Weds, Fri 2 pm–7 pm*), has temporary exhibits about lesser known Russian writers in rather incongruous white-washed 17th-century surroundings.

Ulitsa Moskvina

This pleasant little street opposite provides a good view of the monastery. Furthermore, its mixture of art nouveau, classical and eclectic architecture reflects the diversity of the city's cultural life.

Among its buildings are a children's school, formerly the house of Sergey Yesenin's friend **Anatoly Mariengof**, a talent recently rediscovered through the pages of his tragic novella *Cynics*; a branch of the Theatre of Nations at No. 3, long under repair; at No. 8 the house of Princess Trubetskaya who became the wife of architect **Osip Bove** (in those days it was considered way below her station for a woman of the nobility to wed an architect); and a museum devoted to the history of the Bolshoi Theatre, under equally total reconstruction.

 Starina and Almaz

At No. 24 are two very upmarket but relatively low-priced souvenir shops, the first selling antiques, notably icons, and the second jewellery, including gold, silver and diamonds.

 News Bar

This theme bar opened several years ago with a novel attraction, a plentiful choice of international newspapers for browsing as you sipped your beer or coffee. Somewhere along the way the management changed and this feature was lost: the bar has not completely degenerated, though, and retains its original Scandinavian pine decor.
☛ *Open noon–2 am. Tel: 925-3777. Major CC.*

Budapest Hotel

The News Bar occupies a corner of the building of the Budapest Hotel, which spans the length of Petrovskiye Liniyi. The hotel looks moderately impressive from the outside, though its new porch is a product of recent cosmetic changes.

The Budapest is in fact a better-than-average central Moscow hotel both in price and service, more tranquil and less crime-ridden than the Rossiya and Intourist, with something of an old-world atmosphere into the bargain.

 It boasts a quiet but non-descript first floor English pub, while the restaurant is one of the oldest in the city, its pompous decor virtually unchanged since opening in 1856. Its food – Russian with a very faint nod towards Hungarian cuisine – is reasonably priced for the experience. However, don't expect quiet here in the evening: like most such locations, diners are treated to a more-or-less raucous musical show.
☛ *Restaurant open noon–11 pm. Tel: 923-9966. Cash only.*

Neglinnaya Ulitsa

Follow Petrovskiye Liniyi to its end onto the street which, as its name suggests, replaced the unsavoury, marshy Neglinka River (*see* Walks 1, 2) when it was re-directed into a pipe in the late 18th century. The river,

STEAK RESTAURANT AND BAR

AT UNCLE GUILLY'S, WE HAVE MADE MOSCOW HOSPITALITY OUR SPECIALITY...

The best Steak Restaurant and Bar in Moscow is named in honour of one of the most famous Muscovites, Vladimir Guilyarovskiy. A turn-of-the-century writer and artistic figure Guilyarovskiy wrote about the everyday life of 19th century Moscow. He was a real connoisseur of good food, drink and hospitality.

Situated in an authentic cellar dating back to the year 1700, "Uncle Guilly's" has become famous for its exquisite blend of Russian and American cuisine featuring 100 percent USDA beef. The wine list and the unique ambiance and decorations add special flavour to the historic atmosphere of this restaurant

**Open:
12 noon to 12 midnight at
6 STOLESHNIKOV PEREULOK,
(a minute's walk
from the Dolgorukhy
statue).**

**Tel: 229-2050,
229-4750,
fax: 229-4295.**

however, did not immediately benefit from the change, since affluent locals built illegal private drains into it to dispose of their sewage. It took decades to create the relatively sweet-smelling and leafy avenue you see today.

Sandunovsky Baths
(Sandunovskiye Bani)
Turn left onto Neglinnaya, then right before the street opens out into an avenue. At No. 14 is the city's top bath house, which was built by Vera Firsanova, a wealthy timber merchant's daughter, at the end of the last century.

The sumptuous interiors reflect the extrovert socialite natures of Firsanova and her flamboyant penniless Guards officer husband, who goaded her into the project. Its luxurious neo-baroque statues and jagged arabesque archways alone should be reason enough to experience this Russian *banya*. If you can, come with a Russian friend to explain the ropes, and leave valuables behind.
☛ *Open 8 am–10 pm (kassa until 8 pm), closed Tues. Tel: 925-4631.*

 ### Uzbekistan Restaurant
The faded oriental beauty of this restaurant and the charm of its little terrace café may not be enough to compensate for the undistinguished food, from a country whose cuisine is not highly prized.
☛ *Open 11 am–midnight. Tel: 924-6053. Cash only.*

Petrovsky Passage
Return via Neglinnaya past the buildings of Russia's Central Bank towards the centre. On your right stands Petrovsky Passage, a two-lined shopping arcade which runs through to Petrovka. It bears a superficial resemblance inside to GUM, but is cleaner, quieter and more generally yuppified, with its modern finishings betraying signs of an overhaul by a Turkish company.

Of its eateries, the relaxed café atmosphere of **DiStyle** seems the most attractive, while the second floor Italian restaurant **Belfiori** and its busy ground floor **Della Palma** café tend to be overpriced.

 ### Rocky's Bar and Café
An American-style café run, like most such ventures in Moscow, by the Irish. Rocky's biggest plus is the size of its helpings: with a salad and burger, you can be bursting at the seams for under $30.

On the other hand, if you just need a snack, you might be content to pay a visit to the snackbar housed in a London bus opposite, very popular with locals.
☛ *Open 11 am–midnight. Tel: 921-2529. Cash only.*

Central Department Store (TsUM)
A few years ago, discerning shoppers and experienced Muscovites would come to this modern monstrosity to look for scarce items rather than visit the glass-roofed palace on Red Square. Nowadays, though, GUM's ugly sister TsUM is just a confusing mixture of old and new, and not nearly as much fun to shop in.

Kuznetsky Most
Turn left from Neglinnaya into Kuznetsky Most, a lively

pedestrian street. In English, its name means "Smith's Bridge" and stemmed from the smiths who lived and worked nearby at the Cannon Forge (after which the parallel Pushechnaya Ulitsa was named).

The bridge itself duly disappeared along with the Neglinka River, though it has recently been excavated and may be put on museum display at some point in the near future.

By the early 19th century, Kuznetsky Most had changed completely, as shops and stalls appeared selling French perfume and cosmetics. Even the street sweepers were stylish, since upper class offenders were brought here by the police to atone for their crimes.

Another aspect of Kuznetsky Most was its abundance of bookshops, which still define its appearance today. This is a particularly good area for buying maps and guide books, especially ones about lesser known parts of the country which are often unavailable elsewhere.

Zwemmer's Bookshop
This branch of Zwemmer's London bookshop chain remains something of an oddity. It has the appearance of an ordinary English bookshop, specialising in art and fiction with small selections of guidebooks, English language textbooks and others. In theory, the prices are the same as in London, but in fact many are marked up.
☞ Open 10 am–7 pm, except Sun. Tel: 928-2021. Major CC.

Ulitsa Rozhdestvenka
Half way up, Kuznetsky Most crosses this street, named after the **Monastery of the Nativity** at its northern end. In 1948, it became Ulitsa Zhdanova, named after the man who was Stalin's ideology chief at the end of the dictator's reign. The street reverted to its original name in 1989 in perestroika's first bout of name-changing.

Iberia Restaurant
Unlike other Georgian eateries in Moscow which are closer to being cafés, Iberia (at No. 5/7) is a restaurant in the full sense – although priced at a level which is still welcome for Moscow: two can feast here for about $50.

As well as a full menu and choice of Caucasian wines, it has the added attraction of a very civilised, colourful interior and Spanish-style music, in the form of violin and piano, adding charm to evening dining here.
☞ Open noon–11:30 pm. Tel: 928-2672. Cash, AmEx only.

Tosakhan Restaurant
The Tosakhan Restaurant at No. 12 could be described more as a Japanese cultural centre than a restaurant. Diners enter through a "pebble garden" to prepare

them for the oriental atmosphere of the place. Once inside you can choose between a European-style restaurant and smaller traditional Japanese rooms with low tables. Japanese cuisine is one of the most expensive in Moscow and Tosakhan is no exception.

☛ Open noon–2 pm, 6 pm–10 pm. Tel: 925-6990. Major CC.

Savoy Hotel

The Savoy, another recently restored turn-of-the-century hotel – in Soviet times named the Berlin – stands at the southern end of Rozhdestvenka, its small and gilded interior betraying its style and exclusivity.

 The Savoy's excellent restaurant carries on the hotel's original traditions of fine cuisine and service in a splendid rococo hall. Prices, as you might expect, are high. The adjoining casino is one of the classiest in the city.

☛ Restaurant open noon–midnight. Tel: 929-8600. Major CC.

Le Stelle del Pescatore

One of Italy's most famous restaurant chain, Le Stelle del Pescatore is situated on Pushechnaya Ulitsa, suitably next to the Alitalia offices. Its menu includes delicious seafood in a light breezy interior. Expect to pay over $50 per head for a full meal.

☛ Open 10 am–2 am. Tel: 924-2058. Major CC.

Stroganov Institute

Walking north down Ulitsa Rozhdestvenka stop briefly at No. 8, a large mansion distinguished by its blue and white tiled exterior and fountain near the entrance.

The building began life in the 18th century as the residence of the powerful nobleman Count Vorontsov, whose estate and gardens once stretched down to the nearby Neglinka River.

Though originally classical in style, the new facade was added in the 1890's when the building was taken over by the Stroganov School of Applied Art. Now the Institute of Architecture, it maintains a strong tradition of expert instruction in sculpture and other art forms as well.

Church of St. Nicholas of the Bell-Ringers

(Tserkov' Nikoly v Zvonaryakh)
This little church, further down on the same side, was also commissioned by Vorontsov and built by the baroque period architect Karl Blank in 1762. Its name comes from the former settlement here, occupied by bellringers of the Kremlin's Ivan the Great bell.

Convent of the Nativity

(Rozhdestvensky Monastyr')
Another monastery founded in the 14th century, the Convent of the Nativity is easily accessible and provides a uniquely peaceful haven from the roar of

nearby traffic. Like many convents in its time, it served as a prison for disobedient wives of high-ranking citizens: it was here that Prince Vassily III sent his wife Solomoniya.

The central Nativity Cathedral was built after a fire in 1500 and has survived almost unchanged. With its cross-shape and layered *kokoshniki* topped by a single dome, it is reminiscent of the Cathedral of the Saviour in the Andronicus Monastery (*see* Greater Moscow, "Moscow Icons").

Trubnaya Ploshchad

Emerging on the Boulevard Ring half way up a steep hill, below you on the left is this rather unattractive square, its name taken from the Russian word *truba*, meaning pipe, referring to the Neglinka River which runs in pipes below. In the last century, there was a market here specialising in birds and hunting dogs: today the area is still in the throes of a lengthy restoration.

The route of this walk now goes right, but you can take a detour first towards the Garden Ring Road.

ШКОЛА СОВРЕМЕННОЙ ПЬЕСЫ

😃 **Modern Play School**

The small theatre building on the corner of Neglinnaya and the Boulevard has a grand period interior, small stage area and one of the most successful companies to have emerged in Moscow over the last five years.

With visiting actors who include some of the undisputed stars of the Russian stage and screen, their first major success, *Why the Tails?* was a delightfully frivolous adaptation of Chekhov's story "The Proposal".

😃 **Tsvetnoi Bulvar, Old Circus**

The route of the Neglinka River follows another leafy avenue to the Garden Ring. This area is notable for three buildings on its left side, the first of which, the Mir cinema is jointly run with the French and shows mainly European films.

Next to the Tsvetnoi Bulvar Metro station is the Central Market (*Tsentralny Rynok*), a place to come for fresh vegetables, fruits, meat, beans and spices from all over the former Soviet Union, though current restoration work inside has driven remaining traders out onto the street.

In between the two, the building of the Old Circus is a likely stop on many visitors' itineraries. Built in 1880 by the entrepreneur Albert Salamonsky, it was virtually rebuilt by Finns in 1989, and remains home to one of Moscow's two excellent circus troupes (the other is situated further from the centre, near to Metro Universitet). Famous clown Yuri Nikulin heads this company. ☛*Shows usually daily (except Tues) at 7 pm, also Sat and Sun at 3 pm and Sun at 11 am. Tel: 200-6889. Tickets can normally be found at the Circus box office in advance, on sale in metro and street ticket booths, as well as from the inevitable touts at the door.*

😀 Obraztsov Puppet Theatre

Walk on towards the Garden Ring, cross underneath it and walk up the incline to the left. Moscow's premier puppet theatre, named after its founder and long-time artistic director Sergei Obraztsov, who died in 1993, is on the right, immediately recognisable from the elaborate clock mechanism mounted on its front wall.

Inside, the theatre has considerable charm with a small museum of puppets and puppetry, as well as a well-established, much-loved repertoire of shows for adults and children alike. From the former, *Don Juan* and *Concert Extraordinaire* are both worth catching, communicating without language problems and relying on a healthy sense of fun. They are normally performed at weekends at 7 pm.
☛ *Tel: 299-3310.*

Ulitsa Sretenka

Retrace your steps to Trubnaya Ploshchad and back up the hill along the Boulevard, now continuing to the crossroads with Ulitsa Sretenka. In Moscow's early days, during the time of the city's founder Yuri Dolgoruky, this area was a village called Kuchkovo Polye. It was ruled by the boyar Kuchka, a long-standing rival to the Muscovite prince. Although Dolgoruky was finally victorious over Kuchka, sending his enemy to execution, the boyar's sons had final revenge when they killed Yuri's son Prince Andrey Bogolyubsky.

Nowadays, this area is controlled by another contender for power in Moscow, the extravagant and virulent nationalist Vladimir Zhirinovsky. Based in the headquarters of his mis-named Liberal Democratic Party on Rybnikov Pereulok (a left turn off the boulevard), he has been buying up much of the area's property. There is even a rock music shop named after him on the corner.

U Sretenskikh Vorot Restaurant

Situated on Bolshaya Lubyanka, the road leading off the Boulevard to the right, is a small lively restaurant highly acclaimed for its unpretentious and easy-going atmosphere. The food is deeply Russian, with heavy and greasy dishes, but if that meets your taste you won't be disappointed.
☛ *Mon–Sat noon–9 pm. Tel: 924-9252. Cash only.*

Sukharevskaya Ploshchad

Emerge from Sretenka onto the Garden Ring at this lively square, which before the Revolution was Moscow's largest flea market. Sukharevskaya Market appeared after the 1771 plague as a result of tight controls on the sale of second-hand goods and operated only on Sundays.

Riddled with fakes and stolen goods, it gave rise to a host of entertaining anecdotes. In one, a woman trader had bought a painting supposedly by artist Ilya Repin, and came to show it to the artist. Repin inscribed it "This is not Repin, I. Repin" – as a result of which the owner promptly took it back to the market and sold it for ten times its original price.

The market was not the only thing on the square to disappear after the Revolution. One of the most tragic acts of 1930's destruction wrought in Moscow was the demolition of the slender Baroque Sukharev Tower. Built in 1700 as another monument to Peter the Great's victory over Sophia, it was dedicated to the "Streltsy" general Sukharev who had remained loyal while the rest rebelled.

Always rich in legend, the tower was even

believed to have magic powers; a satanic book was supposedly hidden within its walls. Stalin hoped to find the book, so rumour goes, and when he failed, decided to destroy the tower; the official reason given was that the road needed to be widened.

Sklifasovsky Institute

This large classical mansion on the other side of the Garden Ring is striking both for its architectural splendour and for its history. The building was begun in 1792 by Count Nikolay **Sheremetyev**, at the request of his mistress (later wife) the serf actress Praskovia Zhemchugova-Kovalyova (*see* Greater Moscow, Kuskovo).

Praskovia wished to atone for her life of sin through the good works of endowing this shelter for the homeless and hospital for the poor. Though they subsequently married, and the Countess died before construction was finished, Sheremetyev vowed to make the hospital a memorial to his wife.

For this he commissioned the St. Petersburg-based Italian architect **Giacomo Quarenghi**, who created the fine semi-circular Doric colonnade which survives today. In the centre of the ensemble is a church, with hospital wards occupying the wings.

In 1919 the whole complex became the First Aid Institute, named after Nikolay Sklifasovsky, who in the 19th century introduced Russia's first public ambulance service. Today it still provides emergency care to accident victims.

9. Myasnitskaya, Maroseika, Solyanka and the Hills Around

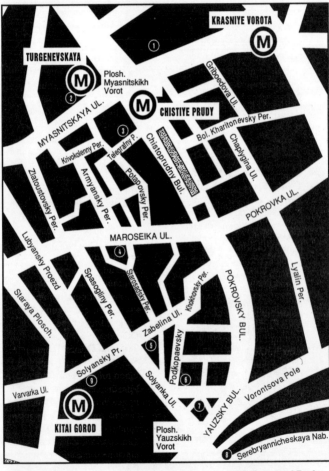

1. State Statistics Committee
2. Perlov Tea House
3. Menshikov Tower
4. SS. Cosmas and Damian Church
5. St. John's Convent
6. St. Nicholas Church
7. SS. Peter and Paul Church
8. Trinity Church
9. All Saints Church

A walk through some of central Moscow's lesser-known back streets, a hilly part of town with a cultural mix engendered by its once multiracial inhabitants – Ukrainians, Armenians and a mostly German foreign community.

Though buildings here are of mixed age and some later constructions seem incongruous, the streets remain picturesque wholes.

STARTS FROM: Metro Turgenevskaya, Chistiye Prudy
ENDS AT: Metro Kitai Gorod

DIRECTIONS: If you want to visit the first three stops on this walk, exit from Metro Turgenevskaya and turn **right** in the underpass to emerge on the outer side of the ring. Otherwise turn **left** in the underpass and emerge onto Myasnitskaya Ulitsa on the inner side of the Boulevard Ring.

Myasnitskaya Ulitsa

One of the radial streets leading towards Lubyanka Square, Myasnitskaya connects it with three of Moscow's railway stations (*see* Walk 10). Its present-day name comes from *myasniki*, the butchers who once lived and worked here, though in Soviet times it was named after **Sergey Kirov**, the Leningrad Communist Party chief whose funeral procession passed through here on the way to the Kremlin.

Kirov was killed in 1934, supposedly by an envious Stalin, who saw Kirov's popularity in the country's second city as a threat to his own central authority. His death marked the beginning of the Stalinist terror.

 ### State Statistics Committee
(Goskomstat)

Looking across the Boulevard, you will see the State Statistics Administration at No. 39, Moscow's only building by the French futurist **Le Corbusier**, and also his first major work anywhere in the world. Construction began in 1929 and the building was completed in 1936.

Le Corbusier was an enthusiastic partisan of the young Soviet Union and "worked for the U.S.S.R. with all my heart," as he later wrote. Many are thankful that he didn't manage to realise further his plans for the city: they would have involved the demolition of even more of old Moscow than fell victim to other grand designs.

 ### Taburna Miramar

Hidden away opposite the above monster in the first right turn off this part of Ulitsa Myasnitskaya, Bolshevistsky Pereulok, Taburna Miramar is a small, cozy restaurant/bar serving mainly Mexican and Cuban dishes. Relaxed and welcoming, Miramar's food is both tasty and colourful – without putting too much strain on your pocket.
☛ *Open 10 am–midnight. Tel: 924-1986. Major CC.*

Regina Gallery

If you're already in this area, take a look at this small art gallery at No. 36. A few years ago it burst onto the scene with a series of attention-catching exhibitions and happenings, such as the killing and serving up of a piglet to an audience of journalists.

Though it now stirs up less commotion and has moved to sparkling new premises, Regina maintains its reputation as one of Moscow's most innovative contemporary art galleries. ☛ Open Tues–Sat, noon– 7 pm. Tel: 921-1613.

Moscow City Post Office

Cross the square onto the inner side of the Boulevard and you will see the Moscow City Post Office, a pre-revolutionary building which, if little else, provides a more elegant setting for postal business than the Central Telegraph on Tverskaya.

Yushkov House & Perlov Tea House

The first two buildings on the right hand side of Myasnitskaya as you approach the centre are worth a look. The first (No. 21) was the house of wealthy socialite General Ivan Yushkov, built by Vassily Bazhenov (see Pashkov House, Walk 6) at the end of the 18th century. Despite reconstructions, the beautiful corner colonnade in particular still reflects the classical spirit of the original.

If this building seems standard for Moscow, its neighbour, at No. 19, is quite definitely not. Its Chinese facade, complete with dragons, snakes and other regalia, and pagoda on top were commissioned by the S.V. Perlov tea company, owners of the building. They were expecting to host the regent to the Chinese Emperor, Lee Hung Chang, on his Moscow visit at the end of the last century. Unfortunately, there was another Perlov tea company in the city at the time, and whether in spite of or because of the first Perlov's generous deed, Lee chose to try the hospitality of the rival.

Chistoprudny Bulvar

As the name, which means "clear ponds" in English, suggests, this part of the Boulevard Ring is distinguished by the rather murky body of water situated at its lower end.

The first monument visible just beyond the tram junction in the centre is a statue of the liberal early-19th century writer and diplomat **Alexander Griboyedov** (1795-1829), associated with the Decembrist movement and later killed by a mob while on a diplomatic mission in Tehran. Beneath the statue is a bas-relief of characters from his most famous work, *Woe from Wit*, a social satire that became a major source of modern Russian sayings.

 Café Anna Tram

If you're looking for a moveable feast (or at least snack) you could try and board the Café Anna, a tram/streetcar complete with small café which runs from here approximately on the hour, from noon to 11 pm.

Built in the 1940's, it used to take government officials on city tours along a route near the Kremlin that is now defunct. For the last five years Café Anna has been running as a private venture, on a route which loops round via Novokuznetskaya to the St. Daniel's Monastery and back.

The tram's interior retains its original decor, with kitsch additions like pink curtains and fairy lights. The food is a Russian-Caucasian mix and cheap for Moscow.

NOSTALGiE

🔴 Café Nostalgie
🍴 Another stylish eatery – of the stationary kind – is a five-minute walk down the Boulevard inside the Bykov Children's Cinema Centre at No. 12-A. This is Moscow's first post-modernist café, combining Stalinist marble à la Moscow metro with wooden archways characteristic of the old Russian merchant class.

Here you can expect decent service, tasty food, or simply a pleasant atmosphere for whiling away the afternoon with a cappuccino or glass of wine.

In the evenings live jazz is played by local celebrities, and sometimes groups from farther afield.
☛ Open 8 am–11:30 pm, admission free to 7:30 pm, then $5 (women), $10 (men). Concerts start 8:30 pm. Tel: 916-9478/9090.

🎭 Sovremennik Theatre
Opposite the café, across the pond, is a white building in neo-classical style. Built in

the 1920's by Roman Klein, this building was originally the "Kolisei" cinema, used by the great director Sergey Eisenstein for his "Proletcult" workers' theatre. The current theatre troupe didn't come here until 1974, though they quickly made a name for themselves for their lively and politically daring work.

The Menshikov Tower
Leave the Boulevard by the right turn closest to Myasnitskaya, Telegrafny Pereulok. In a courtyard to the right you will see a very tall baroque tower, the **Church of the Archangel Gabriel**, known more commonly as the Menshikov Tower.

Alexander Menshikov, Peter the Great's ambitious right hand man, commissioned Ivan Zarudny to build a baroque church with internal and external sculptural reliefs, features then associated with churches built by the Naryshkin family. However, the wealthy Menshikov would not be satisfied with just a beautiful church: he added a wooden spire which made it higher than the Kremlin's Ivan the Great bell-tower, and an expensive English clock which chimed every quarter hour, an unheard of luxury in Russia which even the Kremlin's Saviour's Tower didn't possess.

In 1722, 15 years after its completion, Menshikov received his come-uppance – the spire was destroyed by lightning and the clock duly dismantled. His own career

Central Moscow | Myasnitskaya

161

ended soon afterwards, when Peter II ascended the throne in 1727.

By way of contrast, next door is the cosy little 19th-century **Church of St. Theodore Stratilates**. Both churches are now functioning again.

Krivokolenny Pereulok

Turn right at the end of Telegrafny into another quiet back street that runs parallel to Ulitsa Myasnitskaya. Krivokolenny Pereulok is the closest thing Moscow has to an Armenian quarter – note the building at No. 11, the offices of Moscow's "Ararat" cognac factory.

Large quantities of the former Soviet Union's finest spirit are bottled in Moscow, though the end product isn't what it used to be. A combination of Armenian energy shortages, disintegrating economic links and abuses such as doctoring have adversely affected quality and made many people turn to cheaper imported cognacs, or vodka.

Following the road to the left, turn round for the best view of the Menshikov Tower. Of some interest also is the house at No. 4, once owned by the poet and distant relative of Pushkin, Dmitry Venevitinov. Returning from exile, Pushkin took Moscow by storm here with his reading of the verse play, *Boris Godunov*. According to an eyewitness, audience reactions ranged from cold sweats to amnesia!

 Samovar Restaurant

Reached by returning to Myasnitskaya Ulitsa via Bankovsky Pereulok,

Samovar is a standard fare Russian restaurant with prices that are average for Moscow (expect to pay $40-$50 a head).

Its speciality is the collection of spotlit samovars around the room, and the 20 varieties of black and green tea that are served in the traditional Russian way with one pot for strong brew, another for boiling water.
☛ *Open Mon–Sat noon–9:30 pm. Tel: 921-4688. Cash only.*

Armenian Lane

(Armyansky Pereulok)
Turn left from Krivokolenny into this side street, Armyansky Pereulok, which took its name from the Armenians who settled here in the 18th century.

The first was the merchant and philanthropist Ivan Lazarev, whom Catherine the Great rewarded with permission to buy land and build factories. His house, on the right at No. 2, is distinguished by the bronze lions on the gate. A restrained but grand classical mansion built by serf architects, it now houses the Armenian Embassy. The prominent obelisk in front of the house is a memorial to Lazarev's sons, who donated the building to an Armenian school.

The Lights of Moscow Museum

The building opposite, No. 3, the Lights of Moscow Museum was the 17th century chambers of Protopopov, a courtier of Tsar Alexey Mikhailovich. It now houses one of Moscow's many tiny eccentric museums.

"The Lights of Moscow" displays the history of the city's street lighting from gas through turpentine and incandescent kerosene to electricity, which first appeared in the Church of Christ the Saviour in 1883.

If the many lanterns fail to interest, the museum also has a decent collection of old sketches and photographs of the city.

☛ *Open Tues–Thurs, 1–4 pm. Tel: 924-7374.*

Continue down the lane past the recently restored No. 11, the estate of Prince Gagarin and the childhood home of the poet **Fyodor Tyutchev**, to emerge on the busy thoroughfare which to your right is called Ulitsa Maroseika and to your left Ulitsa Pokrovka.

Ulitsa Maroseika

Maroseika takes its name from the street's inhabitants, the *malorossy* or "little Russians", as the Ukrainians were once called. They settled there after Ukraine was devastated by war between Russia and Poland, and broken up by a treaty signed in 1683. The house at No. 11 became their first legation.

To your right on both sides of the street are buildings by Matvey Kazakov. One is a mansion with fine sculptures that was once inhabited by Field Marshal Rumyantsev, a hero of the Russo-Turkish war of 1768-74, and today is the Belorussian embassy.

Opposite the embassy is the austere green **Church of SS. Cosmas and Damian**, with cubes and cylinders gracefully hidden by willows and offset by the giant modern glass-and-steel structure situated behind it. The church has a reputation as one of the most liberal and progressive in Moscow.

Maharaja Restaurant

One of a new wave of exotic and not-so-expensive restaurants to hit Moscow, Maharaja has been much praised by Westerners and Indians alike for its contribution to the Moscow culinary scene. Set in a pleasant cellar that was once an inn serving the nearby SS. Cosmas and Damian Church, Maharaja serves subtly spicy food amid authentic Indian chaos and spontaneity. Expect to pay about $50 for a meal for two.

☛ *Open noon–10 pm. Tel: 921-9844/7758. Major CC.*

Starosadsky Pereulok

This leafy lane's name means "old garden" and was once the site of orchards, where green-fingered Prince Vassily III grew and tended his rare plants.

As the lane bends sharply to the right, you pass an 18th-century classical mansion, a well-preserved example of pre-1812 architecture with a central portico and jutting wings characteristic of its period.

Further down, you come to the huge 18th-century gothic cathedral whose broken spire was visible from

Central Moscow | Myasnitskaya

Armyansky Pereulok. Now a film studio, this was once a Lutheran church used mainly by Germans who lived in the area. Foreigners first moved here during the enlightened reign of Alexey Mikhailovich, thus incurring the wrath of the Ukrainians who had come to Moscow with the express purpose of preserving their Orthodox religion. Though packed off to a special area on the left bank (*see* Walk 10), the "far abroad" foreigners drifted back towards the centre in the next century.

You now emerge onto one of Moscow's most attractive spots, whose first landmark is the white **Church of St. Vladimir-in-the-Old-Gardens** (*Tserkov' Vladimira v Starykh Sadakh*), the work of Alevisio, best known as the architect of the Kremlin's Archangel Cathedral.

St. John's Convent
(*Ivanovsky Monastyr'*)
The bleak, ruined towers and broad-domed church of the St. John's Convent are a contrast to the light airy church of St. Vladimir opposite.

Not surprisingly for an institution founded to mark the birth of Ivan the Terrible, it had an unpleasant history, becoming a prison for noble-women such as the unhappy Elizabeth, illegitimate daughter of the Empress of the same name, and much later for victims of Stalin's NKVD. On a lighter note, though, the nuns here were once famous for their knitting — perhaps this side of the convent's activity is due for a revival.

Khokhlovsky Pereulok
Turn left past the monastery entrance into the area which was once the heart of Moscow's Ukrainian

The Best of Classic Russian Cuisine...

Prepared by former Kremlin chefs, with accompaniment from high-class musicians and club performers, gives the **AROMAT** Restaurant its very special flavour. With a wide choice of fish and vegetarian dishes and special main courses as well as service from an experienced and professional staff, **AROMAT** is the ideal choice for intimate evening dining. Open 7 pm–4 am.

AROMAT,
Ulitsa Rogova 12, building 2.
Metro Shchukinskaya.
Tel.: (095) 947-2645; fax: 947-0024.

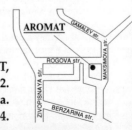

community. The street's name comes from *khokhly*, the tufts of hair Cossacks wore on their shaven heads; the word has been preserved to the present day as a slang term used by some Russians for Ukrainians.

Mazeppa's Chambers
(Palaty Mazeppy)
A few yards up Kolpachny Pereulok, the first left turn, are the 17th-century chambers of **Ivan Mazeppa**, a maverick Ukrainian *hetman* (chief) and contemporary of Peter the Great, whose wiliness and shallow loyalties made for an exciting life, but eventually led to his downfall. An arch-plotter, he turned against Peter during the 1708 war against Sweden and after the Russian victory at the battle of Poltava was forced to flee to Turkey.

Podkopayevsky Pereulok
Turn down Podkopayevsky Pereulok, the next right from Khokhlovsky. About half way down is a large red-brick manor house, the former summer residence of "Time of Troubles" Tsar **Vassily Shuisky**. When his brief and bloody reign ended in 1610, his wife Maria became the first prisoner of nearby St. John's Convent.

The newly restored and functioning **St. Nicholas Church** (*Tserkov' Nikoly*) at the bottom provided this street with its name, which comes from the Russian word *podkopatsya*, meaning "to dig under". More than 500 years ago robbers tunnelled into the then-wooden church on this site. Taking the metal mounting from an icon and valuables from the altar, they made their escape, but not before one had been killed by the collapsing tunnel – the Almighty was on hand to punish them after all.

Ploshchad Gorkovo
Turning left from Podkopayevsky into Podkolokolny Pereulok you soon emerge onto this rather bland square. There is little left which betrays its former notoriety as one of Moscow's steamier quarters, known then as the Khitrovo Market.

In the last century, it attracted the dregs of society, with ex-convicts, robbers and fallen aristocrats gathering here. Parents turned their children out on the streets to beg, and girls became prostitutes from an early age. Every category of scoundrel had their own special inn here and slept in hostels of varying degrees of seediness and filth.

The slums and taverns of Khitrovo provided inspiration to **Maxim Gorky** for his famous play and Moscow Arts Theatre hit *The Lower Depths*. Needless to say, the area was cleaned up in the 1930's by Stalin.

Petropavlovsky Pereulok
Bear left into Petropavlovsky, another lane named after the church situated on it. **SS. Peter and Paul Church**, built in 1700, is a typical example of late Baroque and has a number of famous icons, many taken from St. John's Convent.

If you don't make a habit of going inside churches, this one should be an exception – it never closed during the Soviet era and is one of the most radiant of Moscow's smaller churches.

Central Moscow | Myasnitskaya

165

The Silversmiths' Guild

Turn right into Yauzsky Bulvar, the southern end of the Boulevard Ring, and left onto Yauzskaya Ulitsa. The beautiful turquoise baroque bell-tower in front of you is part of the ensemble of the ✝ **Trinity Church in Serebryaniki** (of the Silversmiths).

This area was once home to the guild which minted coins and made icon frames for the Tsar. Strangely, the bell-tower's ground floor is used for services today while the church proper remains padlocked.

Ulitsa Solyanka

For more information about the busy road and river junction you have now reached and descriptions of more sights beyond the Yauza River, *see* Walk 11. Otherwise walk or take a trolleybus back to Metro Kitai Gorod along this busy street.

The name Solyanka derives from the Tsar's Salt Court, a place for processing and selling the mineral, situated where house No. 1 now stands. The most striking landmark is at No. 14, a classic example of the post-1812 Moscow Empire style built by Domenico Gilliardi. It became the Court of Wards, a charity which raised funds for orphans and the elderly by means of gambling and money lending. It is now the Academy of Medical Science.

Café Khinkalnya

On the corner of Ulitsa Solyanka and Solyansky Proyezd is Café Khinkalnya, Moscow's best snack bar selling Georgian food. If you can bear a stand-up table and the rather chaotic serving style, you can expect a tasty and filling meal for very low prices.

✝ Church of All Saints in Kulishki

(Tserkov' Vsyekh Svyatykh v Kulishkakh)

As you arrive at Metro Kitai Gorod, look out for the little 14th-century Church of All Saints in Kulishki on your left: the name *kulishki* refers to the ground on which the church was built, a burial place for the fallen from the battle of Kulikovo Field, Muscovite Prince Dmitry Donskoy's great victory against the Tatars.

Slavyanskaya Ploshchad

The non-descript new name of this square (meaning "slavic") says nothing about its past. In Soviet times it was named after leading communist Viktor Nogin, and before the Revolution was Varvarskaya Ploshchad, site of the Gates of St. Barbara. On these gates hung the miracle-working icon of the Virgin of Bogolyubovo, cause of a tragedy in the 18th century.

In 1771, the year of plague, the icon was taken down from its mounting and made accessible to the crowds. As it was the custom to kiss the icon, the epidemic naturally worsened, and Moscow's enlightened Archbishop Amvrosy had it removed again. For his pains he was followed by an angry mob to the Don Monastery and murdered.

The Gates themselves were pulled down in 1930, a victim of Stalin's grand reconstruction plans.

= JUSTUS =

For expertise in legal and consulting services in Moscow, it pays to come to the experts. With an experienced staff of lawyers, economists and accountants, JUSTUS offers specialist advice in a broad range of fields, including:

Public Relations
Including coordination of advertising campaigns, pricing and marketing of goods

Management Consultancy
Selection of business partners, within Russia and abroad, analysis and management planning

Legislation and Taxation Advice
Preparation of documents to meet anti–trust law requirements, as well as full legal services for your company

Standardization
Preparation of documents for rapid receipt of quality certificates, plus examination of goods and adaptation of any product to the market

Ecology
Services and experience in the field of ecology, from examinations to preparation of documents

For a fuller idea of how we can help you meet your legal and business needs in Russia, contact JUSTUS at:

**Suite 3020, Mayor's Office Building
New Arbat Street 36, Moscow**

**Tel.: (095) 290-8923
Fax: (095) 290-8463**

10. The Foreigners' Settlement, Nobles' Estates & Three Railway Stations

1. Lefort's Palace
2. Military Hospital
3. German Cemetery
4. Tank Academy
5. Resurrection Church
6. Old Believers' Church
7. Physical Education Institute
8. Epiphany Cathedral

This walk visits the relics of Moscow's former foreign community, some elegant out-of-town estates of the nobility, as well as two of Moscow's most colourful and lively squares, *Razgulyai* and *Tryokhvokzalnaya* (Three-Station).

The "German Suburb" (*Nemetskaya Sloboda*) was a colony of about 30,000 foreigners moved here by Tsar Alexey Mikhailovich in the 17th century in one of many attempts in Russian history to keep an eye on the activities of non-Russians. One of the initiators of the resettlement was the Russian Orthodox church, which feared the "contamination" of Russians by "godless" Catholics, Anglicans and Lutherans.

This walk is lengthy, so some parts are optional, and where applicable connecting public transport routes are given.

STARTS FROM: Metro Baumanskaya
ENDS AT: Metro Komsomolskaya

Baumanskaya Ulitsa

This is one of the busier areas of the former "German Suburb". Emerging from the metro, you see a street which is in its way picturesque but bears little resemblance to the original foreign quarter, despite the large-scale recreation map on a nearby wall.

When restrictions on the movement of foreigners were lifted, some residents (by now predominantly German, unlike the original settlers, who were mainly British) remained here into this century, occupying the apartment blocks which now line the street.

Nemetskaya Sloboda Restaurant

Situated at No. 23, this restaurant claims to revive the traditions of the taverns of the foreign community. You might expect European

cuisine here, but the food is as Russian as in any ordinary *traktir*. Prices are average for Moscow.

Open noon–11 pm. Tel: 267-4476. Cash only.

The House of Anna Mons

To get a glimpse of the older quarter, turn left down Baumanskaya Ulitsa and left again down Starokirochny Pereulok (Old Kirche Lane), immediately after the market (Basmanny Rynok). At No. 6 is a small yellow mansion with a pillared facade, the house of Anna Mons, who was Peter the Great's German mistress for 12 years and one of the many reasons for the Tsar's frequent visits to the quarter.

Lefort's Palace
(Lefortovsky Dvorets)
As you reach the end of Starokirochny Pereulok you will see to your right the rather grim-looking main entrance to Lefort's Palace. It was built at the very end of the 17th century for the former Swiss mercenary Francis Lefort, close friend of Peter the Great.

The palace became a scene of wild parties which united the foreign community and the Tsar's entourage – in many ways, virtually a royal residence. It had some peculiar customs, such as the rule that visitors had to stay at least 72 hours, and was an island of Western fashion: men shaved and wore powdered wigs, habits that must have shocked Peter's conservative critics.

Lefort died of drink soon after the palace was built and it eventually passed to Alexander Menshikov. Following several reconstructions, and damage in the 1812 fire, it acquired its current sober appearance, and now houses Russia's military archives, which contain documents relating to every conceivable campaign from Peter's wars against the Turks to recent events in Chechnya. Its doors are firmly closed to the public, but you might be able to get a glimpse of the inner courtyard from the entrance gate.

Count Bestuzhev's Palace
The German quarter stretched along both sides of

the Yauza River. If you cross to the far side, there's much worth seeing, although this part requires a lot of walking. For those with less time or energy, turn right down Vtoraya (2nd) Baumanskaya Ulitsa past Lefort's Palace to rejoin the walk at Lefort's Bridge (see page 172).

On the way you will pass the Bauman Technical Institute, another severe-looking palace, its bland facade broken only by occasional two-columned loggia and a central sculpture by Ivan Vitali portraying the triumph of reason and enlightenment. Its original owner, Count Bestuzhev-Riumin, was an 18th-century Russian equivalent of Bismarck who masterminded foreign policy for most of the century, particularly during the reign of Elizabeth, when his relationship with the monarchy was most intimate.

The palace only assumed its current appearance later, though, under the influence of the Russified Italian architect **Giacomo Quarenghi**, one of the masterminds of classical St. Petersburg. His finest contribution here is the back facade, adorned by a beautiful rotunda.

Across the Yauza: Detour

From the end of Starokirochny Pereulok, take the

second left turn down Malaya Pochtovaya Ulitsa and right down Gospitalny Pereulok, through what may be one of the most unpleasant and chaotic of the many building sites in inner Moscow.

 Crossing the river, you come upon the reason for the street's name: Russian Military Hospital No. 1 occupies a fine classical structure built by Ivan Yegotov, pupil of Matvey Kazakov, on the site of a hospital first commissioned by Peter the Great.

Cemetery of the Presentation of the Virgin

(Vvedenskoye Kladbishche)
Follow Gospitalnaya Ulitsa up to the square, fronted by the main hospital entrance, and take any tram one stop north (i.e. left past the facade of the hospital) to this cemetery.

Despite its Russian name and Orthodox appearance, much of this cemetery is occupied by the graves of foreigners, who are still buried here in tangible evidence of the German quarter.

Wandering down the main pathway is a peaceful experience, bringing many German, French and Italian graves into view. Some are Russified, some not, including one of a Victorian English family – John and Mary Pickersgill of Howgrave in the County of York.

At the central crossroads of the cemetery, the white chapel with a blue dome is dedicated to the Erlanger family, Germans who converted to Orthodoxy. Shortly afterwards, another smaller pathway leads off to the right to an obelisk in the distance. This is a monument to fallen French soldiers from the 1812 war.

Ironically, foes are juxtaposed with allies – nearby is a memorial to fallen French pilots of the Normandy-Niemen squadron who fought the Nazis on the Eastern front, among them Maurice de Sein, posthumously made a Hero of the Soviet Union.

† SS. Peter and Paul Church

(Petropavlovskaya Tserkov')
Returning two stops by tram to Gospitalnaya Ulitsa, this bright 1711 church, built for the soldiers of Lefort's regiment, stands on your left. It's worth a look inside for the beautiful 18th century iconostasis and several individual icons, such as a copy of the Pochayev Virgin on the left of the altar.

This madonna and child has a European flavour – both are wearing crowns. The original is at the Pochayev Lavra in Western Ukraine. On the right side is the figure of St. Nicholas, encased, except for the face and hands, in a gold cover. The crosses above it are believed to be in memory of fallen soldiers.

Catherine the Great's Palace

Turn right along Krasnokursantsky Proyezd, to approach the huge red palace, built for Catherine the Great by Giacomo Quarenghi and Domenico Gilliardi over a period of 25 years. Architecturally, this was probably a case of too many cooks spoiling the broth, and the result is a heavy and staid facade.

Catherine, at any rate, refused to live there and her son, Paul, turned it into a barracks. Now, perhaps appropriately, it's Russia's Malinovsky Tank Academy, which doubles as an occasional venue for rock concerts. The 16 giant grey ornamental Corinthian columns, though, are a work of art in themselves.

Lefort's Garden
(Lefortovsky Sad)
The garden behind the palace is much older, dating from the time of Peter the Great, who also had a palace on this site. Once endowed with romantic cascades and bridges, it remains a pleasant riverside park, and is reached from Krasnokazarmennaya Ulitsa, the next right turn, which leads back to the Yauza River.

Lefort's Bridge
(Lefortovsky Most)
This is the oldest surviving river bridge in Moscow, and the first stone bridge over the Yauza; Lefort's Bridge was built in 1781 to give access to Catherine's palace.

Church of the Resurrection in the Pea Fields
(Tserkov' Voskresenya v Gorokhovom Polye)
Take the #24 trolleybus three stops from outside Lefort's Garden (two stops if you didn't cross the river), and continue on foot up Ulitsa Radio to the large round-domed church at the top of the hill.

The Church of the Resurrection is the only work of Matvey Kazakov on this street, which takes his name. The church once stood in a vegetable patch (hence its name, *gorokhovoye polye*, the pea fields), owned by nobles from the nearby estates. At the time, this area was completely outside the city.

Old Believers' Church
Take a brief detour to the right down Tokmakov Pereulok to see one of Moscow's more extraordinary, and forgotten, churches, hidden behind residential blocks on the right side of the road. Built in 1914 by the architect I. Ye. Bondarenko, the Old Believers' Church was one of Russia's last art nouveau buildings, with exterior wall paintings and a triangular roof raised on four pillars above the church itself.

It was used by the Pomorye sect from Northern Russia, who had no priests or altars, and whose icons were displayed, contrary to Orthodox canons, facing in all directions around their churches. After years as a factory, the church was recently returned to the sect, but because of the poor public transport they still prefer to worship at Preobrazhenskaya Ploshchad (*see* Greater Moscow, "Moscow Icons").

The Razumovsky Palace
(Dvorets Razumovskogo)
Return to Ulitsa Kazakova, and head for the Razumovsky Palace, one of the local country estates, now occupied by the

Institute of Physical Education.

It was built in 1803 for one of Russia's foremost 18th-century families by **Nikolay Lvov**, an architect more closely associated with St. Petersburg than with Moscow. This shows in the palace itself, which seems unusually grand for the latter city. Note the magnificent columned entrance, and the extensive wings, a feature created later by Empire style architect Afanasy Grigoriev.

The Demidov Mansion
(Usad'ba Demidova)
Take the next right from Ulitsa Kazakova and turn left onto Gorokhovsky Pereulok. On the left is another out-of-town mansion, built by Kazakov for industrialist Count Nikita Demidov, grandson of a Tula gunsmith who so impressed Peter the Great with his craftsmanship that he was made a factory owner.

The building's current status as an engineering institute makes it comparatively accessible. You should be able to walk in and visit the Golden Rooms, drawing rooms with exquisite gold carvings on panels, doors and mirrors, and flowery ceiling and wall paintings, typical of pre-1812 Moscow interiors – and, therefore, quite rare.

Staraya Basmannaya Ulitsa
Leaving the Demidov Mansion, turn right onto Staraya Basmannaya. Originally named after the Bakers' Guild, which provided *basman* bread for the Tsar, Staraya Basmannaya

became a favourite residential area for nobles in the time of Catherine the Great. It is dominated by two churches, with the bright blue Epiphany Cathedral visible at its far end.

Where you should now be standing is the **Church of St. Nikita the Martyr** *(Tserkov' Nikity Muchenika)*, an enormous and rotund Baroque church built by the architect Prince **Dmitry Ukhtomsky** (1719-75), teacher of Bazhenov and Kazakov among others.

The House of Muravyov-Apostol
The attractive house at No. 23 is currently undergoing a major overhaul and may not be properly visible for some years. Still, through the scaffolding you may spot the bas-reliefs on either side of the portico. The house belonged to Ivan Muravyov-Apostol, Catherine the Great's education minister.

Its most recent function, however, was as Museum of the **Decembrist Uprising**, commemorating the revolt by progressive guards officers in December 1825 which aimed to establish a constitutional monarchy in Russia. Muravyov-Apostol's three sons were all involved in the rebellion; one was hanged, one committed suicide and the third was exiled in its aftermath.

House of Vassily Pushkin
Further down on the right at No. 36 is the wooden classical house of Alexander Pushkin's uncle, Vassily. Pushkin himself was a frequent visitor, and it was here

that he became acquainted with Moscow literary society.

Count Musin-Pushkin's Mansion
(Usad'ba Grafa Musina-Pushkina)
Next door is Kazakov's mansion of Count Musin-Pushkin (no relation of the poet), a cultured historian of the Catherine years, best known for his discovery of the original manuscript of *The Lay of Igor's Host*, a medieval tale of the heroic but reckless deeds of a Russian prince.

Ploshchad Razgulyai
This square was once the centre of Moscow's drunken nightlife (*razgulyai* means "have a good time"), and its rowdy patrons must have caused many a headache for the good Count Musin-Pushkin. In recent years, feeble attempts have been made to resurrect that atmosphere.

One restraining factor, however, is the large domed
✝ Epiphany Cathedral
(Yelokhovsky Sobor) which stands in the centre of the square; its official title is the *Bogoyavlensky Sobor*.

Built in the middle of the last century, it became the seat of the Russian Patriarch in 1943, when World War II put the Orthodox Church back in favour, and it remained so until the restoration of St. Daniel's Monastery in 1988.

It is still an important holy place for Russians, and the Patriarch often conducts services here on important occasions here. The interior is a magnificent whole, though none of the icons,

paintings or other features is of particular value or note.

Other buildings on the square are neat and well-preserved, and its tranquillity provides some relief from the heavy traffic nearby. They are a curious mixture: a "Private People's College" attached to the church, a library named after Pushkin, and the pre-revolutionary offices of a society of evangelists from Volgograd. In the central garden is a statue of Nikolay Bauman, a hero and victim of the 1905 revolution.

Razgulyai Restaurant
Finding decent refreshment here nowadays isn't as easy as it once was, but if you come during the day, you should have no trouble getting into this small restaurant. Razgulyai was one of the first of perestroika's cooperative restaurants to open in Moscow.

Rather than bask in its fame, however, and charge extortionately as many such places now do, it has very reasonable prices. You can choose to dine in one of three halls, decorated with traditional patterns from Gzhel porcelain, Khokhloma varnished wood or Palekh lacquer boxes.
☛ *Open noon–11 pm. Tel: 267-7613. CC.*

Three-Station Square
(Tryokhvokzalnaya Ploshchad)
Take a #22 trolleybus from beside the Epiphany Cathedral to its final stop, and head towards the rail bridge leading into this very large and crowded square. Three varied turn-of-the-century stations, with trains

departing to destinations as far away as Helsinki and Peking, stand alongside several Soviet-era buildings.

Leningradskaya Hotel, Casino Moscow

The wedding cake building that dominates the entire scene is the indifferent Hotel Leningradskaya. On its premises is Casino Moscow, one of Moscow's first, most popular and reputable casinos, run by a Scottish businessman and pillar of the Moscow foreign community who goes by the name of "Jacko".

A small but characterful bar here is extra reason to visit, if you're looking for a taste of Moscow's gambling scene.

☞ *Casino 2 pm–5 am, bar 6 pm–5 am. Tel: 975-1967. Major CC.*

Kazan Station

(Kazansky Vokzal)
Entering the square under the railway bridge from the Leningradskaya Hotel side, the rich and complex struct-ure on your right is disting-uished by its evocation of early Russian style. It was built by the versatile **Alexey Shchusev**, one of the few architects whose fame spanned the pre- and post-revolutionary periods (as, in fact, did the construction of the station, 1912-26).

The tower in the form of a stepped pyramid atop the entrance is a copy of the Suyumbeka Tower in Kazan, named after a 17th-century Tatar princess, who ordered that it be erected at night so as not to be visible to her. (The result was a leaning tower, though its list was not repeated on this replica). The fortress-like building to the left of the station, part of the ensemble, is the Railway-Workers' Culture House.

Yaroslavl Station

(Yaroslavsky Vokzal)
The most impressive building opposite is Fyodor Shekhtel's magnificent Yaroslavl Station, which offers a fantastical start to any journey on the Trans-Siberian Railway.

Built at the height of the architect's career in 1902–04, it fuses Art Nouveau with motifs from the wooden architecture of the Russian north. The majolica panels on the walls are also by Shekhtel. The main hall and ticket office contain panels showing scenes from the life of northern peoples.

Adjoining it is the dull, neo-classical Leningrad Station, notable only for the fact that the terminus in St. Petersburg is identical to it. The Metro station which serves them both, Komsomolskaya, is one of the most fascinating on the Metro system (*see* Walk 12).

A Word of Warning

This square is a place of transit for hundreds of thou-sands of people a day. Most do not dwell here for more than a few minutes if they can possibly help it: Russian railway stations nowadays have a reputation for attract-ing the worst elements of society and have a high crime rate. So it's advisable to appreciate the square's attractions in company, and then to depart promptly by metro.

Central Moscow | The Foreigners' Settlement

11. Across the Yauza

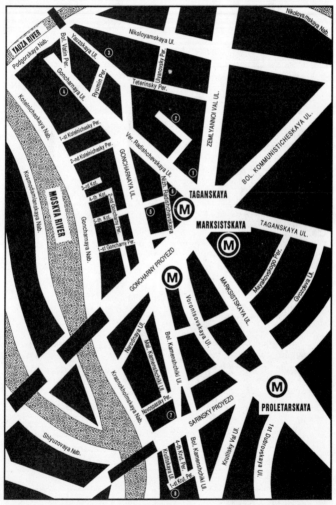

1. Taganka Theatre
2. Vysotsky Museum
3. Yauza Hospital
4. St. Nikita's Church
5. Assumption Church in Gonchary
6. St. Nicholas in Bolvanovka
7. New Monastery of the Saviour
8. Krutitsy Mission

A walk beyond the Yauza River into a quiet, hilly part of the city, originally home of some of Moscow's former artisan guilds, or *slobody*, and a centre of metal-working and ceramics in the 16th century. The guilds were placed on the far side of the river to prevent the spread of fires, a common occurrence in the guilds in other parts of the city.

Beyond the Garden Ring, which passes under Taganskaya Ploshchad, the scenery changes dramatically: most older settlements have been obliterated, but its grim modern roads are still relieved by two fine church ensembles – the New Saviour Monastery and the Orthodox Church residence at Krutitsy.

STARTS FROM: Metro Taganskaya
ENDS AT: Metro Proletarskaya

😀 Taganka Theatre

Exit the metro from the Circle Line station to emerge on the northwest side of Taganskaya Ploshchad. On the corner opposite is the red brick building of the Taganka Theatre. Its new stage, the foundation of its reputation, opened in 1964.

During the "stagnation years" of the 1970's and early 1980's, the Taganka stood out as one of the main centres of cultural opposition. Most of the credit for this goes to **Yuri Lyubimov**, its brave and talented director, and to actor and gravelly-voiced bard **Vladimir Vysotsky** who died in 1980. Vysotsky's biting social commentary struck chords in the hearts of his countrymen: a statue of him in his most famous role, Hamlet, stands in the tranquil inner courtyard of the theatre.

More recent history, however, has been far from tranquil, in a way all too typical of the conflicts which have destroyed similar institutions. After Lyubimov's return from exile in 1987, a bitter struggle for ownership and use of the theatre has brewed between the director and opponents, headed by his one-time ally Nikolai Gubenko, with the company now divided into two factions.

While Lyubimov's repertoire performs on the Old Stage, Gubenko now leads a new company who have control of the Taganka's New Stage; their first three productions there have been competent, but lacking the spirit of the original.

СОДРУЖЕСТВО АКТЕРОВ ТАГАНКИ

Vysotsky Museum

To the left of the Theatre a small lane, Nizhny Tagansky Tupik, takes you round to this small museum dedicated to the memory of actor, poet and bard Vladimir Vysotsky; it opened in July 1992 on the 12th anniversary of his death.

Enter the courtyard of No. 3, a somewhat seedy and semi-derelict block of communal flats, and circum-navigate a courtyard for some reason strewn with rusty barbed wire and aban-doned military hardware to enter through its left entrance. The museum is in Flat 2, a tiny simple room which communicates, despite its meagre exhibits, the devotion of millions of Russians.

☛ *Open Mon, Weds, Thurs, Fri, 2–6 pm. Tel: 915-7578.*

Diner 24

Just beyond the theatre on the approach road leading up from the Garden Ring is a Moscow novelty which deserves further investiga-tion, a diner which claims to be American. In fact, the chef is American, the restaurant itself under Russo-German ownership, and the decor tasteful. You should be able to have a relaxed meal here, and you can expect to be well fed for under $25 per person.

☛ *Open 24 hours. Tel: 915-3248. Cash only.*

Taganskaya Ulitsa

Returning to your starting point, walk past the Taganka Theatre entrance away from the metro along this street, once the site of the Tripod-makers' Guild.

This area of the city (*Zayauzye*, meaning "beyond the Yauza") was occupied by producers' cooperatives, which differed from guilds like the Silversmiths' (*see Walk 9*) in that they were economically independent of the Tsar's court, and had, until the mid-18th century, some political autonomy.

The great 18th-century Russian thinker **Alexander Radishchev** (1749–1802) lived on this street, and in Soviet times it was named after him. In 1790 Radishchev wrote his famous work, *A Journey from St. Petersburg to Moscow*, travel notes which described the lamentable plight of the lower echelons of society. For this he was exiled, and the book was published only in 1905. A bust of the writer stands in a small square on the left of the street, 100 metres away.

Batashov Palace

(Dvorets Batashova)

Descending the hill towards the river, you pass the front gates of this sumptuous classical mansion, now Hospital No. 23 or the Yauza Hospital. They are guarded by two very curious black lions with flattened faces – which, unlike most other such animal sculptures in Moscow, are smiling.

The palace was built in 1798 following a design by Rodion Kazakov (a talented architect of the day, often confused with the great Matvey), for the iron foundry owner Ivan Batashov. Their family history was a dark one; his brother Andrei, the original manager of the foundries, was a homicidal

Nightclubbing Highlights!

CLUB MOSKOVSKII

К Л У Б

МОСКОВСКИЙ

In the heart of Moscow on Tverskaya Street, Club Moskovskii offers stylish entertainment in an elegant interior combined with the highest standards of service. As well as its discotheque, casino and acclaimed restaurant-bar with European cuisine, Moskovskii has regular weekend special guest appearances by stars of Russian and foreign rock.

Club Moskovskii is open every day from noon–8 pm and 10 pm–6 am. Guarded parking. Ulitsa Tverskaya 6, close to Metro Okhotny Ryad. Tel.: 292-1282.

CLUB TITANIK

Titanik's three decks and large dance floor with room for 1,000 guests, all decorated in the original style of the ocean liner, have already made it a favourite in Moscow's style and music circles. The state-of-the-art club has a 16 kilowatt Turbosound system, with outstanding lighting, lasers and special effects. A second room offers a quieter meeting place, with restaurant, casino and billiards.

Club Titanik is open Thursday-Sunday, 10 pm–6 am, entrance $15. Leningradsky Prospekt 31 (in the Young Pioneers Stadium). Metro Dinamo. Tel.: 213-4581, 213-6182.

КЛУБ

·ТИТАНИК·

maniac who bribed investigators generously to keep them away from the piles of bones in his cellar.

After his brother's death, Ivan took over the foundries, improved conditions and compensated the families of the deceased, for which actions he received the Order of St. Vladimir. The palace, later bought by the Golitsyn family, is marvellous, both as a whole and in its details.

Library of Foreign Literature

(Inostranka)

As you descend further, the modern complex on your right before the embankment is one of Moscow's largest libraries; it houses the city's collection of foreign literature, three million books in 127 languages.

Following a major overhaul in recent years, it now accommodates, as well, the offices and resource centre of the British Council, the French Cultural Centre and the United States Information Service (USIS) library.

A few hundred metres along the Yauza embankment from here is a classic example of recent tendencies in Moscow's social life. When it opened a few years ago, the nearby Union Café (adjoining the Union supermarket) was a brave new venture, a chaotic westernised student-style café of a kind which Moscow had sorely lacked.

Today, the decor and menu are still the same, but the clientele is a far cry from the early days: expect to find yourself in the company of plump, middle-aged, middle-income mafiosi.

Yauza River

The Astakhovsky Bridge leads to the turquoise church and bell-tower across the Yauza River. In the 1812 war against Napoleon, this bridge was the scene of an argument between the Russian commander, Marshal **Kutuzov** and Moscow's governor, Count Rostopchin. Kutuzov wanted to evacuate and burn the city, while Rostopchin hoped to defend it. Kutuzov won, and history proved him right: the exhausted French army entered Moscow but, unable to recover its strength, was shortly forced into retreat.

The waterway beneath has had a chequered history. Beginning as a trade route to the Volga in the 14th century, it declined during the next 400 years, gradually deteriorating into a rubbish dump. It was reclaimed for a time during the early-19th century, but the onset of the industrial revolution finally rendered it a grimy wasteland, "emblazoned by factory waste in all colours of the rainbow", in the words of a 1917 city guidebook. Little has changed to this day.

Illuzion Cinema, Stalin Skyscraper

On the left is a huge 1950's building, one of Stalin's so-called "wedding cakes". This one is partly occupied on the ground floor by the Illuzion Cinema, one of the few repertory cinemas in Moscow, showing regular programmes of old films, both Soviet and foreign.

The rest of the building is given over to luxury apartments. Taking a detour around to the Moskva River side (the confluence is just a few hundred metres away), you can peek inside to admire hallways and lifts which are as grandly beautiful today as when they were built.

Sewing Hill
(Ushivaya Gorka)
From the Illuzion, turn back up the hill along the tiny Bolshoy Vatin Pereulok. This brings you to the Church of St. Nikita-Beyond-the-Yauza *(Tserkov' Nikity za Yauzy)*, also known as Nikita-on-Sewing-Hill *(Na-Ushivoy-Gorke)*, believed to be on the site of the Tailor's Guild. The Russian name for this hill, however, was later corrupted to *vshivaya*, meaning lousey – appropriately enough, since this became a pauper's district.

✝ The little pillarless church is supposedly 17th-century, although there are indications that it stood here as early as the 1470's, the period of Alevisio's work in Moscow. Now associated with the Russian monastery on Mount Athos in Greece, it promises, when restored, to become a genuine beauty spot, with excellent views of the Moskva River and the south bank.

Goncharnaya Ulitsa
Continue along the hilltop on this quiet street, the centre of the Potter's Guild *(Goncharnaya Sloboda)*. Ahead of you at No. 12 stands the mansion of Count Bezborodko, foreign minister during the reigns of Catherine the Great and Tsar Paul, who had the dubious distinction of organising one of the many partitions of

Poland. Built originally by Matvey Kazakov, it suffered greatly from 1930's and 1990's "restorations".

✝ Assumption Church in Gonchary
(Tserkov' Uspeniya v Goncharakh)
Continuing past some 1930's buildings on the right-hand side, you arrive at this festive church ahead on the left; it is a living reminder of one of the specialities of the Potter's Guild. Here, and in fact all over Moscow, the coloured tiles that were the hallmark of local craftsman **Stepan Polubes** are in evidence: decorated with fruit and flower patterns, they run around the drums below the church cupolas and frame the icon on the wall outside.

The church itself, built in 1654, is a pillarless structure with five domes typical of the pre-Baroque era, its red, white, green, blue and gold standing out starkly in an area which has lost most of its historical churches. It is now the headquarters of the Bulgarian Orthodox Church in Moscow.

✝ Church of St. Nicholas in Bolvanovka
(Tserkov' Nikoly v Bolvanovke)
Turn left onto Uspensky Pereulok and head for the slender early-18th century Church of St. Nicholas in Bolvanovka. There is some disagreement over which particular guild was here – either hat-form makers or makers of metal moulds. There is no obvious connection with the main meaning of the word *bolvan*, a fool or blockhead.

American Bar and Grill

On Zemlyannoi Val, equidistant between Taganskaya and Kurskaya is Moscow's second American Bar and Grill (the first is at Metro Mayakovskaya, *see* Walk 3).

The menu is much the same, but two floors here make for a feeling of greater space, while an outdoor terrace gives a welcome escape from summer heat.
☛ *Open 24 hours. Tel: 912-3615. CC.*

Holsten Bistro

Return to Taganskaya Ploshchad by turning right at the church, and you'll come across this little café which provides a good opportunity for a snack or coffee break. The choice of southern European salads and sandwiches is surprisingly good and prices lower than you might expect.
☛ *Open 10 am–10 pm.*

Mercator Club

The Slovenian-run Mercator Club is a German *bierkeller*-style restaurant set in the premises of the Moscow Commercial Club on Bol. Kommunisticheskaya Ulitsa, which leads off Taganskaya Ploshchad.

In summer, the building's elegant courtyard becomes one of Moscow's most inviting *alfresco* restaurants. With its tables shaded by huge umbrellas set next to a central fountain, the noise of the neighbouring streets is a world away. Fish is a speciality, as is the list of Slovenian wines. A full meal should cost $40-$50.
☛ *Open noon–11:30 pm. Tel: 272-3908. CC.*

Bolshiye Kamenshchiki

There is something end-of-the-worldish about Taganskaya Ploshchad: the older city buildings on its west side suddenly give way to vast expanses of roads and unfriendly tower blocks, while the rumbling of the Garden Ring Road underneath supplies a steady stream of noise.

Hints of the Stonemasons' Guild, after which this now ultra-modern street is named, can be summoned only by the most fertile imagination. Try not to think about your new surroundings and skirt round the right side of the square, keeping on the right side of Bolshiye Kamenshchiki, which leads towards the top of the bell-tower peeping over one of the blocks in front of you, about ten minutes walk away.

The New Monastery of the Saviour

(Novospassky Monastyr')
This immense monastery-fortress which confronts you is part of the defensive system which guarded Moscow's southern approaches from Tatar raids

(see Greater Moscow, the Don, St. Daniel's and Novodevichy Monasteries).

Originally situated in the Kremlin, it was removed by Ivan III during Kremlin rebuilding to be established as a super-fortress down-river. In 1613, when the first Romanov **Tsar Mikhail** came to the throne, he made it a burial place for his relatives.

✝️ ◾ **Transfiguration Cathedral**
(Preobrazhensky Sobor)
Turning inside the gate, you are confronted by the Transfiguration Cathedral; in 1649 Tsar Mikhail's son, Tsar Alexey, built it as an imitation of the Kremlin's Assumption Cathedral, over the family tombs. The result is a lofty, richly decorated church, now functioning again.

The frescoes here, paying tribute to the holiness, erudition and royalty of the young Romanov dynasty, are of particular interest. They include the family tree of their predecessors, the house of **Rurik**, starting from Prince Vladimir, who adopted Christianity for Rus', down to the last Tsar, Fyodor, at the top. Mikhail and Alexey both have their portraits here, behind the right choir, and the two dynasties are linked by a painting of St. Theodore and St. Michael, patron saints of the last Rurik and first Romanov. The fine iconostasis was a gift of Tsar Alexey.

✝️ ◾ The smaller **Church of the Sign** behind the cathedral was built 150 years later as a necropolis for the Cherkassky family, relatives of the Romanovs. Beside them, accorded unusual honours because of her marital status, lies Praskovia Zhemchugova-Kovalyova the serf actress and wife of Count Nikolay Sheremetyev, (*see* Greater Moscow, Kuskovo).

Krutitsy Mission
(Krutitskoye Podvorye)
Leaving the monastery, continue a few metres to the corner of the fortress and cross the main road just before the Moskva River bridge. The Moskva River Boat Cruises also visit here, the last stop on their down-

A leader among Moscow Tourism Agencies, Selective Ltd. can arrange the full range of services for foreign tourists and visitors, including:

• Visa support
• Accommodation in all classes of hotel in Moscow, St. Petersburg, Kiev and the cities of the Golden Ring.
• Organisation of tours by bus or car in Moscow, St. Petersburg, Kiev and the cities of the Golden Ring, with professional guides.
• Special all-inclusive tours for school groups.

Contact Selective Ltd. on tel., fax: (095) 326–8510, 329–6432.

stream route, docking on the embankment to the right of the bridge.

Opposite is a lane leading up to this ensemble, distinguished by the green cupolas and red brick of the Assumption Cathedral. The Krutitsy Mission was the residence of the Metropolitans of Moscow, heads of the Russian church while it remained subordinate to Byzantium, from the 13th to the 16th centuries, when they moved to the Kremlin. The mission then became a luxurious country residence, and most of the current buildings date from the late 17th century.

With its lavish decorations and complex architectural touches, it reflects perhaps better than anywhere else the period of enlightenment through which Russia was then passing. Since then, it has several times been saved from neglect and ruin, most recently by the Soviet restorer Pyotr Baranovsky, who worked on it in the post-war period. Currently housing the headquarters of the Orthodox Church's Youth Movement (VPMD), its buildings are once again in need of an overhaul.

✝ Assumption Cathedral
(Uspensky Sobor)

On the right as you approach the entrance is the Assumption Cathedral (the first gateway through which you pass is not the entrance to the ensemble, simply a modern addition). As is customary in such ensembles, this comprises two churches — the lower, heated church for winter use and the upper one for summer worship.

Briefly, when Polish troops occupied the Kremlin in 1612, this cathedral became Russia's main church: it was here that **Kozma Minin** and Prince **Dmitry Pozharsky** took their oath to drive out the Polish invaders.

▲ Terem

The gates themselves are the main attraction here, and especially the Terem, or chamber, above them whose facade is covered with an unbroken layer of ceramic tiles with patterns in relief, lending it a light and festive appearance.

Because of its strange concave shape, the ensemble is better viewed from outside than from inside. Beyond the gates is a courtyard, once the site of one of Moscow's first gardens. The buildings on the far side do not seem connected with the rest — they are part of an army barracks, which were joined to the Mission at the end of the 18th century.

Returning to the main road, take any tram one stop east (right) or walk 5–10 minutes to Metro Proletarskaya.

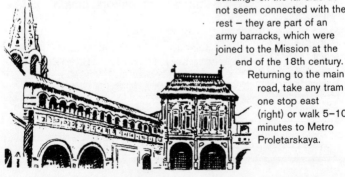

12. Exploring Moscow - By Metro and by Boat

More than just an underground railway, Moscow's Metro is renowned throughout the world for the beauty of its marble "palaces", perhaps the only genuinely positive architectural legacy of the Stalin era in the city.

As well as being far and away the easiest way of travelling around Moscow, the Metro is worth exploring for its own merits. You can either do this on the special Patriarchi Dom tour, or independently following our route.

Another way to see Moscow from another angle is to board one of the river boats which run up and down the Moskva River from May to October.

STARTS FROM: Metro Kropotkinskaya
ENDS AT: Metro Mendeleyevskaya.

History

The first proposals for construction of an underground railway system in Moscow were put forward by the City Duma in 1902; they were rejected as a result of fears of damage to the city's old buildings.

Such concerns had become less important by 1931 when construction started on the *Metropoliten imeni Lenina* (as it is still named and written) on Stalin's initiative. The first line opened in May 1935, and building has continued at a steady rate ever since; even recent economic crisis has not interrupted its progress, and plans exist to extend many lines still further.

When it comes to statistics, Moscow's Metro is impressive indeed. Eight million passengers travel on it daily, more than in London and New York together; 7,030 trains a day run between 150 stations over a length of 243.6 km. Everything is designed to facilitate a hyper-efficient service, though in recent years this has lost a little of its edge.

Trains run at intervals – as frequently as every minute during peak hours – which beat the systems of other capital cities hands-down. Stations are scrupulously scrubbed every night by armies of elderly women, and escalators are guarded by attendants in booths.

Most impressive, though, are the extravagantly conceived and executed stations, which reflect seven decades of Soviet architecture.

Practical Advice

One plastic *jeton* is enough to enter the Metro system, giving unlimited travel until you leave through the gates of another station. Either because of this, or because it is such a convenient point of orientation, many Muscovites use the Metro as a place for meetings, both business and informal; fixing exactly where to meet is accomplished through a complicated system of directions and points of orientation.

If you are looking to explore in a leisurely fashion, then steer clear of the morning and evening rush hours, which can be particularly frantic on the Circle Line; avoid the late evening too, although the Moscow Metro is safer than many in the West.

The Metro system operates from 5 am to about 1:30 am, although connecting elevators between lines stop at 1 am.

Sokolniki Line

(Sokolnicheskaya Linia)
The oldest line on the network, opened in May 1935 between Sokolniki and Park Kultury, linking two of the city's major recreational parks. It now extends south of the river to the University and the prestigious suburb of Yugo-Zapadnaya (the Russian word means "south-west").

The architecture of its central stations remains unsurpassed. Look out for the rich earthy colours in the vast and simple **Kropotkinskaya**, built by Alexey Dushkin (also architect of Mayakovskaya) whose cream-coloured marble columns are reminiscent of giant fantastic plants.

Take a train four stops north from Kropotkinskaya to **Chistiye Prudy** (formerly Kirovskaya), a station which had a vital wartime function. While many stations served as air raid shelters, Chistiye Prudy was the headquarters of the General Staff, where Stalin and Zhukov planned their campaigns against the invading Nazis.

Krasniye Vorota, the next stop, is probably the most architecturally successful of the early stations, with low granite pylons replacing the usual heavy columns, and a curious entrance in the shape of a scallop shell.

Cross to the **Circle Line** at the next stop, **Komsomolskaya**, a station unusual for its upper walk-through galleries. It also includes a majolica panel depicting metro-builders by Yevgeny Lansere.

Circle Line

(Koltsevaya Linia)
All 12 stations of this line were built in the 1950's. The idea was to reflect Moscow's street plan with a circle of intersecting radial lines. Situated beyond the Garden Ring road, the line also connects seven out of nine of Moscow's mainline railway stations.

Serving three major street-level termini, **Komsomolskaya** is the busiest station in the network. More than that, it is a glittering palace, which won a prize at the New York International Exposition in 1958.

Mosaics here are by Pavel Korin, one of the leading Soviet artists of the day, and reflect the most important historical events in Russia, from Alexander Nevsky's victory at Lake Peipus (Chudskoye) against the Teutons in 1242, through to May 1945. The overall design was by the highly versatile (and by then quite elderly) architect Alexey Shchusev, who based it on the trapezium of a 17th-century church in Rostov the Great.

Board a train in the anti-clockwise direction towards **Novoslobodskaya** (the second stop) to admire this station's stained glass panelling, also to a design by Pavel Korin. The arches resemble *kokoshniki*, one of the classic features of Russian church architecture.

The next station, **Belorusskaya**, features mosaics with scenes from everyday life in Belorussia, the destination of trains from the rail station above ground. Cross here to the **Radial** station.

However, you may want to take some more time to investigate other stations on this, the most ornate and colourful line. Among its highlights are the revolutionary mosaics at **Kievskaya**, and marble bas-reliefs of sport and recreation at **Park Kultury**.

Beyond-the-Moscow-River Line

(Zamoskvoretskaya Linia)
So-called because it serves the Zamoskvorechye area south of the Moskva River, this line began operation in 1938. It now connects southeastern suburbs with Leningradsky Prospekt, the main road leading to Sheremetyevo airport and St. Petersburg.

There are some interesting stations on the northern part of this line, notably **Sokol** with its unique double staircase. **Belorusskaya** radial station was one of the first on this line, built with rare pink marble and onyx from eastern Siberia.

The real masterpiece, Alexey Dushkin's **Mayakovskaya**, is one stop to the south. A prizewinner at the New York International Exposition in 1938, its columns are made of stainless steel and the semi-precious stone Orlets, frequently used by the Russian firm Fabergé for production of its jewellery.

The mosaics on the ceilings are copies of Alexander Deineka's socialist realist paintings. Thirty-three in number, they portray as a background the sky at different hours, progressing from day to night and back to day again. During World War II, Mayakovskaya was the headquarters of the Anti-Aircraft Defence Forces, and its extensive communications network enabled Stalin to address the nation from here.

Teatralnaya (formerly Ploshchad Sverdlova) was built in 1940, and is devoted to the art of the national republics of the Soviet Union. Costume designs on the ceiling come from a porcelain factory outside Moscow.

Cross here to the **Arbatsko-Pokrovskaya** (dark blue) line, and the intersection station Ploshchad Revolutsii.

Arbatsko-Pokrovskaya Line

Built in 1944 – construction continued throughout World War II – this line runs from the east at Shcholkovskaya (the city's main bus station), through Izmailovsky Park, ending at Kievskaya, junction with the circle line and Kiev Station. There are plans to extend it to Victory Park *(Poklonnaya Gora)* in the west.

Ploshchad Revolutsii is one of the most striking stations in Moscow, its archways guarded by lifesize bronze sculptures of Red Army soldiers and partisans, who give way at the station's other end to peacetime statues of sportsmen and families. Adjacent stations at **Kurskaya** and **Arbatskaya** are also devoted to war themes. From **Arbatskaya** cross to **Borovitskaya**.

Serpukhovskaya-Timiryazevskaya Line

Built mostly in the late 1980's, this ought to be called the "Perestroika Line". With greater intervals between trains and more frequent accidents, it seems to embody the problems faced by the Metro in economic crisis. It runs north to south, and connects new housing estates at either end.

Take a train north to **Chekhovskaya**, opened in 1988 and dedicated to the writer Anton Chekhov. Pictures at either end depict the writer himself and his Moscow memorial museum. Others, made from small pieces of marble, decorate the side walls, with cherry blossom from his famous orchard and scenes from his beloved Crimea. In the centre of the hall are metal stage curtains, lights and flowers.

The next station, **Tsvetnoi Bulvar**, is the stop for the Old Moscow Circus. A stained glass panel at the end depicts circus life, including a portrait of current circus director Yuri Nikulin. Here also is the latest in metro ventilation – the air in the station is changed every 15 minutes.

Next is **Mendeleyevskaya**, junction with Novoslobodskaya, named after the famous chemist Mendeleyev who created the periodic table. Hence the decorations of this station, resembling chemical bonds and molecules.

Other Lines:

Kaluzhskaya-Rizhskaya Line

This line began operation in 1958, and is now Moscow's longest. In fact, at various stages of its history, it has been the longest underground railway line in the world.

It also runs north to south, and its most interesting stations are on the original northern section, like **VDNKh**, serving the All-Russian Exhibition Centre, or **Rizhskaya**, for the Riga Station, its yellow colouring representing the amber found in the Baltic.

Filyovskaya (Fili) Line

The central section was built as a branch of the first 1935 line and is characterised by similarly spacious halls and deeply coloured marble.

The western extension to the government residential area at **Krylatskoye** is the Moscow metro's only substantial aboveground stretch.

Taganskaya-Krasnopresnenskaya Line

Beginning operation in 1966, this line was built almost entirely in Brezhnev's "stagnation era". This is reflected by the pompous, gaudy and sometimes even plain hideous appearance of some of its stations. It runs northwest to southeast.

The Metro Museum

To find out more about the technical aspects of operations on the Moscow Metro, visit this little museum, situated just up the stairs above the militia post at the southern exit of Metro Sportivnaya.

Its exhibits show everything you could want to know about the metro system – different kinds of equipment, past and present, signalling points, escalator models, reconstructions of a driver's cabin, ticket barriers, a model train and even the first ticket ever sold.
☛ *Open Mon 11 am–6 pm, Tues–Fri 9 am–4 pm.*
Tel: 222-7309.

Moscow by Boat

Riverboats cruise the Moskva River through the centre of the city between May and October. If you choose a fine day, it's a peaceful way of avoiding the crowded and noisy streets – as well as seeing a different view of Moscow.

DIRECTIONS: You can board the river boats at any stop. These are at Kievskaya (Metro Kievskaya), Leninskiye Gory (Metro Universitet), Frunzenskaya (Metro Frunzenskaya), Gorky Park (Metro Oktyabrskaya), Krymsky Most (Metro Park Kultury), Bolshoy Kamenny Most (Metro Biblioteka imeni Lenina, Borovitskaya), Ustinsky Most (Metro Kitai Gorod), or Novospassky Most (Metro Proletarskaya).

Cruises run approximately every half hour, with journey time from beginning to end about one and a half hours.

Kievskaya

Close to the centre as well as to a metro station, this is the best place to start a cruise. Nearby is the Kiev Station (*Kievsky Vokzal*), with trains to Ukraine and Southern Europe, built in 1917 by Ivan Rerborg and until recently the only rail station in the city with a Western-style roof over the platforms.

Next door, the **Radisson-Slavyanskaya Hotel**, built in the 1980's and subject of an ongoing feud between Russian and American joint-venture partners, is a centre of Moscow's business and social life.

Beside the pier is the Borodinsky Bridge, the oldest over the Moskva River in the city. It was built by Roman Klein in 1912 to mark the centenary of the Battle of Borodino – hence its military appearance.

As you begin the cruise, the Novodevichy Convent comes into view on your left. It was founded in 1524 by Grand Prince Vassily III as part of Moscow's southern fortifications against the Tatars. The walls visible today, however, are purely ornamental, and date from the end of the 17th century. Their builder, Regent Sophia, was later incarcerated in the convent by her brother, Tsar Peter the Great.

The two most prominent buildings are the Cathedral of the Virgin of Smolensk, built in 1525 in honour of the capture of that city, and Sophia's bell-tower, a slender six-tier structure in Naryshkin Baroque style. Unfortunately the convent is not easily accessible by riverboat (*see* Greater Moscow, Novodevichy).

Leninskiye Gory

Immediately in front of you is the enormous tree-covered expanse of the Sparrow Hills (formerly known as the Lenin Hills), a popular recreation area. In the distance rises the tower of the main University building (MGU), built by Lev Rudnev in 1953 as the crowning glory of the "wedding cake" series.

On the opposite (left) side from the pier the Luzhniki stadium complex covers the entire crook of land. The main stadium is the home of Moscow's Spartak sports club and has a capacity of 100,000. Outside it, an enormous market sells mainly cheap imported consumer goods.

Ahead is a road and metro bridge. The lower part used to be occupied by Leninskiye Gory metro station; it was closed a decade ago and seemingly broken up. The metro tracks were then diverted around the side of the bridge and covered with corrugated metal, giving rise to the ugly tangle of metal and concrete visible today.

The greenery on the right side continues as the Sparrow Hills converge with Gorky Park. The small cluster of churches here is St. Andrew's Monastery (*Andreyevsky Monastyr'*).

The main church of St. Andrew Stratilates was built after the victory against the Tatars in 1591, and the monastery founded later, in 1648. It soon became an educational centre, where monks translated Greek and Latin works into Slavonic and prepared them for publication at the Pechatny Dvor (*see* Walk 2).

Catherine the Great consigned the monastery to oblivion at the end of the 18th century, and its revival has started only recently, with restoration of the churches and transferral of the Patriarchate's Synodical library here from St. Daniel's.

Just behind the monastery, and visible for miles around, is the modern building of the Academy of Sciences, worth investigating for its strange sculptures and space-age gadgets. Both it and the monastery are inaccessible from the river, but can be reached in about 15 minutes on foot from Metro Leninsky Prospekt.

Frunzenskaya Naberezhnaya

This embankment (on the left) was mainly built in the 1930's and is named after Mikhail Frunze, a Civil War hero and military Commissar responsible for army reform in the 1920's.

On the opposite side of the river is the Restless Garden (*Neskuchny Sad*), the 18th-century estate of Prokofy Demidov, who built the Alexandra Palace and a number of outbuildings here.

The beautiful classical palace (not visible from the river) is now another part of the Academy of Sciences; the gardens, frequented at weekends by Tolkien enthusiasts reenacting battles from *The Lord of the Rings*, are an extension of Gorky Park and best reached from the next pier.

Gorky Park

The Krymsky Most bridge marks the place where the Crimean Tatars forded the Moskva River on their raids. Built in the 1930's, it is Moscow's only suspension bridge.

Beyond on the right is the Krymsky Val exhibition complex, housing the Central House of Artists and the New Tretyakov Gallery. The first houses some of the best of Moscow's temporary art exhibitions, the second contains the Tretyakov's post-1917 collection of Russian art (*see* Walk 6).

On the same side slightly further on is the President Hotel (formerly Oktyabrskaya), once used by the Communist Party Central Committee and now just another exclusive Moscow hotel.

Soon the river splits in two, with the Drainage (*Vodootvodny*) Canal (*see* Walk 7) going off to the right round Stone Island (*Kamenny Ostrov*). At this end of the island is the 19th-century red-brick Red October chocolate factory, set up by the German confectioner Friedrich von Einem in 1889 and since then enjoying a reputation as the country's best sweet producer (*see* Walk 7).

Next door is a pretty 17th-century ensemble in Russian Baroque style, the Chambers of the Duma's Secretary-Scribe Averky Kirillov (*see* Walk 7).

On the left side is a small church, all that remains of the Convent of the Conception (*Zachatyevsky Monastyr'*), founded by Irina, wife of Tsar Fyodor I, in the 1580's, in the hope that she could thus overcome her barrenness. She didn't – and as a result Russia was plunged into the Time of Troubles. Most of the monastery was destroyed in the 1930's.

On the next corner (the end of the Boulevard Ring) is the Pertsov House, with fairytale paintings on the exterior by Sergey Malyutin, an example of how the "Itinerant" Movement applied its aesthetic creed to the architecture of Art Nouveau (*see* Walk 6).

After the Boulevard Ring a massive construction site comes into view, its cranes dwarfing the surrounding buildings. The Church of Christ the Saviour, Russia's largest ever church, finished in 1883 and destroyed in 1931, is being rebuilt here. The site was a swimming pool in the Soviet years (*see* Walk 6).

Bolshoy Kamenny Most

The boat stops on the right side in front of the Estrada Theatre, part of the "House on the Embankment" complex built in the 1930's for government officials of the Stalin era (*see* Walk 7).

Built in 1938 by the architects Vladimir Gelfreikh and Vladimir Shchuko, the bridge ahead was made largely of steel and designed to fit in with the architectural ensemble of central Moscow beyond.

Central Moscow | By Metro and by Boat

Why Your Trip to Russia Should Begin with Us

Russian Travel Service can provide any assistance and advice needed to make your trip memorable and safe. Managed by Helen Kates, a Moscow native, RTS is the recommended agent of *An Explorer's Guide to Moscow* for low-cost Moscow, St. Petersburg, and Kiev travel arrangements, which include:

Visa Support • Individual & Group Travel
Bed & Breakfast • Guide/interpreters • Cars & Drivers
Cruises & Tours • Airport Pick-up

Russian Travel Service
P.O. Box 311, Fitzwilliam, NH 03447 • Phone & fax: (603) 585-6534

Central Moscow

The Kremlin on the left side appears in its full glory. Most visible are the 15th-century Assumption, Annunciation and Archangel Cathedrals, a combination of the efforts of Italian and Russian masters under Grand Prince Ivan III and his successors to create a "Third Rome" in Moscow.

Standing high above them is the Ivan the Great bell-tower, built by Ivan the Terrible to house bells from other annexed Russian princedoms. The top was added later by Boris Godunov. The Great Kremlin Palace was built by Konstantin Thon in the last century.

The walls are also 15th-century and Italian-built, with turrets added in the 17th century. Here you can see the Water-Drawing Tower (corner), used to pump river water to the gardens and palaces, the Secrets Tower (the third along), believed to be the site of underground passages, and the Beklemishev Tower (far corner), haunted by a 16th-century nobleman.

Beyond the Kremlin rises Moscow's most famous landmark, St. Basil's Cathedral, with its brightly patterned domes and cupolas, a monument to the capture of Kazan by Ivan the Terrible in 1552 (see Walk 2). The bridge ahead is the Moskvoretsky (also built in 1938), the first on the river to be constructed in concrete, with a pink shade supposed to harmonise with the colours of the Kremlin walls.

On the right side, landmarks include the British Embassy, the 17th-century St. Sophia's Church and its later bell-tower, and the 5-star German-owned Baltschug Kempinski Hotel situated beyond the Moskvoretsky Bridge (see Walk 7).

Ustinsky Most

Before this pier, the Rossiya Hotel is visible on the left – central Moscow's greatest eyesore, built in the 1960's on the site of the picturesque Zaryadye ("beyond the trade rows") district (see Walk 2). Its name survives in the Zaryadye cinema on the embankment, part of the building.

One of the survivors of the old district is the Church of the Conception of St. Anne (*Tserkov' Zachatya Svyatoy Anny*), rebuilt by Ivan the Terrible on the site of a 14th-century church. The original was also connected with a barren Tsarina, Vassily III's wife Solomonia, who prayed here. She proved ultimately fertile and gave birth to a son, but her husband had by this time given up hope and remarried Helen Glinska, mother of Ivan himself. Solomonia arranged for the adoption of her own son, saving him from a likely cruel death.

Beyond the pier is another of the "wedding cake" series, the apartment block housing the Illuzion Cinema (see Walk 11).

Novospassky Most

The last stop on the route, convenient for the New Monastery of the Saviour (visible on the left). Another of Moscow's southern defensive fortresses, it became a burial place for the Romanov family under the first Tsar of the dynasty, Mikhail.

The main Transfiguration Cathedral dates from the time of his son Alexey and is an imitation of the Kremlin's Assumption Cathedral (see Walk 11).

Just through the trees ahead (also on the left) you can see the green cupolas of the Krutitsy Mission (see Walk 11).

If not returning by boat, take any tram one stop away from the river to Metro Proletarskaya.

The Tretyakov Gallery

The greatest collection of Russian art in the world, Moscow's Tretyakov Gallery reopened in April 1995 after a ten-year renovation, with its exhibition space enlarged and improved.

DIRECTIONS: From Metro Tretyakovskaya, turn left out of the exit, cross Ulitsa Bolshaya Ordynka into Maly Tolmachevsky Pereulok, and turn right down Lavrushinsky Pereulok. The gallery entrance is on your left. **OPEN:** Tues–Sun, 10 am–7 pm. Admission R 30,000 ($6); R 6,000 for Russian citizens (half price for students in each category).

The Gallery's History

The Tretyakov Gallery was founded in 1856, the creation of wealthy 19th-century merchant Pavel Tretyakov; Tretyakov was not so much a patron of the arts as a man with a civic conscience, and a passionate collector. His interests went well beyond paintings – he kept an aviary, a pedigree milk herd and a valuable collection of violins, all of which he willed to interested societies at the early age of 28.

However, art was his greatest legacy, and his prolific purchases, notably of the era's new realist art of the "Itinerant" movement, made for a very wide and varied collection. At first, paintings were exhibited in his house on Lavrushinsky Pereulok,

but soon the collection grew too large and in 1874 it was moved into a specially designed building next door.

By the 1880's the gallery had been opened to the public, and in 1892 was presented, together with brother Sergey's European paintings, as a gift to the city of Moscow. Tretyakov spent the last six years of his life as director of the new municipal museum. After his death, artist Viktor Vasnetsov participated in the reconstruction of his house, creating the facade visible there today with its bas-relief of St. George and the Dragon and ceramic frieze in Russian folk style. Tretyakov's statue, displaced in the Soviet era by successive images of Lenin and Stalin, was finally restored to its rightful place.

The collection increased rapidly in size after the Revolution, notably at the expense of churches and other private collections. It grew to include a restoration centre, specialised library, photo archive, and over 100,000 works of Russian art.

Recent major reconstructions and additional building work deprived visitors of the chance to see the greater part of the

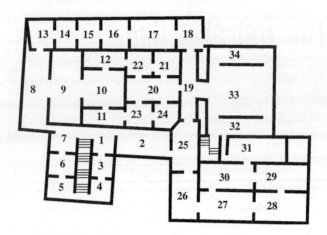

TRETYAKOV, FIRST FLOOR: 1–15: Painting & Sculpture of the 18th–early 19th Century. 16–31: Painting & Sculpture of the Second Half of the 19th Century. 32–34: Mikhail Vrubel, Mikhail Nesterov.

collection for over a decade. Though a few rooms have been open since 1989, the gallery only reopened in April 1995, with ten more rooms and many previously unseen works on show

Inevitably, many have criticised the gallery's new layout – for its stark and impersonal modern rooms, occasionally inept arrangement of paintings and the lack of explanatory notes in English (most of the icon collection is not even labelled in English). However, such quibbles are no reason to forego the opportunity to see the largest and finest collection of Russian art in the world.

The Plan

The Tretyakov Gallery is on two floors, with halls numbered 1 to 62. The exhibition begins on the first floor with 18th-century portraits (Hall 1) and ends, rather strangely, with icons, on the ground floor. This guide follows that numerical order. However, connecting stairways and corridors make it possible to change the viewing order.

Halls 1–15 Painting and Sculpture of the 18th–early 19th Centuries

The display begins with Russia's earliest non-religious paintings. Peter the Great's reforms and Russia's partial Europeanisation brought innovations like oil-on-canvas and three-dimensional painting, previously unknown to Russia. This is mostly a collection of portraiture, reflecting the tendencies of European art of the day but also an intrinsically Russian interest in personality and facial expression.

Hall 1. This room presents mostly the work of "imported" European artists, like the German Georg Grooth and the Frenchman Louis Caravaque. In the early days, when Russian secular artists were thin on the ground, the aristocracy ordered their portraits from foreigners. Ivan Nikitin, the first such Russian artist, sponsored by the Tsar, is also represented.

Hall 2. The sculpture of the period developed in parallel, with artists like Fedot Shubin combining technical excellence with psychological study. Note his bust of the aristocrat and socialite Prince Golitsyn. Ivan Martos, famous for the statue of Minin and Pozharsky in Red Square, demonstrated his talent for cemetery art with the tombstone of Princess Volkonskaya.

Hall 3. Following Nikitin's death without heirs or pupils, the new generation, including artists like Alexey Antropov and Fyodor Rokotov, had to start afresh. The former is represented here by his honest, unflattering depiction of Peter III, the latter by intimate portraits like that of the charming and thoughtful A. Struiskaya.

Hall 4. Many of the artists of the day were serfs, like Ivan Argunov and Mikhail Shibanov. Note particularly Argunov's profound and elegant "Unknown Woman in Russian Costume", one of the few portraits of peasants of the 18th century.

Hall 5. Another great artist of the time was Dmitry Levitsky, to whom this hall is devoted. Levitsky was fascinated by the colour and diversity of everyday life around him. The dominant portrait here is of industrialist and philanthropist Pyotr Demidov, captured in his bathrobe watering his plants. His outstretched hand draws the viewer's attention to an orphanage in the background, which he had endowed.

Hall 6. A hall of minor artists, displaying some of the earliest Russian landscape paintings. The centrepiece is Martos's sculpture of the Greek god Actaeon.

Hall 7. The gallery now moves into the era of Romanticism, with one of its leading exponents Vladimir Borovikovsky. His works

The best of Russian fiction today – in quality translation...

Omon Ra
Victor Pelevin

The best known talent of the younger generation of Russian writers, Victor Pelevin's surreal version of the Soviet space dream has been a major critical success in the West. Published with the highly-acclaimed novella, *The Yellow Arrow*, in a translation by Andrew Bromfield.

Price £7.99
ISBN 1 899414 00 2

"Confirms the arrival of a major talent"
Times Literary Supplement

"A natural story teller with a wonderfully absurd imagination"
The Observer

Published October 1995:

The Life of the Insects and Other Stories
Victor Pelevin

Price £7.99
ISBN 1 899414 20 7

All Harbord Publishing titles are distributed by Central Books, London. For further information, write to:
Harbord Publishing, 58 Harbord Street, London SW6 6PL.

Central Moscow | The Tretyakov Gallery

portray isolated noblewomen, sentimental souls in the ivory towers of the landed gentry, as in the hazy, dreamlike beauty of M.I. Lopukhina.

Hall 8. A large hall where the romantic portraits of Orest Kiprensky face the equally sentimental landscapes of Sylvester Shchedrin. Among Kiprensky's masterpieces are a noble Pushkin, his head turned slightly in contemplation of higher things, and "Poor Liza", the tragic heroine of Nikolay Karamzin's sentimental tale.

Shchedrin brought new qualities to Russian art, both stylistically and geographically, with his gentle and breezy scenes of life in Italy.

Hall 9. This hall is devoted to the versatile artist Karl Bryullov, represented mainly by portraits. His first and most famous paint-ing is "The Horsewoman", a great improvement on the stiff equine portraits of the 18th century, which depicts a beautiful young woman in an ideal, animated setting. Note also the self-portrait, done in 1848 near the end of his life, showing a tired artist, almost groaning under the pressure of reality.

Halls 10–12. The largest of these three, hall 10, is dominated by the huge "Appearance of Christ to the People" by Alexander Ivanov. The artist spent 20 years on this painting and never finished it, hence the some-what gaudy colouring and lack of detail. It reflects Ivanov's view of Christ as a rational, historical figure, an idea which he himself in the end came to doubt. The preparatory sketches of individual figures displayed around the hall appear to have more depth than the painting itself. Ivanov may

excel as a landscape painter, but the decision to devote two whole halls to him (10 and 12) seems excessive – the privilege is accorded to only two other artists. Hall 11 displays works of Ivanov's minor contemporaries.

Hall 13. The works of Vassily Tropinin (*see* Walk 7 for the Tropinin museum) show a fresh and lively interest in the persons he portrays, without the lofty romanticism of the likes of Kiprensky.

Hall 14. Alexey Venetsianov, a believer in the importance of the relationship between man and nature, went out to Tver Province to observe rural life and find subjects for his work. The result was something of a breath of fresh air in Russian art – genuine rural scenes, devoid of idyllic excesses.

Hall 15. The works of Pavel Fedotov, father of the "critical realism" school, really belong in the next section. His works are small-scale and often satirical, portraying characters which resemble the "superfluous men" of the literature of the era. Observe the disillusioned officer of "Encore, Encore Again" and the idle gentleman of "The Aristocrat's Breakfast".

Halls 16–31, 35–37 Painting and Sculpture of the Second Half of the 19th Century
The next section of the gallery contains the nucleus of Tretyakov's collection. Its range is enormous, covering every aspect of Russian realist art, but dominated by the work of the "Itinerant" (*peredvizhnik*) move-ment, whose socially motley collection of artists took their exhibitions round the country to interest people in their work. This

was a movement truly of the people and for the people.

Hall 16. Among its selection of minor realist artists, this room includes Tretyakov's first two acquisitions, Khudyakov's "Skirmish with Finnish Smugglers" and Shilder's "Temptation".

Hall 17. The initial driving force of the Itinerant movement was Vassily Perov, who drew attention to the agony of Russia's peasant classes in his vivid but almost monochrome paintings. He is well represented here with "Troika", three weary peasant children dragging a heavy cart, the massive spread of "Nikita Pustosvyat, a Dispute about Faith", never previously shown, and a fittingly gloomy portrait of Dostoyevsky.

Hall 18. A room dominated by the works of Alexey Savrasov, the Itinerants' foremost landscape painter, who makes the tamest scene look wild and stormy.

Hall 19. This hall is devoted to sea themes – naval battles by Alexey Bogolyubov and portrayals of elements of sea life by Ivan Aivazovsky. The latter's "Storm Breaking over the Black Sea" is magnificently threatening.

Hall 20. The work of Ivan Kramskoy, the ideologue and main portraitist of the "Itinerant" movement, fills the best portrait room in the gallery. Along with famous works like Lev Tolstoy, Pavel Tretyakov and the "Unknown Lady", it has the magnificent "Christ in the Desert", a hunched figure before a radiant sunset, tormented by choice between good and evil.

Hall 21. The colours of Arkhip Kuindzhi are unmistakable, bringing a romantic beauty to his work

And all with an original design... Quality fiction from Harbord Publishing

One-way Ticket
Zinovy Zinik

A collection of quirky, humorous stories from two decades of emigré life by Zinivy Zinik, one of the most distinctive voices writing in Russian today, author of the acclaimed novel *The Mushroom Picker*.

Price £8.99
ISBN 1 899414 05 3

"A scary, hilarious feat of conjuring"

The European

Published January 1996:

Witch's Tears
Nina Sadur

One of Russia's best-known dramatists, Sadur is also an original writer of prose. *Witch's Tears*, her first volume to be published in English, combines black humour with rich veins of poetry and fantasy.

Price £7.99
ISBN 1 899414 15 0

All Harbord Publishing titles are distributed by Central Books, London. For further information, write to:
Harbord Publishing, 58 Harbord Street, London SW6 6PL.

Central Moscow | The Tretyakov Gallery

matched only by its deceptive closeness to reality.

Hall 22. This room displays work of the artists Konstantin Makovsky and Genrikh Semiradsky, exponents of academism, a reaction of the traditional artistic establishment to the "Itinerants".

Halls 23–24. Several minor "Itinerants" are displayed here. In the second room is "The Party" by Makovsky's brother Vladimir, portraying the revolutionary intelligentsia of the day at play.

Hall 25. No Russian artist has captured the rich expanses of the Russian countryside better than Ivan Shishkin. In paintings like "Rye" the life-giving power of the soil, before which the ears of rye appear to be bowing, is tangible.

Hall 26. If Shishkin was inspired by Russian nature, Viktor Vasnetsov's main inspiration came from fairy-tales. In "The Knights", facing you as you enter this room, he instils his heroes with the main traits of the Russian character – cunning, bravery and straightforwardness. Also included is the "Baptism of Rus'", a preparatory work for one of the murals in Kiev's Cathedral of St. Vladimir.

Hall 27. This hall is devoted to the work of Vassily Vereshchagin, who combined his skills as an artist, historian and ethnographer to great advantage. Thanks to him, the humble viewer is transported back to the brutal times of the Middle Ages in Turkestan (Central Asia), as well as seeing the cruelties of war through new eyes.

Hall 28. The historical theme is continued by Vassily Surikov, in whose work the ordinary people takes the dominant role. In his

pictures he displays the real faces of the crowd with its cacophony of emotions. Thus the stubborn Old Believer Boyarinya Morozova, who won't reform, is carried through the streets accompanied by anger, sobbing, prayer and laughter, and in "Morning of the Execution of the Streltsy" a confused and despairing crowd huddles around the execution block on Red Square.

Halls 29–30. While Surikov treats historical Russian types, Ilya Repin portrays those of his own time, in work that is regarded as the crowning glory of the genre. In "Religious Procession in Kursk Province" he presents all the layers and social types of Russian provincial society. He also presents historical themes, like "Ivan the Terrible and His Son Ivan" with heightened dramatic effect – the old Tsar stricken with terror as he clutches his dying son to him, after dealing him a mortal blow. (The majority of Repin's works are currently on tour, hence the current bareness of these rooms. They return late autumn 1995.)

Hall 31. The next hall contains the works of Nikolay Ghé, a highly expressive and dramatic "Itinerant" painter. His most famous works, "What is Truth?" and "Peter the Great Questioning Tsarevich Alexey in Peterhof" illustrate intense psychological duels, between Pilate and Christ, and the Tsar and his estranged son respectively.

Halls 32–34. The gallery's largest room is dominated by a new display, Mikhail Vrubel's "Princess of Dreams" tapestry.
Vrubel was closely linked to the symbolist movement in literature and was one of the initiators of "Russian Moderne", a branch

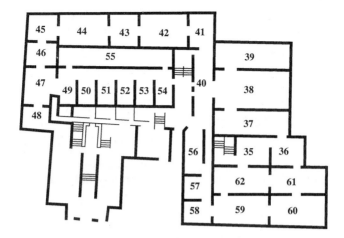

TRETYAKOV, GROUND FLOOR: 35–37: Painting & Sculpture of the Second Half of the 19th Century. 38–48: Painting & Sculpture, end-19th Century, early-20th Century. 49–54: 18th–20th Century Graphics. 55–62: Old Russian Art, 12th–17th Centuries.

of Art Nouveau. His work seems to remove the barrier between real and fantastic, his rich colour schemes making the symbolic figures of his paintings both poetic and human.

"The Princess of Dreams" was originally created for the Nizhny Novgorod Industrial and Artistic Exhibition in 1896, where it appeared in public only briefly.

It was given to the Tretyakov in 1956, having been rediscovered in the wings of the Bolshoi Theatre, but restoration was begun only in 1000, and is still not complete. For comparison, look at the mosaic version on the wall of the Metropol Hotel (*see* Walk 2).

The far side is devoted to Mikhail Nesterov, one of many artists for whom the Revolution brought dramatic changes.

Previously, emphasis was always put on his Soviet-era works, but now the deeply religious paintings of his "Itinerant" period have been given greater prominence.

Nesterov's series on the life of St. Sergius of Radonezh offers a profound spirituality and peace.

Hall 35. Descend to the three remaining halls in this section. The first shows the work of Vassily Polyenov, a versatile artist producing both dark spiritual portraits and fresh, subtle landscapes. Well-travelled and highly educated, he was an exponent of democracy in culture and his activities spread well beyond the realms of painting.

Hall 36. Among the minor "Itinerants" displayed here are works by Sergey Malyutin, an artist of the Talashkino circle, a creative collective similar in aims and style to Abramtsevo, and best known in Moscow for his work on the Pertsov House (see walk 6). Note two famous portraits of cultural figures – Tchaikovsky by Nikolay Kuznetsov and Chekhov by Iosef Braz.

Hall 37. Pavel Trubetskoy's works, whose impressionist style revolutionised Russian sculpture, are spread around several rooms but most appear here. The landscapes are mainly by the great Isaac Levitan. He is often compared to Chekhov for the way his nature scenes teem with mysterious internal life. Most striking here is "Eternal Peace", a classic scene from north Russia of a little wooden church on a river promontory.

Halls 32–4, 38–48. Painting and Sculpture, end-19th & early-20th Century

The Vrubel and Nesterov rooms offered a foretaste of this section, and in reality the divide between this and what preceded it is very vague. Many of the next group of artists were pupils of the "Itinerants", but more concerned with new artistic forms than social issues. Though Impressionism and the retrospective *Mir Iskusstva* (World of Art) movement dominated for a while, Russian art was now more splintered and diverse than before.

The search for new expression, the "Great Experiment", led to the appearance of various avant-garde movements. Unfortunately, the Tretyakov has been ruled by historical events and not artistic categories in its display. With 1917 set as the dividing line between this gallery and its new building, the substantial collection of Futurism has been split and weakened.

Hall 38. A variegated hall, including the almost glaring colours of Nikolay Roerich (*see* Walk 6) and the kaleidoscopic patterns of Filipp Malyavin.

Hall 39. Another room juxtaposing two famous artists, one mainly a landscape painter (Konstantin Korovin), the other a portraitist (Valentin Serov). Their sketchy, bold strokes indicate a tendency towards Impressionism.

Among Serov's masterpieces is the elegant and austere portrait of the actress Maria Yermolova.

Hall 40. A whole galaxy of artists is on display here – the exponents of the *Mir Iskusstva* school. It features artists like Boris Kustodiev, with his characteristically plump and playful "Beauty", Zinaida Serebryakova's marvellous "Self-Portrait at a Dressing Table" and movement leader Alexander Benois' ironic, stylised portrayals of aristocratic life in the 18th century.

Hall 41. The dreamy and nostalgic Viktor Borisov-Musatov has this room to himself. Observe his "Reservoir", with its exquisite colour harmony, portraying two women from a bygone era of lazy days on the country estate.

Hall 42. Two movements, "Blue Rose" and "Golden Fleece", continued the poetic symbolism of Borisov-Musatov. They are represented here by such artists as Nikolay Sapunov, Martiros Saryan and Pavel Kuznetsov.

Hall 43. Now firmly in the modernist era, this hall presents examples of the grotesque and primitivism from artists like Natalya Goncharova and Mikhail Larionov.

Hall 44. The modernist movement was built around the "Jack of Diamonds" group, whose core was made up of artists like Ilya Mashkov, Alexander Kuprin, Robert Falk and Aristarkh Lentulov. All are represented here, but the last deserves special mention for his unusual portrayals of the Ivan the Great bell-tower and St. Basil's.

Hall 45. This room is dominated by the striking red tones of Kuzma Petrov-Vodkin's "Bathing of the Red Horse", whose depth of colour and precision of figures was a clear reaction against Impressionism.

Hall 46. A room of minor avant-gardists, including the Georgian primitivist Niko Pirosmanishvili.

Hall 47. The beginning of full abstractionism in Russian painting is apparent in the works of two of the leaders of the movement, collages by Olga Rozanova and the "anti-illustrative sculpture" of Vladimir Tatlin.

Hall 48. Into this small room are squeezed three more great names of Russian avant-garde – Vassily Kandinsky, Alexander Rodchenko and Kazimir Malevich, the last of whom renounced completely the painting of "things" to initiate the Suprematist movement.

Halls 49–54 18th–20th Century Graphics
The Gallery's very rich graphics collection has been allotted six halls with special dimmed lighting. As exhibits are unable to be shown for more than a few months, they are rotated regularly, with each work being seen for a third of every year.

Attractions here include sketches by architects like Giacomo Quarenghi and Vassily Bazhenov (hall 49), pencil portraits by Bryullov and Kiprensky (hall 50), Vrubel's illustrations to the poems of Lermontov (hall 53) and hall 54, devoted to the World of Art movement, which gave special attention to this genre.

Halls 56–62 Old Russian Art of the 12th–17th Centuries
Probably the best icon collection in the world, this too was begun in the 19th century. In those days, Pavel Tretyakov was one of the few people in Russia to value the artistry of ancient icons: never displayed in public during his lifetime, it was passed to the Gallery only after his death. Including works from all the major schools and artists, it illustrates the form's development from early Byzantine influence on to the appearance and evolution of Russian schools.

Hall 56. A room showing Byzantium's earliest influences on Russian art. The greatest treasure is an early-12th century mosaic of St. Demetrius of Thessalonica from Kiev. Here also are the first, 13th-century icons of Russia's earliest schools, a deisus row (Christ flanked by Archangels) from Vladimir/Suzdal, and the Ustyug Annunciation from Novgorod.

For the Best Seats in the Bolshoi...

EPS Theatre Box Office offers you the best seats in the best theatres and concert halls in Moscow.

Metropol Hotel, Main Lobby, 1/4 Teatralny Proyezd
Tel.: 927-6982, 927-6983

Monday – Friday 10 am–6 pm; Saturday, Sunday 10 am–3 pm.
Call in advance for guaranteed service.

EPS

Hall 57. One of the greatest works of art in the museum, the 12th-century Vladimir Virgin, is displayed here. Painted in Byzantium, it originally stood in Kiev, but was secretly brought to Vladimir by Prince Andrey Bogolyubsky where it became the guardian of his realm. Keeping its original name, it was moved to Moscow when that city became the capital.

Hall 58. In the 13th–15th centuries, the cities of Novgorod and Pskov produced very distinctive icons. With colour schemes that blended deep reds, yellows and browns, they were generally smaller in size, suitable for home use by the powerful local merchant classes.

Hall 59. This hall contains icons of the same period from Byzantium, the Balkans, and another Russian centre, Tver. In this period the Moscow school also appeared, led by the first named artist, Theophanes the Greek – icon-painting had up until then been a purely anonymous trade. The dramatic and expressive Don Virgin, painted at the end of the 15th century, is believed to be his work.

Hall 60. Two of early Russia's greatest icon-painters are represented here, Andrey Rublyov and Dionysius. The first, working at the end of the 14th and beginning of the 15th centuries, produced Russia's first genuinely independent art. Highly poetic and contemplative, works like the Deisus row here capture Russia's suffering at the hands of the Tatars while at the same time observing Hellenic traditions of harmony, colour and beauty. Rublyov's best known and most revered work is the Trinity from Sergiyev Posad, depicting God's appearance in the form of three angels to Abraham and Sarah: their faces reflect the ancient Russian ideal of moral perfection.

A century later Dionysius, represented here by a Deisus row and Hodigitria (Guiding) Virgin, evolved the genre further, developing an exquisite moderation of expression and sparseness of detail in subtly coloured portrayals of heavenly bliss.

Hall 61. More 16th-century icons can be found here, including some from newer schools like Kostroma. Among them are icons and tapestries ordered for the wealthy Stroganov merchant family. Here also is the work of a little-known Russian genius, the sculptor Vassily Yermolin. The fragment of St. George is his only surviving work of this kind.

Hall 62. The last room in the Gallery displays icons of the 17th century, which marked the transition to secular painting. At the time of the church reforms of Patriarch Nikon, a pro-reform group known as the Kremlin Armoury artists, led by Simon Ushakov, brought some Western influences to icon-painting. The most notable change here is the introduction of buildings and landscapes into the backgrounds of their compositions.

Russsky Zal Restaurant

While taking a break from looking at the museum, it makes sense to visit the eateries downstairs. The bistro is a good place for a coffee, snack or beer (local brews are on draught).

For a more leisurely interval, the Russky Zal restaurant provides traditional Russian fare, imaginatively prepared, for around $50 a head.

☛ *Open Mon–Fri 1 pm–midnight; Sat, Sun, holidays, noon–midnight. Tel: 233-1829. Cash only.*

The Pushkin Museum

The Pushkin Museum of Fine Arts and the Museum of Private Collections

The Pushkin Museum is Moscow's main collection of European art, displaying works from the Ancient Egyptian era down to its remarkable collection of Impressionists and Post-Impressionists. The Museum of Private Collections adjoining it opened in 1994.

DIRECTIONS: From Metro Kropotkinskaya, leave by the northern exit (the last carriage if coming from Okhotny Ryad) and cross Ulitsa Volkhonka to the museums.

OPEN: Tues–Sun 10 am–7 pm. Tel: 203-7998, (recorded message) 203-9758. Admission R 25,000 ($5); R 6,000 for Russian citizens.

The Pushkin Fine Arts Museum

The Idea for Moscow's Fine Arts Museum originated in the 19th century, when a group of Moscow University professors decided to create a museum of antiquity for students, consisting mainly of plaster casts of ancient classical sculptures in a specially designed building.

In 1898 architect Roman Klein created a neo-classical structure, with a front portico copied from the Erechtheum in Athens, and an interior including an imitation of the courtyard of the Florentine Palazzo del Podesta.

In 1912 the museum opened under the directorship of Professor Ivan Tsvetayev, father of poet Marina Tsvetayeva.

In the 1920's, the museum's horizons broadened, as it absorbed collections of Western European art originally formed by noble families like the Sheremetyevs, as well as some works from museums like the Tretyakov (Sergey Tretyakov's collection) and that of the Morozov family.

Museum halls are not numbered, nor do they always follow any logical pattern, chronological or otherwise. For the sake of clarity, the Museum's own numbering system is retained here.

Visitors should be warned, also, that there are almost always several rooms closed at any one time. It is advisable, therefore, not to try to take rooms in any order, but decide what you want to see in advance and head straight there.

Ground Floor

Hall 1. Ancient Egyptian Art. Reached from the entrance by initially going straight through one of the courtyards (Halls 14 & 15), then bearing left until you can't go any further. Unlike many of the museums's classical works, all exhibits here are genuine, donated to the museum by the collector Vladimir Golenishchev in 1913.

Covering three millenia, they include a 3,000 B.C. relief of the head of the depository of Isis, and a 15th-century B.C. wood and ivory toilet spoon in the form of a girl in a black wig.

Hall 2. Devoted to ancient civilisations, only the archaeological finds are genuine; this is not a unified collection, with exhibits ranging from Mesopotamia to the Inca and Mayan civilisations.

Hall 3. The first hall of paintings, a collection of unique 1st–2nd century portraits from a necropolis in the Faiyoum oasis in Egypt, a meeting place of Eastern and Western cultures. Here also are several Byzantine icons, mostly dating from the city's decline in the 14th–15th centuries.

Halls 4–6. Several halls devoted to the transition between medieval culture and the art of the Renaissance period in Europe. Hall 4 includes the early religious art of Venice and Pisa, progressing to the appearance of individual talent in such centres as Siena. Hall 5 heralds the Renaissance, and the appearance of more profound and spiritually expressive works including Sandro Botticelli's "Annunciation", and Pietro Perugino's "Madonna and Child".

Hall 7. A room of genuine treasures from ancient Greece and Rome, either from Russian private collections or excavated from original settlements in the Crimea and on the Black Sea coast. They include an exquisite 3rd-century B.C. head of a Greek goddess and a 210 A.D. Roman sarcophagus with bacchanal scenes.

Hall 10. 17th-century Dutch painting. Here are six works by Rembrandt, including his "Chasing the Tradesmen out of the Temple" and the famous, moody "Portrait of Adrian van Rijn, Brother of the Artist".

Hall 11. 17th-century Flemish and Spanish painting. Dominated by the works of Peter Paul Rubens, notably his highly energetic and powerful "Bacchanalia". Another highlight is the El Greco portrait of the haughty and arrogant Castilian noble, Rodrigo Vasquez.

Hall 12. Post-Renaissance Italy, from the 17th and 18th centuries, including the acutely expressionist Caravaggio and the great monumentalist Giovanni Tiepolo, represented here by his "Death of Dido", a scene from Virgil's *Aeneid*.

Hall 13. Paintings from France's Golden Age, the 17th century. The best known artist is Nicholas Poussin, whose desire for justice and reason is reflected in such works as "The Magnanimity of Scipio", depicting a noble and selfless act by the Roman conqueror of Carthage.

Halls 14–15. The Greek and Italian Courtyards. The first is a rather colourless room full of plaster casts, the most interesting of which is a copy of the Erechtheum's portico of caryatids

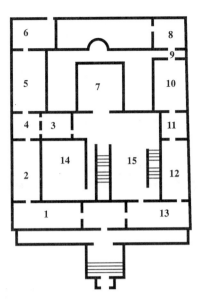

PUSHKIN, GROUND FLOOR: 1: Ancient Egyptian Art. 2: Ancient Civilisations. 3: Early Paintings. 4–6: Medieval-Renaissance Art. 7: Greek & Roman Art. 10: 17th Century Dutch Painting. 11: 17th Century Flemish & Spanish Painting. 12: Post-Renaissance Italy. 13: 17th Century French Painting. 14-15: Classical Sculpture Courtyards.

in Athens. Copies in the Italian Courtyard are more diverse, with works of medieval Italian and German applied art, like the south portal of Freiburg cathedral and Peter Fischer's Nuremburg tomb of St. Zebald.

First Floor

Halls 16-A & 16. Climb the staircase from the courtyard to more plaster casts, these of Aegean and Ancient Greek sculptures up to 400 B.C.

Hall 17. A leap in time to early-20th century painting, from which the exhibition now proceeds in reverse chronological order. It contains an excellent collection of Henri Matisse – intensely colourful, idyllic scenes like "Nasturtiums and 'the Dance'", "Moroccan Triptych" and "Spanish Woman with a Tambourine".

The Picasso section is much more diverse, with a 1912 cubist series of musical instruments alongside "An Old Jew and a Boy" from his "blue" period, and "Girl on a Beach Ball" from the "pink" period. However, World War I and the subsequent Revolution interrupted the Russian collectors' access to Paris, and his later works are not represented here.

Futurism is on show in works from the Russian-born Vassily Kandinsky and Marc Chagall (although Chagall was born in Vitebsk, his work does not appear in the Tretyakov Gallery).

Hall 18. The two wings of Post-Impressionism: glorious Provence landscapes and still lifes by Cézanne, the logical thinker of the French provinces, and the exotic Tahitian nudes of the foot-loose Parisian Paul Gaugin.

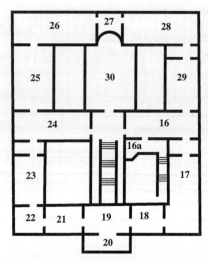

PUSHKIN, FIRST FLOOR: 16, 16-A: Aegean & Ancient Greek Sculpture. 17: Matisse, Picasso. 18: Cézanne, Gaugin. 19-20: Temporary Exhibition Halls. 21: Dégas, Van Gogh. 22: The Impressionists: Monet, Renoir, Rodin. 23: Early 19th Century Painting. 24-29: History of Sculpture. 30: Temporary Exhibition Hall.

Halls 19–20. Temporary exhibition halls.

Hall 21. A hall devoted to near-Impressionists like Eduard Dégas, with his irresistibly charming "Blue Dancers". Vincent Van Gogh's "Red Vineyards in Arles", a scene of feverish activity at dusk on a hot day, was the only painting he sold during his lifetime.

Hall 22. The Impressionists. Leader Claude Monet is well represented, with, among others, his glimpses of Rouen Cathedral at various times of day, and one of his last works, the colourful and pleasing "White Waterlilies".

The great portraitist Pierre-Auguste Renoir's works include a sketch of Paris darling and actress Jeanne Samary (the full portrait is in the Hermitage in St. Petersburg).

Sculptures by Auguste Rodin include a portrait of the romantic poet Victor Hugo.

Hall 23. A room covering tendencies in classical and romantic painting in the early-19th century. Works include a "Napoleon" by the era's greatest portraitist François Gérard, and a small Constable "View of Highgate from Hampstead Heath".

Halls 24–29. A series of rooms presenting an impressive array of plaster, following the history of sculpture from late Classical Greece, through Ancient Rome and medieval Germany to the Italian Renaissance, culminating in a whole room full of Michelangelo copies.

Hall 30. One of the Museum's grandest rooms, this temporary exhibition hall is also the venue for its celebrated series of Christmas chamber concerts, the "December Evenings" series, when Moscow's cultural elite competes for tickets to hear some of the greatest Russian and international soloists.

The Museum of Private Collections

The stern-faced building to the left of the Pushkin Museum as you enter from the street is a much reconstructed residence of the noble Golitsyn family, originally designed by the architect Matvey Kazakov in the 18th century.

In its new incarnation it is the Museum of Private Collections, a branch of the Pushkin, which opened in 1994 after a protracted initiative of writer and art historian Ilya Zilberstein, whose own collection formed its basis.

Instead of displaying art according to historical periods, styles or movements, Zilberstein sought to reflect the integrity of private collections, and thus to maintain a sense of the personality and taste of the collectors themselves. The museum is on three levels, beginning with rooms for temporary exhibitions on the ground floor.

OPEN: Weds–Sun 10 am–5 pm. Tel: 203-7998, (recorded message) 203-9758.
Admission R 15,000 ($3), R 2,500 for Russian citizens. For more information about many of the artists mentioned here, see the Tretyakov Gallery chapter.

First Floor Collections

Yevgeny Stepanov
A thematic collection of animal sculptures is spread through all the rooms on this floor. Stepanov was a Soviet-era veterinary surgeon, whose visits to humble Moscow antique shops brought him such treasures as horses by the great 19th-century sculptor Pyotr Klodt.

Ilya Zilberstein
The largest collection in the museum, covering the first six rooms. Its nucleus consists of drawings and water-colours by almost all major Russian artists of the 18th–early 20th centuries. Best represented is the "World of Art" movement (see Tretyakov Gallery), including Alexander Benois' illustrations to the Pushkin epic poem *The Bronze Horseman*, and theatrical sketches by Lev Bakst and Boris Kustodiev.

Zilberstein's collection of Ilya Repin's work is also sizeable, with over 50 graphic works and oil paintings like the poetic "Summer Landscape at Abramtsevo". One unique room is devoted to portraits of members of the Decembrist movement, painted by Nikolay Bestuzhev in exile in Chita in the 1830's.

Other rooms show classical sketches by architects like Giacomo Quarenghi and Pietro Gonzaga, as well as paintings by Vassily Tropinin, Vladimir Borovikovsky and others.

Sergey Solovyov
One room of Russian 19th-century realist paintings, collected by a rural wood carver who fell in love with Russian art on arrival in Moscow. Its finest works are Vassily Polyenov's "Christ by the Sea of Galilee", a vertical version of a painting in the Tretyakov and Bogdanov-Belsky's elegant portrait of Nikolay Yusupov.

Mikhail Chuvanov
One room of pre-reform icons collected by a prominent member of Moscow's Old Believer community at Preobrazhenskoye.

Second Floor Collections

Leonid Pasternak
A room containing several works by this pupil of Vassily Polyenov and master of the portrait sketch, now better known as father of writer Boris Pasternak.

Svyatoslav Richter
One room of works belonging to the great pianist, who was a prominent collector and exhibition host for many unofficial artists during the Soviet period. Most of these paintings were gifts from the artists themselves, including Robert Falk, Pyotr Konchalovsky and Dmitry Krasnopevtsev.

Alexander Ramm
Two rooms containing a post-war collection by a Leningrad

professor with a very subtle taste and acute sense of quality. It spans the turn of the century, covering the "World of Art" (*Mir Iskusstvo*) movement and formalists like Nathan Altman.

Other highlights are Boris Kustodiev's "After the Thunderstorm", with its fairytale scenes of a Russian village, and Zinaida Serebryakova's sad, elegant "Portrait of Sergey Ernst".

Alexander Tyshler
A room of paintings and a room of graphics by this highly original Soviet artist. Tyshler's peculiar mixture of the romantic and the ironic produces grotesque mythical creatures like the "Girl-Centaur" and series like the "Lyrical Cycle"; other parts of this cycle are in the New Tretyakov.

Alexander Rodchenko and Varvara Stepanova
The museum's largest collection is of works by this modernist pair, who were also husband and wife. It traces Rodchenko's creative path from his cubist period, to Constructivism and work for Vladimir Mayakovsky's literary and artistic journal *LEF*.

In a second room, you can see the ground-breaking results of their experimentation with photography, and joint efforts with Mayakovsky at making the first Soviet advertising posters.

David Shterenberg
One room devoted to an under-rated artist, who was the first Soviet Commissar for the Arts in 1917–18.

The collection was given to the museum by his children, including daughter Violetta, herself an artist who is still working into her eighties. The radiant colours of his portraits and still lifes single out and give meaning to every object he depicts.

Greater Moscow

Novodevichy Convent and Cemetery

Moscow's most famous and beautiful monastery stands next to the cemetery where many of the most distinguished figures of Russian and Soviet history are buried. Nearby is Luzhniki Stadium, today scene of a goods market, while dominating the skyline across the Moskva River, on the Sparrow Hills, towers the new building of Moscow State University.

DIRECTIONS: From Metro Sportivnaya, leave by the northern entrance (the last wagon if coming from the centre), turn right and continue until you see the Convent on your left. By car, or trolleybus #5 or #15, leave the Garden Ring road along Bolshaya Pirogovskaya Ulitsa.

Novodevichy Convent

Founded in 1524 by Grand Prince Vassily III to celebrate the capture of Smolensk from the Lithuanians, the Novodevichy (New Virgin) Convent, nestling in a bend of the Moskva River, soon occupied a prominent position among Moscow's southern fortifications, designed to defend the city against Tatar raids. It also became a place of exile for high-ranking women in disfavour or mourning: since their incarceration was accompanied by presents of land or jewellery, the Convent became one of the richest in the country.

Among those who lived here was the sister of Boris Godunov, and it was from here that Boris himself was called upon to become Tsar by the crowds. Peter the Great's reactionary sister, Sophia, and the woman he married in spite of her, Yevdokia Lopukhina, were also prisoners. From her cell, Sophia organised the 1698 coup against Peter, and as punishment her followers, the *Streltsy* (musketeers), were strung up outside her window, an ordeal which drove her mad.

Though originally designed as a fortress by Godunov, Novodevichy's current walls and towers date from Sophia's time (1685-87) and are purely decorative, the towers topped by festive coronas instead of the usual defensive merlons. The Convent was closed in 1923, and until quite recently was part of the State History Museum. Now it has been returned to the Church and is functioning again, with its grounds and churches remaining open to the public.

Cathedral of the Virgin of Smolensk

(Sobor Smolenskoy Bogomateri)
The monastery's main church was built in 1525, architecturally a more dynamic version of the Kremlin's Assumption Cathedral. The magnificent, lofty interior contains 16th century frescoes on the theme of the reunion of the historic lands of Kievan Rus' under Moscow.

In the triumphal arch in the east wall you can see a painting of a *Hodigitria* (Guiding) Virgin, similar to the Smolensk Virgin icon revered in the Convent. On either side of her, the heavenly host with raised swords are reminders that Smolensk was taken by force of arms. Other paintings show different campaigns, such as the uniting of Tver and Novgorod with Moscow.

The magnificent iconostasis dates from the end of the 17th century, when Sophia, not yet a prisoner, was involved in new work on the Convent. Five-tiered in structure, it is made of 84 thickly gilded linden columns carved in the shape of interwined vines. On the lowest "local" tier of icons, to the left of the altar, is a copy of the Smolensk Virgin icon – the original was kept elsewhere and disappeared during World War II.

Bell-tower

A beautiful slender structure in Naryshkin Baroque style built in Sophia's time, it was a fine complement in the Moscow landscape to the Kremlin bell-tower, and therefore nicknamed "The Bride of Ivan the Great".

Its six tiers serve variously as the Church of St. John the Divine (2nd), belfries (3rd and 5th), most of whose bells predate the bell-tower itself, with a clock face on the 4th tier.

Other Buildings

Among the other churches and chambers in the Convent is the Church of the Transfiguration, standing over the main entrance. Also the work of Sophia, its cubic form and scallop shell *kokoshniki* are more reminiscent of the earlier Kremlin churches than the Baroque style which was prevalent at the time of its construction.

To the right of the entrance are the red brick chambers which housed Yevdokia Lopukhina, and further away, by the corner tower, the prison of Sophia, who sat in mental misery in the Convent she had virtually created herself, after Peter the Great's accession.

U Pirosmani Restaurant

Across Novodevichya Ulitsa is Moscow's first private Georgian restaurant, dedicated to the primitivist artist Niko Pirosmanishvili. It has had a chequered history, with various changes of ownership and variable quality of service and food, but has remained popular with tourists throughout. ☛ *Open noon–4 pm, 6 pm–10:30 pm. Tel: 247-1926. Major CC.*

Novodevichy Cemetery

Adjoining the monastery walls, with its entrance along the wall in direction of the river, is Moscow's most celebrated place of burial, whose distinguished inhabitants have their final resting places marked by monuments of exceptional and pleasing variety – though they are not always easy to find unless you know their coordinates.

The cemetery is divided into numbered sections, each covering a certain period of recent history. Enter through the gates of the new part and turn right at the central square to pass into the old cemetery, past section 2 on your right, which contains many famous cultural figures of the late 19th and early 20th centuries (row numbers are marked on the Central Avenue, the next cross roads).

The most striking grave is that of **Anton Chekhov** (row 15, grave 25), in a curious neo-Russian style reminiscent of that of the Abramtsevo artists. Beside him lies his wife, the actress Olga Knipper, her grave carved with the Moscow Art Theatre's seagull symbol. **Gogol**'s grave (row 12, grave 20) is much simpler, but distinguished by a bust added in 1951, a "present" from the Soviet government which the writer is unlikely to have appreciated. Also in this section are the graves of **Mikhail Bulgakov** (row 21, grave 21), **Konstantin Stanislavsky** (row 20, grave 16), "Itinerant" artists **Valentin Serov** (row 22, grave 8), **Isaac Levitan** (row 23, grave 20) and **Mikhail Nesterov** (row 26, grave 19), and the actress **Maria Yermolova** (row 22, grave 10).

Across the Central Avenue is section 1, containing mainly the graves of communists who for one reason or another were not buried in the Kremlin Wall, like Lazar Kaganovich (row 10, grave 13) scourge of many fine Moscow buildings, and Vyacheslav Molotov (row 44, grave 10), co-initiator of the Nazi-Soviet pact. Stalin's wife Nadezhda Alliluyeva, who committed suicide in 1932 is buried in row 44, grave 20. Among literary figures is another suicide, the poet **Vladimir Mayakovsky** (row 14, grave 13). The only pre-revolutionary graves in this section are those of the Tretyakov brothers, founders of the Tretyakov Gallery, at row 14, grave 12.

Turn back along the Central Avenue, keeping the convent walls on your right, into sections 3 and 4. These two sections have a musical accent, with the first containing composers **Sergey Prokofiev** (row 47, grave 11) and **Alexander Scriabin** (row 40, grave 1) and the second singer **Fyodor Shaliapin** (row 49, grave 1), whose remains were reburied here from their original resting place in Paris. Another interesting grave is that of Andrey Gromyko (section 4, row 18, grave 1), the former Soviet Foreign Minister (known by the international community as "Mister *Nyet*") and titular Head of State until shortly before his death in 1989.

Beyond are sections 9, 10 and 11, the newest in the cemetery. These contain many of Russia's recent cultural elite, whose deaths have followed in quick succession in recent years. They include *War and Peace* director **Sergey Bondarchuk** (section 10, row 9, grave 1) and famed Moscow Arts Theatre actor **Innokenty Smoktunovsky** (section 10, row 8, grave 10).

Turn left and return to the main entrance via the new cemetery. The grave of Nikita Khrushchev (section 7, row 20, grave 1), Stalin's successor and initiator of the 1950's "thaw", who fell from favour and died in obscurity in 1970, is here – he is the only Soviet leader to be buried outside the Kremlin wall. The sculpture on his grave is by the now-emigré artist Ernst Neizvestny. Another sculptor, Sergey Konyonkov is buried nearby (section 8 row 45 grave 1), his grave distinguished by two wooden sculptures typical of his work.

Luzhniki

This massive stadium complex just to the south of Metro Sportivnaya covers the entire crook of land jutting out into the Moskva River. Among its parks and sports halls is the Lenin Stadium, home of Moscow Spartak football club, with a capacity of 100,000 people. As well as football it hosted major events during the 1980 Olympic Games, and currently serves as an enormous anarchic market selling cheap imported consumer goods, especially clothing.

Sparrow Hills
(Vorobyovy Gory)
Take the #28 trolleybus from the eastern end of the complex, or walk across the bridge to this massive tree-covered hill on the

other side (the metro station here has been closed for years and shows no signs of reopening).

At the top, the highest point in Moscow, is a viewpoint, a favourite spot for newly-weds. Though the Kremlin is visible on a clear day, most of central Moscow is too distant, and all you can be sure to see is the area around the Convent and Stadium. Behind is the main University building (MGU), built by Lev Rudnev in 1953 as the crowning glory of the "wedding cake" series.

New Moscow Circus
Across Prospekt Vernadskovo from the park and University, the New Circus is located next to the Universitet metro station. Built in 1971 complete with special ingenious contraptions which rapidly change the floors of the ring, it offers a fun evening out. There's little in it, but the quality of performance is probably slightly higher here than at the Old Circus.

St. Daniel's Monastery

The oldest of the six monasteries built to defend Moscow from the south, St. Daniel's *(Danilovsky Monastyr')* is now the headquarters of the Patriarchate of the Russian Orthodox Church.

DIRECTIONS: From Metro Tulskaya, walk back towards the square (Ploshchad Serpukhovskoy Zastavy) and turn right along Dubininskaya Ulitsa. By car

take Ulitsa Bolshaya Ordynka from the centre, then Lyusin-ovskaya Ulitsa, and turn left at the same square. It can also be visited in Patriarchi Dom's tour of three monasteries.

The monastery was founded in the 13th century by Prince Daniel, who lived a monastic life here and was later canonised. Since then it has had a mixed fate, with periods of disuse and dereliction interspersed with prosperity. It was revived by Ivan the Terrible, and then again in the 1980's, when the Patriarchate returned here from Zagorsk (now Sergiyev Posad), marking the millenium of Christianity in Russia in 1988.

Church of the Seven Ecumenical Councils
(Khram Svyatykh Otsov Semi Vselenskikh Soborov)
The most interesting building in the monastery complex is this 16th century church with 17th century additions, which originally celebrated the unity of Russia, Belorussia and Ukraine, and includes some features of the Ukrainian Baroque.

It was built by Ivan the Terrible, to whom Prince Daniel suppos-edly appeared in a vision with the request to restore the monastery. The church is made up of five chapels, one of which contains a fresco of St. Daniel, which mirac-ulously survived decades during which the church was used as a factory.

Other buildings include the Trinity Cathedral, built in 1838 by Osip Bove and containing a beautiful new iconostasis, and the pretty gate church of St. Simeon the Stylite. However, many are brand new, built in the rather bland retrospective style used by today's church.

Danilovsky Monastery Restaurant

The monastery includes the Patriarch's own hotel and restaurant for church guests. Ordinary mortals can sample the exquisite Russian cuisine too, provided they book in advance and are prepared to pay up to $100 a head.

☛ *Open noon–11 pm. Tel. 954-0566. Major CC.*

Don Monastery

The last in the line of southern defenses to be built, the Don Monastery is famous for its contrasting cathedrals and cemetery within the walls.

DIRECTIONS: From Metro Shabolovskaya, turn right as you exit along Shabolovka Ulitsa and take the second street right. By car, take Donskaya Ulitsa straight to the monastery from Kaluzhskaya Ploshchad, on the Garden Ring.

Alternatively you can reach it directly from St. Daniel's by returning to Ploshchad Serpukhovkoy Zastavy and going straight on, down Serpukhovsky Val and Ulitsa Ordzhonikidze, to turn right down Donskaya Ulitsa. Patriarchi Dom organises a separate tour here.

The powerful-looking Don Monastery was founded in 1591 by Tsar Fyodor after a trying year in which Moscow had almost been captured by the Crimean Tatars. As at the battle of Kulikovo Field in 1380, Dmitry Donskoy's miracle-working icon was brought into play to rout the Tatars, and as a result Khan Kaza

Girei, Russia's latest tormentor, took fright and retreated. The new monastery was dedicated to the icon.

The "Old" Cathedral of the Don Virgin

In the same year, this tiny cathedral was built, a beautifully proportioned church with a slender dome and stepped layers of *kokoshniki*. Note the half moon beneath the cross, denoting the victory of Christianity over Islam. Inside is a copy of the Don Virgin icon, the only one to survive the Soviet era, and two tombs, one of Archbishop Amvrosy, murdered by the mob during the 1771 plague (*see* Walk 2), the other that of Patriarch Tikhon, head of the Russian Orthodox Church in the early Soviet period.

The "New" Cathedral

Beside it, in total contrast, is the "New" Cathedral, a massive Baroque building in the Naryshkin style. Its most notable feature is the magnificent seventier iconostasis, also constructed in the Baroque fashion of the day. The frescoes are unusual: painted by Italian artist Antonio Claudio, they are purely western and totally uncharacteristic of Orthodox art.

The Cemetery

The far side of the monastery includes a cemetery containing some fine works by 18th century sculptors Ivan Martos and Ivan Vitali, surmounting the graves of members of the aristocratic families of the day. They include contemporaries of Pushkin like the philosopher Pyotr Chaadayev, and the famous Moscow architect Osip Bove.

Along the back wall are some marble high reliefs saved during the destruction of the Church of

Christ the Saviour (see Walk 6). When building work on the Church has finished there are plans to return the high reliefs to their original position, although they represent only a small fraction of the whole.

"Moscow Icons"

The Monastery of the Saviour and Andronicus (Spaso-Andronikovsky Monastyr') now houses the Andrey Rublyov Museum of Ancient Russian Art, while the nearby Old Believers' Settlement at Rogozhskaya Sloboda has churches containing fine collections of pre-17th century icons.

DIRECTIONS: From Metro Ploshchad Ilyicha, turn right for the monastery and take trolleybus #45, #53 or bus #152 one stop. For the Old Believers' Settlement, turn left out of the Metro, and take bus #152 in the opposite direction as far as the cemetery.

By car, take Ulyanovskaya Ulitsa from the Garden Ring away from the centre – the monastery will be visible on your left at Ploshchad Pryamikova. For the Settlement continue past the rail bridge and take the first right turn until you see the cemetery on your left.

Monastery of the Saviour and Andronicus
(Spaso-Andronikovsky Monastyr')
Built during the childhood of Prince Dmitry Donskoy, this powerfully fortified but undefended

monastery became something of a Christian sanctuary from the Tatars. It was founded by Metropolitan Alexey, regent of Muscovy and the first head of the Moscow church who was not appointed by Byzantium, after he miraculously survived a ship-wreck. Dmitry returned here in triumph after his victory at Kulikovo Field.

Icon painter Andrey Rublyov, a monk here who had his workshop in the grounds, was buried at the monastery after his death in 1430. His remains have never been located, though a head-stone was uncovered during restoration in the 1920's. Unfortunately, it was lost again the next day in the mud and rubble.

A museum was set up after World War II, combining icons rescued during expeditions into the wilds of central and north Russia, and facsimiles of ancient frescoes created on site. A statue of Rublyov stands outside the main enttrance.
☛ Museum open Thurs–Tues 11 am–6 pm, closed last Fri of each month. Tel: 278-1467.

Cathedral of the Saviour
(Spassky Sobor)
As soon as you enter, you see the Cathedral of the Saviour, a beautiful single-domed church which, while preserving features of the pre-Mongolian school of architecture of Vladimir/Suzdal, included such innovations as kokoshniki or gables, later to be used widely in Moscow churches.

Built in 1427, the church was painted by Rublyov. Most of his frescoes were lost as a result of 18th century changes and the 1812 fire, though traces can be seen in the most remote window areas. The cathedral is open for services.

Church of the Archangel Michael

(Tserkov' Mikhaila Arkhangela)
The baroque church to the left of the cathedral was built by the Lopukhin family, whose most famous member was Yevdokia, Peter the Great's ill-fated wife. Though begun in 1691, Yevdokia's demise, combined with the Lopukhins' involvement in the coup attempt of Peter's son, Alexey, prevented completion. Only when the family returned from exile in 1729 was it finished.

The Icon Museum

Various displays, both temporary and permanent, are spread around the monastery: ask at the entrance *kassa* for details.

The main icon exhibition is dedicated to Rublyov and his pupils. Its greatest treasure is an anonymous 14th century icon of Christ the Saviour, a face from a higher, ideal world giving comfort to an oppressed nation. From the Rublyov school are such icons as the 15th century John the Baptist, in this interpretation a benevolent thinker looking down upon a reviving nation.

The museum has a strong emphasis on the restoration and imitation of ancient art. Much recent work on these and other icons was carried out by the restorer I. Kirikov, who also painted the museum's copy of Rublyov's famous Trinity, depicting the appearance by God to Abraham and Sarah in the form of three angels, the embodiment of the ancient Russian ideal of moral perfection. Note also Rublyov's frescoes from the Assumption Cathedral in Vladimir, copied by N. Gusev in the 1960's, particularly the "Day of Judgement" – portrayed as a happy and triumphant occasion, rather than a scene of punishment and torment, as is usually the case.

In the 16th–17th centuries, icons with multiple scenes began to appear. A superb example of this is St. Nicholas of Zaraisk, with 16 pictures from the life of Russia's best loved saint, with figures which are highly expressive in their nobility and suffering.

Note also the Tikhvin Virgin, painted in the town of the same name in 1680, with vivid scenes which depict both nature and the town's siege by the Swedes in 1612.

Rogozhskaya Sloboda – The Old Believers' Settlement

Reforms in the 17th century introduced by Patriarch Nikon were designed to unite and modernise the Russian Orthodox Church, but instead led to a split: many believers refused to accept them, despite consequent persecution.

The symbol of their disaffection was the way they made the sign of the cross, with two fingers instead of three, but there were many more details over which they disagreed with the official church.

Most "Old Believers" (as they were called) fled to remote parts of Russia, but others held out doggedly in the centre, to be granted freedom of worship in the reign of Catherine the Great.

In Moscow, they were allotted land to bury their dead from the 1771 plague, and built a community round the new cemetery, including two fine churches. Tsar Nicholas I cracked down on them again in 1827, and their churches were sealed until 1905, when more buildings were added to the complex.

The Cathedral of the Intercession
(Pokrovsky Sobor)
This is the main church of Moscow's community of Old Believers, designed in a grand classical style by Matvey Kazakov shortly after Catherine's decree. Its interior is truly magnificent, with an old-world feel unmatched anywhere else in Russian Orthodoxy, mainly because of its icons, which all date from before the schism: Old Believers did not recognise later works, which they felt were tainted by Western influences.

In fact, the collection almost matches that of the Tretyakov Gallery. Its greatest treasure is the iconostasis, including a deis-us row by the Rublyov school, with a Saviour by the artist himself. Another Saviour, kept in a glass case near the southern entrance, dates from the 13th century, a typical example of Byzantine art of the period.

Other icons are representative of other Russian schools, like St. Paraskeva (right hand wall), displaying the bright red colouring of the Novgorod school, or the Virgin of Bogolyubovo (left wall) in the gentler blue and silver shades of Vladimir/Suzdal. The wall paintings were executed in the last century by various artists from the icon-painting village-centre of Palekh.

N.B. While the Old Believers are beginning to open up to the world, their rules are still much stricter than those of the official Church. Women should wear scarves, not hats, when entering, and long skirts are obligatory. During services all visitors should keep to a special area at the back of the church. If you wish to be shown round, apply to the deacon or church elder.

St. Nicholas Church
(Tserkov' Nikoly)
The festive baroque church next door is official Orthodox, but its interior still resembles an Old Believers' church. Note the beautiful eight-point crosses on the doors – Old Believers, unlike the official church, do not recognise the four-point cross used by western Christians.

The Cemetery
A walk in the cemetery shows the wealth and variety of tombs and mausoleums of merchant families like the Ryabushinskys and the Morozovs, on the left of the main path. The white marble grave you see is that of art patron Savva Morozov, accorded unusually high honours despite the fact that he supposedly committed the sin of suicide (some of his family believed that he was murdered).

N.B. Patriarchi Dom organises tours to both these sights. The second, Old Believers' tour also includes a visit to the Preobrazhenskoye Cemetery in the north of the city, home of several smaller, more curious sects, like the Pomorye Division, who don't have a priesthood, and the Filippovtsy, who believe in self-incineration and number just three.

Kolomenskoye

An ancient and beautiful church complex on the banks of the Moskva River, used by the Princes of Muscovy as an out-of-town residence as early as the 14th century, Kolomenskoye remains an oasis of peace today.

DIRECTIONS: From Metro Kolomenskaya, leave by the southern exit (the front wagon when coming from the centre), turn left, then right out of the subway and walk straight for about ten minutes.

By car take Ulitsa Simonovsky Val from Metro Proletarskaya, following its continuation Prospekt Andropova past Metro Kolomenskaya.

Kolomenskoye's name may originate from the refugees from the town of Kolomna who fled here from the Mongols in the 13th century. Later, Muscovite princes were frequent visitors, and in the 16th century, Ivan the Terrible built a luxurious wooden palace on the spot. After extensive additions in stone by Tsar Alexey in the 17th century, the palace came to be described as "the eighth wonder of the world", and foreign ambassadors were ferried across the river to be received there. Although Catherine the Great knocked the palace itself down, other buildings of the same period remain.

The museum, working since the 1920's, is one of the cultural success stories of the Soviet era. Extensive restoration work and archaeological digs were carried out here, under the leadership of restorer Pyotr Baranovsky. In the 1930's, it became the Soviet Union's first open air museum and several wooden architectural monuments were brought to the site.

It also contains a number of indoor craft exhibitions, with plans now afoot to restore the village and even build a tourist complex. Meanwhile, the most arresting thing about Kolomenskoye is that one can find such a rural atmosphere just four metro stops from central Moscow. Until recently there was even a collective farm across the river, connected to the estate by Moscow's last remaining ferry service.

Church of Our Lady of Kazan
(Tserkov' Kazanskoy Bogomateri)
As you enter the complex, this pretty church stands directly ahead on the left, originally adjoining the wooden palace. It was built by Tsars Mikhail and Alexey Romanov in the 17th century in commemoration of the 1612 victory against the Poles; Russian troops had carried the Kazan icon as they successfully laid siege to the Kremlin.

Front Gates
Continue down the hill to the front gates, through which important guests used to pass after arriving from across the river. Since most of Kolomenskoye's buildings actually stand beyond them, the feeling is more as if you are entering, not exiting the fortress.

In the 17th century, wooden lions, sadly no longer in existence, were put in the entrance, connected to a mechanism inside the tower by which they could be made to roar and swish their tails. In the belfry itself was a mechanically chiming clock connected to bells – this and other clocks are displayed in the building's Organ Room. There is also an exhibition of 17th–19th century metalwork by blacksmiths, including ornamental church doors and a four-metre weather cock in the form of birds in a bush.

Administrative Buildings
(Prikaznye Palaty)
Two of the four original buildings have survived, adjoining the gates. The first has a history exhibition in the form of a restored 17th century interior. Beyond it, in the Sytny Dvor, is an exquisite model of Tsar Alexey's palace, ordered by Catherine the Great before she destroyed the original.

This part contains two more exhibitions of interest. One is devoted to wood carving, from axe-hewn church pillars to the intricate village craft of platband carving from Vladimir, Nizhny Novgorod and Kostroma. The second traces the history of ceramic tiles and the work of Moscow craftsmen from the Potters' Guild (*see* Walk 11), with exterior decorations in relief rescued from defunct churches and 18th century flat stove tiles with aphorisms written on them.

Ascension Church
(Tserkov' Voznesenya)
This towering landmark was built in 1532 by Grand Prince Vassily III to celebrate the birth of his son, Ivan, who would later come to be known as "the Terrible". It was once the tallest church in Russia, and its slender tent-roof, based on a wooden architectural style from north Russia, still makes it one of the prettiest. With wonderful acoustics inside, it is a popular venue for concerts.

Beside it are two smaller buildings, the bell-tower of St. George's Church (the church itself was destroyed in the 1930's), and a tower where falcons, one of Tsar Alexey's hobbies, were kept.

Wooden Architecture Museum
Among orchards inside the complex are three buildings brought to Kolomenskoye from remote corners of Russia. The House of Peter the Great, built in the Novodvinsk fortress near Arkhangelsk during the Northern War against Sweden, is open to the public. The bedroom, dining room and servants' quarters are a recreation of 17th century life.

Nearby is a gate tower and a section of wall, from the St. Nicholas Monastery, also near Arkhangelsk. The pyramid-shaped watch-tower and tiny viewing platform are typical of 17th century wooden architecture.

The third exhibit is another tower, this from a defensive fortress in the Siberian town of Bratsk.

Dyakovo
On the next hill, reached by following the riverside path right from the Ascension Church, is the site of the village of Dyakovo, known to have been settled as early as the 1st century B.C.

The hilltop Church of St. John the Baptist (*Tserkov' Ioanna Predtechi*) was built in the 1540's–50's by Ivan the Terrible in honour of his new title – in an attempt to curb the powers of the boyars, Ivan, until then Prince of Muscovy, had effectively made himself the first Tsar of Russia. The church also represents the transition to the tent-roof form; it is regarded as the forerunner of St. Basil's on Red Square.

Izmailovsky Park

Moscow's largest park, Izmailovsky was once the Tsar's hunting reserve and is now the venue for an enormous weekend market.

DIRECTIONS: Metro Izmailovsky Park or Izmailovskaya. The first of these brings you to the hotel complex, fleamarket and old estate (exit left), and to an amusement park (exit right), while the second will take you to wilder forest areas of the park.

By car leave the Garden Ring by Novaya Basmannaya Ulitsa and go straight for 3 km.

Izmailovsky Park

Covering almost 3,000 acres of land in what is now eastern Moscow, this area was a hunting reserve belonging to the Romanov family (then boyars) from the mid-16th century.

In 1663, Tsar Alexey organised an experimental farm there, based around a new estate built on what is now the park's north-western edge. He imported western technology to cope with demand for silk, cotton, paints, medicinal herbs and other products. He even kept a zoo (where the metro station and hotel complex now stand), so close to the estate that he was commonly kept awake at night by the caterwauling of his lions and tigers.

Izmailovo is also one of the dozen or so places in Russia which claim to be the birthplace of Russia's fleet. The infant Peter the Great found an old boat there, probably a gift from Queen Elizabeth of England to Ivan the Terrible, and took it sailing on the ponds, thereby cultivating his famous interest in ships.

Izmailovo Fleamarket
(Vernissazh)

In between the enormous blocks of the mafia-infested, Brezhnev-era Izmailovo Tourist Complex and the Sports Stadium stretches Moscow's largest fleamarket, open Saturdays and Sundays.

Here you'll find everything from carpets to trinkets, from lacquer boxes to *matryoshka* dolls. Quality varies widely, so take your time choosing – many of those selling may well be craftsmen themselves, and are often happy to talk about their work. Bargaining is acceptable but may not always work, and traders will often try to charge foreigners a higher price.

Izmailovo Estate

Instead of heading into the market, turn right before the stadium, walk through a car park and cross the bridge. The stretch of water is part of a system of 37 ponds which Alexey built to irrigate his experimental plots, breed leeches and for many other purposes; unfortunately they have not been carefully preserved.

Soon you arrive at the estate itself. Much has been destroyed but two interesting buildings remain from Alexey's time. The Intercession Cathedral was built in 1672 to commemorate victory over the Poles. Now standing between later buildings, its five massive domes dominate the countryside. Their drums, and the *zakomary* below, are decorated with "peacock's eye" tiling, the trademark of craftsman Stepan Polubes (*see* Walk 11).

Nearby is the Bridge Tower, all that is left of a giant fourteen-span bridge that once crossed the estate's system of lakes. Built in 1671, it was a major architectural and engineering achievement of its time.

AN EXPLORER'S GUIDE TO RUSSIA

"For the adventurous soul... Greenall's
An Explorer's Guide to Russia is a must."
MOSCOW TRIBUNE

*Once you've
explored Moscow
with Robert Greenall,
don't miss seeing
the rest of western
Russia with him
as your guide!*

"Offers a wealth of historical information, maps
and directories, plus tips on customs and habits
in seventeen regions of European Russia."
TIME MAGAZINE

St. Petersburg • Moscow • Volga & Oka
Valleys • Western Defenses • City States
(Novgorod, Pskov) • Russian North

*With our own low-cost bed & breakfast and
guide/interpreter services in St. Petersburg & Moscow!*

$22 (post-paid)

ALSO FROM ZEPHYR

"RUSSIA: PEOPLE TO PEOPLE" (due in 1996):
Lists 1,000 Russians eager to show you
around. Includes name, address, phone,
profession, age, languages and interests.

Also in the PEOPLE TO PEOPLE series ($14 post-paid):
The Baltic Republics • Poland • Romania
Czech-Slovakia, Hungary & Bulgaria

Zephyr Press • 13 Robinson St. • Somerville, MA 02145
USA • Tel. (617) 628-9726 • Fax (617) 776-8246

TRAVEL BOOKS FROM ZEPHYR PRESS

Kuskovo

The palace and park ensemble of the wealthy Sheremetyev family, Kuskovo's interior contains what is probably Russia's best collection of 18th century furnishings; the Orangery houses the State Ceramics Museum.

DIRECTIONS: From Metro Ryazansky Prospekt, take bus #133 or #208 six stops to the palace and gardens.

By car, drive southeast from Taganskaya Ploshchad along Taganskaya Ulitsa, later Ryazansky Prospekt for 4 km, turn left onto Ulitsa Papernika and on as far as the lake on the left.

Kuskovo belonged to the Sheremetyevs since the 16th century, with the ensemble that you see today being built by serfs in the 18th, commissioned by arts patron and public celebrity Count Pyotr Sheremetyev. He spared no expense on his palace, nor on the collection of sculptures and paintings for its interior; its park was also the venue for festivities for the general public, sometimes drawing crowds as large as 25,000 people.

These included drama performed by his serf troupe, made up of the best acting talent chosen from labourers from the family's estates, as well as firework displays.

In the last century, the estate slowly fell into disuse. The famous serf theatre, where the actress and future Countess Sheremetyeva, Praskovia Zhemchugova-Kovalyova (*see* Walk 8 and Ostankino), made her debut, was dismantled. After the revolution Kuskovo became a natural history museum; after extensive research into the Sheremetyev family — many of the family's possessions were lost after the Revolution — it was restored to its original appearance.

The Palace

A fine example of wooden classical architecture of the late 18th century, the Kuskovo palace has a pleasantly restrained and sober appearance. Its central columned portico shelters a ramp, by which carriages brought guests right to the front entrance. They then entered through the grand hallway, decorated by alabaster vases and grisaille murals imitating ancient classical bas-reliefs.

To the left are three drawing rooms. The first two present fine Flemish tapestries with scenes of landscape gardens, which combine with the view of the park through the windows to create an idyllic atmosphere. They are followed by the mauve drawing room, in lavish Baroque style, with busts by Fyodor Shubin showing a powerful and proud Count Sheremetyev.

The next room is the so-called State Bedchamber, more grandiose than the previous rooms with its painted ceiling and gilded vases. Despite its name, no one has ever slept here, nor was this the intention — it was really yet another drawing room.

Passing through smaller functional rooms, you reach the Picture Room, hung with 16th–18th century European art. Beyond it is the White Hall, or Hall of Mirrors, the palace's main reception room. It was also used as a ballroom, and includes mirrors placed in imitation window frames and a ceiling painting, which, combined with the gilded white walls, chandeliers and parquet floor, give an effect of great space and grandeur.

The Formal Garden
The garden, dating from the same period as the palace, is imaginatively conceived and has a wide range of buildings in various European styles – a Dutch House, Swiss House, Italian House and Hermitage, the last roughly symmetrical in appearance and built in the ornamental French style of the day.

Two monuments on its main axis, a triumphal column topped by a statue of Minerva and an obelisk, commemorate the visit of Catherine the Great in 1775 and the election of Count Sheremetyev as a Marshal of Nobility respectively.

The Orangery
This large building facing the palace across the garden had a duel purpose, its central part serving as a banqueting hall and its wings a winter garden with exotic plants, where oranges, lemons and pineapples grew all year round.

Today it houses the State Ceramics Museum, based on the pre-revolutionary collections of the Morozov family and others. As well as examples of the work of Meissen, Wedgwood and other European factories, it traces the history of Russian china from the appearance of the Imperial Factory in 1744 through to the avant-garde "agitational china" of the 1920's (when most art-forms, including ceramics, were directed towards revolutionary propaganda).

The left wing of the building now includes an exhibition-sale of the work of several Russian

ceramics factories, like Shakhty, in southern Russia's coal mining region, with its lyrical and humorous scenes from the lives of the Don Cossacks, or Shchekino, with painted animal toys from the village of Filimonovo.

The Grotto
On the right side of the ensemble closer to the main entrance, this little pavilion was built in the style of a sea king's palace, reflected in the waters of the pond in front.

Its exquisite interior is decorated with sea shells and pebbles brought from the Mediterranean, to resemble a luxurious watery cave.

Ostankino

A second Sheremetyev residence, Ostankino's palace is the main focus of attention for visitors, rather than the gardens. Here also is the complex for which the area is better known to most Russians today – the TV centre and tower.

DIRECTIONS: From Metro VDNKh, take the #11 tram from the near side stop (going right) to the end of the line (5 stops), right outside the palace.

By car, take Prospekt Mira from the Garden Ring for 2 km, and turn left down 1-ya Ostankinskaya Ulitsa. Ostankino can be combined with a visit to the All-Russian Exhibition Centre, whose southern entrance is just three stops away on the same tram.

Ostankino Estate

The village of Ostankino came into the ownership of the Princes Cherkassky, a wealthy noble family, in the 17th century, and the first palaces were built there. In 1743 Count Pyotr Sheremetyev married a Cherkassky heiress and received the land as a dowry.

His theatre-loving son Nikolay decided to build a new stage here for his serf troupe. Rejecting the plans of St. Petersburg architect Giacomo Quarenghi as inadequate for his purposes, he instead commissioned Argunov, his serf architect, to build it. The end result was Russia's best theatre of its time, a palace with sumptuous concert and reception halls, art and sculpture collections, and the latest in theatrical wizardry.

The palace was badly damaged in 1812, and after a century of neglect when most of its valuables were moved to other sites, little was left of the theatre. In Soviet times, however, a museum was set up here, and after painstaking restoration and the return of lost items, it has gradually returned to its former appearance.

The Palace

Sheremetyev's original idea was to build a Palace of Muses and Graces in central Moscow, a grand cultural centre with theatre and museum included. Executed here instead, the result is an elegant, well-proportioned classical structure with a complex of interconnecting side-wings and central columned facades. Like Kuskovo Palace, it is made of stuccoed wood.

The first two main rooms of the palace have a distinctly royal theme. The Blue Hall is believed to have been designed as a bedroom for Catherine the Great,

who died before she was able to visit. Medallions on the wall of her and Peter the Great are by Josiah Wedgwood. Note the grey marble sculptures of Egyptian slaves, copied from an Italian original.

The Crimson Room is so-called because of the deep red velvet covering the walls. The picture frame here was also intended to hold a portrait of Catherine the Great, but her death made it expedient to put her estranged son Tsar Paul here instead.

The western suite contains the palace's art gallery, a feast of colour which combines turquoise wallpaper, ruby chandeliers and multi-coloured window-sill vases.

The paintings themselves are no less prominent, and although most of the original Rubens, Titians and Van Dykes were looted by the French, today's collection of works by minor European painters of the 17th–18th centuries is a worthy substitute.

The Theatre

Now part of the palace interior, the Ostankino theatre, built in 1793, in fact predates it. During reconstructions, the serf engineer F. Pryakhin built a complex device to raise the floor to the level of the stage for balls and banquets. In the process, extra chandeliers were lowered and dummy columns moved out on rails, thus making the stage and auditorium virtually identical.

It was here, in 1797, that Praskovia Zhemchugova-Kovalyova made her last stage appearance, and just 20 years later the theatre finally closed altogether.

Over time, the mechanism was lost, and the hall remained stuck in banquet mode thereafter.

The Pavilions

Connected to the theatre by closed galleries are two side pavilions identical in shape. The Egyptian Pavilion, so-called because of the sphinxes sitting on top of the tiled stoves which heated it, is in the style of a classical atrium, with marble columns and an original Roman statue of the goddess of Health. It served as a concert hall.

The Italian Pavilion, meanwhile, is more sumptuously decorated, as befitting a reception hall. It also serves as a sculpture gallery, its treasures including a 1st century B.C. marble goat from Pompeii, a group portraying the classical hero Milo of Krotos by Etienne Falconet, famous for the "Bronze Horseman" statue in St. Petersburg, and a bronze bust of Voltaire.

Trinity Church
(Troitskaya Tserkov')
Outside the front entrance of the palace, this beautiful 17th century church, typical of the Moscow style of the day, was not connected with the Sheremetyevs. It was built by Mikhail Cherkassy, then the owner of the estate, who was distinguished by being the only man in Peter the Great's court exempted from the Tsar's edict to shave off his beard. Its interior, with a massive nine-tier iconostasis, is mainly 19th century.

TV Tower
When you're in the area you won't fail to notice the Ostankino television tower, the second tallest free-standing structure in the world at 540 metres; with plans in process to raise it yet further in height, it will shortly top the CN tower in Toronto.

Completed in 1967, its original plan resembled the Eiffel Tower, and still shows some features of

that structure, in particular the spread legs at the base. The observation tower 337 metres up is open to the public (bring your passport for entrance formalities), which includes the Seventh Heaven restaurant.

TV Centre
Nearby is the television centre, formerly the nerve centre of the monolithic Soviet giant Gosteleradio (State Television and Radio Committee) and now split between several national and local channels, both state-owned and private. The most dramatic, and tragic, moment in its history came in October 1993, when supporters of the Russian parliament tried to storm the building and gain access to the airwaves.

The All-Russian Exhibition Centre

Still best known under its former initials, VDNKh, the Exhibition of Economic Achievement was a unique monument to the Soviet way of life; the change of recent years has, by a supreme irony, turned it into a microcosm of the new Russia.

DIRECTIONS: From Metro VDNKh, the exhibition complex is immediately visible on the left as you emerge. To go directly to the Botanical Gardens, take bus #24, #85, #803 or trolleybus #9, #36, #73 from outside the Metro. By car follow Prospekt Mira from the Garden Ring.

Kosmos Hotel

Built by the French in 1970, the enormous tower block across Prospekt Mira was once considered Moscow's top tourist hotel, although today, in terms of quality (and to some extent price), it has fallen well behind city-centre competitors. It has just about everything, including a liberal quantity of mafia stooges.

Memorial Museum of Cosmonautics

Before reaching the Exhibition Centre, you will pass a 107-metre tall monument of a rocket shooting up into the sky, connected to earth by a trail of steel. Inside the base is a museum devoted to the Soviet space programme, including a darkened hall which rather unsuccessfully imitates space. Also on view are space suits and modules, including the first Soviet earth satellite and a replica of the cabin of the ship through which Alexey Leonov passed on the first-ever space walk.

☞ *Museum open 10 am–7 pm Tues–Sun, closed last Fri of the month. Tel: 283-7914.*

All-Russian Exhibition Centre (VVTs)

Previously known as the Exhibition of Economic Achievement (VDNKh), this great showcase of socialism once proclaimed the Soviet Union's progress in all branches of science and technology. In the 1930's, Stalin arranged the building of pavilions on this site in the architectural styles of the Soviet republics. They were then filled with goods and exhibits from the respective republics.

Though Khrushchev changed the nature of the exhibitions, dividing them up into branches of industry and agriculture instead of by geography, it remained a display of everything that the country aspired to – but was unable to achieve in reality.

By the beginning of perestroika, its inherent falsity was no longer in any doubt – the contrast between the plenty there and the greyness and poverty of everyday life had become too stark. So when Russia's reformers came to power, VDNKh, like the rest of the country, went commercial. The name was changed to the All-Russian Exhibition Centre, and the pavilions were rented out to business and filled with foreign products.

Visiting the complex today, you may be hard put to find traces of many of its previous "achievements". However, it is interesting in terms of architectural make-up, and also as a perfect illustration of the current mood and atmosphere in Russia. The place has the feeling of a crazy bazaar, clouded by beery smells and smoke from the many *shashlyk* bars. Numerous drunks mingle with equally numerous "New Russians", perusing the complex's electronic goods and furniture showrooms.

The Centre contains 72 working pavilions, and many accessory buildings like cafés, restaurants, theatres and fairgrounds, and covers 254 hectares in all. To see everything would be exhausting, not to say monotonous, so we list some of the complex's more interesting sights, which are not necessarily in its central area.

"Rabochy i Kolkhoznitsa" Statue

The statue of the "Worker and Woman Collective Farmer" stands to the right of the northern entrance. Designed by Vera Mukhina in 1937, and familiar to many as the emblem of Mosfilm, the country's largest film studio, it is considered to be one of the paragons of Socialist Realism.

The Central Pavilion (No. 1)
The first building you reach from the entrance dominates the complex. With echoes of the Admiralty building in St. Petersburg, it was designed to rise above the Exhibition in the same way as the Palace of Soviets (see Walk 6) was supposed to rise above Moscow. Today it contains the "City of Discovery and Creation", full of high-tech toys and holograms for children of all ages.

Education Pavilion
(No. 2, Narodnoye Obrazovaniye)
Originally built in 1954 for an exhibition on the North Caucasus, this high-columned palace on your left used to welcome visitors with palm trees and exotic southern flowers. It still retains its Khrushchev era function, though its teaching aids, toys and textbooks are now more often than not imported.

Round Panoramic Cinema
(No. 124, Kinoteatr Krugovoy Panoramy)
A truly unique building on the left side of the complex (near the southern gate, turn left before Pavilion 1). The idea for a cinema of this kind came from Walt Disney in the 1950's, but it may be that the Soviets beat the great US cinematographer to this invention. In this completely round auditorium, you can stand and observe films on a screen which stretches all round the walls, and listen to a nine-track stereo system blasted from loudspeakers above, below and around you.

Requiring filming from eleven cameras simultaneously, mounted on a special platform, such films are expensive to make, especially for Russia's now-impoverished film industry. The repertoire is therefore small, just four films about travel in the former Soviet Union. However, there are free showings every Saturday.

Atomic Energy Pavilion
(No. 71, Atomnaya Energiya)
One of the most important pavilions in the complex, first as exhibition for the Russian Federation, then for the new industry of nuclear power. Built in the neoclassical style of the day, its entrance used to resemble the halls of the Kremlin Palace.

Nowadays there's no trace of the glory of Russia, or indeed the atom — it's just an ordinary shop, like dozens of others here.

The Fountains
The symbol of VDNKh, reflecting its pomposity and showiness, the fountains are made of bronze, copper and even concrete, covered with gold smalt. The first and most impressive is the "Friendship of the Peoples" Fountain, whose 15 bronze female figures represent the republics of the former U.S.S.R.

Culture Pavilion
(No. 56, Kultura)
Slightly further down on the right, this pavilion is distinguished by the enormous enclosure for its fountain, reminiscent of late 19th century spa town architecture. Inside is the "Filigran" art salon, selling jewellery, china, amber, carpets and other arts and crafts.

Health Pavilion
(No. 13, Zdorovye)
Originally built in the 1930's for an Armenian exhibition, it was

based, far-fetched as it may seem, on 4th–7th century Armenian Church architecture. This is manifested in the building material, red tufa, and the form, a central block with two side wings. Inside you used to be able to see ceiling mosaics and a panel by the artist Martiros Saryan.

As a health pavilion, it became a kind of out-patient clinic, a last resort for people who despaired of finding treatment elsewhere. Now it sells everything from aspirins to iron lungs.

Agriculture Pavilion
(No. 58, Zemlyedeliye)
Midway between the Central Pavilion and Space Pavilion is that formerly assigned to the Ukraine. Representing the main agricultural republic of the Soviet Union, it's not difficult to explain its 1950's conversion.

With its extravagant facade, decorated with coloured tiles to resemble a theatre curtain, it is one of the most striking and overblown buildings on the site, its interior dull by comparison.

Grain Pavilion
(No. 59, Zerno)
Next door is the pavilion built for the Moscow Region exhibition. Built by Dmitry Chechulin, architect of the "White House", Peking and Rossiya Hotels, it is in the style of the "wedding cakes" spread round central Moscow.

Space Pavilion
(No. 32, Kosmos)
This enormous pavilion was built in 1939 in the form of a hangar and originally contained aircraft. This later gave way to an exhibition on space flight, a popular phenomenon of which the Soviet people were genuinely proud.

However, the Space Pavilion has not escaped the fate of most others. It was cleared to make way for a luxury car showroom, but not before staging Moscow's first raves, the "Gagarin Parties", in 1992. Even the smiling photo of Yuri Gagarin, the first man in space, has recently been removed.

Even the two classic aeroplanes outside, the TU-104 and YaK-42, have been turned into shops. Only the "Vostok", a copy of Gagarin's first spaceship, remains untainted by commerce.

The Livestock Display Circuit
(Vyvodnoy Krug)
To the right of and behind the Space Pavilion is one of the few areas of the Centre which still seems to serve its original purpose. In the middle is a short, circular track, and around it viewing stands, crude animal sculptures and pavilions housing horses, cattle and pigs.

It seems that livestock is still a going concern at the Centre, or perhaps it's just that the stench of manure has saved them from displacement by VCRs and luxury furniture. The supreme example is the Pig-Farming Pavilion (No. 47, *Svinovodstvo*), once home to a hog named Napoleon whose enormous testicles brought curious visitors from far and wide.

Beekeeping Pavilion
(No. 28, Pchelovodstvo)
Undoubtedly one of the surprise success stories of the Centre, this little pavilion on the left side near the lake presents a display of beekeeping equipment and a whole range of honeys, combs etc. from all over Russia.

Beekeeping is a favourite pastime for many rural Russians, and the end product is almost invariably delicious. Bring jars with you (the containers provided are inadequate) if you're going to make a purchase. Honey is also sold in the Pond Maintenance (No. 39, *Prudovoye Khozyaistvo*), Livestock Farming (No. 42, *Zhivotnovodstvo*), Breeding of Animals for Agriculture (No. 49, *Vosproizvodstvo Selskokhozyaistvennykh Zhivotnykh*) and Milk Industry (No. 50, *Molochnaya Promyshlennost'*) Pavilions.

Domestic Services

(No. 35, Bytovoye Obsluzhivanye)
Cross the lake by the right or left routes to this fairytale pavilion between them, little known by visitors and abandoned for much of the Exhibition's lifetime. It was built by an artist, not an architect, and embodies features like tobacco leaves in its decor – this was originally the pavilion of the state tobacco combine.

Botanical Gardens

(Botanichesky Sad)
Continue west from the pavilion until you come to a gate, apparently padlocked but on closer inspection broken by the many visitors constantly squeezing through it. This is a back entrance to the Botanical Gardens, a vast and unruly collection of trees and plants. Almost nothing here seems looked after, let alone marked or signposted, and you'll have to walk (about 15 minutes) to one of the two proper entrances just to see a rather crude map.

The exception to the general chaos is the Japanese Garden (*Yaponsky Sad*), reached by taking an immediate right off the lakeside path. Here beautifully tended lawns and flowers, exclusively from the Far East, are set alongside bridges and springs.

Eating in VVTs

It won't be difficult to find food in the Centre – every few yards there is a *shashlyk* bar or ice-cream vendor. However, eating on the street in Russia can be hazardous healthwise, and it might be wise to find a café or restaurant. Newer, smaller cafés like those in the Central and Transport Pavilions are probably preferable to the old Soviet-era places. For a proper meal, restaurants include the Podkova (No. 118), in the style of an old Russian *traktir*, and Astoria (No. 121), situated in an unusual part-wooden Russian-style palace. If you want to be absolutely safe, there is a branch of Kombi's up Prospekt Mira at No. 180.

Tsaritsyno

Famous for the ruins of the great palace of Catherine the Great, which no one ever had the strength to finish building, Tsaritsyno offers rural escape: its lakes and leafy forest are favourites among Muscovites in the summer.

DIRECTIONS: From Metro Tsaritsyno, leave by the northern exit (the back carriage if coming from the centre), cross under the railway bridges and turn right. When the main road bears round to the right, a track to the right leads straight ahead between two lakes.

By car drive as if to St. Daniel's, but continue straight past the market down Varshavskoye Shosse. Turn left onto Kashirskoye Shosse, continue for 2 km and turn left before the railway. In another 2 km turn left under the bridges mentioned above.

Tsaritsyno's huge palace was commissioned by Catherine the Great in 1775, after the Empress took a fancy to a piece of land south of Moscow called *Chornaya Gryaz'* (Black Mud). Proclaiming it to be "heaven on earth", she promptly renamed it Tsaritsyno, the Empress' village.

Architect Vassily Bazhenov began work on the project but the Moorish-gothic neo-Russian buildings he created were not to Catherine's liking, and she decided to knock down all but the entrance gate and the opera house. Matvey Kazakov was commissioned to rebuild the palace, but funds ran out before he could finish.

What remains, then, is a superb ruin of something that never quite existed: enormous palace walls with no floors, windows or roof, a paradise for children of all ages, stunt men, absailers, and the romantically inclined. Tsaritsyno has a reputation for supernatural happenings, too, including a bridge that moved several metres, and even sightings of "humanoid aliens".

For the moment, though, visitors can walk among the ruins (construction work is not really a hindrance, except for a few areas which are fenced off), and strong footwear is an advantage. There are also several acres of forested parkland with follies, while the lakes are popular with fishermen and summer swimmers.

The Museum

Currently there is a new burst of activity at Tsaritsyno. Many of the smaller buildings have been restored and a small museum has been opened, though it only dis-

plays a tiny amount of the fine collection of icons, glass, china and Fabergé eggs, the rest of which are stored in cellars under the ruins, occasionally surfacing for exhibitions abroad.

☛ *Open April through October, Weds–Fri 11 am–6 pm; Sat & Sun 10 am–6 pm, closed Mon, Tues. Tel: 321-0743.*

Arkhangelskoye

Known as Moscow's Versailles, Arkhangelskoye is another favourite for lovers of palace and park ensembles. Although restoration work has closed off the palace, it is still the best preserved estate of its kind in the Moscow area.

DIRECTIONS: From Metro Tushinskaya, take bus #549 for about 30 minutes directly to the Arkhangelskoye sanatorium stop, opposite the back gates.

By car take Leningradsky Prospekt, fork left onto Volokolamskoye Shosse, and just past the city limits turn left onto Ilyinskoye Shosse, which will take you directly to Arkhangelskoye. The park is officially closed, but can be entered through a gap in the fence across the road.

Although the estate was begun in the 1660's, most of the buildings which remain at Arkhangelskoye today date from a hundred years later, when the Golitsyn family, prominent since the time of Peter the Great, devoted large sums of money and attention to its reconstruction. When Prince Nikolay Yusupov bought the estate in 1810, he added new buildings and filled the main house with one of Europe's finest art collections, including works by Van Dyck and Tiepolo.

Unfortunately, the museum, long-closed for restoration, seems unlikely to reopen in the near future, but the park and outer buildings are still worth visiting. A combination of formal gardens near the palace and a landscape park further away, the palace grounds are filled with classical statues and pavilions.

The Palace

Originally built in 1790 by the French architect Chevalier de la Huerne, this simple but elegant classical building took on its current appearance after 1812, when restored and altered by the serf architect Osip Ivanov. He added the current belvedere, by which Arkhangelskoye is so easily distinguished today.

The front entrance has magnificent Triumphal Gates with intricate wrought iron railings, but the back facade is the grander, with numerous statues, a fountain and an ornamental staircase leading down to the French park.

The Park

Fourteen hectares of land behind the palace contain an ornamental garden with more sculptures, mostly 19th century copies of ancient classical works including many lions of varying size and expression.

There are several pavilions and follies, including a little summer house on the right dedicated to Catherine the Great. On the left, meanwhile, is Pushkin Alley, with a statue of the poet erected in 1899 to commemorate the centenary of his birth – he visited and was much impressed with the estate.

The Serf Theatre

On the right side of the park, this faded theatre is a sad example of the way Arkhangelskoye has been neglected in recent years. It contains unique decorations by the Italian master Pietro Gonzaga dating from the late 18th century, used both for theatrical and operatic performances of Yusupov's troupe, and for Son et Lumière productions, of which the Prince was effectively the inventor.

The Yusupov Mausoleum and Colonnade

On the left side, this magnificent structure with its semi-circular colonnade is the last addition to the ensemble. A fine example of pre-revolutionary Neo-Classicism, finished in 1916, it was never used for its intended purpose.

Church of the Archangel Michael

(Tserkov' Arkhangela Mikhaila)
The only survivor from the original 1667 estate, this little church gave the village its name. Situated on the left side overlooking the Moskva River, at some distance from the palace, it occupies the most picturesque spot in the estate and shouldn't be missed.

The Restaurants

Back at the main road, just through the trees is the Arkhangelskoye Restaurant, commissioned personally by the sometime Soviet Prime Minister Alexey Kosygin, one of many officials to own dachas in the area. The restaurant provides welcome refreshment in an otherwise barren area (tel: 562-0328).

For dining in greater style, if you have transport, the pricier Russkaya Izba (tel: 561-4244) is near the Moskva River bridge in the nearby village of Ilyinskoye.

War Memorials

A range of sites in the west of the city are devoted to the heroic defence of Russia in two major wars. The Kutuzov museums and Triumphal Arch celebrate the victory against the French in 1812, while the Poklonnaya Gora complex remembers the Great Patriotic War, four years of battle against Nazi Germany.

DIRECTIONS: From Metro Kutuzovskaya, leave by the western exit (front carriage, if approaching from the centre) and take trolleybus #2, #7 or #39 for two stops for the 1812 museums, and for three stops for the Triumphal Arch and Poklonnaya Gora.

By car, follow Kutuzovsky Prospekt west for 1.5 km. The Triumphal Arch, in the middle of the road, is unmissable.

Kutuzovsky Prospekt

The main road leading west from Moscow is named after the great Russian Marshal of the Napoleonic Wars, Mikhail Kutuzov, whose tactics of evasion wore down the invading French army in 1812 and eventually forced them into retreat.

It took on its present appearance in the 1930's and became a highly prestigious place to live: the "Stagnation Era" Soviet leader Leonid Brezhnev had an apartment here, closer to the centre. Russia's current leadership lives much further out, in the high class suburb of Krylatskoye.

Battle of Borodino Panorama Museum

On the right side of the Prospekt stands a statue of Kutuzov by Soviet sculptor Nikolay Tomsky. Behind him is a museum devoted to the 1812 Battle of Borodino, the main confrontation between the two armies on the approaches to Moscow which, though it ended in stalemate, severely weakened the French army. It displays a panoramic painting of the battle, finished at the centenary by, appropriately, a Russified Frenchman, Franz Roubaud. *Currently closed for repairs.*

Kutuzov Hut

Behind the main museum is a replica of the wooden cabin where Kutuzov and other Russian generals discussed strategy against the French as they approached Moscow.

Against the odds, Kutuzov managed to persuade the others to leave Moscow to the invaders. This proved to be the right decision, and the starved French army was unable to hold the devastated city. The original cabin was burnt down in 1868, but replaced to mark the 75th anniversary of 1812.
☞ *Open Tues, Weds 10 am–5 pm; Thurs, Sat, Sun 10:30 am–5 pm.*

Triumphal Arch

Osip Bove built this 28 metre-high Roman style archway in 1834 during the post-1812 reconstruction of the city. It originally stood on Ploshchad Tverskoy Zastavy, near the Belorussia Station: in the 1930's the road became too busy, but instead of simply knocking it down like many monuments, the Stalinist authorities found it this new and quite appropriate home.

Its sculptural compositions, designed by Ivan Vitali, include top figures representing Glory in a chariot, ancient Russian warriors at the sides, and a frieze depicting the coats-of-arms of the eight provinces whose men fought against Napoleon.

Victory Park
(Park Pobedy)
To the left of the Arch is the Hill of Reverence (*Poklonnaya Gora*), which once provided fine views of the city, and was loved by Alexander Pushkin among others. In 1812 Napoleon waited here vainly to receive the city keys.

A park was created here in 1961 to mark the 20th anniversary of Nazi invasion, while recent construction of the memorial complex was finished in time to celebrate the 50th anniversary of the end of the war, an event attended by many major world leaders.

The park is an impressive and monumental sight, in the grandest Soviet landscaping traditions. A broad avenue with fountains on each side leads off at an angle from the Triumphal Arch to the main body of the complex. Each year of the conflict is marked by a plinth, leading up to final victory in the central square.

Nike Monument
Zurab Tsereteli's rather oversized Victory monument stands at the centre of the square. Its huge shaft, 142 metres high, supports a bronze statue of Nike, the Greek God of Victory, flanked by angels with golden bugles, and is carved with high reliefs of battle scenes and the names of hero-cities of the former Soviet Union.

At the base is a Byzantine-style St. George, standing over an inexplicably chopped Nazi dragon – the warrior is carrying a spear not a sword.

"Anyone interested in Russia and good writing should seek *Glas* out."
– London Observer

GLAS: New Russian Writing presents the best of contemporary Russian writing, deftly translated, in book-length, thematic issues.

Recent issues include:
#8: Love Russian Style
#7: Booker Prize Issue
#6: Jews and Strangers
#5: Bulgakov and Mandelstam
#4: Love and Fear
#3: Women's View

FOR SUBSCRIPTION INFORMATION, OR TO ORDER COPIES, CONTACT:

In the U.K.:
Glas, Dept. of Russian Literature, University of Birmingham, B15 2TT.
Tel: (0121) 414-6044
Fax: (0121) 414-5966

In the U.S., Canada:
Zephyr Press, 13 Robinson Street, Somerville, MA 02145.
Tel: (617) 628-9726
Fax: (617) 776-8246

In Moscow:
Tel./fax: (095) 441-9157

Greater Moscow | War Memorials

Church of St. George the Victor

(Tserkov' Georgiya Pobedonostsa)

On the left stands the first new church to be built in Moscow since the revolution. Tall and slender, it is based on the simple style of the ancient Russian churches of the 13th–15th centuries, though the unusual windows and bronze bas-reliefs are a modern innovation. The latter have caused some controversy – many believe they do not correspond to Orthodox canons. There are plans to build a Catholic church, mosque and synagogue nearby.

Central Museum of the Great Patriotic War

The main building of the complex is a massive museum, containing wartime paintings, posters, sculptures and graphics.

The central Hall of Glory is a unique sight – with the names of all Heroes of the Soviet Union who took part in the war written in golden letters on the walls. In addition, there are six dioramas devoted to the most important battles of the war, from the December 1941 counter-attack near Moscow, through the Battle of Stalingrad in 1943 to the storming of the Reichstag.

☛ *Open daily 10 am–5 pm.*

Open-Air Exhibition

To the left of the museum is a substantial exhibition of weapons of victory, including boats, planes and an armoured train. It seems to serve as a children's playground, as visitors are free to climb through its trenches and bunkers, and play with armour and gun installations, including some weapons captured from the Germans and Japanese.

☛ *Open daily 10 am–5 pm.*

Church of the Intercession

(Tserkov' Pokrova)

Follow Ulitsa 1812 Goda, running north from Kutuzovsky Prospekt between the Triumphal Arch and the Borodino Museum, and its extension Novozavodskaya Ulitsa to this unrelated attraction.

This extraordinary church is one of the finest examples of the extravagant "Naryshkin Baroque" style, with intricate stone carvings set against red brick on the outside, and luxurious iconostases within. In line with the fashion of the day, the painter of the icons, Karp Zolotaryov, was also a portrait painter, and secular themes are prominent. One icon depicts Peter the Great as a young man. In a similar spirit, the Tsar's pew is decorated in the same way as the iconostasis, thus seeming to cloud the difference between saint and still mortal Tsar.

Try to visit between May and October when the upper summer church is open. The lower heated winter church is an exhibition hall used for collections from the Andrey Rublyov icon museum.

☛ *Open daily except Tues and Wed and the last Fri of the month 11 am–6 pm.*

Excursions Outside Moscow

Abramtsevo

A museum-estate set in beautiful countryside to the northeast of Moscow, Abramtsevo become famous for the group of artists who worked there at the turn of the century, combining traditional Russian styles with Art Nouveau.

DIRECTIONS: By local train to Abramtsevo from the Yaroslavl station (Sergiyev Posad or Alexandrov trains), journey time 1.5 hours. A well-tended path leads to the estate from the opposite platform. By car, drive 72 km out of Moscow on the M8 (Yaroslavskoye Shosse) to the village of Vozdvizhenskoye, then turn left to Khotkovo. Before reaching the entrance to the convent, turn left again for Abramtsevo. This trip can be combined with a visit to Sergiyev Posad.

The Estate & Main House

The lush, green countryside in this part of the Moscow Region has inspired artists and writers for centuries, and provides an attractive setting for the small country estate. Abramtsevo was acquired by the devout slavophile writer Sergey Aksakov in the mid-19th century because of its proximity to the Trinity-St. Sergius Lavra. For a time it became almost a headquarters for the Slavophiles in their intellectual battle with the Westernisers.

Later in the century, the estate was bought by the progressive industrialist and art patron Savva Mamontov, who invited such artists as Viktor and Apollinariy Vasnetsov and Ilya Repin (*see* Tretyakov Gallery) to work on collective projects there. Even after the Revolution, artistic traditions continued, as painters like Aristarch Lentulov and Robert Falk lived and worked there.

The main house today contains an exhibition about the estate's two famous owners, with photographs and paintings by Repin, Vasnetsov, Serov and Polyenov. It includes the Red Sitting-Room where Nikolay Gogol read extracts from his *Dead Souls*, and Mamontov's circle gathered to act, read or paint.

Other Buildings

Abramtsevo's character is best appreciated by wandering around the grounds to see the outbuildings constructed by several of the resident artists. The neo-Russian Church of Spas Not Made By Human Hand (*Tserkov' Spasa Nerukotvornovo*, 1880–82), in the woods at the back of the estate, was designed by Apollinariy Vasnetsov with interior icons and other decoration by Viktor Vasnetsov, Vassily Polyenov and Ilya Repin.

White, unimposing, and asymmetrically pleasing to the eye, it is a perfect site for peaceful contemplation. Nearby Viktor Vasnetsov built a children's playhouse, called the "House on Chicken Legs" because of the tree stumps on which it stood.

The Teremok baths, meanwhile, with their traditional but unorthodox folk carvings, were built by Ivan Ropet in 1877. The pleasant interior came to be used as a reception room for guests of the circle.

The Ceramics Studio, near the entrance to the main house, is a wonderful example of the Russian *izba* or peasant hut.

Basically a log cabin, but with intricately carved awnings and platbands, it now houses a craft museum, displaying the works of the studio, which was originally run by Polyenov's sister Yelena. Here you can see some of the finest ceramic works of Mikhail Vrubel (*see* Tretyakov Gallery). ☛ *Open Weds–Sun 10 am– 5 pm. The museum is closed during April and October and on the last Thurs of each month.*

Kolomna

A picturesque but little-known town on the Moskva River, Kolomna was once a major fortress and second city in the Muscovy Princedom. Its main attractions today are the Italian-built Kremlin walls, and numerous churches.

DIRECTIONS: By local train from the Kazan station to Kolomna (Golutvin- or Ryazan-bound trains), journey time 2.5 hours. The #9 tram takes you directly from the station to the local museum (last stop). By car, drive southeast down the M5 (Ryazanskoye Shosse); Kolomna is on your left after the river bridge, approximately 93 km from the centre of Moscow.

History
Kolomna was founded in 1177 as a town in the Ryazan princedom, but soon came under Moscow's influence. It was favoured by Prince Dmitry Donskoy, both as a place for his marriage to a Suzdal princess (by which he managed to unite the two princedoms) and as a point of assembly for troops

on the eve of the historic Battle of Kulikovo Field.

In the 16th century, Vassily III decided to build a stone Kremlin here, the third in Russia after Moscow and Nizhny Novgorod. He hired the Genoese Alevisio brothers, who created a fortress comparable to Moscow's in size – and, if anything, rather stronger.

In more peaceful times, Kolomna became a craft centre, producing special pots from the unusual local black clay. Today it has a machine-building factory, which produced Russia's first tram in 1892, the world's first oil tanker in 1907, and the Soviet Union's first electric locomotive in 1932.

The Kremlin
Start with a visit to the local museum, situated in the Church of the Archangel Michael, then cross the main Moscow road into the Kremlin. The impressive ruined walls you see once rose to 90 feet in height.

Two of its towers are especially worth looking out for: one is the twenty-sided Marina's Tower, once the prison of Marina Mnishek, a woman who in her short, but obviously eventful, life managed to be married to both the false Dmitries and the renegade Cossack Ivan Zarutsky, all of whom rebelled against the reigning Russian Tsar. At night, she was believed to haunt the local townspeople in the form of a magpie.

On the other side of the Kremlin are the Pyatnitskiye Gates, the triumphal entrance used by Prince Dmitry and other important guests. Revered icons used to hang above the entrance, and may one day be returned.

The inside of the Kremlin, like the town around it, is a wonderful cocktail, complete with monumental 17th century cathedral, eclectic and classical churches, and two convents with gothic walls, one of which, the New Golutvin, was the first in Russia to resume its old role during perestroika.

The rest of Kolomna is there for you to discover at your leisure – quiet town streets, river embankments, and the Bobrenyov Monastery across the Kolomna River bridge, founded in honour of the Kulikovo victory.

New Jerusalem

This hilltop monastery and open-air museum on the Istra River to the west of Moscow is an unusual monument to the controversial Patriarch Nikon, and his attempts to make Russia the leader of the Christian world.

DIRECTIONS: By local train from the Riga (*Rizhsky*) station to either Istra or Novoierusalimskaya stations, journey time 1.5 hours, then take any local bus to the "Musei" stop, or walk 15 minutes. By car, leave Moscow by the M9 (Volokolamskoye Shosse) and continue for 40 km. The monastery is just beyond the town of Istra, on a hill to the right.

History

While many Russian monasteries seek to fill their visitors with awe, the subtle ingenuity and architectural excellence of New Jerusalem give it an appeal of a different kind. It was built in the 17th century, part of a grand design to create copies of the sacred places of the Christian world on Russian soil.

Nikon chose this site on a bend in the Istra River because he felt it resembled the Holy Land in its topography – thus, the Istra became the Jordan, the hill beside it Mount Zion, and the monastery, Jerusalem itself.

Resurrection Cathedral
(Voskresensky Sobor)
New Jerusalem's most extraordinary feature is the Cathedral of the Resurrection, completed in 1686 in the "image and likeness" of Jerusalem's Holy Sepulchre, though in contemporary Russian architectural style. German forces occupied the monastery for three weeks in 1941, blowing it up as they retreated from this area in the same year – reconstruction continues today. Its greatest treasures are the ceramic decorations, with tiling in the form of "Peacock's Eye" friezes, portals, and seven unique iconostases.

In stark contrast to the lofty interior of the cathedral is the white plastered underground church of SS. Konstantin and Yelena. Entering by a doorway from the draughty cathedral, the cozy heated stairway gives one the feeling of descending into the bowels of the earth. This subterranean church is the only one of its kind in Russia; its base is six metres below ground level and its belfry just a couple of metres above the grass of the courtyard.

Other Churches & the Museum
The museum occupies the Trapezium and Archimandrite's Chambers, and includes exhibitions on the history of New Jerusalem, ceramics, bell-making, 16th–17th century icons and tapestries, and 16th–20th

century Russian and European art. However, as is the case with many Russian museums today, the Russian Orthodox Church is claiming back its land and property. Part of the complex is already being used as a working monastery.

Outside the walls are the "Gardens of Gethsemane", known for their holy water spring. Here a small open-air museum of wooden architecture, featuring churches from nearby villages, a peasant hut and a windmill, completes a rich and pleasing scene. ☞ *Museum open Tues–Sun 10 am–5:30 pm, all year round. Tel: (8-231) 44375.*

Peredelkino

Set in pleasant forest surroundings, the village of Peredelkino boasts some of the freshest air around Moscow. The house-museum of poet and novelist Boris Pasternak, and the cemetery where he is buried, are its central attractions.

DIRECTIONS. By local train from the Kiev station to Peredelkino, journey time half an hour. By car leave Moscow by the M1 (Minskoye Shosse) and turn left at the 21 km post.

The village of Peredelkino, just outside Moscow to the south-west, is famous as the location of dachas of Russian writers. Though now undergoing a typical process of yuppification, where prized properties are being acquired by Russia's New Rich, it still has some literary residents,

including novelist Andrey Bitov and poet Andrey Voznesensky.

Walking right along the road from the railway station and turning left at the entrance gates ahead brings you to the Transfiguration Church, frequently visited by high-ranking Orthodox priests and even by the Patriarch.

It survived well through the communist era, and its interior still has several ancient icons. The village cemetery is located just opposite the church; by bearing round to the right along the top edge you reach the writers' graves, including the much-loved poet Arseny Tarkovsky, father of the great film director. His son Andrey, who is buried in Paris, is remembered with a simple cross.

Boris Pasternak's grave is nearby, set in a quiet but spacious patch surrounded by pines. This romantic spot was once a gathering place for the literary youth, and is still a place of pilgrimage for many, especially on the anniversary of the writer's death, May 30.

At the cemetery's lower end, towards the stream, is the grave of sculptor Vadim Sidur (*see* Listings, Museums), marked by a headstone etched with a cross shape in Sidur's characteristic style.

The Pasternak House Museum

Continue down the main road from the church, keeping the cemetery on your right, and cross the stream. In about 10 minutes you will see the "Dom Tvorchestva" on your left, a holiday home for writers, luxurious by Russian standards but now mostly empty. In a few yards turn left down Ulitsa Pavlenko.

Its third house is the Boris Pasternak museum, which

opened in February 1990. At one time considered a futurist, Pasternak was really a poet of the old pre-revolutionary school, and though he stayed in Russia after the Revolution he never really accepted it. His overseas fame came from *Dr. Zhivago*, his great romantic novel about Moscow, the Revolution and Russia, for which he received the Nobel Prize for Literature in 1958 in controversial circumstances; under pressure from the authorities, he rejected it.

Pasternak lived here from 1939 till his death in 1960, and the house has been preserved as it was when he died. In fact the staff prefer not to call it a museum – it is simply a place where you can appreciate the poet's spirit.

As you will have guessed from the grave, the writer enjoyed space, and rooms are suitably airy and simple. This enabled him to work fast – here he worked on *Zhivago*, as well as numerous translations of Shakespeare and Goethe (he completed *Faust* in just four months).

The only post-Pasternak exhibit is an easel with a sketch of him on his deathbed, in the room where he died.

☞ *Museum open Thurs–Sun 10 am–4 pm.*

Villa Peredelkino

Across the railway line from the station (it is well signposted) is one of Moscow's few top-class country hotel restaurants, the Villa Peredelkino, set in beautiful woodland behind high walls at Chobotovskaya Alleya, 2. It serves Italian food, as well as offering skiing facilities in winter.

☞ *Open noon–midnight, reservations essential. Tel: 435-1478, 435-1211 (Moscow numbers).*

Sergiyev Posad

Known in Soviet times as Zagorsk, Sergiyev Posad, situated northeast of Moscow, is home of the Trinity-St. Sergius Lavra, Russia's most important and magnificent monastery, founded by its greatest saint, St. Sergius of Radonezh.

DIRECTIONS: By local train from the Yaroslavl station, journey time just under two hours. The Lavra is about 10 minutes walk from the station – bear right out of the station, and walk until you reach Ulitsa Krasnoy Armiyi from where it is visible on your right. By car, drive down the M8 (Yaroslavskoye Shosse) and continue for 80 km.

The Trinity-St. Sergius Lavra
(Troitse-Sergiyeva Lavra)
This magnificent monastery is one of only four in Russian Orthodoxy to have the title "Lavra", accorded to the most influential and powerful. The explanation for its status lies with the regard in which its founder, St. Sergius of Radonezh, is held: Sergius was an ascetic monk of noble birth who settled in the forest with his brother in the 1340's and gradually built up a community of like-minded people.

Hearing of his pure and holy lifestyle, people came from all over Russia for advice and blessing. With his followers he played a major role in the spiritual consolidation of a Russia demoralised by Tatar oppression. Though a man of peace, he made an exception for Prince Dmitry's crusade against Mamai Khan, and gave him vital encouragement in the weeks before the battle of Kulikovo Field.

After being destroyed during a Tatar raid in 1408, the monastery was soon rebuilt, and went from strength to strength. The good management and astute patriotism of its rulers made it extremely wealthy and for several centuries it was the largest land-owner in Russia.

In 1612, after enduring a long and bitter siege by the Poles, it financed the Minin and Pozharsky campaign to throw the enemy out of the Kremlin. It also supported the young Peter the Great's bid for power and sheltered him from the rebellious "Streltsy", thus emerging extremely well from the Tsar's subsequent policy of cutting back the power of the church.

The blackest dates in its history are 1764, when it lost its land, along with the rest of Russia's monasteries, by a decree of Catherine the Great, and 1919, when it was closed by the Bolsheviks. In 1946, however, it reopened, and remains Russia's foremost place of pilgrimage.

Its deeply spiritual atmosphere, as well as its colourful, diverse architectural ensemble, accumulated gradually between the 15th and 18th centuries, and its sumptuous collections of icons, applied and folk art make it an outstanding day excursion.

Trinity Cathedral
(Troitsky Sobor)
Built in 1422–23, the oldest and perhaps still the finest of the monastery's churches was completed on the site of Sergius' grave. Though made of white stone and pre-Mongolian in style, it was the first church to include

kokoshniki, a type of awning over the facades named after the traditional Russian women's headgear it resembles.

Its iconostasis used to include Andrey Rublyov's "Old Testament Trinity", the finest surviving work of ancient Russian art, which is now on display in the Tretyakov Gallery in Moscow; it has been replaced here by a copy. St. Sergius' remains are in a tomb encased by a silver shrine.

Church of the Descent of the Holy Spirit
(Dukhovskaya Tserkov')
Nearby stands this shorter, more slender church, distinguished by the unusual blue dome with a gold band. It is the second oldest in the ensemble, built in 1476 by Pskov masters. This is the oldest surviving church in Russia with a bell-tower contained under its roof – in this case built ingeniously into the drum.

Assumption Cathedral
(Uspensky Sobor)
When, in the 15th century, the monks decided to fortify the Lavra, they raised a huge brick fortress complete with moats and stakes which came to dwarf the Trinity Cathedral. In 1559, Ivan the Terrible commissioned this new blue- and gold-domed cathedral, which when finished 36 years later became the monastery's dominant church.

The interior is bright and sumptuous, with frescoes by members of the highly-acclaimed Yaroslavl school, and icons like the "Last Supper" by Moscow master Simon Ushakov. Adjoining the southern entrance is the tomb of Tsar Boris Godunov, famous for his part in Russia's Time of Troubles at the beginning of the 17th century.

The Refectory and St. Sergius' Church

The large brightly-coloured building on the south side of the ensemble dates from 1692. It is also used as a church, though it originally served as a refectory for pilgrims. The interior is equally lavish, with wall and ceiling painting and an outstanding carved baroque iconostasis.

Also from this period is the little chapel by the Assumption Cathedral, built to mark the site of the holy water well. The well is now once again a gathering place for pilgrims, who come to cleanse themselves with the holy waters. Outdoor services are often held nearby.

The Bell-tower

Building continued into the 18th century with this magnificent bell-tower which, although the tallest in Russia and far larger than any other building, nonetheless preserves the harmony of the ensemble; its successive layers are equal in height to that of other buildings in the monastery.

The base is now occupied by the principal church souvenir and crafts shop in the Lavra, while you can climb the tower for a panoramic view over the monastery ensemble and surrounding countryside.

The Vestry

(Riznitsa)
Set behind the Trinity Cathedral, this building houses the Sergiyev Posad Museum's Old Russian Applied Art collection, one of the first and finest in the country. It contains Russia's best collection of tapestries, which began in the 15th century. Works include a full-length portrait of St. Sergius, possibly made by Andrey Rublyov himself, and the Blue Shroud of Christ, made in the workshops of

the Staritsa Princes, then considered the masters of the genre.

Other outstanding displays are gold and silver items made by the Kremlin Armoury artists and 16th century jewellery from Boris Godunov's workshops on the Volga.

☛ *Open Tues–Sun 10 am–5 pm, by guided tour only.*

The Treasury

(Kaznacheisky Korpus)
Among the monks' cells situated at the back of the ensemble is this wing, also used by the Sergiyev Posad Art Museum. A number of icons are worthy of note – a 14th century *Hodigitria* (Guiding) Virgin thought to have belonged to Sergius himself, and several by the Rublyov school.

There is also an exhaustive display of more recent applied art, notably peasant crafts. A room on wood-carving displays a whole carved pediment from a Volga village hut and a beehive in the shape of a bear. Sergiyev Posad's own crafts like *matryoshka* dolls and clay toys are well represented.

☛ *Open Tues–Sun 10 am–5 pm.*

Infirmary and Church of SS. Zossima and Savvaty

The pretty tent-roofed church in the northeast corner was built in 1638 in honour of these two disciples of Sergius, who built the Solovetsky Monastery on a remote archipelago in the White Sea. Several rooms here are used by the local History Museum.

☛ *Open Tues–Sun 10 am–5 pm.*

The Royal Palace

This festive 17th century building on the north side was built in conjunction with the Refectory. It was the first royal residence to be built as a single unit, unlike previous, 16th century chambers which normally consisted of a series of buildings with connecting stairways and galleries.

The Monastery Walls

The current walls date from the post-1612 reconstruction. They were made extra-sturdy, just in case the Poles reappeared to lay siege, but with some fancy touches. Of the latter, the most noticeable is the northwest Duck Tower (Utichya Bashnya), where Peter the Great was believed to practise his shooting skills on the inhabitants of the nearby pond.

The Toy Museum

Returning in the direction of the station, the Institute of Personality Development on Ulitsa Krasnoy Armiyi houses this unique museum. Most of the exhibits come from a nearby toy factory, one of the best in Russia, and include 19th century dolls, 20th century teddy bears, including a life-size "Misha", the 1980 Moscow Olympics mascot, and a 1959 wooden interplanetary spaceship complete with cosmonauts and detachable capsules.

A number of items from overseas include a 1930's British toy wigwam and canoe for playing "Indians" and Lego models. ☞ Open Weds–Sun 10 am–5 pm, closed last Friday of month. Tel: (8-254) 44101. Address: Ulitsa Krasnoy Armiyi 136.

Chernigov Skeet

While in the Lavra, enquire in the main administrative buildings to the right of the main entrance about visiting another Sergiyev Posad monastery, the Chernigov Skeet on the edge of town. During the 1840's, a string of smaller monasteries was built around the Lavra, of which this quickly became the most famous and revered.

Shortly after its foundation, a nomadic hermit called Philip settled at the Skeet. Intending to build himself a small cave, his enthusiasm resulted in a whole system of underground cells and churches, in the style of the Pechersk cave monasteries in Kiev.

With the discovery of a holy spring, the healing icon of Our Lady of Chernigov was installed, and a group of startsy, wise church elders, arrived. The most famous elder was Barnabas the Comforter, who at one time received 500 people a day, among them Tsar Nicholas II, for whom he predicted the sufferings of 1917.

In Soviet times, the Chernigov Skeet had various new "uses", notably as a home for limbless World War II veterans. Many died here, forgotten by the victorious nation. The nearby Gethsemane Skeet was obliterated except for its walls, and was taken over by a top secret Ministry of Defense department dealing with the storage of nuclear warheads. Until very recently, the monasteries and nearby housing estate were blotted out of local maps.

In the later 1980's, the Chernigov Skeet was partly returned to the church, albeit in a derelict condition. Its caves have survived, as have an underground church and several monk's cells. Some paintings of "startsy" have been preserved on the walls, although their eyes were gouged out by the Bolsheviks in an act of wanton barbarism. Beneath them stands Barnabas' coffin, while above ground the grave of early 20th century philosopher Vassily Rozanov has been restored.

Zvenigorod

Another ancient monastery town, Zvenigorod is famous for its early Russian churches, with works by Andrey Rublyov.

DIRECTIONS: By local train on the Zvenigorod branch line from the Belorussia station, journey time 1.5 hours. Local bus #25 from the station will take you into town, to the Assumption Cathedral, while #23 and #51 will take you further, to the monastery/museum. By car, leave Moscow by turning off the outer ring road onto Rublyovskoye Shosse, and continue for 28 km. to the town.

Zvenigorod is one of the oldest towns of the Moscow Region. Originally built before the Tatar invasion in 1152, it became a satellite princedom of Moscow.

Dmitry Donskoy's son Yuri later ruled here, building a wooden Kremlin and stone churches. The latter have survived, and Zvenigorod is now a pretty backwater, situated on the Moskva River and surrounded by some of the river's most attractive scenery. Its unpolluted waters run through beautiful green valleys and are excellent for swimming.

Just west of the town is an area known as "Moscow Switzerland" (*Podmoskovnaya Shveitsariya*), whose beautiful landscapes were long favoured by party elites for short holidays.

The Assumption Cathedral

At the centre of Zvenigorod is the Assumption Cathedral in the Town (*Uspenskaya Tserkov' na Gorodke*, c. 1400), the most ancient fully preserved architectural monument of old Muscovy.

Built in the aftermath of the Tatar invasion, its simplicity is reminiscent of the earlier, 12th century churches of Vladimir.

If you're lucky enough to visit when a service is taking place (at 6 pm on Sundays and festivals), you'll be able to get inside the building to see a fresco by master icon-painter Andrey Rublyov and his pupils. The icons which Rublyov painted here are now on display in the Tretyakov Gallery.

The Savvino-Storozhevsky Monastery

Sitting at the confluence of the Moskva and the Storozhka rivers, the monastery was founded in 1398 by Savva, a pupil of St. Sergius of Radonezh, and Zvenigorod's second stone church, the Nativity Cathedral (*Rozhdestvensky Sobor*) was built here. All but the cathedral was destroyed during the Polish invasion in the early 17th century, and the current ensemble appeared under Tsar Alexey. The monastery is shared between the Church and a museum.

Its Nativity Cathedral now stands in splendid isolation in the centre. Inside, wall paintings demonstrate the art of four different eras — the 15th, 17th, 19th and 20th centuries, all of which are now visible. The earliest is merely an inscription on the altar, but the best works, dating from 1649, illustrate the acaphist, chants in honour of the Holy Virgin. It also contains some of Russia's finest 17th century icons by painters working in Rublyov's traditions.

The museum has varied collections of 15th–20th century applied art, including jewellery, tapestry icons, majolica, glass and furniture.
☛ *Open Tues–Sun, 10 am–5 pm. Tel: 592-9421/9422 (Moscow numbers).*

Listings

Accommodation

Telephone codes (501) and (502) indicate satellite lines; (095) is the local code for Moscow.

Western Standard, 4 Б зта (\$200+)

Aerostar
A popular, top-class hotel situated on a main road not far from the centre. Rates \$215–\$365, including full buffet breakfast.
Leningradsky Prosp. 37, Kor. 9. Metro Dinamo. Tel: (502) 213-9000, 155-5030; fax 213-9001.

Baltschug Kempinski
See Walk 7. Rates DM 510 upwards.
Ul. Balchuga 1. Metro Kitai Gorod, Novokuznetskaya. Tel: (501) 230-9500, (095) 230-6500; fax (501) 230-9502, (095) 230-6500.

Metropol
See Walk 2. Rates \$340–\$810 (weekend package rates from \$310).
Teatralny Proyezd 1/4. Metro Ploshchad Revolutsii, Teatralnaya. Tel: (501) 927-1000, (095) 927-6000; fax 927-6010.

Mezhdunarodnaya
In recent years notorious for high prices and poor service, this huge perestroika-era complex has come under new management who promise a shake-up. Rates \$220+.
Krasnopresnenskaya Nab. 12. Metro Ul. 1905 Goda. Tel: (095) 253-1391/92, 2760.

National
See Walks 2 and 3. Rates \$310+.
Tverskaya Ul. 1. Metro Okhotny Ryad. Tel: (501) 258-7000.

Olympic Penta
An Austrian-run hotel not far from the centre, close to the Olympic Sports Complex, famous for its Viennese cafe. Rates \$300+.
Olympiisky Prosp. 18/1. Metro Prospekt Mira. Tel: (095) 971-6101, 6301; fax 230-2597.

Palace
See Walk 3. Rates \$360+.
Ul. 1-Tverskaya-Yamskaya 19. Metro Belorusskaya. Tel: (502) 956-3152; fax 956-3151.

Presnja
See Walk 4. Rates \$246+.
Spiridonyevsky Per. 9. Metro Pushkinskaya, Tverskaya. Tel: (502) 956-3010.

Savoy
See Walk 8. Rates \$265+.
Ul. Rozhdestvenka 3. Metro Kuznetsky Most. Tel: (095) 929-8500, 8558.

Radisson Slavyanskaya
See Walk 12, "Moscow by Water". Rates \$280+.
Berezhkovskaya Nab. 2. Metro Kievskaya. Tel: (095) 941-8020; fax (502) 224-1225.

Sofitel Iris
Quieter than central hotels, with good facilities and French restaurant and a free shuttle service to the centre. Rates FF1500 (about \$300).
Khorovinskoye Shosse 10. Tel: (502) 220-8000, (095) 488-8000; fax (095) 906-0105, (502) 220-8888.

Intourist, Middle-range Western (\$100-200)

Art Hotel
Small German-run hotel in Moscow's prestigious southwest suburb, with rooms in art-deco style. Rates DM 175-DM 240.
Prosp. Vernadskovo 41. Metro Yugo-Zapadnaya. Tel: (095) 432-7827, 431-0822; fax 432-2757.

Budapest
See Walk 8. Rates \$80-\$250.
Petrovskiye Linii 2/18. Metro Teatralnaya, Pushkinskaya. Tel: (095) 924-8820, 921-1060.

Cosmos
See Greater Moscow, VDNKh. Rates \$100 (deluxe double \$190).
Prosp. Mira 150. Metro VDNKh. Tel: (095) 217-0785, 0786.

Intourist
See Walk 3. Rates \$155 (deluxe double \$225).
Ul. Tverskaya 3/5. Metro Okhotny Ryad. Tel: (095) 956-8426, 8444.

Peking
See Walk 4. Rates \$95-\$120.
Ul. Bolshaya Sadovaya 5. Metro Mayakovskaya. Tel: (095) 209-2442; fax 200-1420.

Tsaritsyno
Close to the Tsaritsyno Palace, this hotel provides furnished self-catering 1-5-room apartments, normally only for long-term guests. Rates \$30–\$200.
Shipilovsky Proyezd 47-1. Metro Orekhovo. Tel: (095) 343-3621, 4343.

Cheaper, Russian-run (under \$100)

Belgrade
See Walk 5. Rates \$83–\$96.
Smolenskaya Plosh. 8. Metro Smolenskaya. Tel: (095) 248-2841, 1643.

Izmailovo
See Greater Moscow, Izmailovo. Rates \$43+.
Izmailovskoye Shosse 71. Metro Izmailovsky Park. Tel: (095) 166-5272.

Leningradskaya
See Walk 10. Rates \$67+.
Ul. Kalanchovskaya 21/40. Metro Komsomolskaya. Tel: (095) 975-3032, 3570.

Minsk
Rates \$30–\$40.
Ul. Tverskaya 22. Metro Pushinskaya, Tverskaya. Tel: (095) 299-1300.

Moskva
See Walk 2. Rates \$60+.
Okhotny Ryad 2. Metro Okhotny Ryad. Tel: (095) 292-1100, 1000.

Rossiya
See Walk 2. Rates
$50–$70.
*Ul. Varvarka 6. Metro Kitai
Gorod. Tel: (095) 298-
5531.*

Tsentralny Dom Turista
Average Russian hotel far
out in the southwest sub-
urbs. Convenient only for
the Park Place apartments
and shopping centre oppo-
site. Rates $45–$57.
*Leninsky Prosp. 146. Metro
Yugo-Zapadnaya. Tel: (095)
438-5510, 434-2782.*

Ukraina
Another "wedding cake"
hotel, centrally located
(especially for coups – the
White House is just across
the river). Rates $80–$110.
*Kutuzovsky Prosp. 2/1.
Metro Kievskaya. Tel: (095)
243-3030, 2895.*

Cheap, Alternative Accommodation

Bed and Breakfast, youth
hostels and short-term rented accommodation are still
not fully developed in
Moscow. However, already
some systems are springing
up to meet the needs of
budget travellers, as well as
those who prefer in-home
living to hotel accommodation.

**Moscow Bed &
Breakfast**
In-home stays for any length
of time, with a choice of
locations and hosts. Many
also offer guiding and meeting services. See advertisement (pages 41–43) for
details.

Prakash Guest House
A small guest house in the
suburbs on the 16th floor of
a high-rise. Offers singles
and doubles with conve-
niences. $20 per person.
*Ul. Profsoyuznaya 83/1.
Metro Belyayevo. Tel: 334-
2598.*

Traveller's Guest House
Moscow's only youth hostel
type accommodation, on
the 10th floor of a high-rise

block. Double rooms, also
four-bed dormitories for
about $15 a night. Visa
support and travel agency.
*Bol. Pereyaslavskaya Ul.
50. Metro Prospekt Mira.
Tel: (095) 971-4059.*

Airlines

Aeroflot
*Ticket offices: Frunzenskaya
Nab. 4; Petrovka Ul. 20/1;
Korovy Val Ul. 7; Eniseyev-
skaya Ul. 19. Information
tel: 155-5045. Ticket tel:
926-6278.*

Air France
*Korovy Val 7. Metro
Oktyabrskaya. Tel: 237-
2325.*

Alitalia
*Ul. Pushechnaya 7. Metro
Kuznetsky Most. Tel: 923-
9840.*

British Airways
*Krasnopresnenskaya Nab.
12 #1905. Metro Ul. 1905
Goda. Tel: 253-2492.*

CSA Czech Airlines
*2nd Brestskaya Ul. 21/27.
Metro Mayakovskaya. Tel:
250-4571.*

Delta Airlines
*Krasnopresnenskaya Nab.
12, #1102-A. Metro Ul.
1905 Goda. Tel: 253-2658.*

Finnair
*Kuznetsky Most 3. Metro
Okhotny Ryad. Tel: 292-
8788/1762/1758.*

KLM
*Ul. Usachova 35. Metro
Sportivnaya. Tel: 258-3600.*

LOT Polish Airlines
*Korovy Val 7/5. Metro
Oktyabrskaya. Tel: 238-
0003.*

Lufthansa
*Olympic Penta Hotel,
Olympiisky Prosp. 18/1.
Metro Prospekt Mira. Tel:
975-2501.*

**Malev Hungarian
Airlines**
*Kamergersky Per. 6. Metro
Okhotny Ryad. Tel: 292-
0434.*

**Scandinavian Airlines
(SAS)**
*Kuznetsky Most 3. Metro
Okhotny Ryad. Tel: 925-
4747.*

Swissair
*Krasnopresnenskaya Nab.
12 #2003. Metro Ul. 1905
Goda. Tel: 253-8988.*

Transaero
*Hotel Moskva, Okhotny
Ryad 2. Metro Okhotny
Ryad. Tel: 292-7526.*

TWA
*Radisson Slavyanskaya
Hotel #5028. Metro
Kievskaya. Tel: 941-
8146/578-8486.*

Airport Travel

Sheremetyevo 2
Most international flights:
Bus #517 from Metro
Planernaya, Bus #551 from
Rechnoy Vokzal.
*Tel: 578-5633, 578-5614,
578-5634.*

Sheremetyevo 1
Aeroflot flights to St.
Petersburg and Russian
north, all Transaero flights.
*Bus #551 from Metro
Rechnoy Vokzal. Tel: 578-
5971.*

Vnukovo
Flights to most Southern
and Siberian destinations.
*Bus #511 or #511-Э from
Metro Yugo-Zapadnaya. Tel:
234-8656, 234-8655.*

Domodedovo
Flights to Central Asia and
some Siberian cities.
*Suburban train from
Paveletsky Vokzal. Tel: as
Vnukovo.*

Bykovo
Short flights to some cen-
tral Russian destinations.
*Suburban train from the
Kazansky Vokzal. Tel: 155-
0922.*

From Aerovokzal (Metro
Dinamo, Leningradsky
Prosp. 37–A), express
buses run to all internal airports. Connecting buses
run between each airport.
Tel: 155-0922.

Domestic Tickets

Domestic Aeroflot tickets can be reserved and purchased through a number of Moscow travel agents, or from **Intourtrans**, Ul. Petrovka 15/13, 3rd floor, or from the special counters at the **City Air Terminal**, Aerovoksal.

The booking office for **Transaero** flights, both domestic and international, is in the Moskva Hotel on Manezhnaya Plosh. Tel: 292-7526. Open 24 hours.

Art Galleries

Moscow's thriving commercial gallery scene encompasses every artistic direction from the most traditional, figurative and decorative art to the most avant-garde. Some galleries, often occupying former State Exhibition Halls, remain nominally public organisations, while others are entirely private; for the latter, financial security – especially for more experimental galleries – usually comes with some form of private patronage.

Not all galleries have a regular base, with some renting premises for the duration of a set exhibition. The **House of Artists** on Krymsky Val is a centre for this, with its huge collection of halls playing host to a wide variety of exhibitions. In addition, the **Contemporary Art Centre** complex on Bolshaya Yakimanka Ul. is home to a range of small, experimental galleries, most occupying a couple of small rooms each.

A-3 Gallery
Contemporary, conceptualist central Arbat gallery.
39 Starokonyushenny Per. Metro Smolenskaya. Tel: 291-8484. Open 11 am–7 pm, closed Mon, Tues.

Aidan Gallery
Once among the avant-garde leaders, Aidan Gallery has been less active recently.
Novopeschanaya Plosh. 23/7. Entrance 8, Floor 9. Tel: 943-5348. Open by appointment.

Belyayevo Gallery
100 Profsoyuznaya Ul. Metro Belyayevo. Tel: 000 0022. Open noon 7 pm, closed Mon, Tues.

Central House of Artists
Venue for many rotating shows, staged by a wide range of galleries and by artists themselves. Also a regular auction venue/exhibition space for auctioneers Alpha Art.
10 Krymsky Val. Metro Oktyabrskaya. Tel: 238-9634. Open 11 am–8 pm, closed Mon.

Contemporary Art Centre
Adjoining the Guelman Gallery, this complex includes a central exhibition hall, surrounded by a rambling collection of smaller galleries, most of which are avant-garde in direction. Exhibition openings are as much social events, and opening hours are often flexible, or by appointment only, so ring ahead.

Among them, **Dar Gallery**, specialises in naive art (tel: 238-6554). Others include **Laboratory Gallery**, **Studio 20** (tel: 237-3718), **TV** and **Ptyuch Galleries** (tel: 238-9666, 238-4422), **Architecture Gallery** (tel: 231-6654), **1.0 Gallery** (tel: 238-6905) and **Shkola Gallery** (tel: 230-4040).
2/6 Bolshaya Yakimanka Ul. Metro Polyanka.

Dom Khudozhnika
Exhibition space, often geared towards the conventional, in a building which was once the centre of the official Soviet Union of Artists.
10 Gogolevsky Bulvar. Metro Kropotkinskaya. Tel: 291-6218. Open noon–6 pm, closed Mon.

Dom Nashchokina
Attractive small central gallery which has established a reputation with shows of unofficial artists of the 1950's and 1960's.
12 Vorotnikovsky Per. Metro Mayakovskaya. Tel: 299-1178. Open daily 11 am–6 pm, closed Sat, Sun.

Dom Sto Gallery
100 Profsoyuznaya Ul. Metro Belyayevo. Tel: 335-8322. Open noon–7 pm, closed Mon, Tues.

Ensi Gallery
Moscow's only dedicated carpet gallery, specialising in Central Asian and Middle Eastern weaves.
Prosp. Mira 14. Metro Prospekt Mira. Tel: 208-1403. Visits by appointment.

Expo–88 Gallery
Traditional, representational emphasis.
9/1 Ul. Arkhipova. Metro Kitai Gorod. Tel: 925-7242. Open 11 am–6 pm, closed Sat, Sun.

Guelman Gallery
For many, Moscow's premier gallery, run by curator Marat Guelman. Avant-garde, experimentalist emphasis, alongside established sots-art figures such as Komar and Melamid.
6 Bolshaya Yakimanka Ul. Metro Oktyabrskaya, Polyanka. Tel: 238-4422. Open 11 am–6 pm, closed Sun, Mon.

International University Gallery
Leningradsky Prosp. 17. Metro Belorusskaya. Tel: 250-3481. Open 11 am–6 pm, closed Sat, Sun.

Istoki Exhibition Hall
12 Varvarka Ul. Metro Kitai Gorod. Tel: 298-4320. Open 11 am–6 pm, closed Mon.

Kovcheg Gallery
Far from the centre, but a treasure house for shows of 20th century Russian graphics and watercolours. Well worth exploring.
12 Nemchinova Ul. Metro

Timiryazevskaya. Tel: 977-
0044. Open noon–7 pm,
closed Mon, Tues.

Kuznetsky Most Hall
20 Kuznetsky Most. Metro
Kuznetsky Most. Tel: 928-
1844. Open daily 1 pm–
8 pm; Sat, Sun noon–6:30
pm, closed Mon.

"L" Gallery
26 Oktyabrskaya Ul. Metro
Rizhskaya. Tel: 289-2491.
Open 11 am–7 pm, closed
Mon, Tues.

Les Oreades Gallery
A Russian-French partner-
ship, Les Oreades has a
mainstream direction, with
emphasis on landscapes as
well as shows of Russian
folk arts.
25 Tverskaya Ul. Metro
Mayakovskaya. Tel: 299-
2289. Open 11 pm–7 pm,
closed Mon.

Malaya Gruzinskaya 28
A headquarters for unofficial art during the Soviet era,
now a regular exhibition
hall.
28 Malaya Gruzinskaya Ul.
Metro Belorusskaya. Tel:
253-3688.

Manege Exhibition Hall
The huge space of the
Manege is venue to occa-
sional rotating shows, as
well as to the biennial Art-
MIF, a gathering point for
galleries from Russia and
abroad.
Manezhnaya Plosh. Metro
Alexandrovsky Sad. Tel:
202-9304. Open 11 am–
7 pm, closed Tues.

Manege Gallery
Small new private gallery
just opposite the entrance
to the Kremlin. Personable
and attractive collections.
1 Manezhnaya Plosh. Metro
Biblioteka im. Lenina. Tel:
202-8252, 202-9443.
Open daily 11 am–7 pm;
Sun, Sat noon–4 pm.

M'ARS Gallery
High-profile contemporary
gallery, with collections of
unofficial Russian art over
50 years. Far from the centre, but highly professional.
32 Malaya Filevskaya Ul.

Metro Pionerskaya. Tel:
146-2029. Open noon–
8 pm, closed Mon.

Moscow Collection Gallery
In the Tropinin Museum, 10
Shchetininsky Per. Metro
Polyanka. Tel: 238-3968.
Open noon–7 pm; Sat
10 am–5 pm, closed Tues,
Weds.

Moscow Fine Art
38 Arbat Ul. Metro
Smolenskaya. Tel: 241-
1267. Open 10 am–6 pm,
closed Sat, Sun.

Moscow Palette
Small central gallery, which
is also an auction venue for
the "Four Arts" auction
house.
35/28 Povarskaya Ul. Metro
Krasnopresnenskaya. Tel:
291-1124. Open 1 pm–
7 pm, closed Sun, Mon.

Na Ostozhie Culture Centre
6 Savelievsky Per. Metro
Kropotkinskaya. Tel: 201-
5388. Open daily noon–
8 pm, closed Sun.

Na Solyanke Exhibition Hall
1/2 Solyanka Ul. Metro Kitai
Gorod. Tel: 921-5572. Open
11 am–6 pm, closed Mon.

Nagornaya Gallery
10 Remizova Ul. Metro
Nagornaya. Tel: 123-6569.
Open 11 am–7 pm, closed
Mon, Tues.

NB Gallery
Small shows of character at
this Old Arbat gallery.
6/2 Sivtsev Vrazhek # 2.
Metro Kropotkinskaya. Tel:
203-4006. Open noon–7
pm, closed Sun, Mon.

Photocentre
Moscow's premier photo-
graphy gallery, not exclusively commercial. Rotating
shows range from traditional to avant-garde.
10 Gogolevsky Boulevard.
Metro Kropotkinskaya. Tel:
290-4188. Open 12–7 pm,
closed Mon, Tues.

Phoenix Culture Centre
Multi-media venue, whose
shows range from tradition-

al painting, through ceram-
ics, enamels and fashion.
3 Kutuzovsky Prosp. Metro
Kievskaya. Tel: 243-4958.
Open noon–8 pm, closed
Sun.

Rama-Art Gallery
24 Dmitria Ulyanova Ul.
Metro Akademicheskaya. Tel.
124-6151. Open noon–
7 pm, closed Sun, Mon.

Regina Gallery
Avant-garde leader in the
Moscow gallery scene.
36 Myasnitskaya Ul. Metro
Turgenevskaya. Tel: 921-
1613. Open noon–7 pm,
closed Sun, Mon.

Rossia Culture Centre
3 Oktyabrsky Per. Metro
Rizhskaya. Tel: 281-4379.
Open daily noon–8 pm.

Russian Academy of Arts
Conventional gallery space,
its affiliations obvious from
its attachment to one of the
former official Arts bodies.
21 Prechistenka Ul. Metro
Kropotkinskaya. Tel: 201-
3704. Open daily noon–
8 pm, closed Mon, Tues.

Seven Nails Gallery
Small gallery space in the
Russian-American Press
centre building; as its name
suggests, exhibitions are
limited to seven canvases.
2/3 Khlebny Per. Metro
Arbatskaya. Tel: 203-3786.
Open 10 am–7 pm, closed
Sun.

Slavyansky Dom Cera-mic & Porcelain Gallery
Specialist and professional
commercial gallery, which
has staged several selling-
shows of porcelain.
3 Goncharnaya Nab. Metro
Taganskaya. Tel: 915-6821.
Open 11 am–7 pm, closed
Sun.

Unea Gallery
11/2 Sadovo-Chernogryaz-
skaya Ul. Metro Krasniye
Vorota. Tel: 208-5548.
Open 2 pm–8 pm, closed
Mon.

Vostochnaya Gallery
Enterprising, non-conven-
tional space which high-

lights artists from the former Soviet Union, especially the Central Asian republics.
10 Khmeleva Ul. Metro Sukharevskaya. Tel: 208-1167. Open 11 am–7 pm, closed Sun, Mon.

"XL" Gallery
Tiny, one-room gallery with experimental slant.
11-A Ulansky Per. Flat 57. Metro Krasniye Vorota. Tel: 207-2947. Open 4 pm–8 pm, closed Sun, Mon.

Yakut Gallery
Another first-rate avant-garde gallery with immaculate premises; with Guelman and Regina, a leader of the Moscow scene at international level.
5 Dolgorukovskaya Ul. Metro Mayakovskaya. Tel: 973-3452. Open noon–7 pm, closed Sat, Sun, Mon.

Banks

American Express
Full card-member services, cash machine, as well as travel agency. Also exchange and banking services provided by Dialog Bank (for rates, see below).
Ul. Sadovaya-Kudrinskaya 21-A. Metro Mayakovskaya. Tel: 956-9000.

Dialogbank
Accepts Eurocheques, Mastercard, Eurocard (4 % commission) and AmEx card and most travellers' cheques (3 %).
Radisson Slavyanskaya Hotel, Berezhkovskaya Nab. 2. Metro Kievskaya. Tel: 956-9877.

Inkombank
Cash on Visa Card at 1 % commission, also travellers' cheques. Branches throughout the city (for info. tel: 564-8022), including:
Ul. Tverskaya 6/1 (entrance from Kamergersky Per.) Metro Okhotny Ryad. Tel: 292-5594.
Pushkinskaya Ul. 32. Metro Chekhovskaya. Tel: 956-3742.

Elbim Bank
Accepts Mastercard, Visa and Diner's Club (2 % commission) and travellers' cheques.
Mezhdunarodnaya Hotel, Krasnopresnenskaya Nab. 12. Metro Ul. 1905 Goda. Tel: 205-6560.

Menatep Bank
Accepts major credit cards and travellers' cheques, commission 2 %.
Manezhnaya Plosh. 1. Komsomolsky Prosp. 28. Oktyabr Cinema, Novy Arbat 29. All open 10 am–8 pm.

Roscredit
Accepts Visa and Mastercard credit cards and travellers' cheques, 1.9 % commission.
Peking Hotel, Ul. Bolshaya Sadovaya 5. Metro Mayakovskaya. Tel: 209-2317.

Sberbank
All branches handling currency operations accept VISA, Thomas Cook and AmEx travellers' cheques, and Mastercard/Eurocard, VISA, Diner's Club and STB cards (3 % commission on each).

Dobryninskaya Plosh. 36 Metro Dobryninskaya. Tel: 237-4261.

Trubnikovsky Per. 29/31 Metro Barrikadnaya. Tel: 290-5477.

Ul. Gvozdeva 7/4 Metro Taganskaya. Tel: 272-2110.

Ul. Stanislavskovo 14 Metro Pushkinskaya, Tverskaya. Tel: 229-6686.

Ul. Delegatskaya 11 Metro Tsvetnoi Bulvar.Tel: 973-3657.

Astrakhansky Per. 10/36 Metro Prospekt Mira. Tel: 280-9616.

Ul. Chekhova 15 Metro Chekhovskaya. Tel: 299-9085.

Sretensky Bulvar 1/4 Metro Turgenevskaya, Chistiye Prudy. Tel: 924-7478.

Zubovsky Bulvar 13 Metro Park Kultury. Tel: 246-3339.

Buses

Long-distance services leave from the Tsentralny Avtovokzal. Metro Shcholkovskaya. Tel: 468-0400.

For suburban services, there are local stations at the following metro stations: VDNKh, for journeys north (tel: 181-9755). Vykhino, for journeys south-east (tel: 371-5254). Izmailovsky Park, for journeys east. Tushinskaya, for journeys north-west (tel: 490-2424). Yugozapad-naya, for journeys south-west.

Car Hire

Autosun
Grokholsky Per. 29. Metro Prospekt Mira, tel: 280-3600/4310. Sheremetyevo 2, tel: 578-9166

Avis
Berezhkovskaya Nab. 12, 15/1. Metro Kievskaya, tel: 240-9974/9863/2307. Sheremetyevo 2, tel: 578-5646.

Budget Rent-a-Car
Ul. Bolshaya Gruzinskaya 57. Metro Belorusskaya. Tel: 250-3093, 254-4324.

Cinema Trans
Druzhinnikovskaya Ul. 15. Metro Krasnopresnenskaya. Tel: 255-9873, 255-9348.

Eurodollar
Ul. Bolshaya Kommunist-icheskaya 1/5. Metro Tagan-skaya; tel: 298-6146. Sher-emetyevo 2, tel: 578-7534.

Europcar
Krasnaya Presnya Ul. 23-B. Metro Krasnopresnenskaya; tel: 255-9190. Also: Olympic Penta Hotel. Metro Prospekt Mira; tel: 971-6101. Mezhdunarodnaya Hotel. Metro Ul. 1905 Goda; tel: 253-2477.

Hertz
Prosp. Mira 49/11. Metro Prospekt Mira, tel: 284-4391. Sheremetyevo 2, tel: 578-7532.

InNis
Ul. Bolshaya Ordynka 32. Metro Tretyakovskaya. Tel: 238-3077/3044.

Intourservice
Hotel Rossiya. Metro Kitai Gorod. Tel: 298-5855.

Olga
Hotel Metropol. Metro Ploshchad Revolutsii, Teatralnaya. Tel: 927-6972.

Vesta
Hotel Leningradskaya, room 61. Metro Komsomolskaya. Tel: 248-2657.

Children's

Old Circus
Dating from 1880, the Old Circus shows an accomplished range of clown, acrobat and animal acts, which are entertainment equally for adults and for children. Performances at 7 pm on weekdays (no performance Tuesday), on Saturdays at 3 pm, 7 pm, and Sundays 11 am, 3 pm, 7 pm. See Walk 8.
13 Tsvetnoi Bulvar. Metro Tsvetnoi Bulvar. Tel: 200-6889.

New Circus
Prosp. Vernadskovo 7. Metro Universitet. Tel: 930-2816.

Obraztsov Puppet Theatre
Puppet theatre with a rich history, and a pleasant small museum. See Walk 8.
Ul. Sadovaya-Samotechnaya 3. Metro Tsvetnoi Bulvar. Tel: 299-3310.

Durov Animal Theatre
In no way circus, but the Durov Theatre's skilled animal acts have been delighting Moscow children since 1938 – and that's only in their present home. Confirm performance times by telephone.

Ul. Durova 4. Metro Prospekt Mira. Tel: 281-2914.

Cat Theatre
Another Moscow curiosity – small-scale acts with cats, mice and the like, including a celebrated "mice train".
Kutuzovsky Prosp. 25. Metro Kievskaya. Tel: 249-2907.

Children's Music Theatre
Fairytale music performances which have remained constant, and popular, for years.
Prosp. Vernadskovo 5. Metro Universitet. Tel: 930-7021.

Palace of Water Sports
Principle attractions here are the dolphin, seal and whale acts. Shows last an hour, normally Weds–Fri 3, 7 pm and Sat, Sun 11 am, 1, 4, 6 pm.
Mironovskaya Ul. 27. Metro Semyonovskaya, Izmailovsky Park, then trolleybus #22 to Mironovskaya stop. Tel: 369-7966.

Planetarium
Once-grand space show, now long in need of repair. Check in advance whether it's working.
Sadovaya-Kudrininskaya Ul. 5. Metro Barrikadnaya. Tel: 254-1838.

Zoo
Open 9 am–5 pm (winter), 9 am–8 pm (summer).
Bol. Gruzinskaya Ul. 1. Metro Barrikadnaya, Krasnopresnenskaya. Tel: 255-5375, 252-3580.

Church Services

Orthodox

A selective list of Orthodox churches is given here, many of which are also distinguished by their architectural or historical features. Services usually take place:

Mon and Sat 8 am and 6 pm, Sun and festivals 7 am and 10 am, and on festival evenings.

Church of the Archangel Gabriel (Greek Orthodox)
See Walk 9. Telegrafny Per. 15-A. Metro Chistiye Prudy, Turgenevskaya. Tel: 923-4605.

Assumption Church (Bulgarian Orthodox)
See Walk 11. Ul. Goncharnaya 29. Metro Taganskaya. Tel: 271-0124.

Assumption Church, Novodevichy Convent
Metro Sportivnaya. Tel: 245-3168.

Epiphany/Yelokhovsky Cathedral
See Walk 10. Spartakovskaya Ul. 15. Metro Baumanskaya. Tel: 267-7951.

Intercession Cathedral (Old Believers)
Rogozhsky Per. Metro Ploshchad Ilyicha. Tel: 361-5196.

Church of Our Lady
See Walk 7. Ul. Bolshaya Ordynka 20. Metro Tretyakovskaya. Tel: 231-1300.

Resurrection Church
See Walk 3. Bryusov Per. 15/2. Metro Okhotny Ryad. Tel: 229-6616.

Church of St. John the Warrior
Ul. Dimitrova 46. Metro Oktyabrskaya. Tel: 238-2056

Trinity Cathedral, St. Daniel's Monastery
Danilovsky Val 22. Metro Tulskaya. Tel: 235-0708.

Other Denominations

St. Andrew's Anglican Church
See Walk 4. Ul. Stankevicha 9. Metro Pushkinskaya, Tverskaya. Tel: 245-3837.

Baptist Church
Maly Vuzovsky 3. Metro

Kitai Gorod. Tel: 917-0862.
Druzhinnikovskaya Ul. 15/6.
Tel: 150-3293. Metro
Krasnopresnenskaya.

St. Louis Catholic Church
Ul. Malaya Lubyanka 12.
Metro Lubyanka. Tel: 925-
2034.

Church of the Immaculate Conception,
Malaya Gruzinskaya Ul.
Metro Belorusskaya.

Lady of Hope Chapel,
Kutuzovsky Prosp. 7/4/5
#42. Metro Kievskaya. Tel:
243-9621.

Synagogues

Chabad Lubavitch
Polyakov Synagogue
(Hassidic)
Ul. Bolshaya Bronnaya 6.
Metro Pushkinskaya,
Tverskaya. Tel: 202-
7393/7370.

Main Moscow Synagogue
Ul. Arkhipova 10. Metro
Kitai Gorod. Tel: 923-9697.

Marina Roshcha
Synagogue
2nd Vysheslavtsev Per. 5-A.
Metro Savyolovskaya. Tel:
289-2325.

Tkhiya Centre
Ul. Bolshaya Tulskaya 44.
Tel: 952-1317. Metro
Tulskaya.

Muslim Centres

Islamic Cultural Centre
Maly Tatarsky Per. 5/1.
Metro Novokuznetskaya. Tel:
392-9244.

Main Mosque
Vypozov Per. 7. Metro
Prospekt Mira. Tel: 281-
3866.

Cinema

Unlike their European counterparts, all Russian cinemas show films with voice-
over dubbing, which limits
their interest for most non-
Russian viewers (especially
when dubbing quality varies
from professional actors to

a single simultaneous
voice).

Once one of the world's
greatest and most prolific
film industries, the Russian
cinema world has weath-
ered change, both political
and economic, with difficul-
ty. Although quality films are
being made, their chances
at home distribution are
small. After some years of
virtual Western blockade,
foreign films are now widely
shown in Moscow –
although audiences for
them remain disappointing.

Americom House of Cinema
Moscow's only regular
English-language screen
shows new Hollywood films
nightly in two-week runs;
there are extra matinees
and Russian simultaneous
translation at weekends.
After a recent management
change, future quality may
vary. Ticket prices about $8
are compensated for by the
comfort of the venue, plus
full merchandising.
Radisson Slavyanskaya
Hotel, Berezhkovskaya Nab,
2. Metro Kievskaya. Tel:
941-8890.

Kinocentre
The bastion of quality
Russian cinema, Moscow's
Kinocentre has a comfort-
able 1,000-seater hall
which alternates repertory
showings of new Russian
films with classics.
Druzhinnikovskaya Ul. 15.
Metro Barrikadnaya.
Tel: 205-7306.

Museum of Cinema
In the same building as
Kinocentre, but functioning
as a separate entity, the
Museum of Cinema (Musei
Kino) is an art-house par-
adise; its three small halls
show varied repertory pro-
grammes from Russia and
abroad.
Druzhinnikovskaya Ul. 15.
Metro Barrikadnaya.
Tel: 255-9095.

Illuzion
Art-house rep cinema, situated on the ground floor of

the Stalinist skyscraper.
Traditional programmes,
accenting the classics; also
the venue for French-
language showings,
screened by French Cult-
ural Centre. See Walk 11.
Kotelnicheskaya Nab. 1/15.
Metro Taganskaya.
Tel: 227-4353.

Moskva
Despite its relative shabbi-
ness, the Moskva Cinema
(also known as the "House
of Khanzhonkov"), has as
varied a range of quality
cinema as any other venue.
See Walk 4.
Triumphalnaya Plosh. 1.
Metro Mayakovskaya. Tel:
251-5860.

Embassies

Australia
13 Kropotkinsky Per. Metro
Park Kultury. Tel: 956-6070.

Austria
1 Starokonyushenny Per.
Metro Kropotkinskaya. Tel:
201-7307.

Belgium
7 Ul. Malaya Molchanovka.
Metro Arbatskaya. Tel: 291-
6027.

Canada
23 Starokonyushenny Per.
Metro Kropotkinskaya. Tel:
241-5070, 5882.

Denmark
9 Ostrovskovo Per. Metro
Kropotkinskaya. Tel: 201-
7860.

Finland
15/17 Kropotkinsky Per.
Metro Park Kultury. Tel:
230-2143.

France
45 Ul. Bolshaya Yakimanka.
Metro Oktyabrskaya. Tel:
236-0003.

Germany
56 Mosfilmovskaya Ul .
Metro Kievskaya then trolleybus #34 or #17. Tel:
956-1080.

German Consulate
95-A Leninsky Prosp. Metro
Leninsky Prospekt then

trolleybus #33 or #62. Tel: 936-2401.

Ireland
5 Grokholsky Per. Metro Prospekt Mira. Tel: 288-4101.

Italy
5 Denezhny Per. Metro Smolenskaya. Tel: 241-1533, 1536.

Netherlands
6 Kalashny Per. Metro Arbatskaya. Tel: 291-2999.

New Zealand
44 Ul. Povarskaya. Metro Barrikadnaya. Tel: 956-3581.

Norway
7 Ul. Povarskaya. Metro Arbatskaya. Tel: 290-3872.

Spain
50/8 Ul. Bolshaya Nikit-skaya. Metro Barrikadnaya. Tel: 202-2180, 2161.

Sweden
60 Mosfilmovskaya Ul. Metro Kievskaya, then trolleybus #34 or #17. Tel: 147-9009.

United Kingdom
14 Sofiiskaya Nab. Metro Biblioteka imeni Lenina, Borovitskaya. Tel: 230-6333.

United States
19/23 Novinsky Blvd. Metro Barrikadnaya. Tel: 252-2451–2459.

Ex-USSR Nations

Armenia
2 Armyansky Per. Metro Kitai Gorod. Tel: 924-1269.

Azerbaijan
16 Ul. Stanislavskogo. Metro Pushkinskaya. Tel: 229-1649.

Belarus
17/6 Ul. Maroseika. Metro Turgenevskaya. Tel: 924-7031.

Estonia
5 Sobinovsky Per. Metro Arbatskaya. Tel: 290-5013.

Georgia
6 Ul. Paliashvili. Metro Arbatskaya. Tel: 290-6902.

Kazakhstan
3-A Chistoprudny Bulvar. Metro Turgenevskaya. Tel: 208-9852.

Kyrgyzstan
64 Bol. Ordynka Ul. Metro Dobryninskaya. Tel: 237-4882.

Latvia
3 Ul. Chaplygina. Metro Turgenevskaya. Tel: 925-2707.

Lithuania
10 Ul. Pisemskovo. Metro Arbatskaya. Tel: 291-1698.

Moldova
18 Kuznetsky Most. Metro Kuznetsky Most. Tel: 928-5405, 928-1050.

Tadzhikistan
19 Skaterny Per. Metro Lubyanka. Tel: 290-6102.

Turkmenia
22 Aksakova Per. Metro Kropotkinskaya. Tel: 291-6636.

Ukraine
18 Ul. Stanislavskogo. Metro Pushkinskaya. Tel: 229-2804.

Uzbekistan
12 Pogorelsky Per. Metro Dobryninskaya. Tel: 230-0076.

Medical Care

American Medical Centre
2nd Tverskoy-Yamskoy Per. 10. Metro Belorusskaya. Tel: 956-3366.

Euromedical Club - Athens Medical Centre
Michurinsky Prosp. 6. Metro Yugo-Zapadnaya. Tel: 432-1616.

European Medical Centre
Gruzinsky Per. 3/2. Metro Belorusskaya. Tel: 253-0703 (229-7892 outside office hours).

International Medical Clinic
Grokholsky Per. 31. 10th Floor. Metro Komsomol-skaya. Tel: 280-7138.

Sana Medical Centre
Ul. Nizhnaya Pervomaiskaya 65. Metro Pervomaiskaya. Tel: 464-1254.

U.S. Global Health - Columbia Presbyterian
Medincentre, 4th Floor, 4th Dobryninsky Per. 4. Metro Dobryninskaya. Tel: 974-2332.

Museums

Andrey Rublyov Museum of Old Russian Art
See Greater Moscow, "Moscow Icons".
Plosh. Pryamikova 10. Metro Ploshchad Ilyicha, then trolleybus #45 or #53, or bus #152. Open Thurs–Tues 11 am–6 pm, closed last Fri of the month. Tel: 278-1489.

Aviation Museum
Traces the history of Russian aviation from inventor Alexander Mozhaisky, through the great constructors of the Soviet era like Mikoyan, Tupolev and Ilyushin, and on to jet technology.
Ul. Krasnoarmeiskaya 4. Metro Dinamo. Accessible by guided tour only (in Russian), Tues–Fri 11 am, 2, 4 pm. Tel: 212-5461.

Bakhrushin Theatre Museum
An exhaustive display on the history of Russian theatre, from the collection of turn-of-the-century merchant Alexey Bakhrushin.
Ul. Bakhrushina 31/12. Metro Paveletskaya. Open 12 pm–7 pm, Weds & Fri 2 pm–9 pm, closed Tues and first Mon of month. Tel: 235-3783, 233-4848.

Battle of Borodino Panorama Museum, Kutuzov's Hut
See Greater Moscow, "War Memorials".
Kutuzov Prosp. 38. Metro Kutuzovskaya, then two stops by trolleybus #2, #7 or #39. Open Tues,

Weds 10 am–5 pm; Thurs,
Sat, Sun 10:30 am–5 pm,
closed Mon and Fri. Tel:
148-1967.

Andrey Bely Museum
See Walk 5.
Ul. Arbat 53. Metro
Smolenskaya. Open
Weds–Sun 11 am–6 pm,
closed last Fri of month.

Cathedral of the Intercession at Fili
See Greater Moscow, "War
Memorials".
Ul. Novozavodskaya 6.
Metro Fili. Open daily
except Tues, Weds, last Fri
of month 11 am–6 pm.

Central Museum of the Armed Forces
Originally the Soviet Armed
Forces museum, its vast
halls with 600,000 exhibits
dedicated to the Red Army
have been supplemented by
displays on early Russian
campaigns and a section on
the Whites in the Civil War.
Ul. Sovietskoi Armiyi. Metro
Novoslobodskaya, then two
stops by trolleybus #69.
Open Weds–Sun 10 am–5
pm, closed Mon, Tues. Tel:
281-4877.

Chekhov House Museum
The museum is located in
the house on the Garden
Ring where Anton Chekhov
lived with his family
between 1886 and 1890:
he nicknamed it "the chest
of drawers" because of its
unusual shape. This is
where he wrote his first stories under the pseudonym
"Antosha Chekhonte",
worked as a doctor, and
entertained guests like
composer Pyotr Tchaik-
ovsky and artist Isaac
Levitan.
6 Sadovaya-Kudrinskaya Ul.
Metro Barrikadnaya. Open
11 am–5 pm, Weds & Fri 2
pm–7 pm, closed Mon. Tel:
291-6154.

Church of Christ the Saviour Museum
See Walk 6.
Ul. Volkhonka. Metro
Kropotkinskaya. Open daily
11 am–6 pm.

Memorial Museum of Cosmonautics
See Greater Moscow,
VDNKh.
Prosp. Mira, Alleya Kosmon-
avtov. Metro VDNKh. Open
Tues–Sun 10 am–7 pm,
closed last Fri of month.

Darwin Museum
Really just a natural history
museum (though it boasts a
few letters in Darwin's own
hand), the Darwin Museum
contains oddities like
mutants, stuffed models of
extinct species, sculptures
of ancient animals and a
collection of rare books on
zoology and anatomy.
At time of writing the museum was closed for reloca-
tion. Its new address is Ul.
Vavilova 57, Metro
Akademicheskaya; opening
times remain unknown.

Dostoyevsky Flat Museum
A tiny museum devoted to
the great writer's childhood
in the house where he was
born, an outbuilding of the
nearby Pauper's Hospital,
where his father worked as
a doctor. Among the rather
scant authentic exhibits is
the pen with which he
wrote Brothers Karamazov.
2 Ul. Dostoyevskovo. Metro
Novoslobodskaya. Open
Thurs, Sat, Sun 11 am–
6 pm, Weds & Fri 2 pm–
9 pm, closed Mon, Tues,
last day of month. Tel: 281-
1085.

Folk Art Museum
A collection of mainly 17th-
19th century Russian
applied and decorative folk
art. There is a souvenir
shop, and usually a number
of temporary exhibitions of
high quality.
Ul. Delegatskaya 3. Metro
Tsvetnoi Bulvar. Open
Sat–Thurs 10 am–6 pm,
closed last Thurs of month.
Tel: 912-0139, 923-1741.

Folk Graphics Museum
A small and original museum providing an insight into
the Russian folk tradition of
the lubok, or woodcut
prints – a form of expres-

sion used by the poor, who
had no access to icon-
painting, dating from the
mid-17th century.
10 Maly Golovin Per. Metro
Turgenevskaya. Open
Tues–Sat 10 am–
6 pm. Tel: 208-5182.

Glinka Museum of Music
Most renowned for its fine
collection of musical instruments, from balalaikas to
bagpipes, and psalteries of
ancient Novgorod to an
early electronic instrument,
the Termenvox. Rooms are
colour-coded, according to
type of instrument and
region of the world, and
tape recordings of many
instruments can be heard.
Ul. Fadeyeva 4. Metro
Mayakovskaya. Open
11 am–7 pm, closed
Monday. Tel: 972-3237.

Golubkina Museum Studio
Devoted to the impressionist sculptor Anna
Golubkina, a pupil of the
great Auguste Rodin, the
museum combines an exhi-
bition hall and preserved
studio. On display are
famous portraits of Karl
Marx, Lev Tolstoy, and the
weaselly writer Andrey Bely,
and a toned plaster haut-
relief of the Last Supper.
Ul. Shchukina 12. Metro
Smolenskaya. Open Weds,
Thurs, Fri noon–7 pm, Sat &
Sun 10 am–5 pm; closed
Mon, Tues, last Fri of month.
Tel: 202-0683.

Gorky House Museum
See Walk 4.
Ul. Kachalova 6/2. Metro
Arbatskaya. Open 10 am–
6 pm, Weds & Fri 12 pm–
8 pm, closed Mon, Tues.
Tel: 290-0535.

Great Patriotic War Museum
Including the open-air exhi-
bition memorial complex,
Park Pobedy. See Greater
Moscow, "War Memorials".
Open daily 10 am–5 pm.

Herzen Museum
See Walk 5.
27/9 Sivtsev Vrazhek Ul.

*Metro Smolenskaya. Open
11 am-7 pm, Weds & Fri
2 pm-9 pm, closed Mon,
last day of month. Tel: 241-
5859.*

Interior Ministry Museum

A real treasure trove, with
exhibits on the tsarist
police, a complete counter-
feit printing press, the white
flag of the 1993 White
House defenders and a
section devoted to
Chernobyl fire chief Vladimir
Maksimchuk, to name but a
few.
*Ul. Seleznyovskaya 11.
Metro Novoslobodskaya.
Open Tues-Sat 11 am-
6 pm, groups only by prior
arrangement.*

KGB Museum

See Walk 2.
*Lubyanskaya Plosh. Metro
Lubyanka. By appointment
only (tel: 224-1982) or visit
on the Patriarchi Dom tour.*

Kolomenskoye Museum-Reserve

See Greater Moscow,
Kolomenskoye.
*31 Proletarsky Prosp. Metro
Kolomenskaya. Open
Tues-Sun 11 am-6 pm.
Tel: 112-5394.*

Konyonkov Museum

See Walk 4.
*28 Tverskoy Blvd. Metro
Pushkinskaya, Tverskaya.
Open daily 11 am-7 pm
except Mon, Tues, last Fri of
month. Tel: 229-4472.*

Kremlin

See Walk 1.
*Open 10 am-6 pm daily
except Thurs. Includes
Assumption Cathedral (tel:
226-7839), Archangel
Cathedral (tel: 226-7844),
Annunciation Cathedral (tel:
226-7986), Church of the
Deposition of the Robe (tel:
221-7124), Patriarch's
Palace (17th century
applied art exhibition), the
Armoury (tel: 921-4720,
excursion only) and the
Diamond Fund (tel: 229-
2036, excursion only).
Tickets for all museums
except the Diamond Fund
available at entrance.*

Kuskovo Museum-Estate

See Greater Moscow,
Kuskovo.
*Ul. Yunosti 2. Metro
Ryazansky Prospekt; then
bus #133, #208 six stops.
Open Weds-Fri 10 am-
7 pm (6 pm October-April),
closed last Weds in month.
Tel: 370-0130.*

Lermontov Museum

See Walk 5.
*Ul. Malaya Molchanovka 2.
Metro Arbatskaya. Open
11 am-7 pm, Weds & Fri
2 pm-9 pm, closed Mon,
Tues, last day of month.
Tel: 291-1860.*

Lights of Moscow

See Walk 9.
*Armyansky Per. 3. Metro
Lubyanka. Open Tues,
Weds, Thurs 1 pm-4 pm,
and for group tours Tues-Fri
12 pm-4 pm.
Tel: 924-7374.*

Literature Museum

See Walk 8.
*Ul. Petrovka 28. Metro
Chekhovskaya. Open Thurs,
Sat, Sun 11 am-6 pm,
Weds & Fri 2 pm-8 pm,
closed Mon, Tues, last day
of month. Tel: 221-3857.*

Mayakovsky Museum

See Walk 2.
*Proyezd Serova 3/6. Metro
Lubyanka. Open Fri-Tues
10 am-6 pm, Thurs 1 pm-
9 pm, closed Weds, last Fri
month. Tel: 921-9560/9387.*

Metro Museum

See Walk 12.
*Metro Sportivnaya. Open
Mon 11 am-6 pm, Tues-Fri
9 am-4 pm. Tel: 222-7309.*

Moscow City Museum

See Walk 2.
*St. John's Church, 12
Novaya Plosh. Metro
Lubyanka. Open Tues,
Thurs, Sat, Sun 10 am-
6 pm, Weds & Fri 11 am-
7 pm, closed Mon. Tel: 924-
8490.*

Oriental Art Museum

A richly endowed museum
with exhibits from the
Caucasus and Central Asia,
as well as Chinese,
Japanese, Korean and
Mongolian treasures assem-
bled from pre-revolutionary
private collections.
*Nikitsky Bulvar 12-A. Metro
Arbatskaya. Open Tues-Sun
11 am-8 pm. Tel: 202-
4555.*

Ostankino Museum

See Greater Moscow,
Ostankino.
*Pervaya Ostankinskaya Ul.
5. Metro VDNKh, then 5
stops by tram #11. Opening
times unavailable at time of
writing. Tel: 283-4575.*

Alexander Ostrovsky Museum

See Walk 7.
*Ul. Ostrovskovo 9. Metro
Tretyakovskaya. Open
Weds-Mon 1 pm-8 pm,
closed last Mon of month.
Tel: 233-8684.*

Private Collections Museum

See Pushkin Museum
chapter.
*Ul. Volkhonka 14. Metro
Kropotkinskaya. Open
Weds-Sun 10 am-5 pm.
Tel: 203-9578.*

Polytechnical Museum

See Walk 2.
*3/4 Novaya Plosh. Metro
Kitai Gorod. Open 10 am-
5:30 pm, Tues & Thurs
1 pm-8:30 pm, closed
Mon. Tel: 223-0756.*

Pushkin Fine Arts Museum

See separate chapter.
*Ul. Volkhonka 12. Metro
Kropotkinskaya. Open
Tues-Sun 10 am-7 pm. Tel:
203-7998.*

Pushkin Flat Museum

See Walk 5.
*Ul. Arbat 53. Metro
Smolenskaya. Open
Weds-Sun 11 am-6 pm
Guided tours in Russian
only, every 30 minutes, last-
ing 1.5 hours (English by
special arrangement).*

Pushkin Museum

See Walk 6.
*Ul. Prechistenka 12/2.
Metro Kropotkinskaya. Open
12:30 pm-7:30 pm, Sat &
Sun 10 am-5 pm, closed
Mon, Tues, last day of
month. Tel: 202-2321.*

Listings | Museums

Revolution Museum
See Walk 3.
*Ul. Tverskaya 21. Metro
Pushkinskaya, Tverskaya.
Open 10 am–6 pm, Weds
11 am–7 pm, closed Mon
and last day of month. Tel:
299-9683, 299-6274.*

Roerich Museum
See Walk 6
*Ul. Malaya Znamenka 3.
Metro Kropotkinskaya. Open
Tues, Thurs, Sat 11 am–
7 pm.*

Romanov Chambers in Zaryadye
See Walk 2.
*Ul. Varvarka 10. Metro Kitai
Gorod. Open daily except
Tues and the last Mon of
the month 10 am–
6 pm; Weds 11 am–7 pm.
Tel: 298-3235/3706.*

Scriabin Museum
See Walk 5.
*Ul. Vakhtangova 11. Metro
Smolenskaya. Open
10 am–6 pm, closed Mon,
Tues, last day of month.
Tel: 241-0302.*

Shaliapin Museum
The former house of the
great Russian bass Fyodor
Shaliapin, the museum was
restored a few years ago to
its 1910 appearance. It
includes an extraordinary
variety of costumes from his
performances at the
Bolshoi Theatre, and a
recital room where you can
relax to an early recording
of his recitals. Upstairs is
an exhibition devoted to the
opera theatre of art patron
Savva Mamontov.
*25 Novinsky Blvd. Metro
Barrikadnaya. Tel: 205-
6236. Open Sat 10 am–
5 pm, Sun 10 am–4 pm,
Tues 10 am–5 pm, Weds,
Thurs 11:30 am–6 pm. Tel:
205-6236.*

Shchusev Museum of Architecture
See Walk 6.
*Ul. Vozdvizhenka 5. Metro
Biblioteka im. Lenina,
Arbatskaya, Alexandrovsky
Sad. Open Tues–Fri
10 am–6 pm, Sat & Sun
10 am–4 pm. Tel: 291-
2109.*

Sidur Museum
Collection of sculptures
and water-colours of the
famous dissident sculptor,
Vadim Sidur.
*Novogireyevskaya Ul. 37.
Metro Perovo. Open daily
except Tues, Weds 10 am–
7 pm. Tel: 918-5181.*

Stanislavsky Flat Museum
See Walk 4.
*Ul. Stanislavskovo 6. Metro
Tverskaya, Pushkinskaya.
Open 11 am–6 pm, Weds &
Fri 2 pm–9 pm, closed
Mon, Tues, last Thurs of
month. Tel: 229-2855.*

St. Basil's Cathedral
See Walk 2.
*Red Square. Metro
Ploshchad Revolutsii,
Teatralnaya. Open daily
9:30 am–5 pm, closed
Tues. Tel: 298-3304.*

Tolstoy Museum
See Walk 6.
*Ul. Prechistenka 11. Metro
Kropotkinskaya. Open
10 am–6 pm, Weds & Fri
12 pm–7 pm, closed Mon.
Tel: 202-2190.*

Tolstoy Museum Branch
See Walk 7.
*Ul. Pyatnitskaya 12. Metro
Novokuznetskaya. Open
11 am–6 pm daily, closed
Mon, Tues, last Fri of month.
Tel: 231-6440.*

Tolstoy Museum Estate
See Walk 6.
*Ul. Lva Tolstovo 21. Metro
Park Kultury. Open 10 am–
6 pm, closed Mon, last day
of month. Tel: 246-9444.*

Tretyakov Gallery (New)
See Walk 6.
*10 Krymsky Val. Metro
Oktyabrskaya. Open daily
except Mon 10 am–7 pm.
Tel: 230-1116, 230-7788.*

Tretyakov Gallery (Old)
See separate chapter.
*10 Lavrushinsky Per. Metro
Tretyakovskaya. Open daily
10 am–7 pm, closed Mon.
Tel: 233-5223.*

Trinity Church in Nikitniki
See Walk 2.
*Nikitnikov Per. 3. Metro
Kitai Gorod. Open daily
except Tues 10 am–6 pm.
Tel: 298-3451.*

Tropinin Museum
See Walk 7.
*Shchetininsky Per. 10.
Metro Tretyakovskaya. Open
10 am–5:30 pm, Tues &
Thurs 1 pm–8:30 pm,
closed Mon. Tel: 231-1799.*

Tsvetayeva Museum
See Walk 5.
*Borisoglebsky Per. 6. Metro
Arbatskaya. Open Weds &
Thurs noon–5 pm. Tel: 202-
3543.*

Apollinariy Vasnetsov Flat Museum
Devoted to Viktor's lesser-
known younger brother,
who made a name as a
painter, historian, archaeolo-
gist and even astronomer.
One apartment is used as
an art gallery, most notable
for his reconstructions of
life in old Moscow. The second shows where he used
to live, including the studio
where he worked after losing his teaching job to futurist rivals.
*Furmanny Per. 6/21–22.
Metro Chistiye Prudy. Open
Thurs, Sat, Sun 11 am–
5 pm, Weds & Fri 1 pm–
7 pm, closed Mon, Tues.*

Viktor Vasnetsov House Museum
A little wooden house in
Russian Moderne style
designed by Vasnetsov himself, a leading member of
the "Itinerant" group of
artists, displays his personal
belongings and his later
works, including illustrations
to fairy tales.
*Per. Vasnetsova 13.
Metro Sukharevskaya. Open
Weds–Sun 10 am–
4:30 pm, closed last Thurs
of month. Tel: 281-1329.*

Vysotsky Museum
See Walk 11.
*Nizhny Tagansky Per. 3/2.
Metro Taganskaya. Open
Mon, Weds, Thurs, Fri
2 pm–6 pm. Tel: 915-7578.*

Yermolova Flat Museum

See Walk 4.
Tverskoy Blvd 11. Metro Arbatskaya. Open noon– 7 pm, closed Tues, last Mon of month. Tel: 290-0215.

Music, Opera, Ballet

Bolshoi Theatre

Once the temple of official Soviet art, the Bolshoi has suffered badly in the last decade. Its critics accused it of creative stultification, as former Artistic Director Yuri Grigorovich revived old productions; some of the works in its repertoire have been playing as long as 30 years, with a heavy production style that only emphasis their age.

The change of leadership in January 1995 which saw former ballet soloist Vladimir Vasilyev appointed as new Artistic Director was a much-vaunted step towards the new – one which has yet to bear real fruit. Shows at 7 pm, Tuesday–Sunday, plus Sunday matinee. Closed July, August.
Teatralnaya Plosh. 1. Metro Teatralnaya. Tel: 292-0050.

Conservatory, Grand and Small Halls

Moscow's Conservatory has a reputation as one of the world's great musical centres, where an established school and methods of teaching have existed for generations. The stark beauty of its Grand Hall witnesses a number of world-class concerts each year; many of the great musicians who left Russia in the past now return as regular performers, while corporate home sponsors have started to make their mark on a previously-impoverished scene.

The Small Hall is a chamber music venue, where a number of younger musicians also appear; the Rachmaninoff Hall, in an adjoining building, is more often a venue for the Conservatory's student performers.
Ul. Bolshaya Nikitskaya 13. Metro Pushkinskaya, Arbatskaya. Tel: 229-8183/299-0658. Rachmaninoff Hall, Ul. Bolshaya Nikitskaya 11. Tel: 229-0294.

Glinka Museum

Alongside its permanent exhibition of world instruments, the Glinka Museum is a regular concert venue, sometimes offering more avant-garde programmes, as well as occasional world music.
Ul. Fadayeva, 4. Metro Mayakovskaya. Tel: 972-3237.

Gnesin Institute

Student performance venue, situated next to the Russian Academy of Music.
Ul. Povarskaya 30/36. Metro Arbatskaya. Tel: 290-6727.

Kremlin Palace of Congresses

A huge 5,800 seat auditorium betrays the building's origin as a meeting place for CPSU delegates. Artistically, though, the venue is a good one, although best to sit as near the front as possible; performances by the resident ballet company, under Andrei Petrov, are usually worth catching.
Kremlin, Trinity Gate. Metro Alexandrovsky Sad. Tel: 917-2336.

Novaya Opera

Although they have no regular base, *Novaya Opera* (New Opera) are one of the most interesting phenomena on Moscow's musical scene. Set up four years ago by Yevgeny Kolobov, they have more than fulfilled their promise with a series of outstanding operatic premieres, such as Verdi's *I Due Foscari* and Donizetti's *Mary Stuart*. Their concert and opera performances rotate around a number of venues.

Operetta Theatre

The pompously grand auditorium is generally more impressive than the quality of performances at the Operetta Theatre, which combines the Russian genre repertoire with the Viennese classics. It is frequently a venue for visiting dance and theatre.
Ul. Pushkinskaya 6. Metro Teatralnaya. Tel: 292-0405.

Olympic Village

The large hall is an occasional venue for music and ballet performances, as well as rock concerts.
Ul. Pelshe 1. Metro Prospekt Vernadskovo. Tel: 437-5650.

Rossiya Concert Hall

Cavernous modern hall which has considerably more charm than the Hotel Rossiya, of which it is a part. Most frequently a venue for Russian rock-pop, as well as estrada.
Moskvoretskaya Nab. 1. Metro Ploshchad Revolutsii, Kitai Gorod. Tel: 298-1124.

Scriabin House Museum

Preserving much of the atmosphere of the composer's day, the downstairs concert hall at the Scriabin House accommodates an audience of less than 100, for high standard chamber music.
Ul. Vakhtangova 11. Metro Smolenskaya. Tel: 241-1901.

Shaliapin House Museum

The atmospheric White Hall of the great singer's mansion, now lovingly restored, offers occasional vocal recitals.
Novinsky Bulvar 25. Metro Barrikadnaya. Tel: 205-6236.

Shuvalov House Museum

Ul. Povarskaya 30/1. Metro Arbat. Tel: 251-9258.

Stanislavsky Museum

The Onegin Hall of the Stanislavsky House Museum is an occasional venue for chamber music. See Walk 4.

Ul. Stanislavskogo 6. Metro Pushkinskaya. Tel: 299-2855.

Stanislavsky Nemirovich-Danchenko Musical Theatre

Moscow's second opera and ballet company after the Bolshoi, the Stanislavsky Nemirovich-Danchenko Theatre has a considerably smaller auditorium, making for greater intimacy – if less charm – in the surroundings. Artistically, it sometimes beats the productions of the Bolshoi.

Ul. Pushkinskaya 17. Metro Chekhovskaya. Tel: 229-8388.

Tchaikovsky Hall

Although acoustically not outstanding, the Tchaikovsky Hall offers an illustrious musical programme; it is frequently a venue for more "national" forms of art, including folk dance, balalaika orchestras and the like, all of which are well worth catching for their colour. See Walk 4.

Plosh. Mayakovskovo 4/3. Metro Mayakovskaya. Tel: 299-0378.

Nightlife

In a little less than seven years, Moscow's nightlife scene has grown from nothing to rival Las Vegas. Whether taste has kept up with glamour is another matter, and for the foreign eye there's less of interest: clubs and casinos are patronised by New Russians – a loose category which ranges from businessmen through to obvious gangsters – paying prices which are astronomical by world standards in a display of conspicuous consumption which will likely leave you daunted. Musical acts are normally *estrada*, a form which may appear primitive and lacking in variety to an outsider.

More interesting, therefore, is the smaller range of jazz, music and rock clubs; sometimes scruffier and more informal, they have considerably more atmosphere, and are more realistically priced. Unfortunately, also, they are now being edged out in the hunt for space, and many of the pioneering clubs have closed in the last few months. Entrance charge is given, for clarity, in dollars, although is paid in rubles.

Music, Rock Clubs

Arbat Blues Club

Small, informal venue catering to a young crowd, with live blues and rock every Friday and Saturday. Open 8:30 pm–5:30 am, with music from 11 pm. Entrance $10.

11 Aksakova Per. in the "Na Starom Arbate" Theatre Studio. Metro Arbat. Tel: 291-1546.

Hermitage

Stylish central Moscow disco and bar, with techno-oriented disco and occasional live bands at weekends, as well as special party events. Open 10 pm–6 am Friday, Saturday and Sunday. Entrance $10. See Walk 8.

3 Karetny Ryad. Metro Mayakovskaya, Pushkinskaya. Tel: 299-1160.

Krisis Genre

Small cellar bar which has an unusually European feel for Moscow, with live music in the evenings, a welcome informality and refreshingly cheap prices. Open daily noon–1 am, live music from 9 pm (music cover about $3). See Walk 6.

22/4 Per. Ostrovskovo. Metro Kropotkinskaya. Tel: 243-8605.

Tabula Rasa

Stylish small performance club, live music, restaurant, bar and dance floor. Another welcome venue with more style than money. Entrance $10. Open daily 6 pm–6 am.

Berezhkovskaya Nab. 28. From Metro Kievskaya, along the river front in the direction of Mosfilm Studios. Tel: 240-9289.

Voyazh Club

Out-of-centre dance and rock club owned by the rock group of the same name. Entrance $5–$10. Live gigs normally Friday, Saturday, Sunday.

Altufeyevskoye Shosse, 18, kor. 2 Tel: 903-3665, 401-9501.

Jazz Clubs

Art Club Nostalgie

Welcome new jazz club in attractive café surroundings, with live jazz currently on Thursdays, Fridays and Saturdays.

Café open 8 am–11:30 pm, with concerts beginning 8:30 pm; admission is free before 7:30 pm, then $5–$10.

12-A Chistoprudniye Bulvar. Metro Turgenevskaya, Chistiye Prudy. Tel: 916-9478, 916-9090.

Jazz Art Club

For real authentic jazz, this small club, with performances every Wednesday evening opening from 7 pm, is a high-point. Entrance $10, reservations recommended.

Where no formal programme is announced, musicians will frequently appear for an informal jam session. Atmospheric and, for Moscow, refreshingly uncommercial – it's run by enthusiasts.

5 Ul. Begovaya, in the hall of the Vernisazh Theatre. Metro Begovaya. Tel: 191-8320.

Gay

Gay life in Moscow has taken off slowly in the last

four years, with a changing legal situation beginning to allow public gatherings. Most venues have been very flexible ones, appearing for a few months at a time, before moving elsewhere.

Chance

A stylishly-decorated European club with three bars and dance space which opened recently in premises which had been one of the very first gay venues in Moscow. Open every day 11 pm–6 am, with discotheque Thursday–Sunday. Entrance $7–$10. *Dom Kultury Serp i Molot, near Metro Ploshchad Ilyicha. Tel: 956-7102.*

Mainstream Nightclubs

Arlecchino

Successful disco, dance show, bar and Italian restaurant. Entrance $30-$50. Open Friday–Sunday 11 pm–5 am. *Kinocentre, 15 Druzhinnikovskaya Ul. Metro Barrikadnaya. Tel: 268-8500, 205-7306.*

Club Royale

Stylish nightclub/casino, with restaurant, Jazz Bar and occasional live concerts. Entrance $10, $20 upwards on concert nights. Happy hour daily 5 pm–8 pm, drinks half price. *22 Begovaya Ul. part of the Hippodrome. Metro Begovaya. Tel: 945-4842.*

2 x 2 Club

Stylish, intimate club with weekend appearances from Russian estrada stars. Open Wednesday to Sunday, 11–5 pm. *6 Ul. Chekhova, in Lenkom Theatre. Metro Pushkinskaya. Tel: 209-5346.*

Karo-Utopia

New mainstream club occupying the greater part of Rossiya Cinema on Pushkin Square. Entrance $40. *Metro Pushkinskaya. Tel: 229-0003.*

Karousel

Large discotheque, with bar and restaurant. Open every day, 10 pm–6 am. Live music Friday–Sunday. Entrance $30 upwards. *11 1-ya Tverskaya-Yamskaya Ul. Metro Mayakovskaya. Tel: 251-6444.*

Manhattan Express

New York-style restaurant and night club, which has now become, after management changes, a standard New Moscow venue. Frequent special events, shows, live bands. Open daily, entrance $20–$25. *Northwest corner of Rossiya Hotel. Metro Ploshchad Revolutsii, Kitai Gorod. Tel: 298-5254.*

Master

Mainstream discotheque, with weekend live bands. Entrance $10–$25. *6 Pavlovskaya Ul. at the ZVI Club. Metro Dobryninskaya. Tel: 237-1742.*

Metelitsa

New Russian glamour with a large night-club, alongside prime gambling venue, the Cherry Casino. Entrance $30–$50. *21 Novy Arbat. Metro Smolenskaya. Tel: 291-1301, 291-4246.*

Moskovskii Club

Centrally-located mainstream club with quality restaurant. Weekend live performances from estrada stars. Entrance $30–$60. *6 Tverskaya Ul. Metro Okhotny Ryad. Tel: 292-1282.*

Pilot

Disco with young crowd and stylish decorations, plus frequent live bands. Unlike many of its more opulent counterparts, Pilot has a sense of style which goes beyond the pockets of its patrons. Attached to it is Soho, a more intimate 24-hour club with TV screens and electronic games. Pilot shows start at midnight–1 am, open Thursday to Saturday 11 am–6 am. Entrance $10–$20.

6 Tryokhgorny Val. Metro Ul. 1905 Goda. Tel: 252-2764.

Titanik

Decorated in the style of the ocean liner, Titanik is a smaller and more intimate club which opened summer 1995, so far with considerable style. Entrance $15. *31 Leningradsky Prosp. inside Young Pioneers Stadium. Metro Dinamo. Open Thurs–Sun 10 pm–6 am. Tel: 213-4581, 213-6182.*

Restaurants, Cafés

Price Guide for main meal, without drinks

$$$$: very expensive ($75+ per person)
$$$: expensive, $40–$75
$$: moderate, $20–$40
$: cheap, under $20
CC: Credit Cards accepted.

Russian Cuisine

Alexandrovsky

See Walk 3. 1-ya Tverskaya-Yamskaya 17. Metro Belorusskaya. Open noon–midnight. Tel: 251-7987. Major CC. $$$$.

Arkhangelskoye

See Greater Moscow, Arkhangelskoye. Town of Krasnogorsk. Open noon–midnight. Tel: 562-0328. CC. $$.

Borodino

A temple of gastronomy, presenting French cuisine with a Russian slant. *Hotel Aerostar, 37 Leningradsky Prosp. korp. 9. Metro Dinamo. Open 6 pm–11 pm. Tel: 213-9000. CC. $$$.*

Boyarsky Zal

See Walk 2. Hotel Metropol. Open 7 pm–11 pm. Tel: 927-6089. CC. $$$$.

Budapest

See Walk 8. Hotel Budapest. Metro Teatralnaya, Okhotny Ryad.

Open noon–11 pm. Tel:
923-9966. Cash only. $$.

Danilovsky
See Greater Moscow, St.
Daniel's. Danilovsky Hotel,
Bolshoy Danilovsky Per. 5.
Metro Tulskaya. Open
noon–1 am. Tel: 954-0566.
CC. $$$$.

Fyodor
An old world style restaurant named after Fyodor
Kon, builder of the "White
City". A fine selection of
19th century Russian
recipes.
Lubyansky Proyezd 19.
Metro Lubyanka. Open
noon–midnight. Tel: 923-
2578. Cash only. $$$.

Glazur
Two-storey restaurant with
Danish and Russian food,
the latter seeming to hail
from the days of Pushkin's
Moscow.
Smolensky Bulvar 12.
Metro Smolenskaya. Open
noon–midnight. CC. $$$-
2319. CC. $$$.

Imperial
See Walk 6. Gagarinsky
Per. 9. Metro Kropotkinskaya. Open noon–11 pm.
Tel: 291-6063. Major CC.
$$$.

Kropotkinskaya 36
See Walk 6. Prechistenka
Ul. 36. Metro Kropotkinskaya. Open noon–5 pm,
6 pm–11 pm. Tel: 201-
7500. Major CC. $$$.

Laguna
See Walk 3. 1-ya
Tverskaya-Yamskaya Ul. 15.
Metro Belorusskaya. Open
noon–midnight. Tel: 251-
9381. Major CC. $$$.

Le Romanoff
See Walk 7. Baltschug
Kempinski Hotel, Ul.
Balchuga 1-A. Open 6 pm–
11 pm. Tel: 230-6500. CC.
$$$$.

Lomonosov
See Walk 3. Palace Hotel,
1-ya Tverskaya-Yamskaya Ul.
19. Metro Belorusskaya.
Open noon–3 pm, 7 pm–
11 pm. Tel: 256-3152. CC.
$$$$.

Nemetskaya Sloboda
See Walk 10. Baumanskaya Ul. 23. Metro
Baumanskaya. Open
noon–11 pm. Tel: 267-
4476. Cash only. $$.

Razgulyay
See Walk 10. Spartakovskaya Ul. 11. Metro
Baumanskaya. Open
noon–11 pm. Tel: 267-
7613. CC. $$.

Russkaya Izba
See Greater Moscow,
Arkhangelskoye. Ilinskoye.
Open noon–10 pm. Tel:
561-4244. Cash only. $$$.

Russky Zal
Tretyakov Gallery. Lavrushinsky Per. 12. Metro Tretyakovskaya. Open Mon–Fri
1 pm–midnight, Sat/Sun
noon–midnight. Cash. $$.

Samovar
See Walk 9. Ul. Myasnitskaya 13. Metro Lubyanka.
Open Mon–Sat noon–9:30
pm. Tel: 921-4688. $$.

Sirena
Generally considered
Moscow's best private
restaurant, serving mainly
fish dishes, but for a price –
expect to pay $100 a head.
Ul. Bolshaya Spasskaya 15.
Metro Komsomolskaya.
Open 2 pm–midnight. Tel:
208-1412. CC. $$$$

U Arsentyicha
See Walk 2. Bolshoy
Cherkassky Per. 15. Metro
Ploshchad Revolutsii. Open
noon–11 pm. Tel: 927-
0755. CC. $$.

U Babushki
See Walk 7. Bol. Ordynka
Ul. 42. Metro Tretyakovskaya. Open noon–11 pm.
Tel: 230-2797. CC. $$

U Sretenskikh Vorot
See Walk 8. Bol. Lubyanka
Ul. 24. Metro Lubyanka.
Open Mon–Sat noon–9 pm.
Tel: 924-9252. Cash only.
$$.

Yakor
See Walk 3. Per. Sadovskikh 12. Metro Mayakovskaya. Open noon–10 pm.
Tel: 299-2951, 209-5444.
Cash only. $$.

Georgian, Caucasian, former Soviet Cuisines

Aragvi
See Walk 3. Tverskaya Ul.
6. Metro Okhotny Ryad.
Open noon–11 pm. Tel:
229-3762. Cash only. $$.

Baku-Livan
See Walk 3. Tverskaya Ul.
24. Metro Pushkinskaya,
Tverskaya. Open 11 am–5
pm, 6–11 pm. Tel: 299-
8506. CC. $$$.

Guria
See Walk 6. Komsomolsky
Prosp. 7. Metro Park Kultury. Open noon–10 pm. Tel:
246-0378. Cash. $.

Iberia
See Walk 8. Rozhdestvenka Ul. 5/7. Metro
Kuznetsky Most. Open
noon–11:30 pm. Tel: 928-
2672. Cash or AmEx. $$.

Kolkhida
Another excellent value
Georgian restaurant.
Sadovaya-Samotyochnaya
Ul. 6. Metro Tsvetnoi Bulvar.
Open noon–11 pm. Tel:
299-6757. Cash. $.

Mama Zoya's
See Walk 6. Sechenovsky
Per. 8. Metro Kropotkinskaya. Open 11 am–10 pm.
Tel: 201-7743. Cash. $.

Mziuri
See Walk 5. Arbat Ul. 42.
Metro Smolenskaya. Open
noon–11:30 pm. Tel: 241-
0313. $$.

Shakherazada
See Walk 5. Novy Arbat 11.
Metro Arbatskaya. Open
noon–midnight. Tel: 291-
9004, 203-4962. CC. $$$.

U Pirosmani
See Greater Moscow,
Novodevichy. Novodevichy
Proyezd 4. Metro Sportivnaya. Open noon–4:30 pm,
6 pm–10:30 pm. Tel: 247-
1926. CC. $$.

U Yusepha
Still Moscow's only Jewish
restaurant, and something
of a community centre.
Evening reservations vital.

*Dubininskaya Ul. 17. Metro
Paveletskaya. Open
noon–11 pm. Tel: 238-
4646. Cash only. $$.*

Uzbekistan
*See Walk 8. Ul. Neglinnaya
29. Metro Teatralnaya,
Okhotny Ryad. Open
11 am–midnight. Tel: 924-
6053. Cash only. $$.*

French, Other European Cuisines

Anchor
*See Walk 3. Palace Hotel,
1-ya Tverskaya Yamskaya
Ul. 19. Metro Belorusskaya.
Open noon–5 pm, 7 pm–
1:30 am. Tel: 956-3152.
CC. $$$$.*

Arbat Club
*See Walk 5. Plotnikov Per.
12. Metro Smolenskaya.
Open noon–midnight. Tel:
244-7641. Major CC.
$$$$.*

Baltschug
*See Walk 7. Baltschug
Kempinski Hotel, 1 Ul.
Balchuga. Open 7 am–
10:30 am, noon–3 pm,
6 pm–11 pm. Tel: 230-
6500. CC. $$$$ ($$ for
smorgasbord).*

Budvar
German/Czech food and
beer in a hardly glamourous
but consistently well-per-
forming restaurant.
*Kotelnicheskaya Nab. 33.
Metro Taganskaya. Open
noon–midnight. Tel: 915-
1590. Some CC. $$$.*

Café Taiga
The Aerostar Hotel's popular, practical restaurant,
well-known for its good
value Business Lunch and
Sunday Brunch.
*Aerostar Hotel, Leningrad-
sky Prosp. 39. kor. 9. Metro
Dinamo. Open 7 am–
11 pm. Tel: 213-9000, ext.
2741. CC. $$.*

Ekipazh
*See Walk 4. 5 Spiridon-
ievsky Per. Metro Mayakov-
skaya. Open Mon-Fri
5 pm–5 am, Sat/Sun 1 pm–
5 am. CC. $$.*

El Rincon Espanol
*See Walk 2. Hotel Moskva,
Okhotny Ryad 2. Metro
Okhotny Ryad. Open
noon–11:45 pm. Tel: 292-
2893. CC. $$$.*

**El Rincon Espanol:
Tablao Flamenco**
Spanish tapas restaurant-
bar, with great paella.
Nightly flamenco shows at
8, 10 pm, midnight, 2 am.
*Pushkinskaya Ul. 13/8.
Metro Teatralnaya, Pushkin-
skaya. Open noon–5 am.
Tel: 229-7023. CC. $$.*

Evropeisky Zal
*See Walk 2. Hotel
Metropol. Teatralny Proyezd
1/4. Open 11:30 am–
10:30 pm. Tel: 927-6039.
CC. $$$.*

Greek Restaurant
Greek cuisine in delicious
and reasonably-priced set
meals at Moscow's best
floating restaurant.
*12 Krasnopresnenskaya
Nab. (M/S Alexander Blok).
Metro Ul. 1905 Goda.
Open 12:30 pm–
5:30 pm, 7 pm–10:30 pm.
Tel: 255-9284. CC. $
(lunch), $$ (set dinner).*

Karousel
*See Walk 3. 1-ya Tverskaya
Yamskaya. Metro Belo-
russkaya. Open noon–6 am.
Tel: 251-6444. CC. $$$.*

Le Chalet
Swiss-French cuisine,
including delicious fondues
and Caesar's Salad in a
refined ski lodge setting.
*Korobeinikov Per. 1/2.
Metro Park Kultury. Open
noon–midnight. Tel: 202-
0106/2611. CC. $ (set
lunch), $$$.*

Les Champs Elysees
Genuine French food, ser-
vice and atmosphere, but
difficult to get to unless
you're staying in the hotel.
*Sofitel Iris Hotel,
Khorovinskoye Shosse 10.
Open 7 pm–10 pm. Tel:
488-8000. CC. $$$.*

Maxim's
A branch of the famous
Paris restaurant, recently
opened by Pierre Cardin

himself. One of the city's
most expensive eateries,
with meals at up to
$150–$200 a head.
*National Hotel. Metro
Okhotny Ryad. Open
6:30 pm–11:30 pm. Tel:
258-7000. CC. $$$$.*

MKhAT Club
*See Walk 4. Kamergersky
Per. 3. Metro Okhotny
Ryad. Open noon–4 pm,
6 pm–3 am. Tel: 229-9106.
Cash only. $$.*

Mercator Club
*See Walk 11. Bol. Komm-
unisticheskaya Ul. 2-A.
Metro Taganskaya. Open
noon–11:30 pm. Tel: 272-
3908. CC. $$$.*

Night Flight
*See Walk 3. Tverskaya Ul.
17. Metro Pushkinskaya,
Tverskaya. Open noon–
5 am. Tel: 229-4165. CC.
$$$ (lunch $).*

Old Square Piano Bar
*See Walk 2. Bolshoi
Cherkassky Per. 8. Metro
Ploshchad Revolutsii. Open
5 pm–5 am. Tel: 298-4688.
Cash only. $$.*

Paradise
*See Walk 2. Moskva Hotel.
Open 9 am–midnight
(breakfast 9 am–noon). Tel:
292-2030. CC. $$$.*

Praga
*See Walk 5. Arbat Ul. 2.
Metro Arbatskaya. Open
11 am–midnight. Tel: 290-
6171. Cash only. $$.*

Presnja
*See Walk 4. Presnja Hotel,
9 Spiridonievsky Per. Metro
Mayakovskaya. Open 12–
3 pm, 7–11 pm. Tel: 203-
6689, 956-3010. CC.
$$$$.*

Savoy
*See Walk 8. Hotel Savoy.
Metro Kuznetsky Most.
Open noon–midnight.
Tel: 929-8600. CC. $$$.*

Stanislavsky Club
*See Walk 3. Tverskaya Ul.
23. Metro Pushkinskaya,
Tverskaya. Open 1 pm–
4 pm, 6 pm–6 am. Tel: 564-
8004. Major credit cards
except AmEx. $$$.*

Listings | Restaurants, Cafés

Strastnoy 7
See Walk 8. Metro
Chekhovskaya, Pushkin-
skaya. Open noon–11 pm.
Tel: 299-0498. CC. $$.

Teatro Restaurant
See Walk 2. Hotel
Metropol. Open 11 am–
2 am. Tel: 927-6739. CC.
$$$.

U Dyadi Gilyaya
See Walk 3. Stoleshnikov
Per. 6. Metro Okhotny
Ryad. Open noon–midnight.
Tel: 229-2050, 229-4750.
CC. $$.

Vienna
See Walk 3. Palace Hotel,
1-ya Tverskaya-Yamskaya Ul.
19. Metro Belorusskaya.
Open 5 pm–11 pm. Tel:
956-3152. CC. $$$$.

011
See Walk 4. Sadovaya-
Triumfalnaya 10. Metro
Mayakovskaya. Open
1 pm–midnight. Tel: 299-
3964. CC. $$$.

Italian Cuisine: Pizza, Pasta

Artistico
See Walk 4. Pushkinskaya
Ul. 5/6 (entrance from
Kamergersky Per.). Metro
Okhotny Ryad. Open
noon–midnight. Tel: 292-
0673. Major CC. $$$.

Fantasia
See Walk 4. Tverskoy
Bulvar 10/12. Metro
Pushkinskaya/Tverskaya.
Open 10 am–2 am. Tel:
292-0216. Cash only
(rubles or dollars). $$$.

Bar Italia
See Walk 5. Stary Arbat 49.
Metro Smolenskaya. Open
noon–midnight. Tel: 241-
4342. CC. $$.

Ciao Italia
Small new café offering
decently priced tasty food
in a pleasant setting.
Zemlyanoy Val 18/22. Metro
Kurskaya. Open 8 am–
4 am. Tel: 917-9363. Cash
only. $$.

Dorian Gray
See Walk 7. Kadashev-

skaya Nab. 6/1. Metro
Biblioteka im. Lenina,
Borovitskaya. Open
noon–midnight. Tel: 237-
6342. CC. $$$$.

Gelateria
One of the first such west-
ern-type cafés to appear in
Moscow, it is now one of
many, and not as cheap as
it could be. A pleasant
place to spend the after-
noon, all the same.
Prosp. Mira 58. Metro
Prospekt Mira. Open
9:30 am–11:30 pm. Tel:
280-9679. Cash only. $.

Le Stelle del Pescatore
See Walk 8. Pushechnaya
7/5. Metro Kuznetsky Most.
Open 10 am–2 am. Tel:
924-2058. CC. $$$.

Patio Pasta
See Walk 3. 1-ya
Tverskaya-Yamskaya Ul. 1.
Metro Mayakovskaya.
Open noon–midnight.
Tel: 251-5861. CC. $$.

Patio Pizza
See Walk 3. The glass
veranda at Hotel Intourist,
Ul. Tverskaya 4. Open 24
hours. Tel: 292-0891. CC.
$$.

Patio Pizza
See Walk 6. Ul. Volkhonka
13-A. Metro Kropotkinsk-
aya. Open noon–midnight.
Tel: 201-5000. CC. $$.

Pescatore 90
A club-type restaurant with
genuine Neapolitan pizza
and fish dishes, and, most
important, popular with
Italians.
Prosp. Mira 36. Metro
Prospekt Mira. Open
noon–midnight. Tel: 280-
2406. CC. $$$.

Pizza Hut
See Walk 3. Ul. Tverskaya
12. Metro Pushkinskaya,
Tverskaya. Tel: 229-
2013/7840. Also at
Kutuzovsky Prosp. 17.
Metro Kievskaya. Tel: 243-
1727/9964. Open 11
am–10 pm. CC. $$.

San Marco
See Walk 5. Arbat Ul. 25.
Metro Arbatskaya. Open

noon–11 pm. Tel: 291-
7089. CC except AmEx.
$$.

Santa Lucia
See Walk 3. Hotel Intourist
3rd floor. Open noon till the
last guest leaves. Tel: 956-
8413. CC. $$$.

Villa Medici
Relaxing and trouble-free
meals of fine Italian food, a
good place for a quiet
evening meal.
Olympic Penta Hotel. Metro
Prospekt Mira. Open
6 pm–10:30 pm. Tel: 971-
6101. CC. $$$.

Villa Peredelkino
See Excursions,
Peredelkino. Chobotov-
skaya Alleya 2, Peredel-
kino. Open noon–midnight.
Tel: 435-1478, 1211. CC.
Reservations essential.
$$$.

American Cuisine

American Bar & Grill
See Walk 3. 1-ya
Tverskaya-Yamskaya Ul. 2.
Metro Mayakovskaya. Open
24 hours. Tel: 251-2847.
CC. $$.

American Bar & Grill-II
See Walk 11. 59 Zemly-
anoy Val. Metro Tagan-
skaya. Open 24 hours. Tel:
912-3615. CC. $$.

Bourbon and Beefsteak
New café bar, offering "the
juiciest joint in town" if you
believe its publicity (we
think they mean meat!). $10
set lunch, and 5:30–7 pm
Happy Hour.
8/10 Bryusov Per. in the
House of Composers. Metro
Okhotny Ryad. Open noon–
midnight. Tel: 229-7185,
229-6563. CC. $$.

Diner 24
See Walk 11. 72 Zemly-
anoy Val. Metro Tagan-
skaya. Open 24 hours. Tel:
915-3248. Cash only. $$.

Exchange
One of Moscow's best
steakhouses.
Radisson Slavyanskaya
Hotel. Metro Kievskaya.

Open 6 pm–11 pm. Tel:
941-8333. CC. $$$.

TrenMos
Komsomolsky Prosp. 21.
Metro Frunzenskaya. Tel:
245-1216.

Chinese Cuisine

Fast Food Fans
The latest in Moscow fast
food brings "chicken in oys-
ter sauce" and other dishes
to the masses.
Komsomolskaya Plosh.
Metro Komsomolskaya;
Novoslobodskaya Ul.
Metro Mendeleyevskaya;
Marksistskaya Ul. Metro
Taganskaya. Open 10 am–
10 pm. Cash only. $.

Golden Dragon
See Walk 7. Bol. Ordynka
Ul. 59. Metro Dobrynin-
skaya. Open noon–5 am.
Tel: 231-9251. Also at Ul.
Plyushchika 64 (tel: 248-
3602) & Ul. Kalanchev-
skaya 15-A (tel: 975-5566).
CC. $$.

Lily Wong's
See Walk 3. Hotel Intourist.
Open noon–midnight. Tel:
956-0300. CC. $$$ ($$
for set lunch).

Panda
See Walk 4. Tverskoy
Bulvar 3/5. Metro
Pushkinskaya/Tverskaya.
Open noon–11 pm. Tel:
298-6565, 202-8313.
Major CC. $$$.

Peking
See Walk 3. Ul. Bolshaya
Sadovaya 1/7. Metro
Mayakovskaya. Open
noon–4 pm, 6 pm–11 pm.
Tel: 209-1387. CC. $$.

Indian Cuisine

Maharaja
See Walk 9. Ul. Pokrovka
2/1. Metro Kitai Gorod.
Open noon–10 pm. Tel:
921-9844, 7758. Major
CC. $$.

Moscow Bombay
See Walk 3. Ul. Nemiro-
vicha-Danchenko 3. Metro
Pushkinskaya. Open
noon–11 pm. Tel: 292-
9739. MC, Eurocard. $$.

Tandoor
See Walk 3. Tverskaya Ul.
30. Metro Mayakovskaya.
Open noon–11 pm. Tel:
209-5565. Major CC. $$.

Mexican Cuisine

Azteca
See Walk 3. Hotel Intourist
20th–21st floors. Open 24
hours. Tel: 956-3490. Also
at: Novoslobodskaya Ul. 11.
Metro Novoslobodskaya.
Open 24 hours. Tel: 972-
0511. CC for purchases of
over $50. $$.

La Cantina
See Walk 3. Ul. Tverskaya
5. Metro Okhotny Ryad.
Open 8 am–midnight. Tel:
926-3684. CC. $$.

Santa Fe
New Mexican food and styl-
ish decor in a spacious
setting, encompassing sev-
eral restaurant areas and
bars. Good value and
quality cuisine.
Mantulinskaya Ul. 6. Metro
Ul. 1905 Goda. Open
noon–2 am. Tel: 256-
1487/2451. CC. $$.

Taburna Miramar
See Walk 9. Bolshevistsky
Per. 5. Metro Chistiye
Prudy. Open 9 am–10 pm.
Tel: 924-1986. Major CC.
$$.

Asian Cuisine

Japanese Noodles
See Walk 5. Stary Arbat 31.
Metro Arbatskaya. Open 10
am–11 pm. Tel: 241-0886.
Cash only. $.

Manila
The only Philippine restau-
rant in Moscow – and one
of the city's more exotic.
Ul. Vavilova 81. Metro
Leninsky Prospekt. Open
noon–midnight. Tel: 132-
0055. CC. $$$.

Tokyo Restaurant
See Walk 3. Hotel Rossiya.
Metro Kitai Gorod. Open
noon–11 pm. Tel: 298-
5374. CC. $$$.

Tosakhan
See Walk 8. Ul.
Rozhdestvenka 12. Metro

Kuznetsky Most. Open
noon–2 pm, 6 pm–10 pm.
Tel: 925-6990. CC. $$$$.

Tropicana
See Walk 5. Novy Arbat 21.
Metro Smolenskaya,
Barrikadnaya. Open 4 pm–
6 am. Tel: 291-1134, 2045.
Major CC. $$$.

Cafés & Bars

Amadeus
Pleasant atrium-café with
reasonably priced
American-style food; fried
chicken and apple pie
especially recommended.
Radisson Slavyanskaya
Hotel. Metro Kievskaya.
Open 11 am–midnight. Tel:
941-8020. CC. $$.

Artists' Bar
See Walk 2. Hotel
Metropol. Open noon–
midnight. Tel: 927-6065.
CC. $$$.

Armadillo Bar
See Walk 2. Khrustalny Per.
1. Metro Kitai Gorod. Open
5 pm–5 am, weekends from
noon. Tel: 298-5091. Cash
only. $$.

Baku-Livan
See Walk 3. Tverskaya Ul.
24. Metro Pushkinskaya,
Tverskaya. Open 10 am–
10 pm. Tel: 299-8506.
Cash only. $.

Begemot
See Walk 4. Spiridonievsky
Per. 10. Metro Mayakov-
skaya. Open 10 am–mid-
night (1 11 pm Sun). Cash
only. $.

Café Confectionery
See Walk 2. Hotel
Metropol. Metro Ploshchad
Revolutsii, Teatralnaya.
Open Mon–Sat 10 am –
8 pm. Tel: 927-6066. CC.
$$$.

Café Français
Garden-style café serving
not only French, but a
whole host of other
cuisines.
Sofitel Iris Hotel, 10
Khorovinskoye Shosse.
Open noon–10:30 pm. Tel:
488-8000. CC. $$.

Café Kranzler

See Walk 7. Baltschug
Kempinski Hotel. Open
10 am–11 pm. Tel: 230-
6500. CC. $$$.

Cappuccino

One of the best interiors of
Moscow cafés, with deli-
cious coffee and pizza.
Suvorovsky Bulvar 12.
Metro Arbatskaya. Open
8 am–10 pm. Tel: 290-
1498. CC. $.

Cinema

Under the same ownership
as the above, with similar
menu and prices; handy for
the Cinema Centre.
Druzhinnikovskaya Ul. 15.
Metro Krasnopresnenskaya.
Open 10 am–11 pm. Tel:
255-9116. CC. $.

Holsten Bistro

See Walk 11. Taganskaya
Plosh. 88. Metro Tagansk-
aya. Open 10 am–10 pm.
Tel: 915-1130. Cash. $.

Krizis Zhanra

See Walk 6. Per.
Ostrovskovo 22/4. Metro
Kropotkinskaya. Open
noon–12:30 am. Tel: 243-
8605. Cash only. $.

Margarita

See Walk 4. Malaya
Bronnaya Ul. 28. Metro
Mayakovskaya. Open 2 pm–
midnight. Tel: 299-6534.
Cash only. $.

Moosehead Bar

See Walk 7. Bol. Polyanka
Ul. 54. Metro Dobrynin-
skaya. Open noon–5 am,
Sat, Sun 10 am–5 am. Tel:
230-7333. CC for purchas-
es over $20.

Nostalgie

See Walk 9. Chistoprudny
Bulvar 12-A. Metro Chistiye
Prudy. Open 8 am–
11:30 pm. Tel: 916-
9478/9090. CC. $$.

Palm's Coffee Shop

See Walk 5. Valdai Centre,
Novy Arbat 11. Metro Arbat-
skaya. Open 11 am–11 pm.
Tel: 291-2221. CC. $$.

Rocky's

See Walk 8. Kuznetsky
Most 11. Metro Teatralnaya,
Okhotny Ryad. Open

11 am–midnight. Tel: 921-
2529. Cash only. $$.

Rosie O'Grady's

See Walk 6. Ul. Znamenka
9/12. Metro Arbatskaya.
Open Sun–Thur noon–
midnight; Fri, Sat noon–
1:30 am, Sunday brunch
12:30 pm–6 pm. Tel: 203-
9087. CC. $$.

Vienna Café

Popular winter garden café,
famous for its wines and
pastries, also full buffet
meal.
Olympic Penta Hotel. Metro
Prospekt Mira. Open 11:30
am–5 pm, 6 pm–10:30 pm.
Tel: 971-6101. CC. $$$.

River Transport

As well as the regular boat
services which run along
the Moskva River from May
to October (see Walk 12),
hydrofoils (raketi) connect
the Northern River Station
with the many artificial lakes
to the north of the city.
Three routes operate:

The Moscow Canal

(Kanal imeni Moskvy)
All raketa routes follow the
Moscow Canal, one of
Stalin's major construction
projects which connects
Moscow to the River Volga
at Dubna; built by forced
labour, the casualties
involved in its construction
were huge.

This route runs from the
Moskva River in the city to
the town of Kimry, via a
number of artificial reservoirs, which are favourite
recreational areas for
Muscovites for swimming,
windsurfing, sailing and
fishing. The canal includes
eleven immense locks and
eight hydro-electric power
stations.

Tishkovo Route

This raketa takes you to the
Pestovskoye Reservoir,
famous for its fishing, and
for the surrounding country-

side; in autumn, this is a
prime spot for mushroom-
ing. There is a sanatorium
here, specialising in treatment using peat.

One of the intermediary
stops, Zeleny Mys, is a
short way from the beautiful
but ruined 19th-century
gothic palace of Marfino,
as well as the village of
Fedoskino, famous as the
original production centre
of Russia's lacquer boxes.

Pansionat Route

This route connects
Moscow with the
Klyazminskoye and
Pirogovskoye reservoirs.
Klyazminskoye is a sailing
centre, Pirogovskoye excellent for swimming and surrounded by beautiful forest.
Alighting at Chiverevo,
you're a walk away from the
village of Zhostovo, famous
for its painted tray production.

Directions:

From Metro Rechnoy Vokzal
follow signposts to the river
station (also named
Rechnoy Vokzal). To the left
of the main building, hydrofoils (raketi) depart to the
above-mentioned destina-
tions. Services are infre-
quent, leaving about every
hour, so check times before
travelling.

Shopping

Shopping Centres, Department Stores

The appearance in the last
two years of many Western
brand-name outlets has
changed the face of
Moscow. Today, the shop-
per's problem may be
choice (or price) rather than
scarcity. Here, therefore, we
list only the larger and more
established outlets.

Arbat Irish House

See Walk 5.
Novy Arbat 19. Metro
Arbatskaya. Tel: 291-7461.
Open 9 am–9 pm.

Detsky Mir
For children, see Walk 2.
Teatralny Proyezd 2. Metro Lubyanka. Tel: 928-2234. Open 8 am–9 pm.

Europe Centre (Roditi)
See Walk 5.
Ul. Novy Arbat 21. Metro Barrikadnaya, Smolenskaya. Tel: 291-7814. Open 10 am–9 pm.

GUM
See Walk 2.
Krasnaya Plosh. 3. Metro Ploshchad Revolutsii, Teatralnaya. Tel: 921-5763. Open 8 am–9 pm.

Petrovsky Passazh
See Walk 8.
Ul. Petrovka 10. Metro Teatralnaya, Okhotny Ryad. Tel: 923-6055, 928-5047. Open 9 am–8 pm.

Sadko Arcade
A large, empty, Swiss-run mall in the exhibition centre with expensive boutiques selling sports goods, porcelain and food, and several restaurants and cafes.
Expocenter, 1 Krasnogvardeisky Proyezd. Metro Ul. 1905 Goda. Tel: 255-2650.

TsUM
See Walk 8.
Ul. Petrovka 2. Metro Teatralnaya, Okhotny Ryad. Tel: 292-1157. Open Mon–Sat 8 am–9 pm.

Valdai Centre
See Walk 5.
Novy Arbat 11 Metro Arbatskaya. Tel: 291-1083.

Food

Shopping for food in Moscow is no longer the problem it used to be. Supermarkets (formerly accepting only hard currency, now taking only rubles) have mushroomed in recent years, as have private shops, while the old state shops now have much better selections (and are usually cheaper).

Credit cards are normally only accepted in the first category. We list here only

the better-established 24-hour shops (many smaller venues also work around the clock), as well as the colourful local markets.

24-Hour Shops

EML
Smolenskaya Nab. 2/10. Metro Smolenskaya. Tel: 230-0980, 241-9281. Major CC.

Novy Arbat 46
Metro Barrikadnaya, Smolenskaya. Cash only.

Merlin
32 Zemlyanoy Val. Metro Kurskaya. Tel: 917-0215. French food and wine. Major CC.

Privat Bordo
Hotel Rossiya. Metro Kitai Gorod. Tel: 298-3616. Major CC.

Food Markets

Supplied with produce from outside Moscow, often from the south or the Caucasus, Moscow's markets were long proof that private enterprise improved supply. Today, they are pricier than most shops, although may well offer fresher, home-produced or more exotic goods. Most have large flower sections, and sellers are experienced bargainers.

Cheryomyshinsky
The biggest and priciest market in the city.
Lomonovsky Prosp. 1. Metro Universitet.

Danilovsky
Mytnaya Ul. 74. Metro Tulskaya.

Dorogomilovsky
Mozhaisky Val 10. Metro Kievskaya.

Leningradsky
Well-stocked and unusually clean.
Ul. Chasovaya 11. Metro Sokol, Aeroport.

Rizhsky
Prosp. Mira 94/6. Metro Rizhskaya.

Tsentralny
Once the mecca of market traders, the Central Market has long been closed for restoration – and is set to be converted, at Mayor Luzhkov's orders, into a department store-style emporium.
See Walk 8. Tsvetnoi Boulevard 15. Metro Tsvetnoi Boulevard.

Souvenirs

The obvious place to go for souvenirs is the Izmailovsky market, or "Vernissazh" (see Greater Moscow, Izmailovo), open on Saturdays and Sundays only. Alternatively, there are many shops and stalls on the Old Arbat (see Walk 5), and an open-air artists' market outside the Central House of Artists on Krymsky Val (see Walk 6). All will generally accept cash rubles or dollars.

However, these markets are geared towards tourists and their dealers are often unscrupulous. Though their choice is much narrower, the best bargains are usually to be found in the city's Art Salons (*Khudozhestvenniye Salony*), listed here. All accept payment only in cash.

12 Ul. Petrovka
A selection of paintings, jewellery and clothing, plus inexpensive art books.
Metro Teatralnaya, Okhotny Ryad. Tel: 924-2988. Open Mon–Sat 9 am–8 pm.

Moskovsky Fond Kultury
See Walk 7. Pyatniskaya Ul. 16. Metro Novokuznetskaya.

Salon Iskusstva
A large shop selling paintings, all kinds of handicrafts and much more besides.
Bolshaya Yakimanka Ul. 52. Metro Oktyabrskaya. Tel: 238-9523/7913. Open Mon–Sat 9 am–8 pm.

Tsentralny Salon
A wide range of items, whose presence or other-

wise can be difficult to predict. Interesting in particular for hand-woven items such as rugs from Dagestan.
Ukrainsky Bulvar 6. Metro Kievskaya. Tel: 243-9468. Open Mon–Fri 10 am–7 pm, Sat 11 am–7 pm.

Books

A number of second-hand book stalls and kiosks have appeared in the area of Novy Arbat and Nikitskiye Vorota (Metro Arbatskaya), with some titles, including art books, in English. You may also want to visit the weekend book market in the Olympiisky Stadium (Metro Prospekt Mira), mainly for Russian books. All major hotels have small and pricey bookshops with reasonable selections of guidebooks, art books and some fiction. Otherwise try the following:

Biblio Globus
See Walk 2. Ul. Myasnitskaya 6. Metro Lubyanka. Tel: 928-3567. Open Mon–Sat 10 am–7 pm (lunch 2–3 pm). Cash only.

Dom Knigi
See Walk 5. Novy Arbat 26. Metro Arbatskaya. Tel: 290-4507. Open Mon–Sat 10 am–7 pm (lunch 2–3 pm). Cash only.

Inostrannaya Kniga
See Walk 4. Ul. Kachalova 16. Metro Barrikadnaya. Tel: 290-4082. Open 10 am–7 pm Mon–Sat (lunch 2–3 pm). Cash only.

Shakespeare and Co.
A branch of the famous Paris bookshop is due to open in October 1995. For readers of Russian, there is already a Russian bookshop here, called "Ad Marginem", good for literature, philosophy, history.
Novokuznetskaya Ul. 28. Metro Novokuznetskaya.

Teatralniye Knigi
See Walk 8. Strastnoy Bulvar. Metro Pushkinskaya, Chekhovskaya. Tel: 229-9484. Open
Mon–Fri 11 am–6 pm. Cash only.

Zwemmers
See Walk 8. Kuznetsky Most 18. Metro Kuznetsky Most. Tel: 928-2021. Open Mon–Sat 10 am–7 pm. Major CC.

Sport & Leisure

Botanical Gardens
See Greater Moscow, VDNKh. Botanicheskaya Ul. 4. Metro Vladykino. Tel: 482-1373.

Chaika Complex
Tennis courts and swimming pool.
Korobeinikov Per. 1/2. Metro Park Kultury. Tel: 202-0474, 246-1344/0263.

Dinamo Stadium
Home of the famous Moscow football club.
Leningradsky Prosp. 36. Metro Dinamo. Tel: 212-7092.

Gorky Park
See Walk 6. Krymsky Val 9. Metro Park Kultury, Oktyabrskaya.

Hippodrome
Horse racing track: meetings begin 6 pm Wed and Fri, 1 pm Sun.
Ul. Begovaya 22/1. Metro Begovaya. Tel: 945-4516.

Izmailovsky Park
See Greater Moscow, Izmailovo. Narodny Prosp. 17. Metro Izmailovsky Park.

Krylatskoye Sports Complex
The olympic cycle racetrack, velodrome and rowing canal.
Ul. Krylatskaya 2. Metro Krylatskoye. Tel: 140-0347.

Losiny Ostrov
110 square kilometres of evergreen and deciduous forest spreading across and outside the north-east of the city. Known as the "lungs of Moscow", it is also home to elks.
Metro Shcholkovskaya.

Luzhniki Stadium and Sports Palace
See Greater Moscow, Novodevichy. Metro Sportivnaya. Tel: 201-0955.

Moscow Country Club
Krasnogorsky Raion, Nakhabino village (electric train from Riga Station). Tel: 504 0407.

Olympic Health Club
Top-class centre with swimming-pool, solarium, saunas and massage.
Olympic Penta Hotel. Metro Prospekt Mira. Tel: 971-6101.

Olympiisky Sports Complex
Olympiisky Prosp. 16. Metro Prospekt Mira. Tel: 288-3777.

Serebryany Bor Beach
Beaches on a lake formed at a bend in the Moskva river. Very popular, and cleaner than most Moscow beaches.
Metro Polezhayevskaya, then any bus west. Tel: 199-4619.

Slavyanskaya Health Club
Radisson Slavyanskaya Hotel. Tel: 941-8020.

Sokolniki Park
Large park with extensive amusements, including a Sports Palace.
Sokolnichesky Val. Metro Sokolniki. Tel: 268-6958.

TsSKA Sports Palace
Home of the Army football and other sports clubs, as well as of the popular TsSKA Ice Hockey team.
Leningradsky Prosp. 39. Metro Dinamo. Tel: 213-2288.

Tumba Golf Course
Ul. Dovzhenko 1. Metro Universitet. Tel: 147-8330.

Theatre

Despite its illustrious history – one which, perversely, flourished under the communist regime, which gave an urgency to its context –

Moscow theatre today is going through a period of uncertain reassessment.

As commercial pressures affect the logistics of maintaining the previous large repertory companies, some directors have created a style which is more geared towards entertainment. Prime among them is **Roman Viktyuk**, a phenomenon of the 1990's whose company performs on the stages of a number of existing venues. Otherwise, recent critical plaudits have gone to small-stage productions, such as those at the Tabakov Studio, Satirikon and U Nikitskikh Vorot stages.

GITIS Theatre

Small house-theatre stage for the Russian Academy of Theatre, better known by its former title, GITIS. Also the venue for performances by the Bat Cabaret. See Walk 4.
Bol. Gnesdnikovsky Per. 10. Metro Pushkinskaya. Tel: 229-8661.

Hermitage Theatre

Director Mikhail Levitin's style is geared towards the absurd, with a special emphasis on works adapted from writers of the Oberiu school, such as Daniil Kharms. See Walk 8.
Karetny Ryad 3. Metro Pushkinskaya. Tel: 209-6742.

Lenkom Theatre

Mark Zakharov's theatre is one of the popular, and critical, successes of the 1990's. Recent premieres include the energetic musical *Marriage of Figaro*, as well as classics like *The Seagull*, and an excellent *Sorry*, with the wonderful Inna Churikova in the lead role. See Walk 8.
Ul. Chekhova, 6. Metro Pushkinskaya. Tel: 299-0708.

Theatre Na Maloi Bronnoi

Small classic-oriented stage, now going through a new lease of life with director Sergei Zhenovach, whose three-part adaptation of Dostoyevsky's *The Idiot* was a high-point of the 1995 season. See Walk 4.
Ul. Malaya Bronnaya. Metro Pushkinskaya. Tel: 290-4093.

Maly Theatre

Devoted to the classics, especially Russian history plays by the likes of Alexei Tolstoy, the Maly has long abandonned its pioneering pretentions. See Walk 2.
Pl. Teatralnaya 1/6. Metro Teatralnaya. Tel. 923-2621.

Mayakovsky Theatre

Established theatre which boasts opulent productions of comedies and the classics. See Walk 4.
Ul. Bolshaya Nikitskaya 19. Metro Arbat. Tel: 290-4658.

Modern Play School

Intimate comedy played on the small stage of a beautiful building. Their first production, the three-hander *Why the Tails?*, is an ongoing success. See Walk 8.
Ul. Neglinnaya 29/14. Metro Tsvetnoi Bulvar. Tel: 200-0756.

Mossovet Theatre

Unusual for its ability to fill its large auditorium for classics as well as curiosities like *Jesus Christ Superstar*. The small "Beneath the Roof" stage is the venue for some of the best experimental productions in the city. See Walk 4.
Ul. Bolshaya Sadovaya 16. Metro Mayakovskaya. Tel: 299-2035.

Moscow Chekhov Arts Theatre (MKhAT)

The Chekhov Arts Theatre's august history is rarely reflected in the quality of its new productions. It has a beautiful auditorium, complete with historic photo gallery, but for interesting theatre, try something on the adjoining Small Stage, particularly *The Deadly Number*, a premiere by the Tabakov Theatre Studio. See Walk 4.

Kamergersky Per. 3. Metro Teatralnaya. Tel: 229-8760.

Moscow Gorky Arts Theatre

Tverskoi Bul. 22. Metro Pushkinskaya. Tel: 203-8791.

Obraztsov Puppet Theatre

Puppet theatre with a rich history, and a pleasant small museum. Adult shows include *Concert Extraordinaire* and *Don Juan*. See Walk 8.
Ul. Sadovaya-Samotechnaya 3. Metro Tsvetnoi Bulvar. Tel: 299-3310.

Pushkin Theatre

Originally the stage for director Alexander Tairov, the Pushkin has become a solid repertory theatre in recent years – there's little ground-breaking in the repertoire today.
Tverskoi Bulvar 23. Metro Pushkinskaya. Tel: 203-4221.

Satira Theatre

Plosh. Mayakovskovo 2. Metro Mayakovskaya. Tel: 299-6305.

Satirikon Theatre

Under Konstantin Raikin (son of the Soviet Union's greatest comedian and the theatre's founder, Arkady Raikin) the Satirikon has created a very successful style of energetic, lively shows, while on the small stage more experimental theatre flourishes.
Ul. Sheremetevskaya 9. Metro Rizhkaya. Tel: 289-7844.

Sfera Theatre

Karetny Ryad 3, Hermitage Garden. Metro Pushkinskaya. Tel: 299-9645.

Sovremmenik Theatre

In its time a ground-breaker with a reputation to match the Taganka, Galina Volchek's Sovremmenik has done less outstanding new work, although casts are first-rate. See Walk 9.
Chistoprudny Bulvar 19-A. Metro Chistiye Prudy. Tel: 921-6473.

Listings | Theatre

Stanislavsky Drama Theatre

Come here for the more experimental work, like *The Marriage* or *Bald Brunet* (with rock and film star Pyotr Mamonov in the lead) rather than its other repertoire. See Walk 3.
Ul. Tverskaya 23. Metro Pushkinskaya. Tel: 299-7224.

Tabakov Theatre-Studio

With its tiny basement auditorium, the Tabakov Studio, led by one of Russia's greatest actors and teachers, Oleg Tabakov, is among the most exciting of Moscow's stages. Catch their war musical, *Bumbarash*, or *The Deadly Number* (performed on the small stage of MKhAT).
Ul. Chaplygina 1-A. Metro Chistiye Prudy. Tel: 928-9865.

Taganka Theatre

Once the bravest of Moscow theatres, the Taganka has now become one of its saddest, in recent years destroyed by internal struggle. Its wonderful large stage now rarely sees work worthy of the space. See Walk 11.
Plosh. Taganskaya. Metro Taganskaya. Tel: 272-6300.

U Nikitskikh Vorot

Another lively studio space, which bears the distinctive hallmark of director Mark Rozovsky. Audience contact is very immediate, and some of their productions, like *Uncle Vanya*, are outstanding. See Walk 4.
Ul. Gertsena 23/9. Metro Pushkinskaya. Tel: 202-8219.

Vakhtangov Theatre

A heavy, out-dated mainstage repertoire is enlivened by shows from visiting directors such as Roman Viktyuk, as well as Petr Fomenko, whose *Guilty Without Guilt* is unmatched. See Walk 5.
Arbat Ul. 26. Metro Arbat. Tel: 241-0728.

Young Viewers' Theatre

Henrietta Yanovskaya is one of Moscow's most adventurous directors, who has staged alternately excellent versions of Chekhov (*Ivanov and Others*), musicals (*Jacques Offenbach*) and classics (*Heart of a Dog*). Her husband Kama Ginkas staged a brilliant 1995 small-stage version of Dostoyevsky, *K.I. from Crime*. See Walk 3.
Per. Sadovskikh 10. Metro Pushkinskaya. Tel: 299-5360.

Train Stations

Leningradsky Vokzal

Trains to Tver, St. Petersburg, Novgorod, Pskov, Karelia, Estonia and Finland.
Metro Komsomolskaya. Tel: 266-9111, 262-4281.

Yaroslavsky Vokzal

Trains to Sergiyev Posad, Yaroslavl, Vologda, Arkhangelsk and the Trans-Siberian route.
Metro Komsomolskaya. Tel: 266-0218.

Kazansky Vokzal

Trains to Ryazan, Tatarstan, Central Asia, western Siberia, Samara and some southern destinations.
Metro Komsomolskaya. Tel: 266-2843.

Kursky Vokzal

Trains to Tula, Vladimir, Nizhny Novgorod, eastern Ukraine, Crimea and the Caucasus.
Metro Kurskaya. Tel: 266-5846.

Paveletsky Vokzal

Trains to central southern Russia – Voronezh, Volgograd, Astrakhan.
Metro Paveletskaya. Tel: 233-0040.

Kievsky Vokzal

Trains to Kaluga, Bryansk, Chernigov, Kiev, western Ukraine, Odessa, and central and southern Europe.
Metro Kievskaya. Tel: 240-7345.

Belorussky Vokzal

Trains to Smolensk, Minsk, Poland, Germany and Lithuania, Europe.
Metro Belorusskaya. Tel: 253-4464, 266-9213.

Savyolovsky Vokzal

Trains to Uglich, Rybinsk.
Metro Savyolovskaya. Tel: 285-9000, 266-9007.

Rizhsky Vokzal

Trains to Riga.
Metro Rizhskaya. Tel: 266-1372, 266-9535.

For 24-hour general inquiries, call any number between 266-9000 and 266-9999.

Rail Tickets

Tickets for long-distance journeys normally need to reserved in advance from special booking offices
Intourtrans sells international tickets at Ul. Petrovka 15/13. Metro Teatralnaya, Okhotny Ryad, 1st floor, and domestic tickets from Ul. Griboyedova 6/4, Metro Chistiye Prudy, right-hand building, as well as from Intourtrans, Leningradsky Vokzal 2nd floor.
Advance booking for CIS citizens is at the building between Yaroslavsky and Leningradsky Stations, except for St. Petersburg tickets, which are sold at Leningradsky Vokzal 2nd floor.

Travel Agents

Aeroros

Ul. Chernyakovskovo 3. Metro Aeroport. Tel: 151-8661.

Alpha Omega Travel

Lubyansky Proyezd 5, room 12. Metro Lubyanka. Tel: 956-2997.

Griphon Travel

Hotel Ukraina, # 743. Metro Kievskaya. Tel: 243-2395.

Skytour

Leningradsky Prosp. 33-A. Metro Dinamo. Tel: 945-3230.

Index

For Art Galleries, Hotels, Museums, Theatres, Music, see Listings (page 245).

Central Metro Stations, with Russian Names

• Transfer/Interchange Station

Circle Line
Кольцевая линия

• Prospect Mira
Проспект мира

• Komsomolskaya
Комсомольская

• Kurskaya
Курская

• Taganskaya
Таганская

• Paveletskaya
Павелецкая

• Dobryninskaya
Добрынинская

• Oktyabrskaya
Октябрьская

• Park Kultury
Парк культуры

• Kievskaya
Киевская

• Krasnopresnenskaya
Краснопресненская

• Belorusskaya
Белорусская

• Novoslobodskaya
Новослободская

Sokolnicheskaya Line
Сокольническая линия

• Komsomolskaya
Комсомольская

Krasniye Vorota
Красные ворота

• Chistiye Prudy
Чистые пруды

• Lubyanka
Лубянка

• Okhotny Ryad
Охотный ряд

• Biblioteka imeni Lenina
Библиотека им. Ленина

Kropotkinskaya
Кропоткинская

• Park Kultury
Парк культуры

Zamoskvoretskaya Lino
Замоскворецкая линия

• Belorusskaya
Белорусская

Mayakovskaya
Маяковская

• Tverskaya
Тверская

• Teatralnaya
Театральная

• Novokuznetskaya
Новокузнецкая

• Paveletskaya
Павелецкая

Serpukhovsko-Timiryazevskaya Line
Серпуховско-тимирязевская линия

• Mendeleyevskaya
Менделеевская

Tsvetnoi Bulvar
Цветной бульвар

• Chekhovskaya
Чеховская

• Borovitskaya
Боровицкая

Polyanka
Полянка

• Dobryninskaya
Добрынинская

Kaluzhsko-Rizhskaya Line
Калужско-рижская линия

• Prospekt Mira
Проспект мира

Sukharevskaya
Сухаревская

• Turgenevskaya
Тургеневская

• Kitai Gorod
Китай город

• Tretyakovskaya
Третьяковская

• Oktyabrskaya
Октябрьская

Arbatsko-Pokrovskaya Line
Арбатско-покровская линия

• Kurskaya
Курская

• Ploshchad Revolutsii
Площадь революции

• Arbatskaya
Арбатская

Smolenskaya
Смоленская

• Kievskaya
Киевская

Filyovskaya Line
Филевская линия

• Kievskaya
Киевская

Smolenskaya
Смоленская

• Arbatskaya
Арбатская

• Alexandrovsky Sad
Александровский сад

Tagansko-Krasnopresnenskaya Line
Таганско–красно-пресненская линия

• Taganskaya
Таганская

• Kitai Gorod
Китай город

• Kuznetsky Most
Кузнецкий мост

• Pushkinskaya
Пушкинская

• Barrikadnaya
Баррикадная